*Lord Leverhulme*

*By the same author*

MARCONI

SIR OLIVER LODGE

Portrait by Augustus John

W. P. JOLLY

# *Lord Leverhulme*

A BIOGRAPHY

CONSTABLE LONDON

*First published in Great Britain 1976*
*by Constable and Company Ltd*
*10 Orange Street London WC2H 7EG*


*ISBN 0 09 461070 3*

*Set in Monotype Bembo*
*Printed in Great Britain by The Anchor Press Ltd*
*and bound by Wm Brendon & Son Ltd*
*both of Tiptree, Essex*

# *Contents*

# *Illustrations*

# *Acknowledgements*


Many people have helped me with this book but I must particularly thank those whose assistance was invaluable. William Lever's grandson, the third Viscount Leverhulme, gave me much of his time at Thornton Manor to illuminate several aspects of the story. David Orr's interest in the project allowed me access to a mass of historical material at Unilever House and at Port Sunlight, and led to me meeting past and present employees of the Unilever Corporation who so willingly contributed their special knowledge. Some of the more difficult research was taken off my hands by Anne Jolly and Maureen Jolly who also provided advice and encouragement in a dozen ways during the writing of the book.

It is a duty to acknowledge the help of the following libraries and other institutions, and a pleasure to remember the efficiency and kindness of their staff: the British Library at Colindale and at the Patent Office, the Public Record Office, the Bolton Evening News, the National Maritime Museum, the London Library, the Penzance Library, the Beaverbrook Library, and the Trades Union Congress Library.

For permission to quote or reproduce illustrations, I am indebted to Viscount Leverhulme, the Unilever Corporation, the Trustees of the Lady Lever Art Gallery, the Public Record Office, Crown Copyright, Lord Citrine, Mr Nigel Nicolson, and a number of authors and publishers, all of whom are acknowledged in the Notes and Sources (page 236).

# 1

# *Bolton*

The child remembered being lifted on to someone's shoulders. It was a winter evening and a rowdy mob was passing along the main street at the end of the quiet cul-de-sac where he lived. He was held up high so that he might catch a glimpse of the effigy of Czar Nicholas, a straw-stuffed uniform hung with fireworks, being escorted by an excited crowd to a bonfire in the town centre.

In January 1854 indignation and patriotic fervour swept Britain. Anti-Russian feeling, whipped up by the popular Press, labelled Nicholas as a bloody oppressor who supported the reactionary Hapsburg régime against the legitimate aspirations of the Hungarian nationalists. The *Morning Advertiser*, the newspaper of the licensed victuallers, was particularly bellicose. Its pro-war views, passed second-hand over the bar with the drink, often exerted influence on excitable customers whose patriotic sentiments were further inflamed by the ballads and monologues of pub and music hall entertainers.

In Bolton, where the child watched the mob carry off its dummy victim, public houses provided relief for many working people in a miserable existence dominated by brutal working conditions and squalid homes typical of the turbulent communities that had spread around the once attractive old towns of the industrial north of England.

When the child grew to be a man he built a model factory in a garden village. Later still, his own effigy was carried by angry crowds in procession through the streets of London and Florence.

William Hesketh Lever was born in Bolton, Lancashire, on 19 September 1851. In London the Great Exhibition celebrated the triumph of the Victorian age, and in Paxton's huge glass hall were displayed many examples of the skill with which engineers had translated rudimentary laboratory inventions into the reliable machines which were the core of British industrial success. But there were no engineers to convert the concept of an industrial Britain into a smooth-running social structure. Bolton had once been a picturesque little town set amid streams and valleys, but now it was judged by Engels to be one of the worst in industrial Lancashire. Conditions in the poorer parts of the town were very bad, with an exceptionally high infant mortality rate, and appalling sanitation which no doubt contributed to the severe typhus epidemics. The Reform Bills had not yet enfranchised the working classes and the Chartist movement still had many supporters. Industrial Bolton was in a period of disturbed and unattractive adolescence, with its fast-increasing population subject to religious, political, and social passions which were often violently expressed.

Although insulated from the surrounding poverty, the affluent business and professional families of Bolton were distressed by the living conditions which society imposed upon their fellow citizens. Many were also conscious that they themselves, and their children, were excluded from certain positions by reason of their Nonconformist religious views. It was into such a middle-class, Nonconformist family that William Lever was born: the first of two sons who came between six older and two younger sisters.

Lever was an old family name which dated back at least to the fifteenth century in Lancashire, and was found too in the names of districts near Bolton: Great Lever, Little Lever, and Darcy Lever. William Lever's grandfather was a manufacturer of quilts and counterpanes in Bolton and had at one time been quartermaster of the local Militia. His son James – William's father – was born in 1809 and, after some time at a private school, he attended Rivington Grammar School for four years, leaving when he was fourteen.[1] He was apprenticed to John Brimelow, the leading grocer in Bolton, and, as was customary for apprentices in those days, he lived on the premises and was strictly supervised at all times by his master. It was a hard life for a young boy: he started by 'trucking out' orders to customers' carts outside the shop. At sixteen he suffered a blow when his father died and the family was left 'somewhat straitened', but he was able to continue his apprenticeship and obtain a thorough training in all departments of the very extensive Brimelow business. Soon after he 'came out of his time' he accepted an offer to manage a grocery business for Messrs Sheldon & Sons in Swan Street, Manchester. He went to live with Mr and Mrs Sheldon and they exerted a profound influence upon his future life and hence, at one remove, upon that of his son William Lever.

The Sheldons were Congregationalists, and the guiding principle of their household was the 'Nonconformist conscience', characterised by a religious emphasis on prayer, preaching, and Bible reading, and by great concern with material and moral self-improvement. The Lever family had always been members of the Church of England, and James himself had from childhood attended the Bolton Parish Church. But under the Sheldons' influence he began to go to the Grosvenor Street Chapel in Piccadilly, Manchester, and soon became a most active member, teaching in the Sunday School and serving as Mission Secretary.

Among the friends and acquaintances he met in the Congregational Church and at the Sheldons' house were many who worked actively in various fields of social reform and philanthropy. One such acquaintance was a close friend of David Livingstone. The great Nonconformist missionary and explorer became one of James Lever's heroes, and Livingstone's much publicised exploits during the time when William and the other children were growing up often formed the topic of family conversation. The most important friendship James Lever made at church in Manchester was with Eliza Hesketh, the daughter of a cotton mill manager, and they were married in April 1839.

Soon after his marriage he was offered a partnership in a business in his native Bolton. A fellow apprentice from Brimelow's, who had gone as an assistant in a wholesale grocery warehouse owned by a widow, had prospered there to the extent of becoming the lady's partner in business and marriage. The couple decided to extend their trade into the retail side, and James Lever was given the opportunity of becoming a partner with special responsibility for the new shop they proposed to open. He accepted, and when he returned to Bolton from Manchester he brought with him business skill, a devoted wife, and a Nonconformist conscience, all of which reacted together in the prevailing conditions of social upheaval to produce those qualities characteristic of the Victorian middle-class families whose enterprise contributed so much to the shape of the twentieth century.

James Lever's home in Wood Street, Bolton, where most of his ten children were born and brought up, was one of a row of simple, single-fronted Georgian houses with three stories of unplastered brick, a small garden at the back, and a front door opening on to the pavement and facing similar houses on the other side of the street. William Hesketh Lever was born in this house in 1851 and spent there the first dozen years of his comfortable, happy childhood.

# 2

# *A shilling a week*

James Lever and his wife had been married over twelve years when their seventh child, William, was born in 1851. Their first child, born ten years earlier, had been a daughter: something of a disappointment perhaps to Victorian parents, even to radical Nonconformists. When her second, and third, and fourth child were also girls, Mrs Lever could not hide her mortification, although her husband cheerfully denied that he minded. Nevertheless, he was doing well enough in the grocery business to be thinking about setting up on his own, and he must sometimes have brooded on the fact that he was into middle-age with, as yet, no son growing up to help him and eventually take over the business. When the fifth child and the sixth were also girls, congratulation and condolence needed careful phrasing.

So many previous disappointments greatly intensified the rejoicing when their seventh child was a boy. Christened William Hesketh Lever, he assumed a privileged place in the family, and particularly in the affections of his mother who had so keenly felt the old superstitious guilt at not 'giving her husband a son'. There were three more children after William, making ten in all. One was a boy, James Darcy Lever. But having a younger brother reinforced rather than weakened William's feeling of being a special person compared with the other children, who, like their parents, readily accorded him this distinction.

The world in which William passed his early childhood was small and comfortable. His friends were the children of neighbours, the modestly well-to-do trade and professional people who lived in Wood Street, Bolton. At six years old when he and his friends were ready for school most of them were sent to a well-regarded establishment run by the Misses Aspinwall in a house just across the road from the Lever home. The little school took girls of all ages, and boys up to nine years old. There was a friendly, almost family atmosphere, and the Christmas term ended with an address by the senior Miss Aspinwall, followed by cake, and a 'negus' of hot lemon and port, carried around by the head girl in a Staffordshire bowl, the boys sipping from one side and the girls from the other.

With William at Miss Aspinwalls' was Jonathan Simpson, a boy of his own age who was his closest friend and remained so all his life. Another pupil was Elizabeth Hulme, a draper's daughter who lived in Wood Street. She became his childhood sweetheart and eventually his wife, and the two of them used to say afterwards that they never remembered a world without each other in it. When William Lever became a young man it was thanks to the little dame school that he was able to spare himself the hazard of having to expose his intimate feelings and risk rebuff in the normal adolescent search for a wife and a best friend.

The Lever household in Wood Street was conducted in accordance with the principles of Congregationalism which James Lever had absorbed when he was managing the Sheldon grocery business in Manchester, and living with his employer's family. He had become a teetotaller and non-smoker in Manchester, and now in his own home in Bolton smoking and drinking were banned. There was a Bible-reading every weekday, and on Sundays the whole family walked to morning and evening service at the local chapel. Most of the children also attended the early morning and the afternoon Sunday School, where their father often took his turn as superintendent. James Lever hated gambling, and never played cards himself, but the atmosphere in the house was in no way exceptionally repressive, and he would watch cordially when his family and friends played a game without stakes. Occasionally he attended the theatre, more often a concert. He was happy to encourage his children to do so too, and as they grew up the boys and girls were freely permitted to attend dances given by their friends.

When William became nine he left Miss Aspinwalls' and, with his friend Jonathan, went to another private school near by. Then when he was thirteen he – and Jonathan – went to the Church Institute, a Church of England school in Bolton with a headmaster of strong personality who attracted to his establishment the sons of families who might have been expected to patronise the less conformist Bolton Grammar School. If James Lever had any lengthy debate with himself before sending his son to a Church school it might seem to have been scarcely worth while since he took William away at fifteen and put him into his grocery business.

William had not been a bright scholar, nor was he good at games, although he enjoyed swimming and gym. He certainly seemed to have little enough confidence in his own academic ability. Writing when he was nearly fourteen to a friend who was a year or two older, he ended his letter, 'Please excuse all mistakes as I have put the words together myself.' Nevertheless he would have preferred not to have to leave school. He wanted very much to become an architect. His mother, too, wanted him to stay on. She had set her heart on her elder son becoming a doctor. But these were Victorian times, and his father took William into the business, as a few years later he took his younger son James. It was a bleak day when William, almost unnoticed, slipped away from the school where he had made little impression, and it was galling for him to see left behind Jonathan Simpson, who went on to bring credit on himself and the school by qualifying as an architect.

As he prematurely began his working life he somewhat wistfully kept up his friendships with those whom he had left at school, and he carried forward hobbies and interests from childhood, but now with a new purposefulness.

Like many other young boys he had been sufficiently interested in carpentry to make a rabbit hutch, but, more remarkably, for *his* hutch he constructed a tray which fitted on the roof and contained soil in which to grow food for the rabbits. It was an early manifestation of his predilection for complete systems and self-contained communities, but, however tempting, it would be too fanciful to claim it as a first application of the principle of vertical diversification which subsequently governed much of his business strategy.

Continuing with his carpentry after he left school, William built an aquarium, a greenhouse, and a grotto in which he kept the collection of ferns he was assembling: evidence not only of his increasing skill in the use of hand tools but also of his continuing interest in the social microcosm, especially one conceived, constructed, and furnished with inhabitants by himself. He bought and learned to use a microscope, he took lessons in French and shorthand. He extended his reading beyond boys' adventure stories and the *Bab Ballads* to Dickens and Shakespeare, supplementing his private study of literature by forming a serious reading circle with a few young friends. He undertook a regular programme of physical culture at the Bolton Swimming Baths and at a gymnasium in the town. In short, he tried to take account of each hour of the day – indeed each quarter of an hour – and to employ profitably in self-improvement every available moment.

Such dedication to industry and activity was in tune with the Nonconformist conscience which guided the lives of many of the prosperous families who were friends and acquaintances of the Levers. It is easy to believe that William's tightly organised programme was to some extent attributable to a conviction of the intrinsic virtue of a busy life, and easier still to believe that some at least of the items on the programme were not so much the natural interests of a boy as the recommendations of Samuel Smiles in his book *Self-Help*, a copy of which had been given by James Lever to his son on the boy's sixteenth birthday soon after he entered the business. Certainly Smiles laid much emphasis on the husbanding of time in the cause of self-improvement, and specifically mentions, among what to modern eyes is a list of intimidating desiderata: reading to good purpose, the use of hand tools, the recording of observations, and physical fitness. When he was a boy William read and re-read the improving chapters, and as a successful businessman he spoke highly of the ideas expounded by Smiles, and often, consciously or subconsciously, used quotations from the book.

By the time William left school and started work the family had moved from Wood Street to a bigger house adjoining the grocery warehouse. His father required him to be up at seven to sweep out, and to take down the shutters ready for the arrival of the rest of the staff and the customers. He had to stack up the orders on his hand trolley, and wheel them outside to the carts in which customers took the goods from the warehouse back to their own retail grocery shops. One of the first jobs he was given was cutting up and packing soap. In those days before proprietary brands of household soap, the wholesaler's supplies came from the factory in long bars which he then cut into suitable lengths and wrapped for his shopkeeper customers. As the youngest apprentice William had a similar but more tiresome job: breaking up into smaller pieces the great lumps or 'loaves' of sugar from the refiners. It was some years later, in 1872, before Henry Tate, who had also started as a grocery assistant, patented and developed a machine to cut sugar into small pieces. The fortune which Tate subsequently made from Cube Sugar allowed him to make very generous gifts to University College, Liverpool, and also to assemble a notable collection of modern British paintings eventually given to the nation with its own gallery at Millbank.

A shilling a week was William's wage; a shilling a week, all found, rising later to two shillings. 'All found' meant that William – and Darcy when he joined the business – had to ask his father for money for all but the most trifling expenses. Not that James Lever was mean, but when he spent he did so with circumspection, and if William asked for money for an outing or some particular purchase his father considered the matter with the care of an astronaut packing luggage. Mrs Lever was less inhibited financially and it was to her that William usually turned on the frequent occasions when he wanted to go to the theatre with Jonathan Simpson. For even with nineteenth-century pit prices such an evening out in Bolton, or on special occasions in Manchester, would have cost William a week's wages.

Like many another boss's son, William soon left the bottom of the ladder for the office. Once at the centre of things the boy began to look at the business going on around him with a precocious understanding and an increasingly confident eye for possible improvement. But, while the boss's son may pass smoothly to a seat in the office, no one, least of all his father, is likely to shower him with congratulations if he at once points out what is wrong with the organisation. Nevertheless William was only eighteen when with great difficulty he managed to persuade his father that even a business with only twenty or thirty employees needed a more sophisticated accounting system than two wire spikes. He was eventually allowed to consult a local accountant and with his help introduce a proper system of book-keeping.

When he had the new accounts organisation running smoothly William found himself dissatisfied with his work in the office, which now presented little challenge to his eager initiative. He was in no doubt that for him the challenge lay in the front line of the business – on the road, securing orders from the retail grocers. To be a commercial traveller would complete his experience within the firm. It would also assuage a certain inner restlessness, not indiscriminate wanderlust but a positive drive, which for the rest of his life would repeatedly send him on well-planned working trips all over the world.

But James Lever felt it to be not quite the thing for the son of the house to quit the respectability of the office for a pony and trap and order book. So, when a vacancy occurred in the travelling staff, William pointed out that to replace him in the office would cost only thirty shillings a week, the wages of a new clerk. He would then be free to do the job of the commercial traveller who would otherwise cost the firm four pounds a week in wages. It was an argument which his father could not resist, and so at the age of nineteen William set out each day with his horse and trap to solicit orders from the retail grocers in the district round Bolton and to deliver to them the goods ordered on his previous visit.

# 3

# *Independence i[illegible]gan*

James Lever's life and the lives of hi[illegible] were dominated by the business. Consequently young [illegible]m was particularly troubled by the need most boys fee[illegible]ccepted in their first job as a useful member of a team o[illegible]Not to be late in the morning, to sweep out the shop a[illegible] it had always been done were sufficient aims for the [illegible] be satisfactory in his father's eyes was enough at the start [illegible]n he began to feel the challenge of his own standards.

His graduation to the office, t[illegible]ion there of his new accounting system, and his relativ[illegible]ndence as a travelling salesman, satisfied for the time h[illegible]o discover a personal identity and a place in the world. [illegible]as no lack of challenge in being a commercial traveller: i[illegible]t for nothing that they were usually the highest paid em[illegible]n Victorian businesses. The demands of his work and [illegible]ne of physical culture, private lessons, reading circles, a[illegible]ctivities, constituted an acceptable pattern of life for a d[illegible] Samuel Smiles. But at nineteen William's preoccupyin[illegible]on was romantic rather than commercial.

When Elizabeth Hulme was [illegible]ears old her father died and her mother moved from [illegible]to Southport. The little group of children from Woo[illegible] Aspinwalls' school, and the Congregational Church w[illegible]t the loss of a playmate. But Lancashire friendships are [illegible]d lasting. Southport was close enough for frequent visit[illegible]the Bolton families never lost touch with the Hulmes. [illegible]eth grew up she felt that her greatest friends were thes[illegible]men and women she had always known, among them t[illegible]s and the Simpsons.

As the members of the group of friends moved towards their late teens the boys and girls began gradually to look differently at each other and the subtly-changing relationships tended to crystallise into pairs. It was noticeable that William was always included in any party made up to visit the Hulmes at the seaside, and that often he himself engineered such a visit when an opportunity might otherwise not have occurred. Soon he and Elizabeth were exchanging letters, but not through the post, which would certainly have attracted adult attention and disapproval. The group had no great difficulty in organising their own discreet communications and in arranging outings and meetings of acceptable propriety at which their romantic interests might nevertheless be furthered. For William's sister Alice was a close friend of Elizabeth Hulme, and by this time Jonathan Simpson was in love with another great friend of Elizabeth who also lived in Bolton.

The letters which William wrote to Elizabeth were filled out with news of the activities of their mutual friends, references being made over and over again to Alice Lever and Jonathan Simpson. But there was from the start of the correspondence little doubt that its real purpose was courtship. William was very much in love, and like most young men in that condition he wrote of his certainty that she could make him happy. Of his own qualities he was less sure, and when he reported to her the details of his self-examination he would only say that he was no worse than most young men. In the intimacy of his letters he was prepared to promise that he would improve himself and do well enough to make her happy. But although he hoped to convince Elizabeth of his present worth and future prospects he did not feel that these would be apparent to anyone else, and he was constantly nagged by the thought that Mrs Hulme would declare him unacceptable as a suitor for her daughter.

When he was twenty-one William's father made him a partner in the firm. James Lever had considered the matter carefully and, taking into account the profits of the business and his son's contribution to them, he decided that the salary of the new junior partner should be £800 per year. After the financial rigours of his apprenticeship William was almost incredulous at such sudden personal wealth. When he worked out how he might spend his salary all the sums gave rosy answers and he could see no financial obstacle to immediate marriage. He excitedly put the matter to Elizabeth and with many qualms decided to make a formal approach to Mrs Hulme.

There is something touching about modest youth unaware of qualities which are obvious to others. A widow is perhaps particularly anxious that her daughter should make a good marriage, but William's recommendations as a son-in-law were quite clear to Mrs Hulme. Indeed had this not been so the two young people would no doubt have heard of it long before. In December 1872 the engagement was officially announced, and in April 1874 William and Elizabeth were married at the Congregational Church in Bolton whose pastor had baptised both the bride and groom. All their old friends and schoolmates were at the church, and the wedding breakfast was followed by a picnic party before Mr and Mrs Lever left to spend their honeymoon at the extreme limits of England in Devon and Cornwall.

After the honeymoon he returned to Bolton, to commercial travelling and to his duties as junior partner. He still thought of himself as an ordinary young man setting out to be an ordinary householder in the pattern of his father and the fathers of his friends. Perhaps, even then when he was only twenty-three, he considered himself to be just a little out of the ordinary because of his luck in marrying the girl he loved and in receiving such a good salary so early in life. He was unashamedly delighted to be affluent, and before he and Elizabeth moved into their first home in Bolton he had doors, mantelpieces, and fittings replaced by others of better quality and the house redecorated. Some relatives and friends of the family thought it rather too grand and stylish for such a young man.

During the previous year he had watched renovation on a far grander scale being carried out at Harwood Lodge, a fine historic mansion just outside Bolton which his father had bought. William had been rather scornful of the way in which his father fretted about the conversion and fussed around the workmen, although he did admire the way in which he found time to visit the house, issuing instructions and supervising details. This had been rather a worrying time for James Lever. Not so much because of the move into a very large house bought with money already earned by the thriving business, but because he had been nagged and prodded by his son until he had reluctantly agreed to transfer the business to bigger, better appointed premises in Bolton. It was a move which to some extent discounted future expansion and profits, and this was an unwelcome anxiety to the older man, whose business style was one in which past success supported present security, while his son felt that present success was the basis for future growth. James Lever, closer in time and early circumstances to the horrors of Lancashire poverty, was aware that his apprenticeship in a grocery shop might easily have left him to be a Mr Kipps without benefit of legacy. William's apprenticeship had been a very different matter and it was hardly surprising that his father glanced contentedly down from the plateau he had reached to the valley below while the young man was keen to dare the heights above.

There was no doubt about the excellent standing of the business. There was more money about, and more working people were able to afford a sufficiency of food and some domestic goods. An efficient grocery firm was well placed to exploit this new prosperity, and James Lever's was such a firm. He had built up a good clientele, his son's drive was ideally suited to the expanding phase of the national economy, and there was a competent and loyal staff whose pay and conditions of service were good for that time. The relations between management and staff were excellent, and William made an early contribution in this field by organising parties for the employees and their wives. These were simple affairs held in a storeroom done up for the occasion. Tea was served on long trestle tables and after the meal there was musical entertainment and dancing.

In the years following his marriage, William's principal work for the firm continued to be on the road, where he was successful in winning new customers and in returning most evenings with a well-filled order book. The best-selling lines were butter, eggs and potted meat, with starch, mustard, and black-lead to complete a typically Victorian shopping list. Another profitable commodity in the grimy North was soap. Among the varieties which he could offer his customers was one stamped 'Lever's Pure Honey Soap', a laundry soap delivered by the manufacturer in bars a yard long which were cut up in the warehouse into convenient sizes. As the working-class standard of living rose the most spectacular increase in Lever's sales was in butter and eggs, which came largely from Ireland and the mainland of Europe. To secure a sufficient quantity of perishable dairy produce at reasonable prices became a problem, and William went to France and to Ireland to find additional sources of supply.

In 1877 young Lever found time one afternoon to go a little farther than usual from Bolton and he got some orders in a village on the way to Wigan. He persevered in that direction and the trade grew swiftly, possibly because the only exclusively wholesale grocer in Wigan was on the point of failure. By 1879 it had become patently absurd to send such a large volume of goods from Bolton to Wigan when much of it had already passed that way while being carried from Liverpool to Bolton. To end this situation William Lever went to Wigan, bought out the failing wholesale grocer, and established there under his own managership a branch of Lever and Co. of Bolton.

When William Lever took over his first independent command at Wigan he was free to put into practice ideas which eventually hardened into the fundamental principles ruling his business life.

He visited Ireland, and in half a dozen of the principal market towns he appointed agents whose job it was to make themselves known in the district and buy butter and eggs from the farmers as they brought their produce in from the country for sale. By thus cutting out middlemen he got a cheaper product, and by improving on the somewhat haphazard local handling methods he got a better product. He organised his own packing and despatch centres to ensure that the butter and eggs reached England quickly and in prime condition, and from his office in Wigan he carefully monitored the performance of his organisation across the water, spotting faults and quickly ordering their elimination. A natural taste for invention and his long-standing interest in carpentry prompted him to devise an improved crate for eggs. In conjunction with his brother Darcy, who also worked for Lever and Co., he patented the design, which was made up in large numbers and shipped across to be used in Ireland.

Having secured a good, cheap product it was axiomatic to Lever that his personal ownership should be publicly acclaimed. In this way he would reassure his own customers, probably capture other companies' customers, and perhaps expand the market by creating awareness of the product in people who had never before bought it in any form.

Lever applied this policy to the butter, very competitive in price and quality, which he was now able to obtain in large quantities from Ireland. He identified his product with the brand name 'Ulster Fresh Lumps' and advertised it vigorously in the newspapers of north-west England. It was a good product, and the intensive advertising campaign in the Press was very successful. The butter sales of Lever and Co. expanded in a most satisfactory, not to say remarkable, fashion.

The detailed progress of the butter venture and its successful outcome were meticulously recorded and charted by Lever, who had made dynamic stock and finance control into key features of his accounting system as soon as he took over in Wigan. He instituted a scheme of forecasting for three months ahead the trading activities of every department of the business. At the end of the period the forecast was compared with actual events and the lessons learned were incorporated in policy for the future. By 1881 the business prognosis was so encouraging – at least to an expansionist like Lever – that Jonathan Simpson was commissioned to design and build new premises in Wigan.

Simpson had already, in 1879, designed for his friend a new house in Bolton standing in three acres of ground. The client, no doubt, would frequently have been found looking over his architect's shoulder, for Lever was always excited at the prospect of a new house. He sold this one in 1881 because business kept him more and more away from Bolton, and for a short time he and his wife lived in Wigan in a house where he at once had the internal structure and decoration improved, while he himself built on to the drawing-room a conservatory containing a rockery and a collection of ferns. But he was back in Bolton again in 1881 when he bought a big new house there, close to the one he had recently sold. Whatever practical reasons dictated his frequent changes of home, he loved the challenge of a new house and rarely failed to put in hand extensive improvements as soon as he was in. But when the improvements were completed and he could see no scope for major reconstruction or development he was restless for a new challenge.

By 1884 the Wigan branch had amply justified the new premises designed by Simpson. The firm of Lever and Co. was now the biggest wholesale grocer in the area, outside Liverpool and Manchester, and the profits had grown correspondingly. William Lever and his wife were living in comfortable enough style but their expenditure was probably only a fifth or a tenth of his personal share of the profits of the business. It was all well established and running smoothly.

In the summer of 1884 Lever and his wife spent a holiday in the Highlands and Islands of Scotland, accompanied for part of the time by Jonathan Simpson. When they were being rowed among the islands one day Lever revealed to his friend how disenchanted he was with the even course of life as a successful wholesale grocer. He had heard of a small island for sale in the Orkneys. Here was a bigger challenge than a house and a garden. He was considering retiring from the business to take his money, his energy, and his ideas to a remote and exciting life off the northern tip of Britain.

# 4

# *Sunlight soap*

The idea of retiring at thirty-three to an island in the Orkneys was an aberration. It was a natural enough extension of that urge to improve property which continually pushed Lever on from one house to the next, and this impulse was understandably excited by the prospect of a primitive house surrounded by wild moorland, cliffs, beaches, and perhaps a croft or two, all belonging to him. But to gratify this impulse by retiring would have been to suppress the overriding drive which directed his life in the ceaseless activity of business expansion and innovation.

Once back in Lancashire from holiday, to the bustle of prosperous trade, and the gratifying sales figures in his office, the pastoral dream faded, though not for ever, and was replaced by a lustier ambition. His success in the general grocery trade made him one of many, like his father, who had prospered with the increasing spending power of the Victorian working classes. Now in 1884 he determined to try to make his name a household word by becoming the master of one particular grocery item which would be manufactured to his own specification and marketed in his own aggressive manner. From 1884 into the nineties he strove to capture the leading position in the soap trade, and it was during this quest for commercial supremacy that he saw a businessman's vision of the working people exalted by their own efforts under his direction.

The essence of Lever's new project was the marketing of high quality soap in wrapped tablets under a heavily advertised brand name. The imported butter, 'Ulster Fresh Lumps', had already pointed the way towards the advertised brand name, and the firm had for some years sold a bar soap stamped 'Lever's Pure Honey'.

Thus the only radical innovation introduced by Lever was cutting soap into tablets which were each wrapped in parchment-like paper. Perhaps he was inspired by his early labours cutting up soap in his father's warehouse, perhaps he thought of Tate whose cube sugar replaced the old sugar loaves. More likely he was aware that laundry soap in wrapped tablets was already on sale in the United States.

Although Lever had some experience with brand names, of a primitive kind, the use of such names had by 1884 become a complex matter. 'Lever's Pure Honey' soap, so called because of its yellow colour, had first been sold just a year before the passing of the 1875 Trade Mark Act which laid down the conditions to be satisfied by a brand name if it was to enjoy protection in Britain. 'Pure Honey' did not satisfy these conditions, and other soaps using the same name were made and sold by competitors.

Lever in 1884 believed absolutely in the critical importance of a good brand name. When he returned from his Scottish holiday and decided upon the new venture, the first positive step he took was to visit a patent agent who specialised in Trade Marks. This man had lists of names chosen to satisfy the 1875 Act which required that Trade Marks should not, for instance, describe the product or make implications about its quality. Lever looked through the lists and saw nothing which at once excited his enthusiasm as a name for his soap, but he wrote down half a dozen possibilities and went away to consider them further. During the next few days he ran through the short-list scores of times in his mind, trying to consider each word from every commercial and psychological viewpoint. Gradually he felt that one word was beginning to stick out more and more above the others. As the feeling became stronger his interest was sharpened by the sudden thought that someone else might step in and snap up 'his' name. He hurried back to the patent agent and asked him to register 'Sunlight' as the Lever brand name. It was a good choice because it turned out that the word was admissible as a protected Trade Mark not only in Britain but in most foreign countries as well.

In the beginning 'Sunlight' was a house name rather than a true brand name; under this title Lever sold several different varieties of soap. Most manufacturers made more than one kind of soap in their factory. The exact types and proportions of tallow, vegetable oil, and resin used by the 'soap-boiler' gave each product a characteristic colour, smell, hardness, store-life, lathering quality, etc. Lever wrote in an advertisement, 'NO SINGLE MANUFACTURER is equally successful in the boiling of every soap he makes. . . . BY SELECTING ONLY THE BEST SOAPS from each maker, we present a uniformity of quality, under "Sunlight" Brand, obtainable from no individual maker in the United Kingdom.'

Under the 'Sunlight' brand name Lever sold a Pale soap, a Mottled, a Brown, and – in keeping with his uninhibited taste for improvement – a special soap, made to his own recipe, which he claimed would wash clothes 'by itself' without the need for prolonged rubbing, scrubbing, and pounding. This soap was naturally a favourite of Lever's and he made it the particular subject of his growing aspirations in advertising. Metal signs were displayed on railway stations throughout the north of England, carrying the name 'Sunlight Self-Washer Soap', and a line from Shakespeare which Lever thought might help to sell the product: 'See how this becomes the house.'

The soap-boilers were individual master craftsmen of a type thrown up by the industrial revolution; working men who added intelligence and flair to skills acquired during years of hard experience. A mistake by one of these high-priests could ruin a whole melt of steel, a brew of beer, or a boil of soap. Many of the first-class soap-boilers were aware of their importance to the firms' profitability, and the behaviour of some of them had in it a hint of the *prima donna*. In the factories which produced 'Self-Washer' for Lever the soap-boilers were not happy with the unfamiliar recipe they were required to make up for an outsider. Some of Lever's customers, too, were not happy with the smell of the soap, the way in which it sometimes exuded drops of oil, and the hard, rancid skin which formed on the surface. Customers complained to Lever, he complained to the manufacturers, and the soap-boilers said that Lever's recipe was incorrect.

But Lever felt that the advantages of his self-washer soap outweighed its obvious disadvantages and that all would be well if only the manufacturers exercised reasonable care in its production. His commercial obstinacy would not tolerate any suggestion of giving up his favourite soap or of allowing a major change to be made in the recipe. He was encouraged in this attitude by the sales, and by one day hearing a woman in his warehouse ask for 'some more of that stinking soap'. Apparently her customers considered the soap to be excellent value and were quite prepared to tolerate the smelly skin which could easily be removed by wetting the soap and rubbing it to and fro a few times in the hands.

The painful relations between Lever and the manufacturers of his soap were exacerbated beyond toleration when they added to their manifest disapproval of his recipe the injury of squeezing him on prices. He was dissatisfied with the way they were doing their job, and in such circumstances his reaction was always fierce, and usually prompted by the knowledge, or the firm belief, that he could do better himself. The more he considered the pros and cons of sacking his manufacturers and making his own soap, the more he was attracted by the idea. The market was right, with soap sales rising and raw material prices falling. In his own factory he would be able to experiment to get exactly the right recipe, and he would be certain that the manufacturing processes were carried out correctly. Most important of all, he would then be in control of his own supplies of soap, and 'Sunlight' would be a better product and a stronger and more personal brand than it had ever been before. There was in Warrington a small soap works which was losing money – in Lever's opinion because its output was too low. The output required to make it profitable was, he reckoned, just about equal to the amount of soap he could absorb in his own wholesale market. The occupation of that factory and the manufacture there of his own 'Sunlight' soap became his immediate target.

Like some successful generals, Lever never willingly undertook an operation unless he had available an abundance of resources. In the Warrington operation, to secure himself a position as a soap manufacturer, he needed capital. His father, now well over seventy, saw no advantage in moving from the wholesale grocery trade into a risky venture in manufacturing. Neither was his younger brother, James Darcy Lever, very enthusiastic; he was not nearly so robust as William in temperament or physique and, until illness forced his complete retirement, his commercial role was always a subsidiary one. He went much further and faster into big business than he would have wished, pulled along by the slip-stream of his older brother.

But in spite of their misgivings Lever was eventually able to enlist the support of his father and brother, and he secured some twenty-seven thousand pounds of capital without going outside the family. This was ample to enable him to take over the Warrington factory and machinery on a six-year lease, and to leave him sufficient funds for development. The Lever brothers moved in one day in August 1885 and were fortunate to find a first-class soap-boiler among the staff they inherited. His first task was a series of experimental boils to get exactly the right formula for 'Sunlight'.

Soap is a substance called sodium stearate which has a long thin molecule with a knob on the end, like a drum-stick. The knob end of the molecule has an affinity for water, while the stick does not. Consequently in a soap solution there are many such molecules at the surface, each with the knob in the water and the stick poking out of the surface.

But the stick end of the soap molecule has an affinity for oils and greases. Hence when dirty hands are washed in soapy water the stick ends of the soap molecules pick up from the skin the natural oil, and the dirt trapped in it. Natural oil and dirt are carried away in the soap solution, whereas pure water would hardly have disturbed the natural oil or the dirt in it.

When soap is manufactured, oils or fats, which contain derivatives of stearic acid, are boiled for some hours with caustic soda (sodium hydroxide). The products of the reaction are sodium stearate (soap) and glycerine. These can be separated from each other because glycerine will dissolve in brine but soap will not. The jelly-like soap so produced is pressed into moulds and then dried to give hard blocks which are cut up into bars.

The original formula for Lever's 'stinking soap' had contained a very large proportion – about 90 per cent – of vegetable oil. Lever and his soap-boiler, in amicable collaboration, modified the recipe in a series of experimental boils at the end of 1885, and finally settled on 25 per cent tallow (animal fat), 24 per cent cotton oil, 9 per cent resin, and 42 per cent copra or palm oil. By January 1886 the recipe was right, they had solved the various processing difficulties, and were consistently producing good quality soap up to the maximum capacity of the plant, which was about twenty tons per week.

Within two years of leasing the Warrington factory Lever could undeniably claim that the move had been a great success. He learned his trade as soap manufacturer by doing most of the managerial jobs himself at first: sales, finance, advertising, personnel. Almost all his decisions were demonstrably correct in so far as they led to greater sales, production, and profit. This early success gave him an overbearing confidence in his own ability at every aspect of management, and he never fully delegated the appropriate responsibilities to the senior executives he subsequently appointed to the expanding company.

During this two-year period Lever built up a pattern of business activities which became almost as characteristic of his company as the 'Sunlight' brand name. He advertised aggressively: in the Press, on railway stations, and through his own monthly trade paper, *The Lancashire Grocer*, which carried articles and items of general interest as well as technical material, prices, and advertising copy directed at grocers. He packed his soap in individual cartons because the paper wrappers gave insufficient protection to the product if it was carelessly stored or displayed. He fought successfully the first of many law suits, significantly in 1886 against competitors who imitated his label and used it on their own soap until prohibited from doing so by court decisions under the Trade Marks Act. But above all during this period he drove on remorselessly for growth and expansion. Once the sale of 'Sunlight' was flourishing in Bolton and Wigan he pushed out to Liverpool and Manchester, and once established there he went out further and further until he was making profits from Plymouth to Scotland, and then he cast out across the water to countries abroad.

To keep pace with such an explosive expansion of sales was quite beyond the original capacity of the Warrington factory. It was only frenzied improvisation and organisation by Lever which kept the demand satisfied. Collars were fitted around the tops of the boilers to increase their capacity, overtime was worked, and Lever nagged and cajoled manufacturers to deliver extra boilers, machinery, and new wooden buildings to house it all. By the end of 1887 the maximum factory capacity had gone up from twenty tons of soap a week to about four hundred tons, and glycerine – a by-product used in the pharmaceutical and explosives industries – was being purified and sold.

More capital was needed to support such a growth rate and Lever never lost his contempt for the bankers who lacked confidence in him when he had already achieved so much. But nevertheless he raised the money by a business reorganisation which made the grocery business into a limited liability company in which the Lever family still held a large interest. The company was henceforward run by a managing director, although either Lever or his father served as chairman in the period up to 1898. In that year the old man died, and soon afterwards the firm changed its name to that of its managing director, who was now the controlling shareholder and chief executive. After half a century of sturdy progress Lever and Co., wholesale grocers, finally faded away.

The raising of capital was not the only fundamental problem which beset Lever during the frantic two years of growth at Warrington. He found that his site was too small to accommodate the extra factory buildings, storehouses, and loading facilities which he needed. His landlord appreciated the situation and when Lever sought to lease more land the rent asked was punitively greater than that for the original site. Furthermore, Lever said later, the negotiations over the new lease dragged on so long that, desperate for supplies to fulfil the rush of orders, he actually started to put up buildings on the new land before the lease was signed.

It was an intolerable situation for a man of Lever's temperament. He had satisfied himself that he was able to solve any problem in the growing business as long as he had control. But if some part of the operation was in the hands of outsiders then he was vulnerable to their incompetence or cupidity. As a seller

Lever's birthplace in Bolton

Young Lever and dog

Lever at 26

of soap he had been bedevilled by manufacturers, and so he had rented a factory to make his own product. Now that he was being squeezed by the landlord of his factory the obvious step to take was a further one along the path of vertical diversification by owning the means of manufacture and the land on which it stood. He must move from Warrington to his own site. Even as he was negotiating with his landlord for more land, this was in his mind, and the extra buildings he erected were wooden and temporary so that they could be classed as 'tenant's fixtures' and taken away if required.

Prospecting for a suitable site was a matter of urgency but it was, too, a pleasure. Lever loved to pore over a map or plan, he had a sense of geography and a feel for the life of the land, and he enjoyed the pioneer thrill of tramping over rough country. He and William Owen, the architect who had done some work for him at Warrington, picked out likely places from the Ordnance Survey sheets and then went to inspect them. They failed to find what they wanted in Lancashire so crossed the Mersey to Birkenhead on the Cheshire side.

Lever was looking for cheap land that he might improve for himself, and after his Warrington experiences he wanted to be sure of plenty of room for expansion. But he was particularly aware that two aspects of the business were – as yet – not under his control: transport and the supply of labour.

The site eventually selected was a dank and dreary mixture of flat fields, marshes, and muddy creeks between the Mersey and the railway to Birkenhead. It was close to Bromborough Pool, an anchorage far enough up the river not to be liable for dues to the Liverpool Dock and Harbour Board. Cargoes could conveniently be carried on barges between the big ships in the Pool and quays constructed on the works site. This made a considerable saving in the cost of incoming raw materials and it enabled Lever to drive a hard bargain with the railway for the transport of his soap to other parts of Britain. If their rates did not suit him he could use coastal freighters loaded straight from the factory. 'That is the only kind of logic – the logic of a strong position – that I have ever found the railways would listen to.' Lever commissioned his architect to try to purchase about fifty acres of the desolate land.

Once the negotiations for buying the land were in progress between its owners and his agent, Lever went off to the West Country for an ambitious and energetic holiday, the planning of which had for some months been a pleasantly diverting activity during the vigorous struggle of his metamorphosis from local grocer to national soap-maker. It was to be a caravan tour of the Somerset and North Devon coasts, then across the peninsula to the south coast of Devon and Dorset. The trip took several weeks during splendid weather in August and September, and Lever and his wife were joined at different times by various of the friends from their childhood to whom they always clung closely.

As planned by Lever the holiday had about it more than a hint of a progress. He designed and had specially constructed a very large caravan with a cosy living-room and sleeping accommodation for five. To pull this impressive vehicle he imported from Ireland a magnificent pair of greys. A further touch of style was added to the party by the presence of one of the Lever pets, a very large St Bernard dog. A family servant was taken along to do the cooking.

The Irish greys proved unequal to hauling the heavy load up the steep gradients, and so a driver and an extra pair of horses were hired each day to take them on to their next stop. For one particularly long and difficult hill they had a team of eight horses. It was small wonder that the strange party, neither gipsy nor gentry, created a stir when it passed through the country and seaside villages. Many of the locals, especially the children, were disappointed that they were not a circus or performers of some sort, but nevertheless when they stopped for the evening in a field or on a beach they seldom lacked an audience.

One of the friends they invited to join them was Jonathan Simpson, and often Mrs Lever rode on ahead in the caravan while he and Lever followed on foot. The two men tramped side by side through the warm high-banked Devon lanes. The threads of their lives had first run parallel over thirty years before and, since then, through childhood and adolescence until close friendship was reinforced by professional ties in manhood when Simpson often executed commissions for Lever. The tiny child at Miss Aspinwalls' who made Jonathan his first friend, the waif-like lad of fifteen who went diffidently and unwillingly into his father's warehouse, had grown into the self-confident man of affairs, short, thick-set, with piercing blue-grey eyes, and just the vestige of a paunch kept in check by regular physical exercise.

As they walked together under the blue West Country sky, brilliant yellow celandines in the grassy hedges shone in the sunlight, and the two men discussed reclaiming swampy land round a muddy Mersey creek, to carry factories, railways, warehouses – and eventually homes. For Lever no doubt revealed to Jonathan the hope of which he spoke publicly some months later, 'to build houses in which our work-people will be able to live and be comfortable – semi-detached houses, with gardens back and front, in which they will be able to know more about the science of life than they can in a back slum, and in which they will learn that there is more enjoyment in life than in the mere going to and returning from work and looking forward to Saturday night to draw their wages.'

# 5

# *The Village*

By the end of 1887 the purchase of just over fifty acres of the land in Cheshire was completed. Lever, with plenty of capital and a large empty site, was able to savour the bliss of a planner's dream come true: a blank sheet of paper and the certainty that men and materials were waiting to give substance to his sketches. His experience at Warrington, and what he knew about the factories of his older established competitors, gave him firm ideas about the conditions he intended to create in his new soap works. The buildings were to be well spaced, with plenty of light and fresh air to make his employees healthier, happier, and more productive; and the blocks were laid out in a pattern designed to ensure the most efficient juxtaposition of storage, production, transport, and administrative facilities.

He had no difficulty in thinking of a name for his creation on the muddy wastes by the river Mersey – it would be called 'Port Sunlight'.

Lever's son said of him,[1] 'He was never happier than when seated in front of a plan with a drawing-board, ruler, and T-square ready to hand. . . . With him it was never a case of leaving everything to the architect and settling the bill when the work was finished. Expert advice he wisely sought and freely acknowledged, but the plan and the lay-out of Port Sunlight were his own, and so, in the main, were the plans of the works and the buildings in the village, and in many cases of the houses also. The architects he employed all looked upon him as unique amongst their clients. He did not employ them – he collaborated with them.' Over the years many architects made their contributions to Port Sunlight and the projects they undertook were interesting and lucrative. But 'collaboration' with their ebullient client sometimes proved irksome and they must occasionally have felt more non-commissioned than commissioned.

In March 1888 a party crossed the river from Liverpool and then, on the high tide, went by private steam barge up the creek to the site, where Mrs Lever cut the first sod with a silver spade formally presented to her by the architect. All the 'Sunlight' travellers were invited to the ceremony, which was followed by a banquet back in Liverpool at the Bear's Paw restaurant. Lever made a characteristic speech ridiculing those 'who think we have just held our mouths open and success has dropped in. I do not know whether you have heard the story about Mahomet. When he was told to trust in God and leave the camels free, he replied, "Tie them up and trust in God." That, I hope, will always be our motto.'

Not even the combination of Lever's hustle and the dedicated industriousness of Victorian builders could quite eliminate the interval between sod-cutting and topping out. Lever filled part of that interval with a trip to North America, during which he covered many thousands of miles, fitting in as much sightseeing as he could manage between business engagements. He travelled with his brother-in-law, W. F. Tillotson, who owned and ran the *Bolton Evening News*. They wanted to see at close quarters something of American business methods – in particular advertising, in which field Lever was sure that he would find ideas which could profitably be imported into Britain. He also organised agencies for the sale of Sunlight soap in the United States. During a brief excursion into Canada he went to see an old childhood friend who had recently emigrated from Lancashire and was now entrusted by Lever with the agency to introduce Sunlight into Canada. Meanwhile, the building work back in England had gone well and in January 1889 production began at Port Sunlight.

The first stage of construction had been relatively modest, the main object being to provide the capacity to take over from the Warrington works with the minimum disruption. But the factory, or 'soapery', and the offices, which were the first blocks erected, were designed to be able to cope with an immediate growth in production and were planned eventually to be part of a much more ambitious scheme. In addition to the factory and office, the first phase included the construction of a substantial wharf which barges could use when the high tide flooded the creek.

In 1886 Lever Brothers' annual production of soap had been about 3,000 tons, and two years later, in the last year at Warrington, it was over 14,000 tons. The first year at Port Sunlight saw a rise to nearly 16,000 tons. Then, once they were settled in the new works, annual production rose at a steady rate of several thousand tons each year.

By now Lever knew quite a lot about soap-boiling, but he relied heavily upon his technical experts for the improvements in equipment and processes which were continually being introduced to keep production up and costs down. He chaired a committee which met regularly to consider such matters as the conservation of heat, economy in raw materials, and the more efficient recovery of the by-product, glycerine. Commercial security was an important consideration, his competitors being anxious to discover the secrets of the intimidating vigour of the cuckoo in the soap trade. It was not unknown for a member of the senior staff at Port Sunlight to be dismissed because he had carelessly and unnecessarily revealed details of some process to the factory workers.

Lever rarely took advice about the administrative side of the business. He once wrote a note to a senior assistant about such a matter, 'I am always glad to have your free expression of opinion on all matters that I may discuss with you. But until I do discuss a matter with you, I think that you will agree with me that it is not within your province to lay your views before me. . . .' From his office at Port Sunlight he controlled with supreme confidence the affairs of his company at home and abroad, giving orders verbally to those executives who could be summoned to his presence and sending written directives to those farther afield. He answered correspondence and issued a stream of written instructions, dictating at tremendous pace, often to two or even three girls simultaneously so that what one missed another would get, and not a moment of his time was wasted in repetition.

Very early in the expansion of Port Sunlight he had an office specially constructed high above the huge new general office, with glass walls so that he could see everyone at work, and at once telephone to the appropriate supervisor if he saw one of the clerks slacking. Such surveillance seems strangely remote from today's labour relations, but there is perhaps a certain contemporary flavour about the reported occasion in the United States when Lever employed a private detective agency for some weeks to observe and report on the behaviour of one of his managers who was suspected – unjustifiably, it transpired – of laziness.

It was nine months after the banquet at the Bear's Paw restaurant when Lever put in hand the housing scheme he had mentioned there in his speech after the cutting of the first sod at Port Sunlight. In December 1888 a start was made on plans for an entrance lodge and twenty-eight cottages, and building began in the spring of 1889. There was nothing niggardly about the design. Each of the Port Sunlight houses had a kitchen, scullery, bathroom, and either four bedrooms or three bedrooms and a parlour. There were open spaces and lawns maintained in uniform neatness by the Company, each house had its own front and back gardens, and if the tenant wished he could have an allotment. The whole estate, which grew rapidly, was laid out with wide roads and footpaths, and a general theme of old English architecture with a wealth of half-timbering. Every attempt was made to screen the works buildings and the railway sidings from the direct view of the houses. Nevertheless the tall chimneys could hardly be concealed, nor sometimes could the smell be ignored. It was hard ever to escape a sense of the presence of the factory which gave life to the village. All the householders worked for Lever Brothers and the tenants' agreements, like their jobs, were subject to a week's notice of termination from the Company.

The Port Sunlight Village was Lever's first tentative interpretation of profit-sharing. This had been much discussed as a tool of industrial relations since the long-running success in France of Leclaire's experiment, which nevertheless had rather petered out when he died and his decorating business was left in less dedicated and competent hands. The speech Lever made to his employees at a works outing in 1890 showed that he had already adopted what he later called his unsentimental approach to the subject, although at that time he had no very clear practical ideas which might make his scheme the significant step forward he sought to achieve in industrial practice:

'We must remember that there is no sentiment in business, and no room for any fads. Any arrangement that is made must benefit the masters as well as the men, or it will not last. If it did last, it would be a species of charity which no working man would care to have. The way it can be made a success is by the workers making the profits larger, and that can be done by improving the quality of your service, avoiding waste, and by conscientious dispatch of your duties. . . . What we propose to do with the proportion of profit devoted to the workers is to apply it to the building of houses to be let at a reduced rental. . . .'

In 1890 there was little more to Lever's scheme than a promise of better living conditions and a hope for more dedicated workers.

There was nothing new about such schemes, and indeed one of the most famous, at Saltaire in the north of England, had been inaugurated when Lever was a baby. Titus Salt was born in 1803 in Yorkshire to Nonconformist parents. He established the alpaca wool industry and owned a very large number of mills around Bradford. In 1851 he decided to move his mills and workpeople to a model factory and village in the countryside by the river Aire. Salt's declared aim was to draw around him a population who would be contented and happy. By the time he died in 1876 his town was well established and he had made personal gifts to it of a Congregational Church in the Italian style, a Sunday School for eight hundred, a Club and Institute, Almshouses, an Infirmary, and a large park and recreation ground.

Nearer Lever's own age was William Hartley, a Lancashire Nonconformist born in 1846. He started as a lad in the grocery trade and went on to manufacture his own jams at Aintree, near Liverpool, and he set up there the Hartley Village. He was a pioneer in profit-sharing and made large gifts to hospitals and to Liverpool University, and he contributed about half a million pounds to the Methodist movement.

Of the model villages developed contemporarily with Port Sunlight the best best known was Bournville, set up by the Cadbury brothers, who were Quakers, manufacturers of cocoa and chocolate, pioneers of industrial welfare, the first firm in

Birmingham to introduce a half-day holiday on Saturday. There was a strong religious background to their business and for many years they had a popular morning service attended by the work-people. George Cadbury did not believe that it was not necessary for a factory to be in a town and the workers in a slum. In October 1879 the Cadburys moved into the country to their Bournville factory which was provided with a recreation ground and swimming pool, first-class dining-rooms and kitchens, and sixteen semi-detached houses for the foremen. By 1901 there were 370 houses and George Cadbury handed the estate over to trustees for the Charity Commission. There were over 1,000 houses in 1923 by which time Cadbury had surrendered all private interest both in the capital and revenues of the estate. Some houses were sold to the tenants, and well under half the estate was occupied by Cadbury employees. As his company flourished and the City of Birmingham expanded towards Bournville, Cadbury was concerned that he might find himself back in the 1878 situation of running a factory surrounded by city slums. It was largely to prevent this that he bought so much land and gave such personal attention to the planning and administration of his model estate, and was thus led to a close connection with the wider Garden City movement.

Thus the Village at Port Sunlight was one of many such schemes, large and small, which had grown up by the turn of the century and were a sufficiently well-known aspect of industry at that time for Bernard Shaw to use such a model village at the end of *Major Barbara* as a concept in which an armament magnate, a Salvation Army worker, and a scholarly advocate of religious freedom could find common cause. In this literary use of the model village, Shaw was half a century behind Disraeli, in whose novel *Coningsby* appears the paragon of all industrial development, Millbank, believed to be based upon the Barrow Bridge Mills which were already thriving in Bolton in 1851 when Lever was born there. Where other successful businessmen might set up an Oxford college or a racing stable, the Victorian Nonconformists inclined to favour a modern university or a model village.

When the first factory block at Port Sunlight was being built, and a month or two before he put plans in hand for the first houses in the Village, Lever made arrangements for his own accommodation. He rented, and subsequently bought, Thornton Manor near the village of Thornton Hough in the centre of the Wirral peninsula. It was not exactly 'over the shop' nor even within sight of the factory chimneys, but it was close enough to Port Sunlight for him to summon directors, senior executives, and their wives to dinner, after which the men would have an informal business discussion. The manor house stood in a fine park with woods beyond, and during his first years there Lever used to provide an annual picnic party in the grounds for the workers from Port Sunlight and the villagers from Thornton Hough.

Under the wing of the Manor the village of Thornton Hough became, like the Village at Port Sunlight, another favoured satellite, the closely cherished object of Lever's zeal for improvement. It was a picturesque little community with whitewashed thatched cottages, but nearly all of them were insanitary and almost ready to collapse. Within a few years of setting up home at Thornton Manor Lever had bought the land between the house and the village, and most of the village too. He knocked down the old cottages, not without opposition from some occupants who had spent a lifetime in them, and in their place he built houses like those at Port Sunlight. He put up a school – designed by Jonathan Simpson – a girls' orphanage, shops, and a club, and he laid out a fine recreation ground. He also commissioned, from Jonathan Simpson's son, a Congregational Church which was an elaborate and expensive replica, faithful, inside and out, to the Norman style. During this almost complete remodelling of the village the blacksmith's forge had to be demolished to make room for one of the larger projects. Lever had it replaced by a fine new half-timbered smithy, complete with a young chestnut tree planted in front.

Inevitably Thornton Manor itself went under the improver's T-square. The improver's wife claimed that never during her marriage had she lived for any significant period without workmen in her home. The Manor had been built in the middle of the nineteenth century in Gothic style, and now Lever made it into a very much bigger house reproducing many of the features of an old Elizabethan manor-house. He gave great attention to the gardens and grounds, being particularly pleased with the two-acre kitchen garden. He built a fernery, as he had done before in several of the other houses he had lived in, and in this connection he wrote to a friend, 'I had no idea that the love of ferns entitled a man to the jaw-breaking title "Pteropodist" [*sic*]. I have always been a lover of ferns. . . . I feel now that I must have been a Pteropodist all my life without knowing it, like the man who found he had been speaking prose all his life. . . .'

A particularly impressive addition to the park was a water vista: canal, lagoon, swimming-pool, and an artificial lake three feet deep dotted with small shrub-covered islets where water-fowl lived and nested. All bird life was carefully conserved except for the wild duck which were encouraged to breed on the lake to provide sport for the gun. Lever himself gave up shooting when he was about forty-five but, reflecting his old father's attitude to card games, he was happy to breed and rear duck for his friends to shoot, although characteristically he made a penetrating and pungent analysis of the cash flow in this expensive operation: 'Up goes ten shillings, bang goes twopence, and down comes half a crown.'

Making a Victorian Gothic house into a much larger neo-Tudor one is likely to involve some remarkable construction work, but there could have been nothing quite so surprising to the architect and builders as the strange shelter they were required to fit on top of the house in a corner made by sharply sloping areas of roof. There was little more to the shelter than a glass roof with some support at the side, and it contained a bed where Lever slept every night in the open air, a very large bath, and a cupboard for dumb-bells. In the worst of weather the wind blew strongly through the exposed sides and it was not unusual for the coverlet to be dusted with snow.

Not many would have relished the prospect of going up to such a bedroom on a winter's night, but how attractive the morning warmth deep under the snowy bedclothes must have seemed when faced with the thought of stepping out on to the freezing roof. Lever got up at five o'clock, did a twenty-minute stint of physical exercises in a room furnished with various expensive pieces of gymnastic machinery, then he had a cold bath, a cup of tea, and worked at correspondence until breakfast at seven-thirty. Such a mortifying régime seems more likely to have been fulfilling a spiritual need than maintaining a businessman's physique.

If Port Sunlight was the expression of Lever's business principles, then Thornton was the realisation of his domestic ambitions. These two establishments presented a stream of challenges to his eager mind during the 1890s. This was, too, just the time, during his late thirties and early forties, when his habits of thought and behaviour were becoming fixed, and the two environments moulded his future life.

When Lever first came to Thornton Manor his son, and only surviving child, had just been born, and the proud father was able to savour the unfolding of a mature family life in the setting of his own, now considerable, affluence and business influence. He liked to entertain on a large scale and he soon built rooms grand enough for his purpose. At his regular Christmas party there would be fifty or more personal friends and relatives seated at dinner, and on Christmas Eve he would assemble domestic staff, family, and guests, and read to them from Dickens's *A Christmas Carol*. On more formal occasions Mrs Lever often had to carry much of the weight of keeping the party going, while Lever engaged in close conversation with a business friend, occasionally glancing affectionately and proudly at his attractive, statuesque wife playing hostess so well. Sometimes Lever would conduct his conversations while pacing up and down a drawing-room – he showed something of a 'quarter-deck' syndrome – and in his gardens he liked a path that encouraged a brisk stimulating promenade rather than a gentle sensual meander to enjoy the flowers and shrubs.

Thornton Manor was the base from which Lever began to appear in public life and eventually to make his entrance into politics. But perhaps the occasion on which he first became the subject of animated national discussion was in 1889 when he was involved in one of the controversies about art which editors of Victorian journals could rely upon to fill columns with unenlightened indignation of the kind provoked by education arguments today.

The big new rooms at Thornton Manor needed pictures to grace the walls, and Lever became a collector. His original interest was in the Victorian artists, and his first important acquisition a painting by Millais, several of whose most significant works he later bought, including *Sir Isumbras at the Ford* and the portrait of Tennyson. Lever was a keen attender at the Royal Academy's exhibitions, and in 1889 he purchased there a painting exhibited by W. P. Frith, A.R.A. It was called *The New Frock* and showed a little girl holding up a white pinafore. By July of that year the painting, with the title changed to *So Clean*, was the centre-piece in advertisements for Sunlight soap, which carried in addition a strong recommendation from a titled doctor. Frith complained publicly, and Lever was amazed that anyone should question what an owner did with an object which he had purchased in the open market. Many papers featured the controversy but *The Pall Mall Gazette* made the most of it with a series of interviews with interested parties, of whom Millais was perhaps the most interesting as the painter of *Bubbles*, the earlier, famous Pears soap advertisement. Sir John Millais said he had no complaint if the reproduction was good. He was by then sixty and had moved some way from the original ideals of the Pre-Raphaelite Brotherhood towards an appreciation of the values of Lever's commercial world.

# 6

# *Soap combine*

Keen advertising in favourable trading conditions contributed largely to the huge success of Lever's early years as a soap-maker. Later, in painfully evident reciprocity, the Company was severely damaged by bad publicity during a difficult period.

The controversy about Frith's painting did not deflect Lever from using works of art in advertisements. For his part he welcomed the extra publicity and he declared, too, 'My opinion is that Mr Frith is rather pleased.'[1] Lever never felt constrained to treat art esoterically and was in no way embarrassed to find it decorative, interesting, or useful. Of another painting he bought at the Royal Academy he said, 'It is only a moderate picture but very suitable for soap advertisement.' He saw no need to distinguish artists commissioned to draw advertisements from other employees of the soap business. But style might transcend anonymity – more often than Lever recognised. He wrote that he had seen an advertisement for Sunlight[2] 'which seems to me to be most excellent. Who is this Mabel Lucie Attwell who is the artist? I always understood that we had a rule that artists' names would not appear on the drawings. I know that in the case of Hassell we have varied it because whether he signed the work or not it was obvious whose work it was. I have never heard of the name of Miss Mabel Lucie Attwell before and it seems to me that unless we are really compelled, it is better that the name of the artist who works for us should be left off the advertisement. It would only send all other advertisers to them which is scarcely fair to ourselves.'

Lever found many of his advertising ideas in the United States. He bought from an American soap-maker the famous slogan

'Why does a Woman look old sooner than a Man?' It was a disturbing question and it sold soap. Lever had no reservations about the overtones – so familiar today – of such a slogan. Sunlight released the working-class housewife from some of the drudgery of the steaming wash-tub in the stone-floored scullery, and any increase in sales must, he believed, be for the public's own benefit.

'Won't wash clothes' was another slogan with a transatlantic origin. It appeared in newspapers, on hoardings, and on the old horse-drawn buses, advertising 'Monkey Brand', a scouring powder originally produced in America and bought by Lever for manufacture in Britain.

As well as the instant message of picture and slogan, Lever employed the written word at some length in his campaign to create a market for his soap among the multitudes of the working class, whose spending power and literacy – both relatively newly acquired – made them an ideal target for such advertising. The first thing to do was to tell them why they needed the product, and Lever himself prepared most of the first booklet issued, entitled *Sunlight Soap and How to Use It*, in which, as he said, 'everything was brought down to the level of a working man's needs.'

The promotion literature was not all instructive: there was an element of interest and entertainment included to keep the reader turning the pages. A traditional interest of the working class was indulged with an account of the tribulations of a titled lady.[3] 'The Lady Gwendolin's Lament' told in verse how this unfortunate lady's fading charms had not responded even to expensive treatment from beauty specialists until one day when a fellow aristocrat, the Lady Mary Bright, appalled by her friend's appearance, gave her the secret to restore her good looks:

> This article, if you but try,
> Will realize each hope.
> Go send your maid at once, and buy
> A box of Sunlight Soap.

By 1899 the *Sunlight Year Book* was a handsome illustrated book of nearly five hundred pages which, with perspicacity verging on cunning, Lever arranged to have sent to the masters and mistresses of elementary schools. This particular piece of enterprise brought protests from competitors, and the Secretary of the Soap Makers Association complained[4] that 'the Mistress of a Board School has been distributing advertisements and prizes in connection with Sunlight Soap. . . .'

It was Lever's introduction of gift schemes from America which caused most rumpus in the trade. When Lever ran his first scheme it was in a modified form which made it appear worthier than a simple appeal to acquisitiveness. The prize was two thousand pounds, but the participating members of the soap-buying public did not get it. It was, instead, divided among charities chosen according to votes sent in on tokens from Sunlight cartons. Those who had bought the soap and sent in their tokens had to be content with the chance of a minor prize. The *Illustrated London News* of 19 October 1889 contains an account of a rescue at sea performed by the lifeboat *Sunlight Number 1*, a gift to the R.N.L.I. by the votes of users of Sunlight soap in the competitition of 1887.

This 'improved' scheme was very soon replaced by the standard one in which certain prizes were awarded for particular numbers of tokens collected and sent in. Typically, a competitor with twenty-five thousand tokens got a motor car and several bicycles, the retail price of his prizes being rather more than that of the immense quantity of soap purchased to get the tokens. Clearly the economics of such a promotion were finely balanced, and it was only profitable if the redemption rate (i.e. the percentage of issued tokens returned) was fairly low, and if a large fraction of the extra sales generated was maintained without the need to repeat promotions frequently. At first Lever's gift schemes were very successful and sales increased considerably. But when his competitors stopped complaining and began to imitate, schemes multiplied rapidly to the point where a manufacturer had insufficient time to recoup the cost of his promotion from increased sales before the faithless token-collectors he had just won were snatched away from him by a rival's promotion.

The gift scheme became Lever's albatross, although in this case the other soap-makers each suffered a similar incubus. He tried abandoning schemes altogether, or giving almost worthless prizes, but the consequent fall in sales was alarming. Customers had grown accustomed to expect a prize by way of discount on the price they paid for their soap. Eventually Lever gave Sunlight soap itself as the prize, because he said that by arrangement with his grocer the recipient could 'easily convert the Soap into money'. The details of this scheme were well thought out and it was a much improved economical proposition, but nevertheless by 1906, when raw material prices rose suddenly and hard times came to the soap industry, cut-throat advertising and promotion schemes had become an intolerable burden to Lever and everyone else.

An unusual aspect of Lever's advertising strategy was derived almost certainly from his own experience as a commercial traveller and from his conviction that personal knowledge of the customer and the circumstances of his life were vital to any commercial project. The business line of a large manufacturer normally ends with the wholesaler, but Lever always felt – in any activity – an urge to have the whole system under his hand. He had a force of men, called District Agents, whose job was penetrating the homes of the public to demonstrate the superiority of the product and to report to Port Sunlight anything of significance they saw or heard in the houses. The Lever Brothers' journal carried many stirring calls to the D.A.s to knock on doors every minute of the day and extol the virtues of the Company's products. The exploits of the more enterprising were featured as an example to others. Thus D.A. Bramwell reported that at a wedding party he had stopped each one of the lady guests and asked which household soap she thought was the best. Fifteen out of nineteen chose Sunlight or Lifebuoy. The latter being a new brand which made use of some residual oils unsuitable for Sunlight because of their strong odour. It contained carbolic acid, a germicide whose very strong smell effectively masked that of any other ingredient. One of the duties of each D.A. was to report any outbreak of infectious disease so that a spurt of local advertising might direct anxious minds to the sanitary qualities of Lifebuoy.

One Lever publicity agent, more senior and more romantic

than the D.A.s, was a Swiss called Lavanchy-Clarke. With his huge mane of hair and flamboyant clothes he looked less like a Lever employee than a poet. He was a widely travelled, inventive man, among whose many interests was a keen concern for the welfare of the blind, and he had been largely responsible for the international adoption of the Braille system. When his fertile mind turned to advertising he was impressed by the vigour of the Sunlight campaigns and obtained an introduction to Lever, who interviewed him, listened to his ideas, and gave him a job publicising Lever products on the Continent. He poured out ideas for the Company, ranging from sound proposals for serious commercial developments to wildly successful publicity stunts.

He obtained rights in a very early cinematograph system and at various exhibitions gave popular shows to which admission was obtained by producing a token cut from a Sunlight packet. When the cinematograph machines were brought to London to give open-air demonstrations at night, using back projection on to screens cut in Sunlight advertising hoardings, the crowds that collected to see the moving pictures were so enormous that the police had the shows banned. One of his greatest coups was to organise, one Easter Monday on Lake Geneva, a Fête des Blanchisseuses, a washing competition to which all the washerwomen from the towns around the lake were invited, being brought to the site in specially chartered steamers and given a banquet afterwards. Nothing like it had been seen before. The holiday crowds poured in, and the event, with suitable reference to Sunlight, was reported in the Press all over Europe and even in America.

In more serious style it was Lavanchy-Clarke who did most of the preliminary work in the setting up of Lever's first overseas soap factory, 'Savonneries Helvetia', and he became its first manager.

By the end of the nineteenth century Lever owned, or was building, soap factories in Switzerland, Germany, Canada, the United States, Holland, and Australia, with plans to build more, and with agencies selling Lever products in most parts of the world. In addition to Sunlight, these products now included Lifebuoy soap, Monkey Brand, Vim and Lux. This last product had been a poor seller under its original name, 'Sunlight Flakes', which described it exactly. But renamed Lux and briskly advertised it prospered and survived.

The growth of Lever's business in the early days had made some soap manufacturers feel, then, that perhaps he might be invited to join their Association. But when his competition began to damage their sales all over Britain and abroad, the older manufacturers decided that it had now become essential to draw him into their trade organisation and its deliberations.

In the soap industry, as elsewhere, individuals tended to cling together for self-defence when they felt themselves to be threatened in times of crisis. As early as the 1850s the soap-makers of the north of England had come briefly together to fix prices during a period of uncertainty about the supply and price of raw materials due to the Crimean War. This loose grouping of companies broke up after the war, and it was not until 1867 that a general financial crisis prompted the formation of the Soap Makers Association. The new Association had no very rigid constitution, and no very clearly defined objectives. It did not intend to fix prices in any formal way, although some attempt was made to co-ordinate alterations in price throughout the country, but it was able to represent the interests of the trade as a whole to Government and other authorities. For much of its existence the members of the Association tended, in bad times, to compete with each other even to the extent of going against agreements made within the group, while in good times the Association became little more than a jovial dining club and, as one member remarked, 'our competition and rivalry become like a game at billiards or cricket'.

During such a euphoric period – before Lever Brothers started to make soap at Warrington – a suggestion was made that Lever and Co. be invited to join, but it was turned down because they were only 'buyers of soap'. A few years later Sunlight was being advertised and sold all over the country, breaking the tradition of local markets and causing members of the Association to bicker among themselves and complain bitterly about unfair competition from Lever and from some fellow members who were taking their own measures to match Lever's methods. In 1889 the members felt that Lever must be persuaded to join, in the hope that this might lead to a reduction in the amount of soap flooding the market and to some curbing of the Sunlight promotion schemes.

Lever agreed to join, although he never took very seriously the acrimonious discussions and loosely framed policies of the Association. He was not a popular member, and he considered this to be a matter for self-congratulation. After attending a Soap Makers' dinner in London in 1891 he wrote in his diary, 'very pleasant evening – all London makers complaining of Sunlight. . . .' In 1903 he accepted the Presidency of the Association's Northern section, less from a commitment to its principles than because the office befitted the powerful position he had now reached in the soap trade. But then in 1905, after over fifteen years of membership of an organisation which irritated him with its lack of bite and which barely served his interests, Lever resigned, saying blandly, 'there is no special reason at all – except that after long experience we have failed to find any benefit in continuing members . . . with kindest regards. . . .' A year later Lever was himself proposing a new grouping of soap manufacturers: not in any sense an aimless, cosy club, but a hard-centred combine with very clear immediate commercial objectives.

Twenty years or more of study and experience of industrial relations had led Lever to the firm conviction that there was an identity of interest shared by Capital, Management, and Labour, and that the fundamental criterion for lasting success was, 'the production of more goods with less labour in fewer hours, so as to allow for larger wages and a bigger margin for profit. . . .' He believed that a rise in wages, or a cut in wages, forced upon one side of industry by another, and not associated with some change in working hours, efficiency, or output, was quite pointless and, in the long term, damaging to everyone including the general public. He thought that profit-sharing was, at worst, a demeaning charity, if it was simply doled out to the worker with nothing in return. He believed in a sort of commercial second law of thermodynamics which said that an improvement in the organisation of an industrial system can only be achieved as a result of properly directed effort, and any kind of passive mixing and muddling must in the course of time lead only to a general degradation of the system.

He certainly applied this principle to Combines, by which he meant the combination of workers into Trade Unions, or the combination of manufacturers into Trusts. It was this latter type of combination which was very much in his mind in 1906. Three years before at Port Sunlight he had said, 'In my opinion the principles that govern Combines are just as old as the law of gravitation and just as immutable. . . . It is an iron law, and any manufacturer who feels competition keen today and seeks relief in combination with other manufacturers in the same line of business, thinking thereby to avoid what he calls cut-throat competition, unless he can prove to himself that such combination will enable him to produce cheaper goods and to save expenses, will be simply putting off the evil day, and the firms he has combined with will simply drag each other down, down, down, until they disappear. Their place will be taken by men who are producing more cheaply, with probably improved machinery and other better conditions.'

If, on one of his rather irregular attendances at the meetings of the Soap Makers Association, Lever looked around with this speech in his mind, he would have seen little to give him confidence in his fellow members' ability to satisfy his criteria for successful combination. There were one or two manufacturers, Joseph Watson of Leeds for instance, whom Lever found compatible, but any combine conceived and planned within the framework of the Association would surely have inherited far too many bad habits. When Lever resigned his membership in 1905 his sales were at their highest level and, looking at the ineffectual way some members complained about his competition, he would have been justified in thinking that the easiest and safest way of combining with some of the manufacturers would be to bide his time until poor management had still further eroded their position, and then buy them out.

But although in 1905, with his sales breaking previous records, Lever could be somewhat patronising about his competitors, there were trends in his own accounts which were disturbing enough taken alone. When in addition there was a startling rise in the price of raw materials in 1906, Lever's own position was in jeopardy.

Diminishing returns and fierce competition from rivals' promotions meant that Lever had needed a disproportionately large advertising budget to achieve an increase in his sales. The frenetic thrust and counter-thrust of the promotion battle reached a ridiculous pitch. One particular Lever promotion seems to catch the flavour. Men dressed in bright blue uniforms and capes, with hats bearing the words 'Sunlight Soap' in gold, distributed to a bemused public free samples of soap and a book called *How to Become Rich*, written appropriately enough by Barnum of 'The Greatest Show on Earth'.

The rise in the price of raw materials which took place in July 1906 was unexpected and particularly alarming. It was not just one of the irregular peaks and valleys that most of the industry had for years muddled over and welcomed improvidently. This was a sharp and very high leap on to what most believed would almost certainly be a very long plateau. There was consternation among soap manufacturers, amounting almost to panic in some cases. Lever even considered saving costs by a radical change in the sacrosanct formula for Sunlight, but he decided instead to reduce immediately the weight of the sixteen-ounce bar by one ounce. By early August he had approved the printed notices to be placed inside the flaps of the delivery cartons telling retailers of the change.

When the whole industry had appreciated the critical nature of the situation the Northern manufacturers invited Lever to a meeting in Liverpool on July 27th. It was ostensibly to discuss the glycerine market, but would clearly be overshadowed by apprehension about the huge cost of advertising and the rise in raw material prices which menaced the future progress of the industry like two masses of loose snow hanging over a mountain road. By the time Lever came to the meeting he had already put machinery in motion effectively to raise his prices by reducing the size of the Sunlight bar. If he could in addition exert his influence on the whole industry then there could be more economy, greater efficiency, and the sales of soap need not fall, but might indeed be pushed still higher. He arrived at the meeting with his own house put in order, and set upon making a positive bid to form a Soap Trust.

Lever laid before the anxiously receptive audience his views on the advantages of a properly constituted Manufacturers' Combine, pointing particularly to the success achieved by the Coats combine in the sewing thread industry. His contention was that the economies of combination – reduced marketing expenditure, advantages of bulk buying, and the sharing of certain manufacturing and administrative facilities – would allow the increased cost of raw materials to be absorbed by the manufacturers without raising prices at the risk of a cutback in consumption and a fall in profits. (The arrangement for the 15 oz. bar already under way at Port Sunlight was an attempt to make the customer pay the same for consuming less.) Lever's was in no way a proposal for another talking-shop to replace the old Association whose individual members so often flouted agreed policy. The new Combine was to be based on firm financial interdependence which would be achieved by the constituent companies exchanging large blocks of shares.

Less than a week later, on August 2nd, Lever had a meeting with the principals of the firms of Watson, Gossage, and Crosfield at which they discussed the delicate matter of an agreed valuation for each firm, which was an essential preliminary to an exchange of shares. Lever and Joseph Watson, two prime movers in the negotiations, met in London on August 4th to discuss tactics and further contacts. By September the number of big firms throughout the whole country who had agreed to join the Soap Trust was, Lever believed, more than sufficient to ensure its success. He was pleased, too, that a number of smaller firms had also asked to join, because this would help to disarm criticism that the Trust was a grouping of powerful manufacturers which would not be in the interest of smaller businesses and the public. Inevitably some firms, big and small, were not able to agree to the suggested valuation of their assets and would not join. Such a group, outside the Trust, must have viewed it with some apprehension and would have been happier to see it disintegrate.

Lever was in charge of the financial planning, very much in the driving seat, and intending to remain there when the negotiations were completed and the Soap Trust a going concern. He arranged to increase the capitalisation of Lever Brothers from four million to twelve million pounds, the extra shares created to be exchanged for those of the other companies joining the Trust. He also bought two small soap companies, which had for a long time been his targets for take-over and would now be added to the bigger fish which had come voluntarily to hand.

In the early stages Lever and Watson made every attempt to keep the scheme secret. They were worried that the delicate preliminaries might be frustrated by shareholders, shopkeepers, or members of the public with misgivings about the motives or the consequences of the combination. As more companies asked to join the Trust, and especially as some refused to do so, the chances of a leak increased. But by September Lever and Watson felt that although disclosure must be imminent, it could not now spoil the plan. They themselves were busy carrying out the first of the economies for which the Soap Trust had been formed. They decided how many agents might be dismissed – gradually, to avoid a damaging outcry. They cancelled advertising campaigns worth many thousands of pounds which had been provisionally scheduled for the national and provincial Press. It was October before the newspapers published the story about the Trust, first as a simple report and then, particularly in the Northcliffe papers, as a swift crescendo of hostile comment. Lever, who had wished for the dominant role in the Soap Trust, now found himself the principal target of a vituperative newspaper campaign.

The *Daily Mail*, *Daily Mirror*, and *Evening News* carried such headlines as: 'Soap Trust Arithmetic – How 15 ounces make a pound', 'Dismissal of employees begins', and 'Trust Soap Already Dearer'. There were allegations that the Trust was trying to corner the market in raw materials, and was prepared to use 'unsavoury substances' in its soap. There were disparaging references to the labour conditions at 'Port Moonshine', prominently published views from shopkeepers and the public hostile to the Trust, and readers were urged to boycott Sunlight soap and were given the names of non-Trust products to buy instead.

On 23 October 1906 Lever's son wrote to him from Trinity College, Cambridge, 'I can quite understand how worried you must be about the attitude of the Press towards the Combine. What a frightful concoction that was in the *Daily Mail* of yesterday. I enclose you a cartoon from yesterday's *Daily Mirror* in case you have not seen it but I expect you have. What is the use of trying to make the public cry before they are hurt?'

The cartoon* he enclosed summed up the campaign with a picture of a bloated 'Mr Soap Trust', presumably Lever, dealing roughly with a poor woman who had suggested that her bar of soap was an ounce short, and surrounded by posters showing sackings at 'Port Moonshine' and 'If you don't like it – lump it!' The *Daily Mirror* reproduced the cartoon on postcards which it distributed free to the public so that they might post them to aid the 'fight for cheap soap'. Some of them, with offensive messages, were sent to Lever anonymously.

Northcliffe was personally involved in the remarkable campaign. On 18 October 1906 Lever had received from the *Daily Mail* offices a letter saying,[5] 'I am authorized by Lord Northcliffe to convey to you his sincere assurance that in dealing in the columns of the *Daily Mail* with the question of the Soap Manufacturers' Amalgamation, it is the aim and intention to maintain the strictest impartiality and in no sense to take sides. In quoting the views of dealers and in giving publicity to the correspondence reaching us on this subject, the *Daily Mail* assumes no attitude of hostility towards your firm or any other, but, in the pursuit of its duty as a public newspaper, desires to lay before its readers with perfect fairness all sides of the question. . . .'

Lever at once replied to assure Lord Northcliffe that,[6] 'I have never for a moment thought that a high-class newspaper could be actuated by any other desire than perfect accuracy and impartiality. If there is any point which arises where I can be of assistance in ensuring accuracy, I shall be very glad at any time to hear from you.'

This cool exchange of statements of disinterested good faith did not stop the campaign. Northcliffe liked to run a strong controversial story that stirred up emotions and showed his papers as champions of the public against powerful adversaries. A campaign against the proposed Soap Trust had much to commend itself to Northcliffe. He was a close friend of Theodore Roosevelt and a firm supporter of his famous activities as a

* Reproduced facing page 120.

'trust-buster'. The President's battle with the oil, sugar, beef, and other Trusts in America had uncovered some sensational instances of dishonesty, graft, and intimidation, and these had been reported fully in the British Press to the sanctimonious amazement of readers confident that 'it could not happen here'. Northcliffe maintained that there was already a Tobacco Trust in Britain and that events might easily move the American way. He saw the campaign against the Soap Trust as opportunely in accord with his own views, in the public interest, and good for the circulation of his newspapers. Furthermore, although Fleet Street hardly felt itself personally menaced by the fifteen-ounce soap bar, the reduction in advertising was another matter. Reporters were set to work to ferret out any potentially useful titbits of information, and the campaign rolled forward, but with such wild acceleration that it looked as though everyone was pushing and no one was guiding. At the end of October Northcliffe apparently sent a verbal message to Lever[7] saying that the campaign could be brought to an end if he would resume advertising at the old level. Lever refused and the consequences of that decision were soon upon him.

In November Lever sales were 60 per cent down on the corresponding period of the previous year, and other firms in the Combine experienced falls almost as great. The effect in the City was to reduce the share value of Lever Brothers by about 25 per cent. At a despairing meeting of the constituent companies towards the end of November it was proposed and carried that the Trust should be completely abandoned. Lever could not bring himself to support the motion, and he and the rest of his team abstained, although it was clear to him that the industry would now revert to the fierce competition of 1905, that the weight of the Sunlight bar would have to be restored, and that with increased costs and much reduced sales Lever Brothers were in for a major crisis. He was quite correct: Sunlight sales, which had been built up by intense advertising, were now savagely cut by bad publicity. It was ironic that there should be such conflict between Northcliffe, the pioneer of sophisticated advertising through agencies, and Lever, one of the earliest big spenders on newspaper advertising. Northcliffe's action when Lever tried to reduce his advertising budget suggested that the symbiotic relationship lacked benevolence even if it could not fairly be called parasitic. The front page of the *Daily Mail* trumpeted, 'Public Opinion Smashed the Soap Trust'.

Brooding on the disastrous turn that his fortunes had taken in just a few months, Lever felt that there could rarely have been such an obvious combination of injury and insult. There was little possibility of undoing completely the damage done to the Sunlight reputation, which had taken so long, such care, and so much advertising to establish, but something must be done to brush off as much as possible of the mud. There would too be immense personal satisfaction in throwing Northcliffe's allegations back in his face. Lever was absolutely confident that his character, behaviour, and motives would stand the closest public examination, and he sought advice on the possibility of taking action for libel against Northcliffe's Associated Newspapers. The first legal opinion he was given suggested that the publicity and the violent opinions expressed against the Trust made it very unlikely that any jury would find in his favour. But friends and colleagues thought this to be a false conclusion, and his solicitor took the matter to another barrister who had established a connection with Lever Brothers a few years earlier when he had acted as junior counsel for them in a case against a shipping company about a damaged cargo. There now followed the well-publicised incident which gave F. E. Smith an eagerly seized opportunity to advance his professional and political career.[8]

Smith was in the country for the week-end when a telegram asked him to go at once to London on an urgent legal matter. Waiting for him in his room at the Savoy Hotel was a stack of papers four feet high and a most pressing request for a legal opinion by nine o'clock the next morning. He ordered a bottle of champagne and two dozen oysters and, after working on the papers all night, wrote the laconic opinion, 'There is no answer to this action for libel and the damages must be enormous.'

The case came up on 15 July 1907 at Liverpool before Mr Justice Lawrence. There was a little difficulty in swearing in the jury because so many of those called to the Assizes for jury service were excused this particular case because of some connection with Lever's business. There was tremendous interest in the case all over the country and the public's expectation of fireworks in court was intensified when the star-studded teams of barristers appearing for the plaintiffs and defendants were announced. Leading for Lever Brothers was Sir Edward Carson assisted by another King's Counsel and two juniors of whom one was F. E. Smith, later Lord Birkenhead. For the defendants, Associated Newspapers Ltd, Rufus Isaacs, later Marquess of Reading and Viceroy for India, was assisted by another K.C. and two juniors. Apart from those named, the other five barristers in the case ultimately provided three judges and a Recorder of Liverpool.

During the trial Carson and his team stayed at Thornton Manor and were entertained by Lever in great style.[9] They had the opportunity to absorb the Sunlight ethos and thus establish a more convincing background to their case than might have been obtained by poring over a brief in chambers. The benefit Carson and his men derived from the hospitality and support of their principal witness contrasted strongly with the position in which the opposition found themselves.

Rufus Isaacs and his colleagues for the defence were under some handicap because their principal was not to be available to them during the case. Northcliffe was abroad 'for his health' and had no intention of returning within range of any writ server while the case was on. He had played a strong and not very prudent personal role in the soap campaign[10] and in a note from Paris he wrote, 'none of us can be cross-examined on motives of soap cases . . . if I am examined should be obliged to tell truth and therefore Sir G.L. [*his solicitor*] had from the outset decided that I could not be put into box. . . .' Those who remained to fight the case for him were now equally unhappy about the coming action, and a few days before it was due to open Northcliffe offered Lever a public apology. But by this time Lever was not only outraged, he was confident. He wrote to a colleague,[11] 'They have had their detectives round Port Sunlight, and no doubt myself also if I only knew, for the last eight or nine months and have been interviewing every discharged, disgruntled, dissatisfied malcontent that there is or ever was in Lever Brothers' employ any time during the last twenty-two years. They have raked in all the scrap heaps and refuse heaps they could find. If they had discovered anything that would enable them to still further bully and browbeat us they would have had no suggestion of settlement. . . .'

When Carson got up to make his opening speech for the plaintiffs he was very confident. He put the fundamental matter squarely to the jury: 'This libel, gentlemen, is of a very exceptional and serious character, deliberately carried on for several weeks, and was made with the object of smashing up Lever Brothers.' He enumerated the principal complaints against the defendants, starting with their accusation that the company had behaved fraudulently by deceiving the public about the weight of their soap bar. He went on to describe fully Lever's background of enlightened industrial practice, to refute individually all the allegations made by Northcliffe's papers, and to demand from the jury a verdict with punitive damages as the only way in which the incalculable harm done to Lever and his company could be at least in part redressed. His speech lasted five hours and went on into the second day of the trial. It was a beautifully constructed, splendidly delivered address and when he sat down many in court felt that the job of winning the case was more than half done.

Carson then administered what was to prove to be the *coup de grâce*. He knew that his client would impress the jury with his honesty, and he knew too that Lever was expert in handling difficult questions at meetings and would therefore not crack under cross-examination. Knowing all this, and a little more, Carson waved Lever into the witness box, remarking to the jury, 'And now, gentlemen, I have put my first witness – my client, Mr Lever – into the box: let my learned friend, Mr Rufus Isaacs, cross-examine him to his heart's content, and, when his time comes, I hope he will be able to follow my example and do the same, and call as his first witness his own client, Lord Northcliffe. . . .'

When the court adjourned that afternoon the plaintiff's party returned in good heart to Thornton Manor. They were pleased with Lever's showing in the witness box and his cross-examination had yielded nothing of value to Isaacs.

Next morning as soon as the court assembled Isaacs rose and addressed the Judge. 'My Lord, with the assistance of my learned friends I have carefully considered my clients' position. In view of Mr Lever's statements on oath in the witness box and the impression made both upon myself and my friends, and no doubt upon the court, by those statements, it is impossible for my clients to continue their defence under the lines on which it has been drawn. On their behalf, therefore, and with their full concurrence, I beg to withdraw the plea of justification. But my clients wish to do something more than this. They wish to withdraw unreservedly every imputation made upon Mr Lever's honour and integrity, and to say that they very much regret having been misled into making an attack on him. Under the circumstances the only straightforward and honourable course for a newspaper to take is to withdraw without any reservation of any sort. Having resolved upon this course, my clients do not propose to proceed with the defence of fair comment so far as it is applicable to the minor issues of this case. It is right that they should deal with the case in a generous and proper spirit, and there will be no issue for the jury except damages.'

Carson asked for time to bring witnesses on the question of damages and this was granted. *The Times Law Report* continues, 'An interval followed during which Mr Rufus Isaacs and Sir Edward Carson were seen in conversation.'

To describe what took place between the two leading barristers as a conversation was to underplay a very remarkable courtroom scene. Carson conducted a sort of auction in which the discomfited Isaacs was the only bidder. In the crowded court many could hear the whispered exchanges, and everyone could follow what was going on from the two men's expressions as mounting offers from Isaacs were repeatedly rejected by Carson. Ten, fifteen, twenty, thirty, forty thousand pounds, all met with a shake of the head. But, finally, Isaacs rose and addressed the Judge: 'I am happy to be able to inform your Lordship that this case has been settled, nor will your Lordship be troubled with the next case of "Lever Brothers against the *Daily Mirror*" to which the considerations which govern this case equally apply. My Lord, the defendants are anxious to meet the plaintiffs in no mean, niggardly, or grudging spirit. My learned friend has mentioned to me a sum formulated by Mr Lever which we are willing to pay.

That sum is fifty thousand pounds. It is paid in respect of the two actions, but my friend desires that judgment should be given in this action for the whole of fifty thousand pounds, and taxed costs, and in the action against the *Daily Mirror* for taxed costs alone.'

This was an unprecedented amount to be awarded in a libel action and his Lordship then brought the trial to an end saying, 'It was not merely money that was at stake, but the reputation of the defendants. It would be ungracious for me to express criticism of the articles after the course that has been taken. I will only say this, that if I had been called upon to deal with the articles, and if no more justification had been put forward than appeared from Mr Lever's cross-examination, I should have dealt with them in no hesitating or measured manner. (Cheers) There will be judgment for the plaintiffs for fifty thousand pounds and taxed costs.'

As Lever left the building he was cheered by a crowd outside and, that afternoon, back at Port Sunlight where a day's holiday had been declared, he and his wife got a tremendous reception from over three thousand employees gathered to hear him speak.

Next day the *Daily Mail* reported the result of the case in which, it said, it had been involved because of 'a no doubt mistaken sense of public duty'. A rival paper[12] paraphrased the remark of the dirty old tramp in the Pears Soap advertisement, 'Six weeks ago I *abused* your soap, since when I have *abused* no other.'

In spite of the ringing perorations and the celebrations, this was not the end of the Soap Libel affair. It dragged on for many months with a series of minor actions in which many of the participants revealed various types and degrees of unflattering vindictiveness and self-interest.

Lever was particularly incensed by the manner in which other members of the combine, rushing to loot the citadel which he had dared to breach, obtained substantial compensation from Northcliffe – Watson's getting thirty thousand pounds in cash and a similar amount of free advertising in the *Daily Mail*. Not only was the Soap Trust irreparably shattered, but relations between the firms were now worse than in the old days of the Association.

Lever himself continued to pursue Northcliffe, making use of the fact that lawyers acting for Associated Newspapers had not ensured that the *Daily Mail* and *Daily Mirror* settlements were comprehensive. Sir Thomas Lipton, a grocer who had done with tea what Lever had done with soap, tried to secure a truce between the two men, who were friends of his. But when he came bearing offers from Northcliffe he found Lever bitterly intransigent, and the action dragged on. In a letter to Northcliffe his brother, Harold Harmsworth, wrote of Lever,[13] 'As far as we can learn, he has still at the back of his head an idea that he can get anything up to £250,000. Even the flabby Rufus Isaacs does not think he can get more than £10,000, *in toto*, for the remaining actions.'

There is nothing particularly unusual about a barrister being less sanguine than his client about the outcome of litigation, and no doubt Lever and Isaacs freely exchanged views on the subject. In contrast was the showing of another, supposedly loyal, member of Lever's legal team whose duplicity most would have found distasteful and Lever would have treated with furious contempt.

In one of the minor actions the jury found for Lever, but awarded only £500 damages, much less than had been expected. F. E. Smith, Lever's counsel, wrote to Northcliffe,[14] 'Frankly, the result was a great triumph for you. This is very private. None was more disgusted than I at another *rechauffé*, especially after the extraordinarily liberal offer your people made.' Towards the end of the prolonged soap litigation Smith was meeting Northcliffe secretly – hoping, he said, to arrange a final reconciliation between him and Lever – and he wrote, 'If you feel that you have placed yourself at any disadvantage by discussing the case intimately with me, I am quite willing to withdraw from it – if you don't, I hope you will let us meet anyhow, for, God knows, there are many subjects of interest to discuss besides soap.' The notes made by Northcliffe's confidential secretary gave the impression that Smith was determined to secure Northcliffe's support in his political career, and that 'L', presumably Lever, was 'of no use to me, I don't want his money. Would much rather never have seen him.'

When everything was finally settled the case was reckoned to have cost Associated Newspapers something over a hundred and

fifty thousand pounds, and there was deep gloom over Carmelite House. Of this sum Lever Brothers received ninety-one thousand pounds in damages.

The way in which the courts' award was spent is characteristic of Lever and his domination of the Company. It was accepted without question that the money was his to dispose of. It might very properly have been put into the Company's account; it was after all damages and the Company had undeniably been badly damaged. The fall in sales and the rise in the price of raw materials had forced stringent economies upon Lever Brothers, and all work on new building had been stopped in the Works and in the Village at Port Sunlight. The money might well have been used to resuscitate this building programme. But having with autocratic presumption appropriated to himself the damages awarded to Lever Brothers, he gave it all to Liverpool University, earmarking the gift for the endowment of Schools which reflected his own interests and aspirations: Town Planning, Tropical Medicine, and Russian Studies. In the University library he placed a book containing a full account of the litigation and judgment, so that the record of his fight and his victory might be displayed 'for ever'.

Much that he did in his life, not least his almost obsessional remodelling of houses and gardens, carried a hint of concern about immortality: a suggestion of the name-carving syndrome which causes council estates to be named after aldermen, and leads young Americans to deface the sides of vehicles in an aggressive attempt to make themselves known and remembered.

Of the dozen or so houses that Lever lived in, and upon which he stamped his own mark of reconstruction, the three most important were Thornton Manor, The Hill at Hampstead in London, and The Bungalow at Rivington just outside Bolton and not very far from Liverpool.

As the business expanded, Lever had to visit the London office more and more often. Domestic life with his wife and young son was very important to him, and so in 1893 he looked for a permanent London home. After a short spell in a flat, he and his wife moved into a house near Hyde Park where he was able to get some reconstruction done in the few years they were there. In 1904 he bought The Hill, a very large house standing in extensive grounds on the edge of Hampstead Heath. The first alterations were carried out even before he moved in, and thereafter he poured money and ideas into improving the property. Not all his plans were to Hampstead taste, and those who sought to protect the great public amenity of the Heath were often up in arms at his activities from the earliest days of his ownership when he added two large wings to the house and made very elaborate changes to the grounds which considerably raised the level of the lawns and terracing. It was now possible for the public to see into certain areas of the garden, and so in order to preserve his privacy Lever built a screening pergola around the Heath side of his grounds. It was made of brick, with Doric columns and wooden supports for the climbing plants. Many residents and visitors to Hampstead considered it to be a monstrous disfigurement of the Heath.

The property at Hampstead was in no way cramped, but that at Rivington was on an altogether different scale – a superb estate for a man with a taste for changing the shape of the land, and the means to indulge it. When Lever was approached in 1899 by the owners of the Rivington estate he was at once interested in buying the property. Not only did he grapple to his heart the friends of his childhood, but the places and indeed the moral values too. Bolton had given him a wonderful early life, and some of his happiest times had been spent wandering the fields and moorland around Rivington Pike, a landmark over a thousand feet high and a favourite picnic resort of people from Bolton, Wigan, and other nearby industrial areas of Lancashire. Lever thought that he might make some of the estate available for the recreation of the public. He saw, too, that if he put up a house on Rivington Pike the moor sweeping away in front of the building would provide almost limitless possibilities for landscape gardening on the grandest scale.

The land in the area drained into the reservoirs supplying water to Liverpool, and before completing the purchase Lever asked that the Liverpool Corporation first be offered the property at the price he intended to pay. The Corporation expressed no interest in the proposal so the deal was concluded and Lever at once had a large wooden bungalow with a tiled roof built just below the summit of the Pike. He earmarked some forty or fifty acres surrounding the house for his own use, and offered much of the rest of the estate as a municipal country park to the Bolton Corporation, who gratefully accepted.

Then in 1902 Liverpool Corporation promoted a Parliamentary Bill to obtain statutory powers over much of the land feeding their reservoirs. This included Lever's house and grounds, and the park he had given to Bolton. Lever and others objected to the provisions of the Bill and the matter was eventually threshed out before a Select Committee of the House of Commons. In May 1905 it was ruled that Lever might keep his house and forty-five acres of grounds, and that the proposed park should be taken over by Liverpool, although still maintained for the public benefit. Lever was given the 'right' to provide at his own expense a number of amenities he had planned for the park. Over the years he built roads, restored a fourteenth-century barn to make a refreshment room, established a museum, stocked paddocks with exotic cattle and other animals, and, most ambitious of all, put up on the bank of a reservoir a striking replica of the ruins of the old Liverpool Castle which had been pulled down in the development of that city.

The price to be paid by Liverpool Corporation for Lever's land gave rise to quite unnecessary litigation between the two parties. It is remarkable how often Lever seemed to bring out the worst in public officials. Sometimes it almost seemed that they resented the way he achieved instant reforms by spending his own money, when they were struggling to do much the same using public funds.

Lever offered to let Liverpool have the land for the price he had paid for it plus expenses, but the Corporation refused the offer and the matter was tried before an umpire appointed by the Government. At the hearing, which lasted several days, both sides were represented by counsel, Asquith leading for Lever. The umpire's decision staggered the officials of the Corporation. Lever was to receive almost twice the price he had originally given for the whole estate. The Corporation was now required to approve payment out of the rates of a sum far in excess of that for which they could originally have obtained the land. They lodged an appeal on the unusual grounds that the umpire had been ill at the hearing and not in a fit state of mind to pronounce judgment. Dismissing this appeal in April 1905, Mr Justice Warrington said, 'I am surprised that such a body as the Liverpool Corporation should have put such a plea as that on record. I can only say that there is not a particle of evidence to support it.' At last the matter was settled – to nobody's satisfaction. The inhabitants of Bolton, the nearest town, got most benefit, and the ratepayers of Liverpool paid dearly for what was to have been a gift. Ironically it was decreed that the land should be called Lever Park. Bolton had made Lever a Freeman but, rather unjustly, his stock did not stand so high among Liverpudlians, who were mostly ill-informed about the true course of events. But inside his own long perimeter at The Bungalow the urge to create hills and streams took charge and his excavations and reconstructions were almost Babylonian. The great Japanese garden – with lake, waterfalls, oriental tea-houses, pagodas, exotic ornaments and shrubs – was perhaps the most spectacular feature.

Lever's happy domestic life rested upon the firm base of his three fine, happily never quite completed, houses. To take his houses a little nearer to his own complicated idea of perfection was his greatest, but not all-absorbing, hobby. In London he sometimes went to the theatre several times in a week, and he greatly enjoyed an outing to a variety show or a music hall. In the country he liked riding, and driving his light carriage and pair. He was an accomplished whip and found it particularly thrilling to take a four-in-hand at great pace on the long run from Thornton Manor to Chester, with a stop at an inn half-way for a change of horses.

Company affairs frequently intruded into his home and he gave many business dinners which were an extension of his punishing working day. There were often other, more relaxed parties for old friends and for relatives. He enjoyed, too, the quiet times: a simple meal, sometimes high tea, with his wife; a walk in the grounds with his young son when the boy was not away at school. The Levers were loving parents, taking trouble to make their only child happy, but carefully trying not to over-indulge him. Lever wrote regularly to him at Eton, keeping him in touch with what went on at home. On the day the Select Committee announced their decision on Rivington in 1902 he sent the boy a telegram, and an amplifying letter[15] ending, 'We must be satisfied that it might have been worse.'

In 1905 he wrote to 'My dear Will', care of his housemaster, with details of the boy's finances: a modest account including a few pounds of half-year dividend from Lever Brothers shares. Lever decided that at seventeen his son was ready for a measure of independence.[16] 'It has given me very special pleasure to have been able to arrange for you to have a bank account, and this is so because you have always used your money well and not wasted it. It is a very proud day for your mother and myself when you can draw your own cheques on your own account. With the fondest love, in which your mother joins. . .'.

A few months earlier Lever had been enjoying himself trying out cars on his son's behalf, and he reported to the boy,[17] 'when I came to consider the De Dion motor and other small motors I found that there were objections to each and every one of them. The De Dion is stated to be too noisy, the Swift I tried seems to be too fragile and easily breaks down, as I did not want you to have a perfectly useless machine I decided to go in for the seven horse-power Panhard. I include specification. I am having it for you with a number ten sprocket which will give an average running speed of about 16 m.p.h. . . .'

Always sharp-eyed for useful innovations Lever was himself an early user of the motor car, adding his own characteristic twist to its employment. On a long drive he would take two cars, stopping from time to time to transfer into his own vehicle one of a group of people, travelling in the second car, all of whom he wished to interview on various matters during the journey. True to Samuel Smiles he conserved the minutes, quite prepared to pay for redundancy – in the scientific sense – in equipment or staff in order to save his own time. His dictating to several stenographers simultaneously was an earlier example and, rather less plausible, in his bathroom at The Hill, Hampstead, he had enormous taps fitted so that he had only seconds to wait for his bath to fill.

As Lever Brothers spread over the world, duty and inclination took Lever on many trips overseas. He often made short visits to the Continent, and he crossed the Atlantic a dozen times in just a few years, having to work hard to get the business as well established in Canada and the U.S.A. as it was in Europe. He spent some time in the cotton states of the South, setting up, under a Civil War colonel as manager, seed-crushing plant to produce oil. This was at Vicksburg, the much besieged town upon which Grant imposed the famous 'unconditional surrender'.

Lever enjoyed foreign travel and he managed, more often than not, to take with him his wife and son, or other relatives, to share and enhance the pleasure of the novel sights and customs which he observed keenly. At Monte Carlo he and Mrs Lever visited the Casino but decided that it would be a foolish waste of money to play. He recorded in his diary, 'The best sport was to watch the people – young and old, rich and poor, good, bad, and indifferent – all gathered together. The nervous twitching of the faces of some who were evidently making the game a matter of the most serious importance to them; the lightness of others who cared little whether they won or lost, and the stony stare of the old habitué – all a grand study of human nature.' On that same trip he and his wife went to Egypt, travelling up the Nile in one of Cook's steamers. He was favourably impressed with the moral aspects of the Moslem's religion and, thinking of the continual fund-raising activities by English Christian mission societies, he wrote,[18] 'It appears clearer than ever that the money spent on missionary efforts is worse than wasted; that the same money spent in taking the little children out of the gutters in England, feeding, clothing, and educating them decently until they are fifteen, then putting them in respectable service or the Colonies would do ten thousand times more good.' Lever himself was a builder of churches, a listener to sermons, and a contributor to missions, but on the whole he preferred the ethics to the theology, the ritual to the doctrine, and the Anthem to the Creed.

When Lever made his first round-the-world tour it lasted six months, and he took with him his wife, his son, and his wife's companion-housekeeper. In September 1892 they set out across the Atlantic in the White Star liner *Germanic*. Lever greatly admired many of the American commercial methods. Some of their ideas, imported and modified, had been fundamental to the

success of Lever Brothers. But there was much about the New World that was not to his taste. After nine days at sea he was infuriated by a delay of twelve hours in immigration control on arrival, 'we had to be sacrificed to encourage implicit faith on the part of the American public in the completeness of all the arrangements made by the medical officers for preventing the introduction of cholera. . . .' In contrast a church they attended was altogether too lively, with applause and laughter during the service: 'our older fashioned way is the best.' When they visited Salt Lake City, Lever was – reluctantly – impressed by the beautiful tree-lined streets with streams on both sides. He regarded Brigham Young as 'a clever imposter' and the excellence of the town-planning as a testimony to his cleverness.

They were just too early for the World's Fair in Chicago, where Lever reported that the young people had a jaded look as if the pace of life was too much for them. He wrote, 'I am very much mistaken if the "sweater" has not got a firm grip in Chicago, and it would not take much to convince me that, however much of a paradise it may be for the capitalist, it is the direct opposite for the worker. . . .' As Lever recorded his impressions of the journey he sent them home to the *Birkenhead News* where they appeared as articles subsequently published in a book called *Following the Flag. Jottings of a Jaunt Round the World* by W. H. Lever.[19]

The party sailed from San Francisco for Australia and New Zealand, and as they crossed the Pacific under a clear sky Lever observed that up till then he had thought the blue of certain sea pictures was overdone. In Honolulu they heard a South Sea Island child singing 'Ta-ra-ra-boom-de-ay' and felt a half-affectionate amusement as though the family dog, left behind at home, had come trotting out of the jungle. Noting the dramatic fall in the native population of the Sandwich Islands since Cook's day, Lever commented, 'How shall we judge which is best for the native – which best fulfills the doctrine of the "greatest good to the greatest number"?'

In Australia and New Zealand senior members of Lever Brothers' staff accompanied the party and arranged that they got the opportunity of looking a little more deeply at things than the ordinary tourist. Lever was much interested in the New Zealand Labour Government – a subject of some anxious speculation back in Britain. He came to the conclusion that it was a good government with some sound new ideas about taxation which might tend to break up big estates but which would not bear unduly hardly upon the industrial capitalist.

On the voyage home by P. & O. liner one of the diversions for the first-class passengers was a debate on the merits of Free Trade, with Lever the principal speaker in its favour. The chair was taken by another of the passengers, the Hon. George Curzon, then in his mid-thirties, of whom Lever said, 'He will undoubtedly become a bright and shining light in the Conservative Party.'

Lever himself was now a committed member of the Liberal Party. In July 1892, just before he set out on his first world tour, he had stood as Liberal candidate for Birkenhead, a safe Conservative seat in the past and likely to be even safer in 1892 with the Liberal Party in disarray after Gladstone's first Irish Home Rule Bill six years before. Lever greatly admired Gladstone, who, in 1891, had opened the first of the amenity buildings at Port Sunlight Village, a men's recreation hall and dining-room which was named Gladstone Hall. At the opening ceremony Gladstone referred to Carlyle's prediction that by the twentieth century cash payment would be the principal link between one man and another. 'In this hall,' said Gladstone, 'I have found a living proof that cash payment is not the only nexus between man and man.'

In his speech of welcome Lever referred to the particular debt owed to Gladstone by the soap industry. In 1853 he had removed the duty on soap and in 1861 he had removed the duty on paper. These two measures encouraged the large-scale manufacture of soap and the growth of the cheap, mass-circulation Press, a combination exploited by Sunlight through the medium of advertising, of which Lever said, 'at present this art is little understood, and often looked at askance as something that is undignified and appertaining to the charlatan . . . the Press, next to duty-free paper, owes most to the advertisers, and the day is coming when advertising will take its place as a useful and beneficial art, and when it will be recognized that it is a necessity, in continuous, persistent and successful advertising, that the quality of the articles advertised be irreproachable'.

It was soon after Gladstone's visit to Port Sunlight that Lever was approached to stand for Birkenhead in the general election of July 1892. He was a reluctant candidate, not really wishing to take time from his business for the strenuous campaigning that would be expected of him. He certainly did not wish for a Parliamentary career, but there was no danger of his being elected for Birkenhead, and he accepted the nomination in order that there should be a candidate to encourage Liberal supporters to close ranks and so that the local organisation would be stiffened by a taste of electoral powder and shot. Lever was a lively speaker with a good electioneering style and considerable skill in debate, where he dealt well with impromptu questions. When the count was declared the Conservative was duly elected but Lever had done much better than expected, reducing the majority by half.

Lever fought several more elections, always with a show of reluctance, never in a safe seat, and on most occasions agreeing to stand only because there was for some reason no other acceptable candidate available. Less than two years after his first contest there was an unexpected by-election in Birkenhead caused by the sitting member's sudden elevation to the peerage. Lever had arranged to visit the United States on business and an election campaign was a great inconvenience. He told his local party association that he would pay all the election expenses if they would find another candidate, but that they must find all the expenses if he himself stood. The Liberal association chose to pay for Lever and he ran the Conservative very close.

At the snap election of July 1895 there was no time to consider looking for another candidate and once more Lever did well but was not elected. Then in 1900 he refused to contest the seat in Birkenhead because the Conservative member was away fighting in the Boer War. But he was not allowed to escape his electoral chore and he was persuaded to fight another Conservative stronghold, the Wirral constituency where he lived, and once again he managed to reduce the majority. He had no intention of standing again for Parliament and was glad to give his support to the new prospective Liberal candidate for Wirral. Then, at the very last moment before the 1906 election, this new candidate withdrew and once more Lever came to the aid of the party.

During the dozen or more years spanning these campaigns Lever showed himself to be an unusual candidate in many ways, not least in his moral principles and sporting behaviour, which were not universal among Victorian politicians.

In the course of a speech in 1903 Lever said that he could not understand how a working man could be a Conservative. He was challenged to debate the matter with F. E. Smith before the Liverpool Conservative Working-men's Association. He accepted, acquitted himself well, and rounded off the affair some time later by having two hundred of the Conservative members of the Association as his guests on a tour of Port Sunlight. More disturbing to his keener political supporters than such party manners was Lever's attitude to canvassing. He said,[20] 'I do not look favourably upon canvassing, it is highly improper for an employer of labour to canvass his workmen. . . . Nothing but moral suasion and argument should be employed, and I desire no other result than the wishes of the electors. I have not called upon a single person to ask for his vote, neither have I visited private works or property for the purpose of making an election speech. I should not feel comfortable if I were returned on any basis other than that I represent the principles of the majority of the electors and can serve the borough.'

Lever summed up his general, and unusual, attitude to electioneering in a letter many years later to his son:[21] 'I always endeavoured in the old days to avoid any Port Sunlight building being used for political purposes unless I had arranged similarly for a corresponding use by the Conservative association. The . . . time I was candidate in Birkenhead I was very strict on this, as also in Wirral, and . . . the fact that I held a meeting in Port Sunlight was balanced by the fact that the Tories also held one. In 1892 while I was Liberal candidate for Birkenhead, and a Liberal meeting had been held at Port Sunlight, I took the chair for the Conservative Party at their meeting at Port Sunlight. This was far in advance of the mentality of Liberalism at that time and really I think it did me a great deal of harm because it was not understood.

'I strongly urge you to keep Port Sunlight clear of politics. The Tory Party in that district have educated the people for very many years with the idea that employment gives the employer the right to expect the vote. This runs through every phase of service, including in the old days, the gardener, the butler, and the coachman. I always fought against it and I know it would be equally repugnant to yourself that an idea should get about that because a man happened to work at Port Sunlight and that you and I were Liberals that therefore we had a sort of right of pre-emption on the political opinion of those who worked at Port Sunlight. . . .'

In 1906 the great 'landslide' election swept many surprised Liberal candidates into Parliament, among them Lever, who was not elated at having to face life in Westminster. It is pleasant to record that having got to the House of Commons, Lever put forward a plan for its reconstruction. He proposed to improve the appearance of the Palace of Westminster by rebuilding the Terrace of the House of Commons so that it had two tiers. The Minister of Works did not proceed with the plan.

# 7

# *The House of Commons*

Although it was the Liberal landslide which carried him into the House of Commons, Lever might well have blamed his reluctant presence there upon a certain inherent conservatism. He liked old friends, familiar places, and he tended to go on doing the things he had done before. The tendency to repeat, almost as a reflex, some action which had originally been carefully considered, led him occasionally into difficulty, in business and in his social experiments. In 1906 it landed him in Westminster as a surprised new Member, worried about getting out rather than staying in.

Perhaps he was inspired, or persuaded, to stand in a general election for the first time by his hero, Gladstone, visiting Port Sunlight in November 1891, eight months before Lever fought the Birkenhead seat. After one or two such hopeless contests any aspiring Parliamentarian might expect an offer of a more promising constituency, and it would have been very surprising if such an offer had not been made to a man of Lever's wealth and influence, who had proved that he could attract votes. But Lever was not an aspiring Parliamentarian, he was a perennial prospective candidate.

His reasons for wanting this sterile role are difficult to assess. Perhaps it gave him a little extra standing in the local community; certainly it provided a rather wider audience for his didactic speeches than a Chamber of Commerce or the employees at Port Sunlight. It hardly furthered his wish to improve the lot of the people, because he had no intention of becoming an M.P. In so far as he was inspired by any sense of service it was, in this instance, to the Liberal Party rather than the people. He may possibly have been attracted by the notion of presenting himself as a great man sacrificing himself in a lost cause, like the gallant goalkeeper of a losing football team. But as a frequent employer of lawyers – Asquith, Isaacs, and Smith among them – Lever was well aware how barristers could enjoy a swift journey to fame along the carefully engineered twin track of politics and profession. He may easily have believed that it was important to his own international business aspirations to have some influence in political circles. But Lever's business career, unlike the legal profession, left little room for a parallel political track. As a regular candidate in hopeless seats, as a man who could provide funds, as a host who could offer the use of houses and grounds, he would at least be *persona grata* with political leaders even though he could not expect to be one of them. If in so frequently offering himself to the people with no intention of ever being taken he was being a political tease, then he was overtaken by the fate which is the occupational hazard of the tease. He went on doing what he had always done and in 1906, underestimating the emotions of the electorate, he found himself bundled into the House of Commons.

Lever fought Birkenhead three times and Wirral twice, being returned to Parliament in the January 1906 election at his second attempt in Wirral. He delivered his maiden speech in February 1906, but by the following autumn he had made up his mind to apply for the Chiltern Hundreds and informed the chairman of the local party of his intention. The prospect of a by-election in a marginal seat less than a year after taking office did not appeal to the Government Whips' Office, where there is a traditional timidity about consulting the voters again when electoral promise and government performance stand in such close temporal juxtaposition. The Chief Whip was called to use all his resources of tact and persuasion before Lever would agree to save possible Liberal embarrrassment and retain his seat. A publicly acknowledged condition for Lever's co-operation was that he would only be expected to attend Parliamentary sittings when specially summoned and that he would otherwise be free to pursue his business affairs, which certainly needed his attention in the difficult period after the soap libel. On these terms Lever remained an M.P. until the Dissolution of Parliament, when he did not seek reelection for the Wirral constituency. Instead, in the 1910 election, he contested the Ormskirk division in Lancashire; once more he had agreed to carry the Liberal flag in a hopeless contest. However unconventional it was, Lever's political behaviour appeared to find favour in the highest Liberal circles. In 1911 he was created a baronet. In 1912 he entertained Asquith and his wife at a political garden party held at Thornton Manor, and on the same day the Liberal Prime Minister visited Port Sunlight and made a speech just as Gladstone had done a little over twenty years before.

The fact that he was an unwilling M.P. was not made by Lever into an excuse for indifference towards his duties at Westminster. In the first months of his brief career in the Commons he often caught the Speaker's eye, and he made serious contributions to debates on old-age pensions, housing, and the payment of M.P.s. Such social matters particularly engaged his attention and he seemed to set out immediately to try to persuade Parliament to do for the country some of the things that he had done for Port Sunlight. No doubt, like most new members, he was oppressed by the traditions, the rules, and the procedural obscurities of Parliament. He would too have felt the disappointment of being at the seat of national power yet seemingly excluded from exercising any real personal influence. More than most of the newcomers Lever would have been dismayed and frustrated by the enormous inertia of the democratic legislative process. Whatever the demerits of autocracy it was undeniably swift-acting. When an idea came into Lever's head in his office at Port Sunlight he knew that if he so decreed it would be implemented within weeks or even days. But his early disenchantment with the slow grinding of the Parliamentary machine is evident in the opening lines of a speech he made three months after entering the House.[1] Of the Housing of the Working Classes Amendment Bill he said that 'if the thirty-three Bills passed in the last fifty years have produced no results, is it certain that this Bill would carry things much further?' The report of the rest of his speech, read nearly seventy years later, adds ironic emphasis to his opening remarks. 'If employers in any district could throw the burden of providing houses for their people on the Local Authority it would be to their advantage; but I do not think that a Local Authority should make such a provision to satisfy a demand, and in rural districts the landowner should provide for housing as part of the equipment of his land. The great difficulty in the housing problem is the land question (Hear, hear). The small builder finds the greatest difficulty in getting a small quantity of land. He might buy wholesale, but that is beyond the means of his capital and the needs of the district, and the acquisition of land for two or three cottages is surrounded with difficulties; the landowner is not disposed to cut off a small piece of his property, and fees and costs are out of all proportion to the builder's requirements. If, however, the Bill were so amended in committee that a Local Authority should have increased facilities for acquiring land and leasing it in small quantities to suit the requirements of builders, that would go a long way towards removing difficulties. Powers might be given to advance money on mortgage at a low rate of interest, and the money advanced, taking the form of ground-rent, would encourage building and there would not be competition with individual builders or holding up of land for speculative purposes. . . .' Supporting the second reading of the Bill he hoped 'that in committee close investigation will be given to the policy of giving increased power to the Local Authority to acquire land, but not to conduct the building of the houses'.

In 1907, although it was after his agreement with the Whips about partial withdrawal from Parliamentary duties, Lever seized the opportunity when he drew a place in the ballot for Private Members' Bills. He introduced his Old-Age Pension Bill to provide pensions payable at the Post Office for all persons of both sexes at the age of sixty-five. It was to be introduced gradually, taking in those over seventy-five in the first year, those over seventy in the second, and becoming fully operative in the third year. The opponents of the Bill relied upon the stern companions of moral principle and protection of the public purse. A member of Lever's own party put down a motion for the rejection of the Bill which declared that old-age pensions should be provided jointly by employers and employees, and also by habits of thrift and insurance. Lever did not believe it was practicable to make the scheme depend on a joint contribution from employers and employees, and he went on to say that he was 'not sure that thrift was the highest form of citizenship. No father or mother worthy of the name would hesitate to sacrifice their payments to an insurance company if they were called upon to choose between securing their provision for old age and spending the money to relieve their children in sickness or promote their advancement in life. Many fathers and mothers never had the means to insure yet they had done far more to deserve an old-age pension than if they had saved money by thrift. The method of insurance, even where it was possible for working people to keep up the payments, was costly, because so many small premiums had to be collected weekly. The provision by the State of old-age pensions was as legitimate as the State education of children. The State should do for the individual citizen what it was out of his power to do for himself, and when it was for the advantage of the State and the well-being of the citizen to have it done. . . .'

Lever intended that the pension fund should be financed by an extension of income tax on a graduated scale so that every wage-earner came within the scheme. He believed strongly that such a method of raising the bulk of the nation's revenue would have great advantages. The graduated system, he said, 'should embrace even the man earning twenty shillings a week who might be required to pay twopence in the pound. When we come to the rich man, on the other hand, I see no reason for stopping at one shilling. The man of small wages would, I think, be the better for being included in this scheme. The contribution which he was called upon to pay would make him a more thoughtful citizen. A system of old-age pensions standing upon such a basis would not be open to the objection that it was benevolence or philanthropy.' Lever, with some perspicacity, rejected a suggestion that money to pay old-age pensions might be raised by the nationalisation of the railways:[2] 'In my opinion, the nationalisation of the railways would result in a loss of revenue to the State, though it would certainly benefit the shareholders. I do not believe that money for an old-age pension scheme can be obtained by that means. I would rather advocate the nationalisation of canals, and the providing of improved facilities for motor traffic. If that were done the rates for the carriage of goods would fall, and anyone who wished to buy railway stock ten years afterwards would not have to pay the price which the Government would have to pay for the railways if they were bought by the State now.'

The opposition to Lever's Bill expressed grave disquiet about any increase in taxation, and the further moral objection was squarely stated by one Member: 'A man might have spent all his life, not in working for his country, but in injuring it by his own vicious conduct. He might have been, for the greater part of his life, an idle, drunken blackguard, but at sixty-five he is to be entitled to five shillings a week out of the pockets of the sober and the thrifty. And that is what my hon. friend calls social reform!'

Although the Bill was carried easily when the House divided, it lapsed because the Government allocated it no further time. But in the Budget of 1908 money was provided for a non-contributory old-age pension up to five shillings a week for those over seventy whose weekly income was less than twelve shillings. Even the sternest guardians of the national purse found it hard to be outraged at the scale of benefits, and Lever was pleased that at least a start had been made. In 1909 Lloyd George included in his Budget a proposal for a graduated income tax, and Lever was even more pleased to find that his ideas were, to some extent, coming into effect, albeit desperately slowly by his standards. But this 1909 Budget was the one which precipitated the bitter struggle with the House of Lords and the eventual restriction of its power by the Parliament Bill, forced through the Upper House under the threat that the King would create floods of Liberal peers if it were not passed. These tempestuous days, when the Lords threw out the Budget and there followed the two quick elections of 1910, heralded a batch of social measures including the National Insurance Act and legislation against 'sweated labour'. Such measures were much to Lever's taste, but he counted himself lucky to be out of the House of Commons and not involved in the interminable, bitter constitutional squabbles which he regarded as a waste of time and an unpardonable digression from important works of reform.

It is tempting to speculate on what Lever might have done if he had stayed in Parliament and been given a Ministry. Lloyd George is reported to have said of him[3] that 'he could not work with other men' – but much the same might have been said of Beaverbrook, who, perhaps for that very reason, had a galvanic effect when placed in charge of aircraft production in the 1939–45 War. Lever might well have lifted the Victorian face of industrial Britain, building light, airy factories and model villages in hundreds across the country. Perhaps such Government patronage would have been more acceptable to labour, in the long run, than were Lever's private schemes, and by its nature as well as its scale it might have had a significant effect on the country's labour relations.

Had Lever been offered office early in his Parliamentary career the compliment, the challenge, and the chance of power to initiate change would almost certainly have outweighed the wish to resign, which arose from an unwillingness to sacrifice time from his business in order to assist in a minor way in the painfully slow legislative process. But at the time that Lever first raised the question of resignation – in the autumn of 1906 – the libellous Press campaign against the Soap Trust overshadowed his political life, and indeed every other aspect of his life. Certainly the crisis in the soap industry which led to the formation of the Trust greatly increased Lever's reluctance to neglect his business for what he felt to be frustratingly ineffective work on the floor of the House of Commons. The unfavourable publicity directed at him probably ruled out any chance of ministerial office – although a more distinguished Liberal politician, Rufus Isaacs, was not barred from promotion by similar publicity in the Marconi Scandal a few years later. Whilst the outcry against Lever and the Soap Trust militated against his political promotion it also reinforced the Liberal Whips' unwillingness to accept his resignation and face the ensuing by-election. There were undoubtedly other considerations than the stated business reasons which prompted Lever to consider withdrawing from Parliament. He would have felt it only fair to the Liberal Party to offer his resignation when, as a prominent radical, he was accused of swindling the public. Furthermore he found personal criticism exceedingly hard to bear and ridicule intolerable, and he certainly felt that during the newspaper campaign Members of the House of Commons were gossiping about him behind his back and trying to avoid speaking

Lever by Sir Luke Fildes

Mrs Lever by Sir Luke Fildes

The Warrington Factory

Port Sunlight 1890

to him if they met him face to face in the Lobby or public rooms.

Probably there was, therefore, no incident sweeter to him during his brief and relatively undistinguished Parliamentary career than the reception given him when he entered the House for the first time after receiving the verdict in the *Daily Mail* libel case. The *Daily Telegraph* reported the following day,[4] 'Ministers have had fine receptions on returning from conquest or defeat. Newcomers on their début, old friends on their reappearance have provoked stirring party cheers, but we cannot recall any outburst analogous to that which greeted Mr Lever yesterday. The whole House broke into full cry – Radicals, Unionists, Orangemen, Nationalists and Labour men joined in common chorus of sympathetic cordiality. Mr Lever flushed with gratification and bent his head in gratitude. The House shouted again, and then a diplomatic Member beckoned the honourable gentleman to a more comfortable position. No sooner had he risen to accept the offer than the kindly demonstration was renewed. Whereupon Mr Lever, beaming more brightly than ever, stood up and literally "bowed his acknowledgements" amid cries of "Bravo". A remarkable and unprecedented incident in the modern history of Parliament and a compliment the more to be prized by reason of its spontaneity and generous sincerity.'

Such public vindication after the attacks of the newspapers was personally gratifying, but the material consequences of the whole affair were profound. Lever estimated that by 1909 it had cost him about half a million pounds. There was in addition the incalculable damage arising from the destruction of the Soap Trust, of which much had been hoped, and the emergence of the Co-operative Wholesale Society as a very serious competitor in consequence of the orders it received and retained because it was free from the much publicised taints of capitalism. Furthermore, from 1906 onwards the soap market in the United Kingdom stopped expanding and competition from the margarine manufacturers pushed up the price of raw materials as their sales grew rapidly. Lever pointed out[5] that soap contained 63 per cent fatty acids and margarine 85 per cent, but that margarine sold for two and a half times the price of soap, and 'there is practically no good oil or fat but what the margarine maker can make into excellent food'.

Lever's strategy for the bad times from 1906 to 1914 was the same as in the good years – Company growth. He would create the equivalent of the Soap Trust entirely under his own control by buying other soap firms, he would attack the problem of raw materials by securing his own sources in the tropics, and he would expand the overseas business which was now proportionately more profitable than the United Kingdom trade. These projects required enormous amounts of extra capital, but for the first time the public and the money market had lost confidence in Lever Brothers, and Lever had the mortification of seeing capital issues remaining under-subscribed even though they were floated at terms very disadvantageous to the Company. It was lucky for Lever that he had enjoyed twenty fat years to establish himself in the soap trade. By 1906 Lever Brothers was strong enough to consume other companies rather than be itself taken over, a process which Lever would unquestionably have resisted with manic intensity to the point of self-destruction.

It was lucky too for Port Sunlight that there had been twenty years of prosperity to share. Had it not already grown to a viable community by the time the economies came, it might now be a half-ruined folly like a Palmerston fort, or like another later social experiment of Lever's. A simple list of the buildings which had been put up by the end of Edward VII's reign gives some idea of how well founded was the little township with nearly eight hundred houses, all of high quality, and a permanent population of about four thousand.

The two large schools with well over a thousand pupils; an air-conditioned cottage hospital with a resident doctor and four nurses; a church in traditional style to seat seven or eight hundred worshippers; a large inn built round three sides of a galleried courtyard; a Technical Institute providing a three-year evening course for five hundred students; a museum and a library; an auditorium seating two thousand five hundred which was also used as a theatre and ballroom; a heated open-air swimming-pool and a gymnasium; a men's social club and a smaller club for girls; Gladstone Hall, where eight hundred men could eat their dinners, and Hulme Hall, the women's self-service restaurant seating nearly two thousand, both these halls being also used for meetings, concerts, and dances; a very large general store run by an employees' provident society, a Post Office, and a few specialist shops – butcher, hairdresser, draper, newsagent.

But a catalogue of buildings does not sufficiently indicate the power and vitality which Port Sunlight had acquired, nor its special style and the vigorous spirit which permeated the community. Lever was criticised for mixing, in his own houses and at Port Sunlight, the art and architecture of many periods. But the Village, and indeed the Works, had a distinction which transcended the mere shape and colour of the buildings. The Port Sunlight style embodied above all an almost greedy preoccupation with space, light, air, and freedom of movement. Every aspect of the planning and construction was treated generously and with an acute sense of function.

The first impression made by the Village turned out to have lasting validity: a great deal of open grassland with well-built houses set in groups – never in long rows – the antithesis of a Bolton slum. There were about seven houses to the acre – the Building Act allowed forty-five – and they each had a bathroom and at least three bedrooms. The living-rooms were not less than fourteen feet by twelve, there were no attic bedrooms and the smallest ones were twelve feet by nine. The bathroom and the scullery had hot and cold taps, the copper was designed to convert into a table when not used for the washing, and the little yard leading to the back garden and allotments was paved with brick and carefully sloped away from the house to the outbuildings: water-closet, coal-shed, and ash-bin cupboard.

In the Works area very wide roads with grass verges and well kept flower beds gave a feeling of spaciousness which was startlingly reinforced on entering the buildings themselves. The offices, for instance, were single-storied buildings nearly thirty feet high, flooded with light from a glass roof and huge ten-foot windows in the walls. The factory buildings were similar and had wood-block floors which were warm to the feet and easily kept clean. When artificial light was required it was provided by electricity, and the majority of the buildings were heated by low-temperature steam, conserved from the soap-making process.

Two buildings in particular typified the architectural and social style of Port Sunlight: these were Gladstone Hall and Hulme Hall, both primarily intended to provide midday meals for the many hundreds of employees who did not live in the Village. Gladstone Hall, for men, was large with a high vaulted roof and huge windows. It was starkly furnished with tables and benches where about eight hundred men sat down to eat the dinner they had brought to work with them. No meals were provided, but the staff would cook or warm the men's own food in ovens heated by steam to ensure that there would be no burning. The staff also provided, at no charge, salt, hot water, tea or coffee pots, mugs, trays, and spoons. The walls were hung with many oil paintings from Lever's collection, and the table-tops were arranged to swing over and provide seats with backs when the Hall was used for meetings or concerts. Hulme Hall catered for the many hundred girls and women who poured in to work each day from Liverpool and Birkenhead. It was much bigger than Gladstone Hall – one hundred and seventy feet long and very high – and here the walls were decorated mostly with the original drawings made for soap advertisements. A good meal was provided cheaply, or alternatively the employees' own food was warmed, and as in the men's restaurant, hot water and utensils were provided free of charge.

The thousands of employees who filled the offices and factories and even more so the hundreds who lived in the Village, considered themselves lucky to work at Port Sunlight. The wages were rather better than the Union rate, the working conditions very much superior to anything else likely to be found in the district, and the fringe benefits were considerable. There was about the place a bustling air of success, a sense of high rewards for hard work, a cultivation of efficiency, and a keen corporate competitiveness directed at other, generally less successful, firms. It was an atmosphere attractive to the enterprising working people of northern England, and their social temperament is indicated by the number and character of the clubs and institutions which flourished in the Village. Included in a list of more than thirty was a choral society, an orchestral society, and a silver prize band; three temperance associations and a Bible-reading society; a mutual improvement society and a scientific and literary society; clubs for gymnastics and half a dozen other sports; social clubs, a horticultural society, a women's guild and a division of the St John Ambulance Brigade. These were all controlled by the members themselves, although in most cases the Company made some contribution which might be no more than the free loan of a hall, or could be as important as the paid appointment of a musical director who gave his advice and professional assistance to the musical societies and the Church.

Lever went to some pains to show an interest in all the societies and clubs. He acted as chairman, he presented prizes, he gave talks on social and political affairs, he prepared illustrated lectures on his travels abroad. In 1902 he became a Freemason when he was initiated at the first meeting of the William Hesketh Lever Lodge which had been formed in Port Sunlight by local Masons, most of whom worked for the Company and chose to have the Lodge named after the Chairman. He became Worshipful Master in 1907 and went on to hold offices at national level and to help found no less than seventeen new Lodges.

All the important events in the Village were arranged whenever possible so that Lever could be present. He did not spare himself from the activities which he found unattractive, and although, for instance, he was bored by serious music, he frequently attended the meetings and concerts of the Orchestral society and the Philharmonic society, and it was characteristic of his interest that he arranged for the latter to give a choral concert at the Queen's Hall in London. On these formal occasions in the Village he basked in the warmth of the address of welcome, the vote of thanks, and the applause that was invariably accorded him. He appreciated it like the glow after his cold bath, or the thrill of his name in the Honours List. At less formal gatherings he liked to mix with the employees, enjoying the role of jovial squire participating in the affairs of 'his' community. He did not share Nietzsche's view that familiarity in a superior causes bitterness because it may not be returned.

Over and again Lever declared that in industrial relations he had no time for charity, which, he said, indicated sloppy sentimentality in the employer and was unacceptable to the pride of the working man. Lever's benefactions were made from the profits of his business and were intended to further the interests of that business by improving the lot of the workers. But, charity or benefaction, the money came out of Lever's pocket and there was, no doubt, a possibility of gratitude slipping into injured pride. If this was so then gratitude's notoriously poor memory was given no chance to soothe the pain, for the Chairman was ever-present at Port Sunlight functions, in spirit if not actually smiling acknowledgement of the applause. He might have done better to try to be an acute rather than a chronic benefactor, even if circumstances and temperament denied him the ultimate self-indulgence of anonymity.

Lever tried to give all social matters in the Works and the Village into the control of the employees and residents. When the Bridge Inn was opened in 1900 it was Lever's intention that it should be a Temperance hotel, but after a couple of years some residents asked that a licence should be applied for. Lever felt that he should not impose his own views and so he arranged for a referendum among the residents, stipulating that the women might vote as well as the men, and that a 75 per cent vote in favour of a licence was necessary if he was to give his consent. The outcome was an 80 per cent vote in favour of a 'wet' house. The result surprised Temperance supporters in the Village, and a deputation waited upon Lever urging him to use his absolute authority in Port Sunlight and ignore the referendum. He refused to do so and had no reason to regret the decision because the Inn never became a centre for excessive drinking by residents. This pointed, Lever declared, to the fact that when their homes were good the men were not driven to seek solace in the pub.

That Lever had absolute power over most of the affairs of Port Sunlight was as clear to everyone as it was to the Temperance deputation, and there were occasions when it was exercised 'for the good of the community'. Originally the houses in the Village had their own front gardens, and individual residents managed them with a wide variety of results ranging from neglect, through park-like precision, to riotous displays of multicoloured flowers and shrubs, while some whose taste ran to livestock erected chicken-runs. The effect was displeasing to Lever and to many of the residents, and the front gardens were taken back into the care of the Company and maintained with diligence and uniformity.

During the winter months the Company arranged dances each week in the Auditorium and every girl employed at the Works was invited to two such dances each year. Girls under eighteen were provided with partners by the Company, and the older girls were each allowed to submit the name of a man to the social department who would issue an invitation unless – and this only happened infrequently – there was some reason for thinking that the girl had made an unsuitable choice of partner.

There were among the employees and their families those whose independence led them to regard such power and paternalism, however well intentioned and rarely exercised, as an invasion of their rights. Some excellent employees preferred to provide their own more expensive accommodation rather than bring up their families in the Village. On the other hand there were some excellent employees who were never given the opportunity of a house in the Village. Lever wrote,[6] 'The private habits of an employee have really nothing to do with Lever Brothers providing the man is a good workman. At the same time, a good workman may have a wife of objectionable habits, or he may have objectionable habits himself, which make it undesirable to have him in the village. . . .'

One of the highly organised social events at Port Sunlight in 1909 was the celebration of the coming of age of Lever's son and heir, William Hulme Lever, who had gone from Eton to Cambridge and taken his B.A. there in June 1909 before joining Lever Brothers. His father's ideas about the relative importance of a University education and other attributes in a business career were set down in a letter to his son a few years later.[7] Lever considered that the University man was some five years later in developing after entering a business than the man who had come straight from a High School, but that the University man would outstrip the other by the age of thirty because he had a more orderly mind and a better basis of thought. But he continued, 'there are certain qualities that are born in men that we want to keep in mind apart altogether from their education. If we want an engineer he must be a man with a natural turn of mind to engineering and of an inventive and suggestive type of intelligence. If we want a man for advertising . . . and wish to train him up ourselves we must have imagination. I would always want to separate in advertising the man who controlled the preparation for advertising and the idea at the back of advertising, from the man who drove the bargain for space either on walls or in newspapers or on tramcars. The man who was to drive the bargain on price ought to have no imagination, but be of the hard, practical, Scotsman type of brain. This man, good at driving bargains would be wasteful in using his bargain when he got it. . . .' When Lever was considering business in a general way, advertising often came to the fore in his thoughts. He had always been fascinated by the ways in which people's behaviour might be influenced, whether in the purchase of domestic goods, the casting of their votes, or the organisation of their lives.

His son's coming-of-age celebration was held at Port Sunlight in July 1909. Senior Company executives sat on an organising committee which had its own stationery headed by a photograph of the young man surrounded by the legend 'Celebration by the employees and their wives of Lever Brothers Ltd. and their associated companies throughout the world of the coming-of-age of Mr William Hulme Lever'. At a ceremony in the Auditorium he was presented with an album and an address contained in a silver casket. This piece of silver, specially commissioned in the Italian style from Mappin and Webb, was large, ornate, and, to modern eyes, almost stupefyingly ugly, with classic figures, horns of plenty, enamel plaques showing views of Port Sunlight, a rising sun with the date 1888 and the fully risen sun dated 1909. Over six thousand of the nine or ten thousand Lever Brothers employees all over the world contributed to the fund. The balance of some five hundred pounds was at Lever's suggestion invested in Lever Brothers shares and the income used to provide three scholarships at the Port Sunlight schools, worth about ten pounds per year and awarded on the recommendation of Mr William Hulme Lever.

A letter to Lever from a German some months afterwards illuminates one aspect of the coming-of-age presentation. He explained that he had been a traveller with the Berlin branch of the Sunlight Company, and continued,[8] 'in July 1909 we employees were asked to contribute towards a present for Mr Lever junior on the occasion of his coming of age. As I was then not in a position of giving a contribution of more than five marks, matters were so manipulated that, although I had already worked three years to the full satisfaction of the firm, I was dismissed with a trifling pretext. . . .' He went on to say that he had been unable to obtain new employment. He was a druggist by trade and had an opportunity of buying an agency for three thousand marks, and he asked Lever to lend him this sum: 'you are a rich man, and as I have heard also a good soul, and for this reason I approach you confidently, for you know what life is, and how to reward industry and intelligence, which qualities do not weigh at all with us in Germany. Here everything goes by favour. He who knows best how to flatter and act the hypocrite towards his superiors is highest in favour.'

After some considerable enquiry into the matter Lever explained[9] that he and his son had purposely declined to see any subscription list because otherwise it 'would have been within our knowledge which branch works had not subscribed, and which individuals had not subscribed, and your charge of favouritism as a consequence might have had some grounds. But as I know nothing about the matter your statement is false and unworthy. It is not possible for me to lend you three thousand marks but I have had pleasure in remitting through the Post Office money order for fifty marks as a gift, and hope it will be of service to you.'

While, at the range of seventy years, it is possible to question Lever's good taste in seeking such donations for his son's coming of age, at a very bad time for the soap trade, there can be no doubt about the honesty of his reply to his disaffected ex-employee. In this affair of the subscription lists, as so often in industrial relations of more importance, Lever appears to have been considerate and scrupulously fair in the mechanics of the process while, perhaps, overlooking some vital aspect of the human spirit profoundly affecting the whole matter.

To follow the twenty-first birthday celebration Lever arranged a world tour for his son, accompanied by a young cousin, Robin Lever, and Mr John Cheshire of Lever Brothers who would act as chaperon. Lever, writing as an M.P., obtained letters of introduction for the party from the Foreign Office, India Office, and Colonial Office. Cheshire was required to report regularly to Lever on the events of the tour and to arrange for the two young men to see places and people of interest, and to look over factories and other commercial undertakings. In this connection Lever's sense of fair play towards fellow manufacturers appeared when he told Cheshire not to ask to visit the works of such competitors as Colgate or Proctor and Gamble as they 'might regard it as a liberty'. Yet he had no compunction about setting enquiry agents to investigate a manager, or himself reporting on one of the Company's agents abroad:[10] 'I never found Mr X without he was wearing light coloured kid gloves and was spreading his fingers to get the gloves into a more easy fit. Generally he was extremely well groomed, but after one minute's conversation on business one found that Mr X was thinking more of the dignity of Mr X and his appearance at the club than he was of the sale of oil-cake and the purchase of materials for the Mill. Mr X is a most charming and agreeable person in private life, and if he were an attaché at the British Embassy I am sure he would do great credit to his selection, but as a business man to run a difficult proposition abroad he was a long way short of filling the position.'

Lever and his son corresponded regularly throughout the tour and the *Birkenhead News*, favoured among local newspapers with Sunlight advertising, printed a couple of twelve-inch columns of verse, prefaced,[11] 'The following clever and amusing parody of Longfellow's *Hiawatha* written by Mr W. Hulme Lever, composed during the World's Tour that gentleman is now undertaking, has been sent home by him and has created much interest and amusement at Port Sunlight where the personal and topical allusions are appreciated at their full value.'

From San Francisco the boy wrote to his father,[12] 'We saw Chinatown when here a few days ago. Our guide was an old police detective Captain Glennon. He remembered showing you round, and he also showed Irving around when he was here. Of course, Chinatown since the fire and earthquake, is quite a different place. We went in to see an opium smoker but I think it was more of a showplace than a real den. We have had very little time for writing and so my journal is about a fortnight behind hand. I hope to get it all written up on the "Korea". I will try to send the first volume home. I have written about a hundred pages . . . so it is fairly extensive. . . . It is lovely getting letters when so far away from everybody. . . . If you do stand again [*for Parliament*] my best loving wishes are with you. . . .'

Lever wrote to Cheshire,[13] 'I am delighted to hear of the progress of the tour and of the keen interest all members of the party are taking in the opportunity afforded of studying the outlying portions of the Empire and of countries beyond the seas. . . . All is going well here and I am now in the middle of an election so have very little time for writing. . . . We have raw materials very dear in the soap trade and are consequently not able to evolve any startling scheme of advertising or make any great expenditure in that direction. . . .'

The Company's local agents were expected to play their part in the tour arrangements, and on one occasion Lever apparently had some misgivings that the young men might have been entertained rather too well at a party. The local agent in Kobe wrote to reassure Lever about a photograph that had been sent to him, 'this is a flashlight picture of a characteristic Japanese banquet. Like any other similar gathering these affairs have their varying conditions. But in this case you may rest assured that everything was within bounds and as you would have had it if personally present. To your son and party the whole thing was an immense joke and treated as such. . . .'[14]

In addition to leading the tour, Cheshire was expected to keep his commercial senses tuned, since Lever's mind was at this time much preoccupied with the Company's interests overseas. Lever wrote[15] to thank Cheshire for his letters, which, 'are invaluable to me as giving me a thorough insight into the educational value of the trip. I am glad to know that Hulme is taking a keen interest. . . . When you receive this letter you will have arrived at entirely fresh ground of the greatest interest. Japan is just wakening up to take its share in western civilisation. . . . Messrs Crowther are rather anxious for Lever Brothers to open a Soap Works in Japan. I have no doubt that the time may come when such a proposition may demand attention. But our trade in

Japan is not yet sufficiently advanced for us to do so. I may explain that the policy I have adopted is first to get trade in the country of sufficient magnitude to justify the establishment of Works. Only after having reached that point does the question of having Works become feasible. There is no doubt that whoever enters into Japan in its development stage will greatly benefit in years to come by having secured a foothold in the early days. I believe Lever Brothers are in this position as far as soap is concerned, but we are not yet sufficiently advanced to entertain the question of Soap Works. However, you might, by keeping your eyes open, let me have your views after your return. . . .'

Back in Port Sunlight, Lever was not only coping with an election but was also launching what he regarded as one of his most important experiments in industrial relations.

Lever's strongly held view, and one which he expressed frequently, was that profit-sharing as practised in the second half of the nineteenth century was a failure. It was a problem he had given much thought to over the years. In a speech to the Woolwich Chamber of Commerce in 1909 he claimed to have 'first made public utterance on the subject' twenty-one years before. The conclusion he reached over this long period about an acceptable profit-sharing system was, inevitably, strongly influenced by his fairly advanced views on industrial relations generally. But the co-partnership scheme he eventually evolved also contained to some extent the sturdy Nonconformist principles of his childhood, and some of the less worthy punitive elements, too.

Fundamental to all Lever's ideas about business was his concept of the three sides of industry: Capital, Management, and Labour. In the very simplest sense, Capital and Labour represented fixed charges upon the trading surplus, and what was left for Management – the profit – was a variable amount which depended on the success of the business. In this simple case the Capital is considered to be provided by Debenture holders who draw interest at a fixed rate, in much the same way as Labour will draw a fixed wage. Management, sometimes called the employer, might complicate the picture by supplying some of the capital, but if this was by way of Ordinary shares it did not violate the principle that the variable reward received by Management, or employer, was what remained after the fixed payments to Capital and Labour. There was nothing to complicate Labour's role. As Lever said, 'the position of Labour is this – it comes to the employer and says, "I can't store my labour; my labour has to be sold each day, and must be turned to account each day. If I do not make use of today's labour today, I cannot do so tomorrow. ... Now, with Capital, and with commodities you may be able to stand the fluctuating markets; I cannot – my commodity won't keep. In addition to that, I have a wife and family to keep, besides myself, and I must be assured every week of my weekly wage. Whether the product I produce for you realises profit or loss for you, I have nothing to do with that; I cannot have anything to do with it. I must be assured of my weekly wage, and if there is a profit, you are welcome to it. If there is a loss, I cannot help you to share it." Now this is the attitude Labour takes up, and rightly takes up. It practically becomes a Debenture Holder. ...'

In Lever's view the system could be described by the equation, Trading surplus equals Capital's reward plus Management's reward plus Labour's reward. Since Trading surplus was not constant at all times then there must be something on the other side of the equation which could vary with time – this was Management's reward, commonly called profits. To tamper with the system without recognising its governing equation would be imprudent and might easily lead to results quite contrary to those sought. If, for instance, some attempt were made to stop Management receiving the profits, paying instead a fixed sum, then Labour's reward might become the variable quantity and the position of the worker made worse rather than better.

Lever believed that the Trade Unions saw no value in profit-sharing schemes, and he applauded them for implicitly understanding the properties of the wages–profits relationship. It must have surprised some members of his Chamber of Commerce audience to hear him say in 1909, 'I would remind you that Trade Unions have, rightly, set no value upon Profit-Sharing schemes. They have never been interested in them at any time. They have never seen in Profit-Sharing schemes anything worth exchanging for the right to bargain for Labour at the highest market price that Labour can obtain; and I say they are right in that, for through the influence of Trade Unions, Labour has been able to make better terms and better arrangements financially, in the form of increased wages without risks of loss, than could have been made under any system of Profit-Sharing or Partnership. . . .'

Lever made this speech in 1909, the same year that he introduced his Co-Partnership scheme at Port Sunlight, and although his expressed attitude to Trade Unionism was perhaps not general among industrialists, it was certainly the accepted view of those employers who had introduced similar schemes at about this time. It was what might be called the second generation of profit-sharing schemes, which had first started in Britain nearly fifty years before. Their record over the half-century was a dismal one. Of 212 schemes started between 1865 and 1905 only 60 were still in operation in 1912.[16] The gas industry was, however, exceptionally successful with its schemes. Many of the companies producing gas – but not the municipalities – followed the lead of the South Metropolitan Gas Company where in 1890 Sir George Livesey established a profit-sharing scheme which had survived the years, although not without fundamental amendment. The earliest schemes in Britain, like their counterparts in the United States, were intended as an alternative – rarely voluntary – to the Trade Union. In the United States it was the custom to exact from the members of profit-sharing schemes a 'cast-iron pledge not to join a labour movement.[17] Briggs Collieries operated the first great scheme in Britain in 1865 and this was openly anti-Trade Union. In 1872 the management issued a notice that men who stayed away from work to attend a miners' rally would forfeit future bonus payments. This was the beginning of the end for that scheme, with more and more workers choosing the union rather than the scheme, which was discontinued in 1874.

Much later, the South Metropolitan Gas Company made it a condition of employment between 1889 and 1901 that the workman should sign a declaration that he was not a member of the Gas-Workers' Society. The Gas Company's scheme, started in about 1890, was one of the second crop of schemes which grew

Cottages at Port Sunlight

Hulme Hall

Hulme Hall, Kitchen

Christ Church

Sunday School

up roughly twenty years after the peak of the first generation. By 1902 the Labour Co-Partnership Association, which was anxious to extend its schemes throughout industry, recognised that it would be fatal to its purpose to continue to oppose Trade Union membership. The South Metropolitan Gas Company was persuaded to withdraw its restriction and the public attitude of the Association's members was very much in line with the views expressed by Lever in 1909.

Lever considered that he had been practising a kind of profit-sharing – he preferred to call it prosperity-sharing – since the earliest days of Port Sunlight. The funds to provide first-class working conditions in the factory, and to put up houses and other institutions in the Village, all came from Company profits. This money effectively came from Lever's own pocket, since he held most of the Ordinary shares, whose dividend depended on what was left after paying Labour and the fixed interest charges of Capital. But the money was not a charitable gift. Lever had long made it clear that he would have regarded this as sentimental, and that such sentimentality was, he believed, a sign of commercial slackness which would almost invariably lead to the failure of the firm and disastrous unemployment for the workers who were supposed to benefit. The profits he ploughed back into Port Sunlight to make a model factory and estate were intended to give him the healthy, contented, and stable work-force he needed. The excellent labour record there left him in no doubt that his ideas were working at Port Sunlight, and if there was any major flaw it was that there was not yet sufficient accommodation in the Village for all the employees who wanted to live there. Why then did Lever decide that money which might have been used to fill this need should be diverted into Co-Partnership in 1909 when so many such schemes had already failed?

Other people's failure never caused Lever to have misgivings about his own ability to succeed. On the contrary he had a need for lame ducks; striving to make them into golden geese when they were businesses, swans if they were houses or gardens, and sturdy dependable layers if they were workers, white or coloured. There was, too, the fact that with the spread of the Company there were now many employees too far away from Port Sunlight to benefit in any way from the amenities provided there. Above all, however, was Lever's desire not just for a stable, contented work-force, but for employees who would, to his advantage, show just a little of his own dedication to the well-being of the Company. He thought that a properly constituted Co-Partnership scheme would encourage in the workers some of the 'enlightened self-interest' which he identified as the secret of his own success.

There were a number of different broad principles which might govern a scheme.[18] In Britain in the past it had been common to give the worker his share as a cash sum each year which he might spend as he wished. In France it was more usual to put most of the money into a provident fund from which the worker might draw only after he had served the firm for a fairly long period. The purpose of this scheme was to attach the worker to the firm, not so much against Trade Union influences as against the offers of rival employers, although critics from the Labour side pointed out that the consequent sacrifice of independence reduced the workers' bargaining power. More lately in England most of the big schemes had put the worker's share of the profits back into the Company's capital account, giving him the rights and responsibilities of a shareholder. Lever followed the lead of contemporary progressive industrialists and adopted the shareholding scheme with a number of his own characteristic modifications.

The core of the scheme was the formation on 1 May 1909 of the Lever Brothers Co-Partnership Trust. The Trust had power to issue certificates to elected Co-Partners up to a maximum nominal value of half a million pounds. Men and women were equally eligible for Co-Partnership provided that they were at least twenty-five years old and had five years' service with the Company. The nominal value of the certificates issued to a Co-Partner each year might be, say, 10 per cent of his annual salary. These certificates were not in any way negotiable and thus had no cash value, but each year they attracted a dividend or interest calculated according to a formula carefully thought out by Lever. Out of the Company's total annual profit the first payment was a fixed sum to Debenture and Preference shareholders, then a dividend of 5 per cent was earmarked for Ordinary shareholders, and finally the residue was distributed, in proportion to their holdings, to Ordinary shareholders and Co-Partners. Thus if the Ordinary shareholder received 12 per cent of the nominal value of his holding, then the Co-Partner received 7 per cent on the nominal value of all the certificates he held.

Fundamental to these arrangements was Lever's concept of the fixed rewards of Labour and Capital, and the variable reward of Management represented by the Ordinary share dividend which fluctuated from year to year according to the Company's performance. The Ordinary shares were given a 5 per cent start over the certificates because they represented a capital outlay, whereas the Co-Partner was considered to have paid nothing for his certificates.

Thereafter the Co-Partners and the Ordinary shareholders were placed upon the same footing – or more accurately their percentage return on nominal holdings was the same after the initial 5 per cent difference. When a Company had a good year the Co-Partners would get a high dividend, while in a bad year there might be no dividend at all. The total cash dividend on the Ordinary shares – effectively all owned by Lever – was of course very much greater than that of the Co-Partners, who originally totalled just over a thousand, holding certificates of nominal value £114,000, whereas Lever's holding of Ordinary shares was approaching £2 million.

The Co-Partners were split into four classes: Directors, Managers and Foremen, Salesmen, and General Staff. The maximum value of the certificates which might be held by any individual varied with his class, being a few hundred pounds for the lowest class, several thousand for the two middle classes, and an amount decided by the Ordinary shareholders, i.e. Lever, for the Directors.

Arrangements were incorporated in the scheme so that if a man reached retirement age, or died in service, the certificates he had accumulated provided income for himself or his widow. But should a man leave the Company's employment voluntarily before retirement age, or be dismissed, then all his certificates were cancelled. In this way Lever ensured that, apart from pensioners, all those benefiting from the scheme were active Lever

Brothers' employees. But he went further than this and tried to ensure that beneficiaries were not only current employees but dedicated ones too.

To be admitted to the Co-Partnership Trust and to receive certificates, an employee had to sign an undertaking that he would 'not waste time, labour, materials or money in the discharge of my duties, but will loyally and faithfully further the interests of Lever Brothers Limited, its Associated Companies, and my co-partners, to the best of my skill and ability. . . .' If he was considered to have broken this agreement or to have been guilty of 'Neglect of duty, dishonesty, intemperance, immorality, wilful misconduct, flagrant inefficiency, disloyalty . . .' then again his certificates could be cancelled.

The general administration of the scheme was in the hands of the Directors of Lever Brothers, assisted by a committee of three Co-Partners from each of the four classes. In any dispute connected with the trust an employee could appeal finally to Lever as controller of the Ordinary shares.

Each autumn Lever himself decided what allocation of certificates every Co-Partner was to receive for the year. A great meeting was held in the Auditorium at Port Sunlight at which Lever distributed the certificates, personally welcomed those newly admitted to the state of Co-Partnership, and gave a rousing speech on industrial relations, well spiced with the anecdotes that he used so freely on public and private occasions.

In general the workers could expect to receive certificates to the value of 10 per cent of their annual pay, but Lever said,[19] 'if any report came in with regard to any man having committed an act of insubordination, any neglect of duty, or any minor offences, he forfeited any allotment he would otherwise have received during that year. If, on the other hand, an excellent report came in concerning any man, he received more than ten per cent; and if any man rendered the Company exceptional service, he received still more, perhaps many times ten per cent. So that there was always elasticity, and the whole scheme was founded perfectly legally by the shareholders, the only shareholder who was required to vote being the ordinary shareholder. . . .'

The financial terms of the Trust were simple and concise, in keeping with Lever's own, perhaps too naive, view of the interrelation between Capital, Management, and Labour. But the number of certificates awarded to each Co-Partner by Lever was determined by a hotch-potch of criteria which muddled together efficiency, industriousness, and morality. His decisions were personal ones and often based upon the objective and subjective judgment of those he regarded as the 'sergeants and corporals' of the Company. The whole basis of allocation was a mirror of his own standards: the rigid morality, self-discipline, and the work worship of his Nonconformist childhood, and the Victorian acceptance of every man in his place in society. Lever saw no reason why a man should not improve his position, but at any instant in any activity the rank of the participants was clearly defined and hence their proper roles. His autocratic style of running the Company arose from a conviction that his own place in business was pre-eminent, but nevertheless in the presence of a Gladstone, a Lloyd George, or a monarch he was prepared to act the obsequious even sycophantic role he commonly expected of others. In his employees he wished to see all the qualities of the young Lever of grocery warehouse days. Those lacking such qualities were punished, and those who possessed them were rewarded with extra Co-Partnership certificates, often a copy of Samuel Smiles's *Self-Help*, and the possibility of promotion within the Company to any position but the top one. The Co-Partnership Trust contained the essence of Lever's firmly established business principles, but by the years immediately before the 1914–18 War the question of whether there were other, better principles was being asked by young people and young movements.

The Trade Unions remained suspicious of Co-Partnership schemes, disliking their 'paternalism' and fearing that they were intended to attract support from the cause of organised labour. In public speeches Lever echoed the Trade Unions' dislike of paternalism and applauded them for ignoring Co-Partnership benefits in negotiating higher wages. But there was no denying that Co-Partnership dividends were a straightforward donation from Lever's own ample purse, distributed like extra pocket-money to those who behaved well. When there was a minor sympathy strike at Port Sunlight in 1911 Lever made no great issue of the matter, but he did decide that the position of Co-Partners in strikes should be clarified in case there was a more serious dispute in the future, and when it came to the next distribution of certificates, extra shares were given to those who had been particularly helpful in overcoming the firm's difficulties during the strike. However liberal Lever's carefully formulated ideas and public speeches about the Management–Labour relation, the day-to-day working decisions he made in his office remained strongly conservative.

A torrent of decisions was required from Lever all through the early 1900s, and he revelled in the magnitude, pace, and variety of the work. He would take a pile of letters and memoranda, and dictate answers to them at high speed. If he could not instantly think of a reply to one of them it was thrust to the bottom of the pile and by the time it got to the top again he usually had the answer ready. During these hectic years his major activities, any one of which might have occupied a busy man full-time, were making and selling soap, building a model town, replanning industrial relations, fighting elections and sitting in Parliament. From about 1906 onwards, when harder times came to the soap trade, overseas business grew in importance. Then in the search for raw materials he became deeply involved financially and personally in tropical adventure.

# 8

# *South Sea Islands*

No merchant living near bustling Liverpool at the turn of the century could have been unaware of the great financial opportunities to be seized as the tropical countries were opened up to trade. Nor could they overlook the moral problems which the Quakers and others had so effectively exposed a few decades earlier in their successful agitation against British involvement in the slave trade. By 1900 the moral issues of tropical trading were, perhaps, not quite so clear cut. The Cadbury family, whose industrial welfare schemes resembled those of Lever, found themselves in a web of difficulty over cocoa supplies from the tropics.

In 1901 William Cadbury was told that the labour conditions in Portuguese West Africa, where the firm bought cocoa, amounted to near slavery.[1] The reports persisted and in 1905 he persuaded some of his competitors in the chocolate industry to join him in sending out a trained investigator. Fry, Rowntree, and Stollwerck of Cologne collaborated – but not the American manufacturers. The investigator's report confirmed the allegations that the recruiting of contract labour for the 'Cocoa Islands' off West Africa retained many features of the old slave trade. Cadbury was asked by the Foreign Office not to publish the report, and to leave the matter to be dealt with diplomatically. Meanwhile, however, a newspaper, the *Standard*, accused Cadbury Brothers of hypocrisy in concealing the slave conditions under which their cocoa was produced.[2] George Cadbury took legal action and won his case for libel but, thanks to a very effective cross-examination by Carson who appeared for the *Standard*, and to a jury strongly suspected of political bias, only a farthing damages was awarded, although the judge ordered the newspaper to pay the costs of both sides. In 1907 Lever was much more generously compensated when, with Carson on his side, it was his turn to bring an action of libel against newspapers attacking his business morality.

Lever had once had a relatively small investment in tropical trade with a private holding of shares in the Opobo Company in Nigeria, but he first seriously extended his business into the tropics in 1901 when he bought an interest in the Pacific Islands Company whose founder he met by chance on a voyage from Australia. It was the scattered copra business of this Company which attracted his attention. But in the course of trading, the Company had discovered that there were very rich deposits of phosphate on Nauru in the Marshall Islands. A mineralogist confirmed this and also established that there were even richer deposits on Ocean Island, about a hundred and fifty miles away. Ocean Island was British, and Nauru was German, so delicate negotiations were needed before the phosphate concessions on the two islands were granted, and a new company, the Pacific Phosphate Company, founded in 1902 to exploit them.

Lever became a director of the Phosphate Company and played a considerable part in its affairs. This was an uncharacteristic digression from his usually single-minded devotion to the onward drive of Lever Brothers; an act of self-indulgence by an astute businessman who spotted a tempting target of opportunity. Time showed it to be a very rich target indeed, and the episode suggests that, if he had so wished, Lever might have amassed a huge fortune by devoting his talents to a series of divers and unconnected business *coups* rather than by the continuous cultivation of the great spreading tree of Lever Brothers.

In the early 1900s he was looking to the roots of this tree, the raw materials of the soap industry, and in particular to the vegetable oils which came from the tropics. The Pacific Islands Company venture proved to be a false start for Lever in securing his own sources of raw materials in the South Seas because the Company's copra interests were too widely scattered for economical development. It did however lead to Lever setting up his own plantations in the Pacific, and the phosphate deposits on Nauru and Ocean Islands ensured that the false start turned out to be, for Lever, a very lucrative one.

The Pacific Phosphate Company eventually sold its interests in Nauru and Ocean Islands to the British, Australian, and New Zealand governments after the 1914–18 War. The price received was very many times the original investment and was only agreed after protracted and bitter negotiations during and after the Versailles conference. Criticism and acrimonious complaint about the methods of the Company had been continuous throughout its life, and Lever's membership of the Board of Directors did nothing to enhance his reputation as an enlightened capitalist concerned for the general welfare of his workers.

It was alleged that senior members of the Phosphate Company had unethically used information which they had acquired during earlier employment in the Colonial Service; it was claimed that profits were excessive because the royalty paid by the Company was based on false figures which undervalued the phosphate at a quarter of its true price; it was said that the native labourers were unjustly treated, fresh water being sold to them at high prices during time of drought, and strikers being detained in custody.[3]

The problem of obtaining enough labour to work the phosphate deposits was chronic. It was a problem common to most mining and planting companies in the Pacific: to find a labour force more amenable than the indigenous population, most of whom considered that the thrustful Europeans were fools or rogues to impose continuous hard work for cash tokens upon a contented people who could so easily satisfy their own needs in a warm land abounding with natural food. The big commercial organisations wanted to import large numbers of labourers from India or Asia, but this was a matter of international concern at the time and it was the general policy of the Colonial Office to oppose such solutions.

But there were some South Sea Islanders who were attracted by the boom conditions and left home to work in the Phosphate Company's territory. Officials of the Colonial Service in the Pacific remarked that when such natives returned to their own islands they brought back gaudy clothes, venereal disease, and sewing machines.

Back in England, at his central position in the soap industry, Lever quickly learned enough from his relatively subordinate role in this Pacific venture to decide how he should set about securing his own sources of raw materials. Starting in 1902 he sent out expeditions from Port Sunlight all over the world to look into the possibilities of setting up plantations owned and controlled by Lever Brothers. One of these expeditions investigated the conditions in the Pacific. Lever considered their report and then decided upon plantations in the Solomon Islands, growing his own coconuts to produce copra for the Lever mills in Sydney where the oil was extracted and sent to England. Similar plans matured a little later in Africa, and from about 1906 Lever began to re-interpret Port Sunlight in the tropics.

That Port Sunlight and the Solomon Islands were in opposite hemispheres was not by itself sufficient reason for the new plantations having so little about them of the high-minded efficiency of the model soap village. Distance did not significantly attenuate Lever's influence over his agencies in Australia and America, although his frequent journeys abroad ensured that the written or cabled word was reinforced by the memory, or the expectation, of the forceful presence of the 'Captain' himself. But it was several years after Lever's Pacific Plantations were set up that he first visited the Solomons. Furthermore there were no precedents to follow in the Pacific, as there had been at Saltaire and the Hartley Village, when he was building Port Sunlight. He had no first-hand experience of the conditions of life and work in the tropics. Perhaps most important, he did not understand that many locally available white employees were established in the loose habits of those less attractive expatriates who were ready to take a hand in anything which offered a salary – and a chance to make something on the side – for 'managing' natives.

An official of the High Commission for the Western Pacific visited the Solomon Group at the end of 1908 and his report to the Secretary of State at the Colonial Office indicates that Lever's tropical venture had not, in its first year or two, been completely successful in the manner which a liberal businessman would have wished.[4]

'In the very rapid and satisfactory growth of the Protectorate the presence of so wealthy and energetic a firm as that of Messrs Lever Bros. forms a most important factor. With a concession of some 200,000 acres of the best land in the islands and with command of sufficient capital to promote its development, this Company has done excellent work. It is with regret that I felt it my duty to place on record the fact that the local representatives of the firm are in disaccord with the policy and administration of the Resident Commission. This want of harmony may be ascribed to the fact that the firm are infected with the desire to become the controlling factor in the administration of the Group. . . . the aspiration of the firm is, I believe, to obtain some sort of charter for the "running" of the group on their own lines. Nothing could be more fatal to the future prosperity of these islands than the throttling of private enterprise, and this would be speedily accomplished if Messrs Levers obtained the controlling power in the group.'

This certainly suggested that Lever's general policy directives were reaching the South Seas undistorted, and being faithfully interpreted. But criticism in the report of the quality of the local employees indicated that although Lever, on the Bridge, determined the course, he was too remote to know that some of the crew away in the forecastle were a tough lot with unsavoury habits. Certainly he would not have remained unmoved if he had known that some of his staff were said to be 'not infrequently intemperate in their habits', unable to deal with native labour, and inclined to flogging as a demonstration of their dislike of 'niggers'. But what would probably have stuck in his throat more than anything was the statement that, 'At present a very considerable number of the employees of Messrs Levers are persons who have been dismissed for incompetence, or worse, by other employers in the Protectorate.'

In another section of this report to the Colonial Office the turbulent conditions in the Islands are illustrated by an account of a visit paid by the High Commissioner's representative to one of the smaller islands. As they approached the island in their boat, wisps of smoke above the palm trees were the first sign that all was not well. When the party landed they discovered that the store had been smashed and looted. Opened meat tins and other supplies were scattered about, and the burnt out ruins of a large native house still smouldered near by. The white trader was missing, but they met him soon afterwards on his way back from a journey, and broke the news to him of the destruction of his post and the probable murder of the two natives he had left in charge.

It was thought that the crime was the work of a gang who had murdered a white man, Oliver Burns, a few months before. The Burns murder was, in turn, believed to have originated in troubles two years earlier when a native criminal had been captured and held in gaol, where he committed suicide before trial, by hanging himself in his cell. His brother declared that he would avenge the suicide by taking the head of a European.

The obvious and convenient target for the head-hunter was a man called Faddy, a trader of sorts who had been discharged by several firms for total incompetence but had managed to find employment with Lever Brothers. 'A more grotesque figure it would be difficult to find, and his known intemperance and impediment of speech, which made him hardly intelligible, and his more than childish ignorance, make him, and have long made him, the butt of the Western Solomons.' But Faddy had once promised the vengeful native a trip to Sydney and his head was therefore spared in the hope that one day this promise might be kept. So retribution fell instead on the unfortunate trader, Burns, who, happening to be in the district, was followed, tomahawked, and killed.

The wretched Faddy was apparently a typical member of that disreputable element among white settlers, sweating out a dissolute, brutish existence in the remote and lonely islands of the South Seas. This Caliban-like creature appears again in an account of the alleged murder of a native by Alfred Hermes, another employee of Lever Brothers.

A senior official of the Company, Fulton, the assistant general manager, was cruising among the islands. He anchored off one of them and sent his subordinate, Hermes, ashore to the village to find a native woman whom he might photograph. Hermes soon found a good subject but decided to improve her appearance. He took her off to the store, undressed her in front of a number of native men, and handed her new clothes to put on. When he came out of the store with the woman, a group of natives, who were gathered on the beach by the copra shed, muttered angrily at his behaviour. One of them, Aho, more indignant and bolder than the rest, pushed forward and jostled Hermes and told him to get away back on to the boat. The white man at once shouted out for someone to get him a gun, and it was the man Faddy, lurking near by, who ran forward and handed him a revolver. The sudden appearance of a lethal weapon instantly changed the row into a deadly brawl, and Aho, now wildly excited, shrieked out that even though he might be shot he would kill Hermes.

In the subsequent violent affray, watched by Fulton from the deck of his boat twenty-five yards away, Aho was hit in the arm by the first shot fired by Hermes, who then fired twice more and mortally wounded him.

At the local investigation of the killing it was revealed that Hermes had been involved in a number of dubious incidents, among them the purchase of land from natives at exceptionally low prices, and the possession in his service of a native boy who was only ten years old. It was recommended that Hermes be banned from living in the Protectorate, for his own safety as well as for punishment, because it was felt that friends of Aho would almost certainly kill him if he remained.

Believing that the local management of Lever Brothers would try to reverse the ban on Hermes, an official of the Commission wrote to London, 'A sufficiently long catalogue of Hermes's misdeeds could be collected, the compiling of which would incidentally reveal a condition of affairs as regards the treatment of their native labour which would, I am convinced, amaze and horrify the proprietors of the model town of Port Sunlight.' More specifically, the High Commissioner for the Western Pacific considered that there had been 'a miscarriage of justice in the escape of the man Hermes from the gallows'.

During the next two or three years of the life of Lever Brothers' Pacific Plantations the early mistakes in organisation were rectified and principles of land and labour policy were established. But the effect of the Company upon the native customs and conditions in the Islands generally was only superficial. Another Colonial

Office report,[5] on a visit made at the end of 1912, contains none of the criticism of the low quality of Lever Brothers' employees which was such a prominent feature of the 1908 report. But the later report did emphasise that the remote and widely scattered group of islands was still largely undeveloped.

There was nowhere anything approaching a township, the plantations and trading stations were established on the coast but the interior was unexplored by the white population. The islands were decidedly unhealthy, with malaria, blackwater fever, leprosy, dysentery, and a wide variety of skin diseases. In the whole group, which was strung out over nearly a thousand miles, there were three doctors: one provided by the Government, one by the Melanesian Mission, and one by Lever Brothers. Communication with the outside world was provided with the arrival about once a month of the Lever Brothers' steamer or that of another trading company. A Government steamer travelled between the islands within the group and, apart from this, communication was almost entirely by sailing vessels.

A very rough estimate of the native population was 150,000. The white population was 500, of whom 15 were Government employees, ranging from the Resident Commissioner to the carpenter. The report commented that with distances so great, and with means of communication so inadequate, with a native population addicted until recently to cannibalism and still inclined to turbulence, and with the tradition of the bad old days of the 'blackbirding' traffic hardly yet extinct, it was remarkable that with so small an official establishment the Protectorate had made such good progress.

Where there was official criticism of Lever Brothers it was to the effect that the Company had not undertaken sufficient development work, particularly of the land which it leased rather than owned. 'Levers have, up till quite recently, concentrated their efforts almost entirely on their freehold property. They have made no serious attempt to clear or cultivate the lands held on occupation licence. They have done so partly, I think, because it suited them simply to keep possible competition out of the lands so held, partly because expenditure on the freehold land promised an immediate, instead of a remote, return and partly because Mr

Meek [Managing Director of Lever Brothers Pacific Plantations] has an almost superstitious reverence for the virtues of freehold tenure as compared with occupation on licence for 999 years at a peppercorn rent.'

Meek, whose 'reverence' was possibly more for directives from Port Sunlight than for the intrinsic merit of freehold tenure, gave an assurance that more work was shortly to be undertaken, and he cited the shortage of labour as sufficient excuse for slow progress with clearing and developing land. While not fully accepting this explanation, Government officials were well aware that here lay the greatest problem in the industrial development of the Solomon Islands.

The labour position had been improved by the fact that no recruiting of natives to work outside the Islands now occurred, and some natives had returned from service in the notorious Queensland sugar plantations and from Fiji. But recently difficulties had been increased when the minimum age for indentured labour was raised from fourteen to sixteen, and the maximum period of service reduced from three to two years. The labourers never re-engaged when they completed their term, without first returning home for a walk-about, and if they did subsequently re-engage they seemed to have forgotten all they had learned.

Most of the labourers were recruited by the masters of small sailing vessels going among the islands. They would anchor offshore and when the natives came out of the bush down to the beach the master would try to persuade as many as possible to enlist for service in the plantations. For every man he brought back the recruiter was paid a bounty of between seven and ten pounds, while the pay of the labourers themselves was usually six pounds or less per annum. Planters preferred to recruit natives of distant islands to reduce the likelihood of desertion.

There was a general feeling among employers and Colonial Servants that raising the wages would not significantly increase the supply of native labour. The official report affirmed that the Solomon Islander had little idea of the value of money, and if disinclined to work would not be induced to do so by the offer of high wages. Considerable sums of money had come into the hands of the natives from sales and leases of land and from trade in native produce, and many of them were owners of expensive boats built in Sydney or in the Islands.

The employers thought it unfair that they were forbidden to bring in Indians as had been done elsewhere, and they were perfectly willing to pay a higher price for such imported labour. Lever Brothers in particular had put forward schemes to solve the labour problem, but these had been ignored, or perhaps mislaid, in the Colonial Office. The Company had gone so far as to send Meek from the Solomon Islands to India with offers of free land to tempt Indian labourers to come out and work in the plantations. In effect this would have meant that land was transferred, via Lever Brothers, from the indigenous population to coloured men of another race more suited by temperament and industriousness to the needs of twentieth-century commercial development. Whether or not it was recognised as such, this bold piece of social engineering found no favour with the Government who were firmly against the introduction of Indian labour into the Pacific.

Thus by the time Lever first visited his Solomon Islands outpost the more obvious abuses due to bad staff in the early days had been removed, planting and building had gone ahead, and there had emerged a significant pattern of conflict with the Colonial Office over monopoly, land, and labour.

Lever, on one of his world business tours, sailed into the Solomons in December 1913 in the Company's own steamer specially diverted from its normal run to and from Sydney in order to pick him up and take him and his party to inspect all the plantations. His almost obsessive urge to plan and build was excited by the opportunities in his own little colonial possession, and his missionary zeal for good husbandry among the heathen was gratified by the evidence he saw of the results of the orders he had been sending out from Port Sunlight. He wrote:[6]

'On rising ground you see the manager's bungalow, with a well-kept garden in front and line upon line of coconut palms in serried masses for hundreds of thousands of acres in the background. . . . You walk up to the red-roofed, white-sided bungalow, and note the generous and ample width of the verandah all round. . . . In the kitchen garden you see pineapples, oranges, limes, lemons, bananas, grape-fruit, mangoes and all manner of tropical fruit. At the back you see a well-stocked poultry farm with the promise of an ample supply of eggs and chickens and ducks.... Then you come on the main herd of 500 head of cattle – as fine specimens of Shorthorns, Herefords, or Red Polls as ever delighted the heart of a farmer. As you return you pass a bullock team at work, and stop to examine the steam-plough which did such good work in pioneer days before it was known that bullocks would thrive and prosper, but which is little used now, for it costs double in the Solomons per acre to plough by latest up-to-date steam power compared with the old-fashioned bullocks; and so you return to the bungalow, calling on the way at the dispensary where simple medicines are given out to the natives, and to have a look in the sheds provided for native quarters. . . .'

When he visited the Chief's hut in a native village things were not so neat and tidy: 'I noted a wardrobe, three sewing-machines, chairs, table, gramophone, thermos-flask, and other items of civilisation amid general dirt and disorder. Mr Woodford [the Chief Commissioner] states that the natives are making so much money out of copra at present that they have no idea what to do with their earnings or profits, and either waste them on useless purchases or hoard them in some hole in the ground. He said he had no doubt this old chief could produce hundreds of pounds hidden away somewhere. They won't bank their cash, and really, they don't know what to do with it. . . .'

Lever's surprise at the Chief's unused collection of civilised consumer goods was probably much the same as the Chief would have felt about Lever's unused collection of Chinese pots, but to a man of such business initiative it must have been an affront to hear about money – probably originally Lever money – buried unproductively in a hole in the ground.

Probably the day that Lever enjoyed most during his very brief visit to the Solomons was when the steamer took a party over to the island which was the centre of most Lever Brothers property. There, in a few brief hours, he selected the site for the new port, and named it Ladylever. He pointed out that a good road, with a gradient of 1 in 15, could be made up the mountain which overshadowed the harbour, predicting with confidence that bungalows built part way up at a height of 3,000 feet would be in a cool climate and healthy conditions. This was the sort of work he loved: looking at new ground, visualising it clothed with buildings and roads, and then drawing firm lines on maps for the new construction.

But already he had found an even more exciting place than the Solomon Islands in which he could play the part of explorer, missionary, town planner, architect, and tycoon. Now he had a stake in the Belgian Congo, an enormous area of land – almost a kingdom – where, uninhibited by the watchful and intrusive British Colonial Service, he could carry forward virtually without question, his own schemes for the benevolent and efficient management of native land and labour.

# 9

# *The Congo*

The expeditions which Lever sent out all over the world in 1902 and 1903 in search of raw materials to feed Port Sunlight's soap vats reported favourably on two particular sources: the coconut palms of the South Sea Islands and the oil palms of the West African tropical forests.

When the white 'meat' inside the coconut shell is dried it becomes copra, and this copra is crushed in mills to yield coconut oil. The African oil palm bears big clusters of fruit, like large dates, and palm oil is extracted from the soft part of this fruit and also from the kernel of the stone.

The organisation for the production of coconut oil on a fairly large scale was already well established by the opening of the twentieth century. Lever's own steamer brought copra from the coconut plantations of the South Sea Islands to be crushed at his mill in Sydney. But, in the case of the African palm oil, production techniques were still undeveloped.

For generations the African native had gathered palm fruit for his own domestic use. To get oil for cooking, the fruit was stoned, crushed in a crude hand-grinder, and then boiled in water. The liquid was allowed to settle and the oil which came to the top was poured off. It was a tedious and inefficient process. Each family had its own small grinder, or mill, which had to be filled over and over with the stoned fruit and laboriously turned by hand to produce the pulp. It took several hours of steady hard work to yield a few cups of oil.

When the white man came to West and Central Africa he soon put palm oil on his list of commodities which the natives might profitably be persuaded to exchange for the over-abundant products of Europe's factory and textile mills. By 1900 those natives who lived near the rivers – the white man's highways – found that if they cared to prepare a little more palm oil than their family needed, and if they cracked the fruit stones and saved the kernels, then they could sell or barter small amounts of these products at the local trading post of one of the European companies who would export the materials in bulk for processing in factories overseas.

But such a small and uncertain amount of raw material was quite insignificant in relation to the enormous appetite of Lever's soap factories; and its dependence upon the whim of the individual native, deciding to gather a little extra fruit for his hand-mill, was quite inappropriate to the Port Sunlight obsession with optimised utilisation of men, money, and materials. If African palm oil was to be fitted into the great international jigsaw of soap-making and soap-selling, then some way must be found to organise the natives into gathering much more than the fraction of one per cent of the available palm fruit, which was all that was harvested by traditional methods. Machinery must be developed to process the fruit in bulk locally, with much greater speed and higher yield than the natives could achieve. Finally, the source of supply must be assured, and the necessary capital investment protected, by some agreement for the grant of long leases and monopoly. These last requirements led Lever into open conflict with the Colonial Office. The international scandal of the Belgian Congo had made the British Government sensitive about the exploitation of the African native, and the Whitehall nerve was kept exposed by well-organised public opinion outside the Ministry, and by continual prodding within by a group of dedicated civil servants, in particular by Roger Casement.

During the nineteenth century the consciences of the white races of Europe and America finally overcame their reluctance to give up the fat profits that for hundreds of years had been drawn from the slave trade. The fast men-of-war of the British, French and United States navies on anti-slavery patrol so increased the hazards of the middle passage that it was no longer worth while to export black bodies across the sea from Africa. Merchant venturers shifted their interest from the person of the black man to the fruits of his homeland. Anti-slavery organisations watched these developments carefully and found much to disturb them.

The attention of those concerned with African affairs soon focused very sharply upon the Congo region. Since this area had first been opened up by Stanley's exploration, organisations in several countries had tried to ensure that the major Powers should not become involved in squabbles about colonising it. But the initiative in Congo affairs was shrewdly seized by Leopold II of Belgium, a king with a taste and a talent for high finance, who convened an international conference in Brussels in 1876 and set up under his own presidency the Congo Association, which signed treaties with native chiefs and secured power over large areas of territory. In 1885 Leopold's position was consolidated when the Berlin Conference of the Powers established the Congo Free State and recognised him as its autocratic ruler.

But somehow the liberal principles and idealism of that well-intentioned gathering of nations proved ineffective. Certainly the slave trade was largely stamped out. But a new form of oppression replaced it – equally profitable, perhaps not quite so severe, but, if anything, more distasteful because it was a calculated product of modern, 'civilised' minds. Foremost among those minds was that of King Leopold II of Belgium, Sovereign Ruler of the Congo Free State.

The natives of the Congo had long been accustomed to tapping the forest rubber plants for latex, which they cured and took to local European-run trading stations where a price was reached by bargaining in the traditional way. But now, under Leopold's 'System', only the land actually occupied by villages and townships was deemed to belong to the natives. All the rest, the vast majority of the country, the forests and everything in them, was declared to belong to the State, i.e. to Leopold and his associates. The natives were compelled to collect rubber for the agents of Leopold or his concessionary companies, who fixed a price for each kilo brought in. The lower the price fixed by the agent, the greater his commission, and if the agent managed to fix a really low price his commission went up to a disproportionately high figure.

Such a system encouraged single-minded unscrupulousness in

obtaining huge quantities of crude rubber for the considerable gain of the local agents, and for the ultimate profit of the controlling interests in Belgium, where the share price of concessionary companies increased by a hundredfold or more. To sustain this great Congo boom it was necessary for the natives to neglect their farms, to abandon their hunting and trading, and to give their lives to finding enough rubber to meet the almost insatiable demands of their new white masters.

This was no petty commercial exploitation of ignorant natives by sharp traders, common enough in Africa before and since, but a total disruption of a vast community that could only be brought about by systematic coercion. King Leopold and his advisers recognised this and organised the system with brutal effectiveness. The multitude of officials supervising the collection of rubber and other commodities throughout the Congo region was backed up by an armed body of natives, with white officers of several nationalities. This force grew to number several thousand and, with its simple weapons, was quite adequate to police the villages and keep the unfortunate inhabitants up to their endless task of finding rubber or ivory. To make doubly sure that the work was done the army took thousands of women and children and held them hostage in special houses.

Inevitably there were pathetic attempts at opposition by bands of natives armed only with primitive weapons. Immediate ruthless retaliation was the predictable reaction of the occupying power to such opposition, and the punitive forces sent by the State against rebellious villages were given a free hand to murder, rape, and loot, and were often required to bring back severed hands or penises as evidence that the punishment had been satisfactorily carried out.

In the Liverpool offices of the Elder Dempster shipping company a young man called E. D. Morel was in charge of the Congo Department. In handling this business, which sometimes took him to Belgium, Morel began to find that his attention was jogged again and again by certain disturbing features of the ships' manifests. There were enormous increases in the amounts of rubber and ivory taken out of the Congo, and ominously large quantities of arms and ammunition were carried in. Looked at in conjunction with missionaries' reports of atrocities, the papers passing through his office gradually opened Morel's eyes to the way Leopold's system was working. Disquiet grew to disgust and he set out to collect such damning evidence that governments concerned with African affairs would combine to end the King's personal control of the bleeding Congo.

Irrefutable evidence was not alone sufficient. Public opinion had to be aroused, and men of influence had to be persuaded to exert co-ordinated pressure in the right quarters. The organisation of the forces working for Congo reform was centred upon Morel and consequently he could not continue to work for Elder Dempster. He supported himself and his young family by journalism, with some assistance from affluent well-wishers.

In 1903 in the House of Commons, Charles Dilke forced Balfour to accept that the deplorable state of affairs in the Congo demanded action. Roger Casement, the British Consul at Boma in the Congo, was sent into the interior to make a survey. Casement felt deeply for the dispossessed and harried Congolese – indeed for any oppressed people. His report[1] was cleverly written and he gave credit to the new administration for stamping out the slave trade. But he contrasted the prevailing conditions with those he had encountered on a similar journey years before, and he soberly gave evidence of atrocities which were sensational however underplayed. The publication of this report led in 1904 to a public meeting in Liverpool at which the Congo Reform Association was formally initiated with Morel as its Secretary.

Morel and Casement became very close – addressing each other as 'Bulldog' and 'Tiger' respectively – and the friendship was only ended in 1916 by Casement's execution for treason committed on behalf of Irish nationalism. The role of Casement in Congo reform was diligent and unobtrusive propaganda inside Whitehall, while Morel worked indefatigably in public to secure support for the cause in Britain and abroad. Soon there was a crescendo of accusation against Leopold, all more or less reflecting the view of Cecil Rhodes that an audience with the King was 'like a half-hour with Satan'. The list of those who strongly advocated urgent Congo reform included the Archbishops of Canterbury and York, senior Liberal politicians, Mark Twain, Conan Doyle,

W. T. Stead, and most of the principal Nonconformists. Lever does not appear to have actively helped the movement, although two of Morel's most important supporters were wealthy Nonconformist businessmen: John Holt of Liverpool and William Cadbury.

Morel found that neither the businessmen nor the politicians who supported the Congo Reform Association matched his own single-minded idealism. After the 1906 landslide election he was dismayed to find that things moved just as slowly under a Liberal Government as they had under the Conservatives. Casement, too, was sickened by the delays of diplomacy. Disenchanted – with imperialism generally, and with Edward Grey particularly – he wrote in 1907, 'British policy remains always British policy whether it is Ireland, India, or Congo.'[2]

Faced with diplomatic notes and international public outcry, Leopold eventually began a slow retreat. In 1907 he transferred sovereignty of the Congo to Belgium but continued to draw considerable private profits, and the condition of the wretched natives appeared to be little changed. It was however no longer possible to hoodwink international opinion, which was outraged by the cynical manoeuvre. The British Government formally denounced the administration in the Congo, and Leopold's death in 1909 finally cleared the way for integrity and humanity. During the next few years conditions rapidly improved as the Belgian Government abolished repression, introduced reforms, and gradually eradicated the horrors of Leopold's System.

At the height of the great Congo boom attempts were made to extend the System to other territories in Africa, and these attempts were particularly successful in the French Congo. Indeed some of the support for the Congo Reform Association had come from British businessmen who had been excluded from trading in the French Congo by new monopoly concessions. Nevertheless there were those who thought that British West Africa could profitably adopt some of the methods of the Congo Free State. Morel warned[3] that if, 'the desires openly expressed by certain influential persons in this country' were acceded to – that the oil palm forests of Nigeria be declared the property of the British State and the products gathered as the Belgians gathered rubber – then Nigeria would become another Congo. It seems most unlikely that this would ever have come about because successive British Governments and their permanent civil servants in the Foreign Office and the Colonial Office set their faces firmly against monopoly and undue interference with native rights and customs.

It is impossible to believe that Lever, a kind man in most obvious senses, would ever have allowed his business to be tainted with Leopold's openly oppressive methods. In any case an assault by Lever Brothers employees upon the persons or the institutions of the natives in British West Africa would immediately have been stamped upon by the Colonial Office who, in fact, did have sharp disputes with Lever over the protection of some of the natives' commercial rights.

Pursuing his interest in the African oil palm as a source of raw material, Lever in 1908 ordered experiments to be started at Port Sunlight which led to the development of depericarping machinery which would remove the flesh of the palm fruit quickly, efficiently, and on a large scale. He also started negotiations with the Colonial Office for the erection in West Africa of mills and depericarping plant, and for the construction of monorails to bring in the fruit from the surrounding country.[4] As these negotiations proceeded, dragging on for several years, fundamental incompatibilities appeared between the autocratic businessman's concept of free enterprise and the principles of statesmanlike administration of native affairs established and maintained by the professional Colonial Service in Whitehall and abroad.

At the very least Lever wanted exclusive rights over large areas around each factory he erected, and he felt that such rights should be permanent, or very long-term, and should carry freedom to negotiate with the native chiefs for proprietary rights in palm trees or fruit. The Colonial Office, however, were fundamentally opposed to monopoly, European ownership of land, and anything which might take the running of the country out of Government hands. But in spite of what Lever regarded as the unhelpful attitude of the Colonial Office he was sufficiently attracted by the possibilities in British West Africa to buy a well-established African trading firm, MacIver and Company, which gave him a commercial base in the territory. Meanwhile, however, an opportunity occurred to pursue his tropical adventures in an area where his enterprise would be unfettered by the Colonial Office restrictions which had been such an irritation to him some years earlier in the Solomon Islands, and now cramped his style in Africa.

After the Leopold régime ended in 1909 the Belgian Government sent a representative on a mission to Britain to explain the future plans for the Congo and to seek investment. The Belgian emissary, Dr Horn, consulted the chairman of Elder Dempster – E. D. Morel's late employers – and he recommended an approach to Lever.

After his experiences with enterprises in the Solomons and in British West Africa, Lever now knew exactly what he wanted. He had been young during the age of the great explorers and of empire-building. Now he could see a challenge and an opportunity for himself worthy of a chapter by Samuel Smiles. He wanted to create another Port Sunlight in the tropics. Not just the perfect little industrial town which was the ornament of his early years, but more nearly a kingdom – an exotic and wonderfully profitable tropical state such as no one had made before. More prosaically, his experience had taught him what conditions he needed to make sure that he would be truly master of the total project and not subject to the dictates of an obstructive colonial administration.

As a first step Lever sent an expedition to inspect the palm forests. When he had received a favourable report on the abundance and quality of the crop he entered into discussions with the Belgian Government with a view to setting up oil mills in the Congo. His negotiating position was strong and he used it well. He had the resources and the proven nerve and ability to undertake a project on the large scale required by the Belgian Government. His world reputation as a liberal industrialist and humanitarian would bring badly needed respectability to Congo affairs. Almost any concession he sought would seem trivial after the dreadful impositions of the old régime. When the agreement between Lever and the Belgian Government was finally sealed in 1911 it gave him everything he wanted, and the new company set up to run the Congo mills, Les Huileries du Congo Belge, had unprecedented powers and privileges.

Five mills were to be set up, and to serve them the Company was leased nearly two million acres of land which would become its permanent property after thirty-five years, subject to a set production target being reached. The agreement was conditional upon the Company paying its workers a minimum wage and providing schools, hospitals, roads, railways, steamships, and telegraph communications throughout its territory. Lever accepted these conditions much as a masochist might receive a sentence to be birched. He was happy enough to agree that a fraction of the employees and directors of the Huileries should be Belgian, and that a certain percentage of Belgian goods and machinery should be used in setting up and running the factories. What mattered was that the Company had the land, and the management of the Company was firmly in the hands of Lever Brothers, which effectively meant that Lever had gained economic and social control of a large colonial territory.

When Lever set out from Port Sunlight in 1912 to inspect his overseas possessions in the South Seas and in Africa, there is little doubt that he regarded the Congo as the brightest jewel. He made many long trips abroad, combining Company business and sight-seeing, and he looked forward to each of them. But the overseas tour of 1912 was a source of particular anticipatory pleasure, partly because it included a visit to his coconut plantations in the Solomon Islands, but more especially because the long itinerary ended with an expedition by river-boat thousands of miles up the Congo and its tributaries. There was of course no question of this being an expedition into unexplored territory, but it was undeniably strange and savage country, new to Lever, and as he made his preparations for the trip he was conscious again of the little thrills of excitement that he had felt when, as a boy, he read stories of the great Victorian explorers. He decided that, like them, he could keep a diary of his Congo adventures.

The agreement between Lever and the Belgian Government was ratified by the Belgian Parliament, where there was considerable criticism of such extraordinary concessions to a commercial company. That this criticism was eventually turned aside was largely due to the attitude of the Belgian Socialist leader, Vandervelde, who declared that he would have opposed such concessions to any other firm, but that his knowledge of the working conditions at Port Sunlight allowed him to give his approval.

The agreement was signed in April 1911, the first site was cleared and named Leverville, machinery was despatched in August, and the first palm oil reached Antwerp in March 1912. In April 1912, one year after the agreement was signed, King Albert of Belgium received Lever, who presented him with an ivory casket containing the first tablet of soap made from the Congo palm oil.

In December 1912 Lever was ready to inspect the reality which had so swiftly grown from his paper plans at Port Sunlight. He included in his party Lady Lever, the only woman, Dr Horn who represented the Belgian Government, a specialist in tropical medicine, an expert on plantations, a senior engineer, and a cinematograph operator. For most of the journey through the Congo Lever and his staff travelled in one of the Company's wood-burning, stern-wheeler river-boats, which had been specially modified to accommodate them in some comfort. The itinerary, which had some of the features of a vice-regal tour, was to take in the Leverville area and the four other concessionary areas, which had been named after the King and Queen of the Belgians and their two sons.

The boat in which they travelled was the *Lusanga*, as fine a vessel as could be built to navigate the shallow twisting rivers of the Congo. A special large cabin was made for Lever and his wife at the forward end of the saloon deck, and he had a screen of wire mosquito-gauze fitted in front of the cabin to make an insect-free space about eight feet wide. When the boat was under way the breeze often made it cool enough on this private verandah for Lever to feel the need of a light overcoat when he sat there writing letters at eight o'clock in the morning.

He got up at 5 a.m., had a shave, a cup of tea, and a cold bath, before breakfast at six-thirty. He then wrote his letters until about eight-thirty, when he usually presided over a committee of his staff at which they discussed exhaustively every aspect of the Huileries project until lunch at noon. Different officials attended each meeting, depending upon the subject under discussion. As Lever gradually built up his own picture of local conditions and began to formulate his own ideas, he came to the conclusion that his chosen party – his Congo cabinet – was really too large, although he expressed himself in his diary as well pleased with its excellent spirit and temper.

Bedtime for Lever was at nine-thirty, with the boat anchored in midstream, or tied up alongside the bank for the night, ready for an early start at five or six o'clock next morning.

The quoted speed of the *Lusanga* was eleven knots. But the average rate of progress was often nearer four or five knots as she faced strong currents, found weed choking the water intake or paddle-wheel, and often had to go astern to look for a new way round sandbanks silting up the channel. Refuelling, too, was a frequent time-consuming business, with the boat having to stop and buy wood from the stations along the bank where forest timber was cut and stacked for this purpose. Lever, much exercised with thoughts of a labour force for the imminent expansion of Huileries activities, noted that in some cases the wooding stations were owned and organised by natives with no help from white men, 'which shows some ability and might be directed into a more efficient organisation'.*

On one occasion when they needed fuel, a Government steamer had gone up river just ahead of them and the natives had not had time to replenish the wood store. The captain, chief engineer, and mate of the *Lusanga* all gave a hand with woodcutting, and Lever asked his party to help. His doctor was most anxious that Lever should not over-exert himself in the task, 'but he could have spared himself the thought of it as I am no good as a woodsman! There was a dead tree which we [*sic*!] soon had down . . . a magnificent fern of the Hart's Tongue order (Platycerium Grande) was growing on it and I took off its seed fronds to raise stock from it at Thornton.' It was an action much in the image of those plant-hunters who had travelled the world to stock the gardens at Kew and some of the great English country houses.

As the boat pushed up-stream it passed many islands, some large enough to hide the far bank of the river for an hour or more as they steamed slowly past. When they approached some of the smaller islands they could be seen to be floating: large clumps of

* The quotations which follow in this chapter are from Lever's diary. U.H.A.

soil, roots and vegetation which had broken away from the bank and were now twisting and swirling along the water surface, swept rapidly past the ship's side by the strong current. The floating islands sometimes carried quite large trees, and colonies of birds' nests whose occupants seemed happy enough with a home spinning down the Congo like a planet through space.

Occasionally a tropical storm would strike, with thunder and lightning, a cold gusty wind, and torrential rain. These violent storms would last for about an hour and then be followed by light rain for an hour or two before the sun broke through again. The maximum day temperature on the moving boat was in the nineties Fahrenheit, and the minimum at night was about seventy. Sometimes Lever and his wife slept on deck 'and felt all the better for it'. All through the night they would hear the noise of the tropical insects, and early in the morning the sounds of life stirring ashore in a native village, or the ship's crew making ready for the day's work.

During daylight there was the chance of seeing something of the large animals that inhabited the river or were attracted by it. They saw crocodiles splashing about like porpoises in the distance, and early one morning Lever heard a great shouting: 'the cause was that we were passing close to a dead hippo floating on the water. The black crew were very excited, yelled and shouted, and no doubt were greatly disappointed that the captain would not stop the boat to secure this supply of food for them, to their idea just in the best condition for eating – blown up with the gases of decomposition. I understand that if the captain had stopped and the dead beast had been cut up and brought on board, no white man could have survived the smell. One member of our party during a previous visit was invited to eat dead hippo steak and declined because of the smell, which was no reason at all to the native who promptly replied, "You no eat smell – you eat meat – meat very good".'

Travelling in the ship's steam launch they rounded a bend in a tributary of the river and came suddenly upon nine elephants. A member of the party shot one which got away wounded. The great beasts were paddling and swimming in the shallows at a place where boats so rarely passed that the elephants were quite without fear. At one point the launch had to blow its whistle and go astern to avoid running into one big specimen whose lucky survival was due to the intrepid hunters in the party having run out of cartridges. Lever described the elephants as the biggest he had ever seen: 'bigger they looked than Jumbo' – a reference to the most famous of all elephants who was placed on display at the London Zoo, to the almost incredulous amazement of the thousands who flocked to see him. Jumbo was subsequently the centre of a remarkable national controversy when he was sold to Barnum, who exhibited him in America with predictably sensational effect.

The curiosities of the Congo sometimes came themselves to see the white party. Anchored in midstream awaiting the return of the ship's launch with wood, they saw three canoes approaching from a side river. In the canoes were women cannibals: 'their teeth were cut like saw-teeth, their bodies marked with red and white pigment. They had the least clothing on of any previously seen, and that of native make. They were less self-conscious and more at their ease than the three-quarters-dressed women wearing European calico we had seen at the wood-stations. They bargained all their produce – native food – for empty glass bottles, empty biscuit tins etc. etc., and finding plenty of these on board the market rose quickly so that it soon took two or three bottles to purchase the same quantity of manioc* as had been given for one bottle when the market opened. No stock-broker or cotton-broker could have gauged the market better or acted more promptly. They went away cleared out of their wares and happy.'

At about ten o'clock one morning, in the middle of a meeting of the 'oil and fats committee', a couple of hippo swam close to the boat. The committee broke up as everyone rushed to find guns, but 'before the guns came the hippos had gone: which to say the least was distinctly disobliging of the hippos. They might have waited to be shot. If there is anything more vexing than another it is the absolutely total lack of consideration shown by birds, beasts, and reptiles for our strong desire to amuse ourselves by taking pot shots at them. Big game shooting in the Congo

* A native food prepared from maize.

from the deck of a noisy stern-wheeler is not, so far, any success to boast of.' After this incident Lever, who had himself given up shooting many years before, noticed that members of his committees, meeting on deck outside his cabin, allowed their eyes frequently to wander to the swiftly flowing river, hoping to catch a glimpse of some large animal.

Lever's keenness to get ashore and inspect closely everything he could of Congo life was a matter of disquiet to his doctor, who considered that his employer-patient took too many risks for a man of over sixty. To have been over-cautious – or even cautious – in anything affecting a business venture would have been a denial of Lever's established life style. Typically he took the risks – which he considered to be exaggerated – and then exercised his own self-confident brand of prudence by taking more than the medically recommended dosage of quinine. Certainly he contracted no tropical disease, but he believed that the excessive amounts of quinine may have aggravated his deafness, a view that had little medical support.

All the strange things he saw were recorded in his diary with the impressions they made upon him. A lunatic chained to a log. A mother with twins whose destruction would once have been decreed by native custom, 'so here again the white man's influence has been at work or these children would not be alive. . . .' Weapons lying in the bottom of a canoe – 'now we are among the fighting natives.' There was a hint of R. M. Ballantyne in much that he wrote.

He took the opportunity of examining in detail one village and its occupants, before and after nightfall. He noted that the villagers ate baked caterpillars, which he compared with shrimps and whitebait, and hippo meat with 'a smell so strong you could drive a peg in it to hang a coat on'.

'The villagers here are undersized – the women especially so. After dark they all crouch round their fires and eat and chatter like so many monkeys. In fact these groups with many children could easily be mistaken for monkeys. The huts are low and entrance is by a small door on hands and knees. I had a pocket torch and peered into the gloom, and no respectable dog would have fought for one of these huts as a kennel. We turned on the

*Daily Mirror* Soap Cartoon

The Lever family

Thornton Manor

The Hill, Hampstead

electric searchlight, and as its rays reached each group round their fire they bolted in terror into their huts. In the case of the Capita, or chief man of the wood-station, who was dressed in trousers, waistcoat, and a straw hat, he bolted first, and left his wives and children to jam themselves in the door trying to follow him. We tried next magnesium wire, but they enjoyed that, and as to the gramophone, only half a dozen came down to the banks of the river to hear it. But the searchlight had been something that shot across the sky, and whilst a group might not move when it was directed against another group, they could not remain still when it was full in their own faces.'

Lever's party did not often indulge in the sport with the searchlight. More usually when they moored by a village they provided white man's entertainment with fireworks and a magic lantern show. The chiefs were far from overawed and wanted to know where they could buy fireworks to give their own displays. 'If a firework missed going off a derisive laugh was called forth. There must be no misses in dealing with natives. . . .' Lever could not bear derision directed at himself or anything he associated closely with himself. He noted that the natives were particularly excited by the lantern slides of elephants, Congo natives, and (most remarkably) Port Sunlight. They also recognised pictures of King Leopold and King Albert. The inclusion of a slide of King George V caused Lever to complain strongly that they must not use pictures of English royalty, and he also forbade the incorrect flying of the Union Jack which he said was 'no compliment to our King and Country and would leave us without power of answer if either were insulted.'

At one village they found and, at Lady Lever's insistence, took away with them 'a little girl of five years of age who had been sold as a slave by a neighbouring village. The child says her parents sold her. We propose to leave the child to the care of the Jesuit fathers at Womballi tomorrow but will require to give formal notice of her removal to the Chef de Poste at Bandundu, which we will see to being done. She is very bright, intelligent child and one feels tempted to bring her to England to see what she would grow into. But the responsibility is too great to entertain such an idea. . . .' (Twelve years later, in 1924, when once more in the district, Lever was pleased to discover that the little girl had grown up and made a good marriage to a black man who was a dispenser at the local hospital.)

When they went ashore for longer expeditions the white men in the party would walk for twenty minutes and then be carried for twenty minutes in hammocks. Lever reckoned that you could not tolerate much longer of either. There were elephant tracks everywhere, and once they came upon a picturesque hunting party of eight men with spears, bows and arrows, nets for antelope, and loops for climbing trees. The women they met inland were all completely naked and Lever's party considered them to be much less self-conscious than the partly clothed women seen nearer the river. The general feeling among the white men was that dress would improve all but the young women: 'as soon as they pass their sixteenth or seventeenth birthday these native women ought to dress to hide their pendulous tobacco-pouch bosoms and badly shaped figures.' Near the Stanley Falls Lever met a chief, 'about four foot six inches high and of great influence', and compared him, perhaps, with a Lancashire businessman of five foot five inches and also of great influence.

As Lever marched along a forest path, a stocky little figure in topee and bush shirt, he might have day-dreamed of being a great explorer but he was shrewd enough to recognise his own illusions, at least in this matter, and to appreciate that he and others in his party were the merest amateurs. At one Government Post the state of the natives seemed to be very poor. Lever and others were particularly distressed at the condition of one man and wished to find out from Dr Prout, their tropical specialist, whether anything might be done for him. They were a little put out at being unable to find the doctor who was eventually discovered to have been watching a working party from the boat filling casks with water. Lever wrote in his diary, 'no other member was giving a thought to where our fresh water bottles were being replenished'.

Lever not only recognised the limitations of himself and others as explorers, but was prepared to poke fun at their tenderfoot approach to the expedition. 'Our greatest hardship while "roughing it" in the Congo appears to be that there is no starch on board. What is life without starch? How can we maintain our self-respect amidst the more than half-naked cannibals we see when our linen fronts, to say nothing of the light dresses etc. etc. of the one lady of the expedition, are limp and starchless?'

While he realised, perhaps with some regret, that he was no explorer, Lever was quite clear that he was a pioneer. His aim was not discovery but the permanent profitable occupation of the land. That this would be to the benefit of the natives he had not the slightest doubt. If business could be called his religion, then his denomination was soap, and in the Congo he was a missionary for the business of soap. He was completely dedicated and had absolute faith that the spread of the Huileries settlements was for the general good of the world and for the particular material and moral good of those who worked in them. Pioneer was his chosen role; it was a word he used often in his conversation and in his diary. As a pioneer he looked at the things the explorers had discovered, but he looked with the intention of understanding them and using them to make a profit. He looked at the lie of the land, he looked at the way the palm trees grew, he looked at the rivers which carried the trade, but above all he looked at the natives and the way they lived and worked. His experience suggested that, while most business problems would yield to capital and drive, this was not the case with the problem of labour. In the Solomon Islands he had already met some of the difficulties of employing a work force of tropical natives, and he felt that in the Congo the problem of native labour for his vast industrial expansion 'had grown as an ominous dark cloud'.

Fundamental to the Huileries operation was the supply of palm fruit. At that time the fruit growing wild in the forest was gathered by the natives and brought in to depots for sale. This casual supply of raw material appeared to Lever to threaten the whole scheme: 'I do not think we can rely on it as a permanent supply of fruit. We can only depend on our own gathering and cultivation. The fact is the native has few wants. A little salt and a little cloth are his indispensables. After this: beads, brass rods, and other luxuries. Chief Womba at Leverville can be taken as an example. Twelve months ago he and his people were poor and few in number, and were keen to bring fruit. After twelve months or less of selling fruit he is rich and lazy, has ten wives, and his village is about four times the size it was; but he gathers little or no fruit. The people now live on supplying our people with maize etc., which work the women can do, and so it will be all over. The palm tree is in these parts the banking account of the native, and he no more thinks of going to the bank for fruit for money when his wants and ambitions are supplied than a civilised man would.'

Lever saw the lackadaisical ways of the natives not only as a threat to his business plans but also as a crippling moral defect that ought to be rectified. Thus he described one village: 'the natives were apparently strong and well nourished but the system was one where four freemen owned four slaves. The slaves did all the woodcutting and all the other work, the four freemen lived with their wives in indolence. The idea in this village was that work was only for slaves and that it would be a disgrace for a freeman to work. All I saw of the freemen convinced me that they were not quite as blithe and happy as the slaves. The freemen sat on their haunches staring into vacancy, sullen and glum. Their wives were a little bit brighter for they had something to do: water to fetch, meals to cook, etc. as far as I saw of their domestic arrangements. Nor has this system made the freemen virile and courageous. For we heard that when recently a neighbouring village wanted to fight them, they begged of the Government to take them away. . . . Once get the "caste sentiment" against work, and human nature sinks. There is no foxhunting, golf, or other game in this country to take the place of work.'

The identification of idleness as a great sin was consistent with Lever's Nonconformist upbringing, but not so his apparent stretching of the virtue of industriousness to include time-consuming ball games and bloodsports. It was certainly not an indulgence he needed for himself but perhaps he felt that some of the acquaintances of his mature years were more active than industrious.

While his observations led him to believe that most natives were unsatisfactory employees, Lever was inclined to blame this less on them than on their present employers, and to be confident that a more enlightened management would soon raise them to a state of contented efficiency. He commented on the very poor tools used by the natives at a State wooding station: 'a machete and an axe, a hammer and a wedge, no grindstones, no saws. I have never seen a saw mark on a piece of wood for fuel up till now. I think the Europeans a little unreasonable with the native. The excuse is "the native spoils good tools or they are stolen etc. etc." Another thought of mine is that natives must be trained to work to time. At present they work when they please and, like Europeans, procrastinate, so all is confusion. They are only children and, like children, they would work by fits and starts. Regularity of habits must be gradually worked up to. The native material is good, willing and anxious to please the white man.' His sympathetic concept of the native as a child anxious to please is perceptive and touching. He made this one of the fundamental principles of his labour programme, emphasising and restating it on many occasions: 'the native African will be a good workman when better understood. I have only praise for him as far as I can judge. Yet the white man here is always speaking of the "lazy nigger". He is a child, and a willing child, but he wants training and handling with patience.'

Lever's attitude to the native was not likely to find favour with the many Europeans in the Congo left over from the days of the Leopold régime and regretting the passing of some of its features. Their views were exemplified by the President of the Kinshasa Chamber of Commerce who strongly opposed the new Government policy with natives as too extreme a change from the severity of the old days. 'From one extreme of cruelty,' he said, 'the treatment of the native has now passed to the other of imbecility.'

The new soft rules that were complained of, still gave to the captains of Government steamers and other Government officials the power to order the summary flogging of natives without trial. Lever wrote in his diary, 'Some members of our managing staff ask for our similar officials also to have power to flog, to which I am strongly opposed. Temper too much enters into immediate floggings for the system to be a good one.'

Nevertheless, although opposed to flogging, he was swift to recognise – and seek to change – those parts of the new policy whose effect was to reduce the efficiency of his business: 'something ought to be done to give the white man authority. In civilised countries the power of instant dismissal is sufficient . . . some change is wanted in the present law under which a native can be mutinous, insolent, lazy, or drunk, and his white manager can do nothing but either dismiss him, in which case the fare of the native must be paid back to the place where he was engaged, or else the native must be sent to a judge for trial, which wastes always days and sometimes a month.' Lever suggested, and the suggestion was accepted by the Governor-General, that the Company's senior officials be given the power to place wrong-doing black employees in irons at once, and then send them for trial to a judge. He claimed that this would give both partics time to cool down before punishment was asked for from the judge. 'I believe by this system that not one in ten of such cases would ever require to go to trial, and so our white managers' time would be saved.' In Lever's life, business and humanity were partners, not perhaps equal partners, but mutually indispensable.

When, during his expedition, Lever saw something of the Congo missions he found that he was most sympathetic towards those who practised hard-headed Christianity. By coincidence, the hospital of the Bolobo Mission, which he visited, had been built with money raised by a Baptist Missionary Exhibition in Liverpool with which he had been associated.

'In every department except farming this Mission compares most favourably with those we have seen at Kisantu and Womballi, and in medical service it is infinitely superior to either. In fact the medical service at Bolobo Baptist Mission is as near perfect as possible. But it appears to me that this mission falls behind the others in farming and agriculture, and if more attention were given to agriculture it would be better. It is well to teach printing, book-binding, and such trades. But seeing that there is not even one single newspaper published for either whites or natives in the Belgian Congo, it is evident that after learning these trades at the Mission, the natives, after leaving, can have no further use for them. All this show and parade of hand printing, book-binding, compositor's tables etc. which we have seen at all three mission stations is merely a white man's fad. The books, pamphlets, etc. could be printed at one quarter the cost in Europe and in as little time, including time lost on voyage, and the energies of the missionaries concentrated on farming, cattle, and agriculture, which must be the first native industries in the Congo as elsewhere.

'Europe was two thousand years ahead of the Congo before printing was introduced into Europe. If printing by natives is not introduced here for a hundred years, and the next hundred years is concentrated on agriculture etc., the natives will not suffer. But printing and book-binding look like civilisation and progress, and forsooth we must begin at that end. To step out of a compositor's room into a native village is worse than from the sublime to the ridiculous. It would be comedy if it were not for the tragedy of it all.'

The Jesuits, in contrast to the Baptists, gave more attention to farming. Lever approved of the way they taught the natives agricultural methods which tended to make the Missions more self-supporting and less of a burden on home generosity, and also helped the natives in their material lives. The Jesuits were more keenly alert on business matters than the average clergy. Lever had, for instance, to resist their attempts to get the Company to pay for the building of a church and also for teaching carried out by Fathers. 'I must say,' he wrote in his diary, 'I like these Jesuit Fathers very much.'

The Missions, and similar matters which only marginally affected the Huileries, attracted Lever's passing interest, but his close attention was focused on inspecting all the Company's early activities and sorting the bad from the good.

He arrived in Alberta on pay-day. The paying officer sat out in front of one of the buildings at a table with men's paybooks and a pile of notes and coin. Each man's name was called in turn and he came forward to be paid. When one group had been paid a new batch of men was marched into position in military fashion until the whole assembly of some seven hundred had been dealt with. After payment was completed the store was opened and the natives admitted one at a time. Most of them spent all their wages buying cloth, salt, sewing machines, etc., and on one occasion 5,600 francs was paid out in wages and 6,700 francs taken in at the store. The store prices were about 20 per cent lower than those charged by the merchants in the town, so friends of the employees gave them money to purchase goods on their behalf. Lever decreed that as long as the store made no loss the low prices should be retained – 'it brings in the native to work for our rate of pay in preference to working elsewhere.'

Elsewhere the economic advantages of working for the Company had not been so readily accepted. The wives in one village were said to have poisoned six men who wanted to gather palm fruit for the Huileries. But Lever was confident that such opposition would vanish when they saw the material rewards that others were getting.

Communications on the expedition were a source of disquiet, not to say uproar. After noticing and recording how efficiently the native drums carried news swiftly along the river from one village to the next, Lever was not amused to find that his own careful arrangements to have telegrams from Port Sunlight waiting for him at various ports of call were frustrated time and again by a hopelessly incompetent telegraph service.

He was unhappy, too, about the way in which the Company's river craft had been ordered and designed. The stern-wheelers were either too small for comfort or too big for safe navigation. The *Lusanga* herself had damaged her starboard rudder on a sand-bank and thereby delayed Lever's journey. In the choice of the smaller craft the furious currents of the Congo rivers had not been sufficiently considered. One of the launches in which Lever travelled was so unstable that it could never be used without a barge lashed alongside to prevent it from capsizing. Even so the Chairman came very close to being tipped into the dangerous waters. 'If anyone can design a new error in boat-building after seeing our Congo fleet,' he wrote, 'he will deserve a patent for it.'

There were more subtle matters of policy which displeased him. 'If we allow our doctors to add to their income by private practice how can we refuse our engineers, surveyors, agricultural botanists, and chemists, or even our general managers, from giving advice and receiving fees for so doing. . . . In all future engagements of our doctors we must prohibit their receiving fees for private patients. But we leave it to themselves to attend whites or natives not employed by the Huileries if life is at stake or humanitarian reasons require such attendance. But for such services a very stiff charge must be made by the Huileries on account of, and to be paid by, the Huileries to the general Congo Fund for the Suppression of Sleeping Sickness. In short, attendance ought to be given in extreme cases of need to either whites or blacks not employed by the Huileries, and for such attendance a very stiff charge must be made in order to ensure that such calls on our doctors are a matter of life and death . . . it is reported or rumoured that the State doctors in Boma and Banana make about fifty thousand francs a year each by this private practice. The State feels compelled to agree to their doctors holding a private practice because of their responsibility for the general health of the town and for the fact that there are no doctors available except State doctors. We are not in that position.'

No one was spared when matters were threshed out as soon as the party reached Leverville. Not surprisingly Lever subjected his own personal colonial capital to the closest scrutiny. He found much that was wrong: the wrong bricks, the wrong lubricating oil, the wrong tools, poor quality casks sent out from Port Sunlight. 'There is so much to admire and so much to disgust one in our management of Leverville that I cannot say much without saying too much. However, it is a great achievement for a little over twelve months work carried on under great difficulties in the African forest. This work has been accomplished by no more than one third of the white staff present, and the remaining two thirds can claim little or no credit for it. These members of staff have done nothing but hinder and discourage the others.'

Everyone at Leverville felt the impact of Lever's arrival, but no one felt it more than the Company's surveyor. On the very last day of the visit Lever had him out from 5.30 to 6.30 a.m. going round with the town plan making alterations to suit local topography and conditions. The surveyor, with a large working party, was told to alter street lines and drive in pegs to mark the changes. But when Lever returned at one o'clock, having given him what he considered to be ample time, almost nothing had been done. The angry little man took charge of the operation himself, and by just after three o'clock everything was finally settled to his satisfaction.

Many must have returned thankfully to their offices to relax for a while when, after a brief but nerve-racking delay caused by fog, the *Lusanga* sailed away from the little township carrying Lever and his party on their way. On the whole Lever was satisfied, but he brooded on how the organisation must be improved, particularly by putting Brussels, Liverpool, and Port Sunlight in closer touch with the Congo. 'We have no Tom Tiddler's Ground here where we have only to stoop to pick up a fortune. Every ton of oil will need hard work and still harder thinking. For the next ten years we have all got to put our backs into it, and no mistake about it. We are pioneers and we must work and rough it like pioneers.'

By early February they were nearing the end of their time in the *Lusanga* and Lever distributed bonuses to the crew. These sums ranged from 400 francs to those who had been courageous and enterprising in repairing the rudder, to 250 francs for the Chief Engineer, and 100 francs for Coffee the cook, and the same amount for the half-caste Chief Mate. Ordinary members of the crew and the servant boys got a few francs. 'I gave nothing to the Captain because of his getting his rudder bent. He has proved a very good Captain, we could not wish for a better, as far as we have knowledge of him. But I am told he has a weakness for something stronger than tea or coffee . . . the black Purser has been drunk so often I gave him nothing.'

At 11.45 p.m. on February 10th, apparently after the bonus distribution, Lever was awakened by a great splash in the river. 'Our Captain who having not been drinking exactly neat coffee, had fallen twenty feet or more into the river from the deck above. He cut his leg badly and will have to go into hospital. He is otherwise, but for his lack of adherement to teetotalism, a good Captain, and a man one could get attached to, as is so often the case with these victims.' The principles determining the crew's bonus are in some ways reminiscent of the distribution of profits to Co-Partners.

On 12 February 1913 Lever wrote in his diary, 'So ends practically our visit to the Congo. My only regret is that I did not take it twelve months earlier, and if I have another regret it is that I am not yet certain that I can come again this year. . . . It is the most important service that I can render to the business, and if at all possible I intend to come. We have much to do, and we may have many more difficulties than we can forsee today, but we hold winning cards if we play them rightly.'

On the day that he sailed from Africa for home Lever sat in his cabin and wrote, 'I am more confident in our great undertaking than ever, although the difficulties are greater than I judged. We have got hold of something which we can employ all our talents and energies upon for the next quarter century and still find plenty to do. . . . I set to work at once in the afternoon on a plan for the plantation villages.'

# 10

# *Isolation*

So many perils beset Lever Brothers during 1911–13 that the Chairman was needed constantly on the 'Bridge' at Port Sunlight. Yet there were many occasions during this period when a decision was required and Lever was not there to give it. This was particularly the case during the four months of his visit to the Congo. The directors he left behind must at times have felt like ship's officers under a singularly irascible Captain who had set a course at high speed through dangerous waters and then retired to his cabin with an attractive passenger.

The hard work and modest enterprise of his father had provided a safe and comfortable childhood home, and Lever had never needed to glance over his shoulder at poverty. Business meant much more to him than making money. At sixty years of age he was very rich and the possibility of personal financial deprivation was quite remote. Even more than in earlier days he considered it all-important that his life – and that meant his business – should contain some worthwhile project, a challenge to skill and nerve offering the prize of fame and acclamation. His furious, even reckless, pursuit on behalf of Lever Brothers of world domination in the soap market was carried on by a policy of expansion and take-over which might have been considered a sufficiently daunting project to merit single-minded attention. But his ambition looked beyond commercial success – on whatever scale – as once it had looked beyond the Works at Port Sunlight to the Village. He was now obsessed with his African project. He financed it from other departments of the Company which could hardly spare the money, and he devoted to Africa time and effort urgently needed at home in battles which he had entered with gusto and then left to subordinates who were not used to supreme command.

The neglect of the main business in favour of his tropical toy was no fair-weather peccadillo. These were bad times for Lever Brothers, and in 1913 the Company profits were insufficient to cover an Ordinary Dividend. This was a situation Lever dreaded. It was of no importance to him that as holder of the bulk of the Ordinary shares he would be the one to lose most financially, but his over-sensitive pride shrivelled at the thought of the humiliation of admitting failure at the Company General Meeting, and of facing, empty-handed, the Co-Partners in the Auditorium at Port Sunlight.

Lever saved his face, and propped up the Company's credit in the money market, by decreeing that an Ordinary Dividend should nevertheless be declared – the funds to cover it being raised by selling some of the Company's assets in the Pacific Phosphates Company. It was the second time in two years that this long-stop reserve fund had been raided. In 1911 the Company's expensive advertising campaign, so close to Lever's heart, could only be kept going by selling Phosphates shares.

Lever's pursuit of excellence was impelled by an ambition for supremacy. In the business, and perhaps in its colonial extension, supremacy had an intrinsic value not necessarily associated with vanity. But Lever's consuming drive to possess the best and the biggest extended to his houses, gardens and estates; his collections of pictures, porcelain and tapestry; and even to his charity. Often others wanted objects he coveted, or an owner did not wish to sell, or some person or public body opposed his ownership. There was an unending stream of subjects for negotiation and persuasion, argument and litigation: the subjects ranging from the control of a company to the price of a picture. Over and over again there was conflict which Lever often seemed to invite and enjoy. The dust of the arena might almost have been an addictive drug, and the winning sometimes as welcome as the prize.

Overshadowing all the skirmishes and minor battles was the struggle with the Brunner Mond Company which was a ten-year war with its decisive engagements in the 1911–13 period.

Brunner's was a chemical firm with an established position of great strength in the alkali industry. The alkali they supplied to Lever Brothers was soda-ash (sodium carbonate) to be made into caustic soda which was then boiled with the oils and fats to produce soap. The fraction of the raw materials represented by the alkali was nearly 20 per cent by weight, or about 10 per cent by cost, and it was thus a critical element in the soap manufacturing process. Brunner's used the modern Solvay, or ammonia-soda, process to produce their soda-ash, and they had built up a predominant position of their own in the United Kingdom while, in combination with other Solvay Group manufacturers, they controlled the supply of alkali in America and on the continent of Europe. This impregnable position enabled Brunner's almost to dictate the terms on which they would supply the soap-makers. The feeling of being held in the palm of another manufacturer had long rankled with Lever and alarmed his business instincts. For years he had struggled and manoeuvred to get out of this grip but Brunner's had always been too strong for him. The consequent feeling of vulnerability and failure was, for a man of Lever's temperament, made much worse by the fact that Brunner's was very closely associated with Crosfield's, one of the principal participants in the ill-fated 1906 Soap Trust, and in Lever's eyes one of the leading rats who scuttled away leaving him to take the blame and bear the expense when disaster struck.

Lever had been trying to wriggle free even before 1906, but such was Brunner's strength that in Lever's 1904 contract they could insist on stringent conditions among which was a clause nipping in the bud Lever's attempt to set up his own chemical plant. In 1907, when the contract was renewed, Lever was quite unable to wring any worthwhile concession out of his monopolist supplier and he found himself again committed for a long period to buying alkali at a high price. Furthermore, as a check that Lever Brothers were not doing business in alkali with outsiders, they were required to reveal to Brunner's details of all alkali transactions with their associated companies at home and abroad. Even an assurance extracted from Brunner's that they would not supply anyone at lower prices than they charged Lever Brothers was soured by the single exception made for the benefit of

Crosfield's on account of their long and close association with Brunner's.

During the course of a few months in 1911 Lever bought up a number of estates in Cheshire and added some seven thousand acres to the land he already owned there. He had in mind the possibility of extending his town and country planning experiments beyond the Port Sunlight Village to a large part of the Wirral peninsula. As soon as he acquired the land he had a fine wide road cut straight across country to improve communications and thus facilitate the future development of the region. Among the incidentals included in his purchase was the right to appoint a Church of England priest to one of the parishes in his new property. His relations with the Established Church were not at this time very cordial, and he wrote to a friend,[1] 'Lever Brothers are not exactly loved by the Church of England Clergymen in this neighbourhood and I myself am anything but the mild, inoffensive, individual I imagine myself to be, viewed through their spectacles. The *Daily Mail* said I was the "mildest mannered man who ever scuttled competition" and I suppose the Church of England Clergymen, finding Nonconformity and Liberalism to flourish, blame me as the cause, instead of the rising tide of Nonconformity and Liberalism throughout the country.' It was typical of Lever's strong respect for what he regarded as proper authority that, in spite of his strictures on the local clergy, he at once surrendered the gift of the living to the Diocese of Chester in perpetuity.

There was however another incidental to Lever's purchase which was of considerable consequence. Ownership of the land carried with it the mineral rights, and at Lymm there were several hundred acres with rich deposits of salt. This salt – much more so than the development potential of the land above it – was Lever's principal reason for buying the Lymm estate. Salt was the starting point for the manufacture of soda-ash, the raw material which bound Lever so expensively and unwillingly to Brunner's. With a source of salt secured, Lever could contemplate making his own soda-ash, or at any rate he could use this threat as a bargaining point when his contract came up for renewal in the near future. It was not possible to keep secret the purchase of the Lymm estate, and the implications were at once clear to Brunner's, who reacted very strongly. Within months of Lever getting hold of his own salt deposits in 1911 Brunner's raised a very large amount of cash and bought the Ordinary shares of Crosfield's and Gossage's.

The opposing forces were drawn up ready for battle. On one side, Brunner's, with a commanding position in the alkali industry, now owned two soap firms whose joint production was equal to that of Port Sunlight. On the other side was Lever's, with the newly acquired salt, threatening an entry into alkali manufacture.

Personal animosity made the ensuing commercial struggle as implacable as a religious war. Some of the animosity was of long standing, like that between Lever and J. J. Crosfield, who showed how the 1906 wounds still festered by making it a condition for the Brunner Mond take-over of his company that Crosfield shares should never, without his permission, be transferred to Lever Brothers. More recently, ill-feeling had been generated between the management of Gossage's and Lever when he bought up a washing powder firm who had been one of Gossage's best customers for soap, and then successfully sued Gossage's in a particularly acrimonious patent action when they tried to take up the manufacture of the washing powder themselves. Resentments old and new gave extra sting to the exchanges between the opposing sides, and even where no personal animosity had previously existed Lever soon generated it by his aggressive attitude in the negotiations with Brunner's which started at the end of 1911.

Sir John Brunner, whose baronetcy antedated Lever's by some sixteen years, had no ambition to be a soap-maker. Gossage's and Crosfield's were among the very small number of important soap manufacturers in the United Kingdom not already snapped up by Lever, and Brunner's had only bought these two firms to ensure the continuation of their lucrative alkali trade with the soap industry. Sir John's attitude in the negotiations was calm and cool in defence of his own established position as a seller of alkali. His object was to preserve the *status quo*, with Lever and the rest of the soap-makers buying his product.

In contrast, Sir William's negotiating style was a ferment of truculence and vituperation which suited both his purpose and his temperament. He wanted an improvement in the terms of his contract and he had therefore to attack. He claimed that Brunner's entry into the soap trade was in breach of their contractual agreement and that Lever Brothers were consequently released from their undertaking not to make alkali and sell it outside their own group of companies. Whether or not Lever, in the modern manner, turned on 'uncontrolled' temper as a shock tactic to gain negotiating points, there is little doubt that his intense personal feelings occasionally overruled his commercial reason. At one meeting when Brunner offered a new alkali contract of some generosity Lever raged and shouted that he would not be treated like 'a clerk in Brunner's office to be told to make a contract', and subsequently he declared to his own board of directors that 'on no account would he agree to an alkali contract'.[2]

By 1912 each side was more anxious to nip out the salient the other had thrust into its territory than to extend and exploit its own offensive. Brunner certainly had little enthusiasm for his new soap interest *per se*. Lever, deeply involved in securing raw material sources in the tropics, might possibly have sought to develop his salt deposits, but in this instance one long-held guiding principle – vertical integration – was overcome by another: the drive to rule the soap industry by absorbing all serious competition. If he could somehow get hold of Crosfield's and Gossage's, then Lever would double his business in the United Kingdom and do even better in the export market where Lever Brothers had fallen behind these two competitors.

In 1912 the parties had sufficiently clarified their own ideas and motives for it to become fairly obvious that the likely outcome was a settlement which to a greater or lesser extent gave Lever control of Crosfield's and Gossage's, and gave Brunner a sure market for his alkali with all Lever's associated companies. The mechanics of reaching such a settlement was however beyond the skill and powers of the negotiators, one huge obstacle to giving Lever any control of Brunning's two soap firms being the undertaking given to J. J. Crosfield that his company's shares should never be transferred to Lever Brothers. Consequently the struggle had in 1912 reached a stalemate which might easily have remained unresolved if a new factor had not appeared, adding another dimension to the war and leading to a decisive battle.

The new factor was a chemical process called hydrogenation in which relatively cheap oils could be turned into solid fats suitable for making soap, and also for the manufacture of margarine, which was a swiftly growing industry. Crosfield's had bought the patent taken out on the process by Normann, a German, and had developed it on a pilot production scale to the point where they could produce about a hundred tons of hardened fat per week. So high had fat prices been forced by the soap and margarine makers scrambling for raw materials all over the world that the ability to convert cheap oil, particularly the plentiful whale oil, would be a tremendous business asset.

The critical importance of hydrogenation had been widely recognised and several oil-hardening processes other than the Normann method had been patented and developed. By the end of 1911 the exploitation of hydrogenation on a large commercial scale seemed imminent. So Crosfield's decided to take action to establish in Court that the Normann process was the original definitive invention and that they therefore held the master patent. This would mean that in the United Kingdom, and probably in most countries abroad, all other patents would be invalid, and anyone using hydrogenation to produce hard fats would have to pay a royalty to Crosfield's. An action alleging infringement of patent was brought against the owners of a rival hydrogenation process, called Testrup. The action was set down in Crosfield's name but it was in effect brought by Brunner's, who could see the possibility of the Normann process giving them a monopoly position in oil-hardening similar to that which the Solvay process had given them in the alkali industry. The expertise available among the staff of a large company such as Brunner's was invaluable in fighting a patent case where so much depended upon the skill with which details of complicated processes were explained to a Court with little scientific knowledge.

The board of Lever Brothers recognised that if the action were successful then Brunner's would not only control their alkali supply but also another of their vital raw materials.

The owners of the Testrup patent were a relatively small company who were unlikely to stand much chance against the legal, technical, and financial resources which could be deployed by Brunner's. So Lever Brothers took out a licence under the Testrup patent and thus put themselves in a position to be able to go to Court and fight Brunner's in defence of the patent. But owning a patent – even if it were blessed with a legal declaration of validity – was a long way from being able to produce hard fat on a commercial scale. After much deliberation the directors of Lever Brothers – without benefit of discussion with their chairman – signed an expensive agreement with a German firm who not only owned the foreign rights in the Testrup patent but had also discovered and perfected manufacturing tricks not covered in the patent but essential to making it work reliably and economically.

The commercial and legal manoeuvres over the hydrogenation process showed that, at sixty years of age and after twenty-five years or more as a soap-maker, Lever was beginning to stand in a slightly different position relative to Lever Brothers than in the old one-man-band days when Warrington was just behind and Port Sunlight still being developed. He was no longer the sole source of innovatory drive. Indeed, like an old admiral ignoring the invention of the aeroplane, he had needed to be prodded by members of the Board before Lever Brothers belatedly took an interest in the fat-hardening process. Lever was very wary of using hardened whale oil in his soaps, except for Lifebuoy where the carbolic would kill any fishy smell, real or imagined. He believed that the public were prejudiced against whale oil, and he was not impressed by the suggestion that if they were willing to eat it on their bread then they would not object to washing in it. He regarded public goodwill as paramount. As a businessman he cultivated it, and as an individual he coveted it. The vast effort and expenditure on advertising to establish public confidence in Sunlight could easily be dissipated by incautious use of the plentiful whale oil. But though he dragged his feet on hydrogenation he eventually saw that it was an essential component of his business.

The size and complexity of the Company and its associates multiplied the decisions required, while the wide range of Lever's own activities – his property development, his collecting, his politics, and, more than anything, his travelling – meant that more and more frequently these decisions were left to the directors. Often they waited with some trepidation for the Chairman's covering approval of action taken in his absence, knowing that he might take an intense and often unreasonable interest in some matter really too trivial to merit his attention. But they could be reasonably certain of his approval for any action which, in the military jargon becoming fashionable at the time, was intended 'to engage the enemy more closely'. The enemy in Lever's eyes being other soap-makers, and anyone else who hindered his relentless pursuit of growth and the domination of the industry.

Major policy was of course dictated by Lever, not always in concord with his directors, although they rarely dared much more than a muted enquiry by way of criticism. This was however not always the case. J. K. Greenhalgh, a director and financial adviser for many years, objected violently when Lever, needing money for expansion, floated a new capital issue. Greenhalgh maintained that Lever was misrepresenting the Company's rather unsatisfactory financial position by dwelling on past profits and future promise, but not mentioning that the Pacific Phosphates assets had been raided to maintain advertising and to provide an Ordinary Dividend. For Lever, his own faith in the future success of the Company was sufficient guarantee that the public's money would be safe, but to Greenhalgh the only honest guarantee was a balance in the ledger. The disagreement reminded Lever of the arguments with his father about the expansion of the grocery firm over thirty years ago. But whereas Lever had then been able to persuade his father to put family money into the business, he was not able to shake Greenhalgh, for whom it was not just a matter of prudence but of professional integrity and duty to the public who were being asked to hazard their money. Lever floated his capital issue and Greenhalgh resigned as Financial Director. But Lever nevertheless thought so much of his accounting ability that he created for him a special directorship which involved no responsibility for policy. A less obviously talented man would probably have been shipped out of Port Sunlight into the obscurity of some associated company.

Among the few whose advice Lever particularly valued, and who increasingly played a decisive part in the proliferating activities of the Company, were George Harley and J. L. Tillotson. Harley, a Liverpool solicitor, was a close personal friend as well as Lever's and the Company's principal legal adviser. It was he who at the beginning of the century had first sent a few welcome briefs on behalf of Lever Brothers to a promising young northern barrister, F. E. Smith. Tillotson was the son of W. F. Tillotson, who had been one of that close group of young people in Bolton making up the friends of Lever's youth. Tillotson senior founded the *Bolton Evening News* group of newspapers and married Lever's sister Mary. When their eldest son, John Lever Tillotson, went to work for Lever Brothers he was rapidly promoted and joined the Board in 1899.

Harley and Tillotson were prominent in getting Lever Brothers a stake in the hydrogenation process and in setting up the Testrup patent case. In March 1913, thanks largely to technical evidence brilliantly presented by the Company's chemical consultant, the Court decided against Brunner-Crosfield and refused master patent status for the Normann process. Other firms were now free to develop their own plant for the conversion of cheap oils into hard fat. It was for Lever Brothers a most important victory, and Brunner recognised the fact. He at once sought terms with Lever and the agreement was signed, in the victor's tent as it were, at The Hill, Hampstead. It was, though, more of a cease-fire than a final settlement.

Brunner's were not in future to extend further their incursions into the soap trade, and Lever Brothers were not to threaten Brunner's interests in the alkali trade and were to sell to them the salt-bearing portion of Lever's Lymm estate which had triggered off the battle. Lever's companies at home and abroad would buy their alkali from Brunner's or their associates. This was the essence of the new agreement signed at Hampstead; very much a return to the *status quo*, with some improvement for Lever in the detailed provisions. There was however in the new agreement one further provision which was for Lever the nub of the matter. Brunner's would pay to Lever a large share of the profits made by their two soap subsidiaries. Notwithstanding J. J. Crosfield's defensive proviso about his company's shares, Lever had at last got his fingers into the Crosfield–Gossage pie and had every intention of tightening his grip to the stage where he could lift it into his own larder.

Anyone cherishing the illusion that the new agreement would mean a friendly Brunner–Lever alliance, with Gossage's and Crosfield's as willing partners, was soon disabused. One member of the Crosfield family, referring disparagingly to Lever's commercial methods and sensational advertising, said that the Crosfield business 'had not been built up by cutting down the profits of their friends nor had it been built upon bunkum'.[3] The grudges and animosities of the soap and allied industries that had rumbled and grumbled for years continued to do so, still punctuated from time to time with violent eruptions. The 1906 row over the soap combine and the first battle with Brunner Mond were in the past, but Lever was at the centre of others in the future: a dispute when Lever Brothers decided to go it alone on fat-hardening rather than join a price-holding combine of the soap and margarine firms; and violent quarrels with the management of Gossage's and Crosfield's over the soap market in China. Each row brought litigation between Lever and Brunner, and each settlement gave Lever a bigger say in the affairs of Gossage's and Crosfield's, until eventually in 1919 he bought the controlling shares and the two companies were his. The 1906 blow to his pride was amply avenged and a major part of the British soap industry was in his hands. It was the culmination of Lever's unremitting war of attrition which for a dozen years or more had never been long out of his mind no matter how demanding his other projects.

Lever was not always successful in making the legal system further his ambition for commercial supremacy. The Co-operative Wholesale Society was a very serious competitor, making and selling its own soaps. The Cooperative shops naturally pushed their own products and in many cases stocked no other, offering their own brand when asked for a competitor's. Lever believed that if a manufacturer had created a market for his product by expensive advertising campaigns then it was the duty of the retailer to supply that particular product to customers who asked for it. He attempted to get legal sanction for this view but his test case against certain Cooperative shops failed. When he insisted on taking the case to a higher Court his appeal was dismissed, the Master of the Rolls remarking that Lever's view of the duty of shopkeepers to supply his products was 'a somewhat audacious claim to a monopoly without warranty in law'.[4]

Lever was, too, a persistent, even a compulsive, litigator in his private affairs, and, apart from the multitude of Lever Brothers actions, he caused many fat briefs to drop on to the desks of grateful, or at least gratified, counsel, with F. E. Smith and Carson among the principal beneficiaries.

In assembling one of the most important private English art collections he acted with the same directness and vigour as he did in business. Occasionally, perhaps, he showed more gusto than taste, but he was the very opposite of the pretentious connoisseur. He did not see art as too sacred to be subject to the rules of life, and since in his own life many of the rules were commercial, he sometimes shocked the art world by a business-like attitude to its commercial aspects. If the shock gave way to argument then Lever usually relished the controversy, was happy to conduct it in public, and quite prepared to take it eventually to Court like any other dispute.

Lever was particularly interested in English and oriental porcelain and built up a fine collection. In 1911 he bought valuable oriental porcelain which had been assembled by Richard Bennett, a native of Bolton, and he agreed to pay Mr Gover, a dealer, just over a quarter of a million pounds for it. But the terms of the sale were remarkable in that the whole of the collection was at once put on exhibition at Port Sunlight and Lever was required to pay off the quarter of a million pounds in instalments of £13,750 per quarter, with a right to withdraw from the contract at any time. In 1912 when Lever Brothers were hard pressed for cash, Lever, who had paid four instalments, asked Gover to release him from the contract and find another buyer. A dispute arose between Gover and Lever about the custody of the collection while the new sale was being negotiated, and in May 1913 the matter was brought before Mr Justice Darling, with F. E. Smith leading for Lever and Sir Edward Carson for Gover.[5]

Lever wanted to keep the whole of the collection until the new sale had been completed and his fifty-five thousand pounds returned. Carson commented, 'He [Mr Gover] has gone for two years without any interest on this £250,000 and if we can't get a purchaser for the whole collection the china is to remain at Hulme Hall on exhibition and we are still to remain without any interest on our money.'

Mr Justice Darling: 'The difficulty which strikes me is that the plaintiff has trusted Sir William Lever with £250,000 worth of goods with no security.'

Mr Smith: 'If a judgment of Solomon is appropriate here we are perfectly prepared to accept it.'

Mr Justice Darling: 'Solomon isn't here.'

Mr Smith: 'So long as he leaves us sufficient to secure our £55,000 [i.e. four instalments] we are willing to part with the remainder.'

Mr Justice Darling: 'I may take it that Sir William Lever has called upon the plaintiff to sell the whole lot, and I am to decide which of them is to trust the other.'

Eventually the Judge decided in favour of Mr Gover, declaring that he might remove the collection to his galleries for sale. A stay of execution was granted and after much further argument there was, after all, a Solomon-like solution with Lever retaining permanently at Port Sunlight a portion of the collection to the value of the money he had already paid.

In contrast to his uncompromising attitude in the matter of the Bennett collection, Lever was known to have withdrawn discreetly from certain purchases in favour of rivals who, he considered, should be deferred to as people of rank. In one recorded instance[6] Lever commissioned a dealer to bid at Christie's for two pieces of Chinese porcelain, but withdrew his commission when he discovered that Lord Kitchener intended to bid for them. Kitchener got the two pieces but Lever snapped them up for the Port Sunlight collection shortly afterwards when they were put up for sale again on Kitchener's death.

It is hardly surprising, in view of his constant activity in buying and improving houses and estates, that such property was the subject of much of the ceaseless flow of litigation which, like the sound of waves at the seaside, formed an almost unnoticed background to his life. The dispute with Liverpool Corporation went as far as a Select Committee of the House of Commons, and there was a running battle with municipal authorities about The Hill at Hampstead. In 1911 he bought the house next door to The Hill and knocked it down with the intention of adding the grounds to his own garden, from which it was separated by a narrow public path. Lever had to build a bridge across this path to connect his two properties and he offered the Hampstead Borough Council[7] another piece of land he owned, called The Paddock, in exchange for the public footpath. Those who jealously guarded the freedom of the Heath were strongly opposed to the proposal. A neighbour wrote,[8] 'The negotiations went on over many years and raised deep passions. But chiefly I remember that at every critical stage he would end the argument by saying, "I will certainly build over the Paddock".' Lever never built on the land, but so strong was the opposition to the capitalist getting a public right of way, even though he offered more valuable land in return, that he was never able to merge his two properties.

Lever sometimes commented wryly that whatever he did some people would say it was intended to advertise Sunlight Soap. Certainly his motives were scrutinised with suspicious intensity by many who simply could not believe in a liberal capitalist, while less worthy critics were motivated by jealousy and commercial rivalry. Even when he bought the lease of one of London's greatest mansions and offered it to the nation, the gesture was spoiled by a squabble which arose when it was suggested that this would secure some advantage for Lever Brothers in their negotiations with the Government for palm oil concessions in British West Africa.

Stafford House, situated between St James's Palace and Green Park near Buckingham Palace, was the subject of Queen Victoria's remark to the Duchess of Sutherland, whose husband owned it, 'I have come over from my house to your palace.' When Lever bought the lease in 1912 it had twenty-eight years to run before it reverted to the Crown. It was his intention that the mansion should be used to house the collection of the London Museum, with some of the rooms set aside for Government hospitality to foreign visitors. A condition of the gift was that the name should be changed to Lancaster House since it was the gift of a Lancashire man to the Crown which embraced the title Duke of Lancaster. The proposed change of name was viewed with disfavour in official circles but the resistance was overcome. Lever left the details of the transfer in the hands of his solicitors and set out on his journey to the Belgian Congo. By the time he got back things had become complicated and rather sour. Lever wrote to his solicitors, for onward transmission to the Prime Minister.[9] 'My attention has been called to insinuations and innuendoes made during my four months' absence on the Congo by means of questions in the House of Commons, and by Mr W. Moore, K.C., member of Parliament for North Armagh by an interjection, to the effect that I had been actuated by mercenary and improper motives in the offer I made to present to the nation my ownership of the lease of Stafford House. Under these circumstances there is no other course open to me than to withdraw my offer. . . .'

To this Asquith replied,[10] 'I am not surprised that Sir W. Lever should resent the insinuations and innuendoes to which you refer. The publication of the whole correspondence and the answers of the Colonial Secretary have, I think, finally and satisfactorily disposed of any suggestion of the kind.

'It would be a matter of great regret to me if this passing and irrelevant incident should lead to the withdrawal of Sir W. Lever's very generous offer of the lease of Stafford House, of which, subject to certain conditions, the Government had hoped to be able to avail themselves for the advantage of the public.'

Lever was placated by the Prime Minister's letter and by the publication of the Command Paper[11] containing all the correspondence relating to Lever Brothers' concessions in British West Africa. Just over a month after he had returned from the Congo and withdrawn his offer, all was settled amicably again and Lancaster House passed to the nation.

Lever and his wife arrived back in England from the Belgian Congo in March 1913. There had been important developments in the Company's affairs in Lever's absence, but his lieutenants, who had shown unusual and courageous initiative, were relieved to be able to greet him with the victory over Brunner's which considerably strengthened the Lever Brothers position in the home and international soap trade. Lever was convinced that in the Belgian Congo he had taken possession of an asset capable of exploitation on a scale and in a manner which would bring great profit and kudos to the Company and thus wipe out the disappointment attending other attempts to grow raw materials in the tropics: the chronic unprofitability of the Solomon Islands, the swift and total failure of a venture in the French Congo, the painfully slow progress against official obstruction in British West Africa. After a year or two of some adversity with greatly reduced profits and the constant possibility of being out-manoeuvred and taken over by powerful rivals, the way ahead seemed to Lever to be smoother. Dangerous enemies had been defeated and made harmless, and the future of the Company was bright and rosy.

In spite of the rigours of their long journey, much of it in notoriously unhealthy country, Sir William and Lady Lever looked relaxed, fit, and radiantly happy when they were greeted on their return in fine spring weather by friends and employees at Port Sunlight. Both looked younger than their years, and Lever was unashamedly proud of his wife for coming with him on what was undeniably a remarkable journey for a white woman of over sixty. The Royal Geographical Society recognised her exploit by electing her a Fellow, on the motion of Lord Curzon, and Lever himself was honoured by King Albert of Belgium with the Grand Cross of the Order of Leopold II for services to the Congo.

Both Lever and his wife were happy at the successful completion of another of the shared experiences which throughout their married life had contributed to a private relationship of a closeness which would have surprised those who only knew the two very dissimilar public figures. The Congo journey, for all its strangeness, had often been reminiscent of their earliest days together when to press on to Wigan or to cross the water to Ireland had been a business adventure.

There was much to look forward to: settling again into home life at Thornton Manor where the plants in the grounds were touched with spring, recounting their adventures to family and friends, and being reunited with their young son and daughter-in-law who had been married less than a year before in April 1912 with traditional celebrations at Port Sunlight – flags flying, Village decorated, and a day's holiday for all employees. The Levers looked forward, too, to picking up again the threads of their public social life, in particular to the imminent visit of King George V and Queen Mary to Lancashire. It was a time of happiness and confident anticipation for Lever, but hidden just ahead of him was a cruel, sudden tragedy.

On 7 July 1913 the Levers dined with the King and Queen at the home of the Earl and Countess of Derby. While they were there the great wooden bungalow of Rivington Pike was destroyed by fire together with most of the contents, including many works of art and old family records and photographs. It was a deliberate act of arson by militant Suffragettes who left in a prominent position a case addressed to the Home Secretary and containing a message calling upon the King, in the name of the women of Lancashire, to stir the Government into action on votes for women. A further message in the case said,[12] 'If Sir William Lever had been as loyal to us and the Liberal Party as Lancashire is being to its King this would not have happened.' Lever had done more than most to improve women's lot with advanced industrial ideas in his factories and advanced social ideas in the Village at Port Sunlight. He had also spoken publicly in favour of women's suffrage. But this was unknown to the fire-raiser, or considered irrelevant. With the superficial appreciation often shown by political vandals it was decided that The Bungalow was a good target because it was remote, uninhabited and wooden, in a prominent position, and owned by someone in contact with the King. Lever was furious, but at once decided that he would rebuild the house in stone and concrete, 'something they cannot burn'. This instant replanning softened the blow for him and he was flattered when the King sent him a telegram reading,[13] 'Much regret to learn from newspapers that while you were here last night your house at Rivington and its contents were destroyed by fire. I sympathise with you in your loss.' His Majesty enquired further about the damage when he received Lever and his wife again at another function a few days later in Bolton.

For Lever, coming home from the Congo trip meant getting

back once more into the swing of business activity, and this soon entailed travelling abroad again. A few days after the end of the royal visit to Lancashire he went off to inspect associated companies on the Continent. Most unusually he travelled without his wife, who had social engagements at home. He was in Marseilles when a telegram informed him that she was gravely ill with pneumonia following a chill. He rushed back across France and got to her side with no time to spare. She was just able to recognise him before she drifted into unconsciousness and died a few hours later on 24 July 1913. It was a sickening, stupefying blow, and although he soon pulled himself together and to outward appearances carried on as before, the emptiness was always there inside him when he paused to reflect.

Speaking publicly in tribute to her Lever said,[14] 'It would be but a poor compliment to my late wife if I left you under the impression that she was a business woman, that she would make suggestions about the business, and suggestions about building the village and other institutions. She was essentially a womanly woman, and her knowledge of business was nil. . . . But I always told her as soon as I knew myself, exactly how the business was progressing, and I can say, after full and careful thought, that I am convinced that without her great influence there would have been neither a Port Sunlight, nor a Lever Brothers as we know it today. It came because of the confidence she inspired in me.

'During the whole of our married life of forty years, however, early business called me, I never breakfasted alone; she was always up and saw that the breakfast was properly prepared, and I always knew that whatever might happen in the course of the day the great event for her would be my homecoming in the evening. . . . Behind and before all our religion stands the home; civilization is founded upon the home; the centre of the home is the wife. A wife need not be an inspired genius in guiding and directing her husband – genius might be a handicap and not a help – but she can be an inspiration and source of confidence. . . . The greatest inspiration to me has been the wife I was fortunate enough to win.'

There are phrases in this tribute which might stimulate a stirring of the hackles or even make an unreflective feminist reach for matches. But this would be to overlook the fact that the time was over half a century ago, and that the speaker had long before that, given votes to women in a referendum, had asked for them to be appointed to negotiating committees in his factories, had included a large number of them in his first list of Co-Partners, and had taken the wife of whom he spoke on almost every business trip of any length.

Lever showed to a certain degree some of the characteristics of those whom the psychiatrists call schizoid. Such people are said to keep relations with most other humans on a superficial level, to be rather isolated emotionally, and to be inclined to channel natural drives into single-minded pursuit of professional excellence. Their strong urge for power and superiority combined with an inner feeling of vulnerability makes them extremely sensitive to any form of criticism or disparagement and, although the tendencies may be suppressed in youth, in middle and old age there is less mental control and their behaviour is often very aggressive.

With the death of his wife the most important of Lever's personal relationships was destroyed, and any sense of isolation he may have felt was further accentuated by deafness. His hearing had been defective for some time, but when he came back from the Congo it deteriorated very sharply and soon he was physically cut off from those around him, unable to hear more than fragments of ordinary conversation although he tried all types of deaf aid.

The end of 1913 saw Lever at last consolidated in a position of great and growing power in the soap industry. He was rich, he was acclaimed internationally for his liberal views and successful social experiments, but he was widowed, deaf, and lonely. He picked himself up, determined to concentrate his mind on business affairs, and gathering to him the remains of his family he set out in September 1913, with his son and daughter-in-law, on a world tour.

# 11

# *The Lady Lever art gallery*

Between September 1913, when Lever set out with his son and daughter-in-law, and February 1914 when they returned to England, the party visited the United States, Canada, Japan, China, the Philippines, the South Sea Islands, and Australia. The itinerary was strenuous and in all the countries they visited, and at each port of call, Lever occupied almost every waking hour with work; remorselessly visiting factories, negotiating take-overs and mergers, prospecting for new business. Hard work was his life-style, but now he drove himself even harder in the only therapy he found effective to alleviate the pain of the loss of his wife. He extended his commercial interests in the United States, making use of his strength in the fat-hardening business, newly acquired as the result of victory in the struggle with Brunner. He bought out soap companies in Canada, he purchased interests in the two biggest Australian soap manufacturers, he inspected a site in Shanghai and decided upon a first factory in China. It was an extension to the whole world of the expansionist policy which was taking him to a leading position in the United Kingdom soap industry. In the South Seas Lever's son and daughter-in-law went on ahead to Australia, leaving him to visit his Solomon Islands plantations for the first time (p. 98). As he inspected Lever Brothers' coconut forests and installations, and planned the layout of new sites, one of which he named after his late wife, it was hard remembering that less than a year ago he had been doing similar work with her by his side in Africa.

While away on his world tour Lever received at least one letter which assured him that he had not been forgotten in Government circles at home. Lloyd George, then Chancellor of the Exchequer, was raising funds for his Land Campaign and, at the suggestion of B. S. Rowntree, who drafted the letter, he wrote to Lever,[1] 'There is a part of the work of the Land Campaign which I am more reluctant to undertake than any other, namely the collection of the funds which are necessary to carry it on. The fight will be an extremely severe one and if we are to win we shall have to devote very large sums of money to it. A friend of mine had promised me a contribution of £20,000 to the Campaign Funds, and in making my preparations I had this very substantial contribution in mind. Now, however, at the last moment he is putting forward a claim to control the Government policy as a condition of the payment of the money. This of course I cannot for a moment entertain. The withdrawal of this large sum puts me in a very awkward position, for the number of persons to whom I can apply for funds is necessarily limited. You will readily see that it would never do for me to go round cap in hand for a number of small sums. I am therefore writing to ask whether you can help me in the matter. . . .'

Lever, from Canada, sent him a cheque for £5,000 remarking,[2] 'I am sorry I am not at home to do some work in Liverpool for the good cause.' He also took the opportunity to commend again to the Chancellor the merits of graduated income tax, although it is difficult to believe that this would have made much impression on Lloyd George as his eyes flicked from the letter to the figure on the cheque.

Lever was back in England in February 1914 with a month to prepare for one of the proudest events of his life, the visit of King George V and Queen Mary to Port Sunlight. The Works and Village buildings were extra specially cleaned and tidied, and the gardens and grounds clipped, mown, and brushed. Fresh bunting and other decorations; clean protective clothing for the factory workers; a scrub and a polish for the Port Sunlight railway halt; a list of those to be presented; instructions on how to behave in the presence of royalty for workers, villagers, and school-children; a minute by minute timetable of the royal route with allowance made for unscheduled but expected digressions; a rehearsal by Lever and his managers of every likely question and answer that might be raised. All these and much more had been

Huileries, native village

Leverville

Sir Isumbras at the Ford

meticulously planned, and checked personally by Lever, before the afternoon of 25 March 1914 when the Royal Train drew into the station at Port Sunlight and stopped with the carriage door from which the King and Queen would emerge exactly opposite the spot on the platform where Lever stood waiting to greet them.

Guiding the party on the tour, Lever walked a deferential half-pace behind the King and slightly turned towards him. In the film made at the time, the stocky, tough-looking little man is clearly bursting with pride and pleasure at showing the impressive product of his own imagination and drive to King George V, who stood at the very pinnacle of the British Empire and all the traditional institutions that Lever so admired. The royal party inspected the Works and the Village, were cheered by the schoolchildren and, at the Queen's request, visited one of the cottages, before returning to Birkenhead and leaving Port Sunlight to its own private celebrations that evening. A scale model of the Village had been prepared with a cunningly wired electric circuit, so that, at the end of the visit, the King could press a button on the model and thus lay the foundation stone of the Lady Lever Art Gallery, Lever's memorial to his wife.

It was Lever's intention to house in this gallery the majority of the pictures, porcelain, and furniture that he owned, and thus to make available to the public one of the most extensive and important private art collections in the world. He himself considered that the start of the collection had been the purchase when he was a young man of two eighteenth-century Derby Bisque figures, a shepherd and shepherdess, which stood on the mantelpiece of his house in Wigan. In his early collecting years he continued to buy porcelain, added furniture to his interests, and then some bronzes, and a group of etchings by such illustrators as Cruikshank and 'Phiz'. If there was a pattern in this early stage it was a predilection for English pieces of obvious craftsmanship, highly decorative and perhaps romantic, which could be displayed and even used in the home. As he grew richer, and the rooms of his houses bigger, loftier, and more numerous, so the size of his collection began to increase rapidly, and its scope extended to include pictures, tapestry, and sculpture. With the notable exception of his superb Chinese porcelain and some fine French furniture, the collection aimed to be of the very best of British art, and he probably formed the first important collection of English eighteenth-century furniture.

In pictures Lever was fond of the great Victorians, and he had important works by Lord Leighton, Burne-Jones, Sir Luke Fildes, and the Pre-Raphaelites: Holman Hunt, Millais, and Ford Madox Brown. *The Scapegoat* and Leighton's *The Garden of the Hesperides* are indicative of two aspects of Lever's taste: an admiration for great technical skill and realism, and a liking for the richly coloured, decorative composition. With *Sir Isumbras at the Ford* by Millais Lever may perhaps have indulged in an element of self-identification. He would certainly have been attracted by the incidental anecdote connected with the picture: its acclaim as one of Millais's most splendid imaginative works; the undeniable fact that it shows one of the driest horses ever to wade belly-deep in a river; and Ruskin's total condemnation of it as a 'catastrophe' causing Millais to observe that, 'Ruskin said it was not a failure but a fiasco, so I kicked it over in a passion. The hole is there now.' On firmer ground, however, Lever had portraits by Reynolds, Romney, Hoppner and Gainsborough, and other works by Turner, Constable, Landseer, Stubbs, Rubens, and Rembrandt.

Tapestries from Gobelins, Classical and Victorian sculpture, and the finest of English and French furniture, all in remarkable profusion, made up a collection of vast breadth and size.

The combination of great wealth with such a huge collection, comparatively rapidly acquired, might be thought to argue a taste that was indiscriminate rather than eclectic. But such a conclusion is denied by the large number of letters on record in which Lever turned down offers of pieces at reasonable prices and with prima facie grounds for inclusion in his collection. Furthermore, a number of aspects of the way in which he assembled and displayed his pieces indicated that his ideas were positive, if a little unusual.

He felt very strongly that pictures of one period should be displayed in a room with furniture and fittings of the same period, and that the room itself should have walls and ceilings of the appropriate style, even if, in the case of such immovable features as Adam plasterwork, they were copies reproduced by modern craftsmen. He wrote to an architect friend,[3] 'I prefer Georgian dining-rooms as the rooms in which to give large dinners; for small dining-rooms I prefer Tudor. For drawing-rooms I prefer what is called the Adams style; for entrance halls, the Georgian. For a large room such as a music-room, I prefer the period which I should call the Inigo Jones type of Renaissance.'

This concern with completeness of a display, analogous in some ways to his preoccupation with vertical integration in business, appeared in another way in his collection of Wedgwood, where in addition to a comprehensive exhibition of basalts, jasper and other ware, Lever showed the original wax designs modelled by John Flaxman and his associates, and a case containing Flaxman's modelling tools. Lever was interested in the background and the origin of a work of art, and regarded it as a duty and a pleasure to learn as much about it as possible. He wrote to a fellow collector,[4] 'I think a few specimens of the best imitators have an educational influence in all collections, provided they are properly labelled and ticketed.

'I remember a good many years ago I was very proud of a very fine Conjee Hawthorn Pot. This was over twenty years ago and I had purchased it from Duveen's for £600. It was quite equal in quality to the Huth Pot which, you will remember, some five or six years ago was sold by auction at Christie's for £5,900. I bought at the same time from Duveen's a Pot for £5. It was not a modern imitation, as so many are [that] can be purchased at Liberty's for a few shillings, but an imitation made in China by inferior workmen, and certainly not less than a hundred to a hundred and fifty years old, but all the same it was a "wrong un" . . . it was undoubtedly too inky in colour and generally lacked the brilliant translucence of the fine specimen.

'I always found it was of great educational value to me to study these two vases, but my studies were cut short, for one day I had been showing the two to a friend and as I carried these vases from one place to another, generally by putting the lids in my pocket – as you know the lids of a Hawthorn Vase have scarcely any hold on the Pot – and as I was carrying the two in my hands, I inadvertently struck with one of the pots the bronze figure of a boy that I had laid on the floor and whose head had just reached up sufficiently high to break the vase that I carried in my hand. The vase was shattered, and I need not tell you my relief when I found it was the inferior vase that had got the damage and that the brilliant specimen was in the other hand and untouched. I had the inferior specimen patched up, and still have it at Thornton. Sometime when you are there I will show it to you. It is just as good for all purposes as it ever was, and as its value which I paid for it was only £5, the lesson has been worth all the money to me. . . .'

This is not the letter of a man who collected art treasures as one might add shares to a portfolio. He knew his pieces, he handled them, he thought and talked about them. There is a sense of lusty involvement about the bronze boy laid on the floor, and the pot-lids slipped into a pocket. Nor is he ashamed of enjoying a bargain in art whether it was the expensive specimen or the five pound 'wrong un'.

Over a period of many years Lever never missed a Royal Academy Summer Exhibition, and here, as in everything, he was not a man to be content with a half-interest. He was a regular guest at the Academy banquet and each year he entertained Academicians and Associates to lunch or dinner at his Hampstead home. His attitude to the Academy was a reflection of his unaffected view that art was a vigorous part of life, neither to be pampered nor ignored. For Lever life meant business, and if art was a part of life it was certainly a part of business. Using works of art in advertisements was as natural as hanging them in his home or a Works canteen. But if the Academy had to suffer from what many regarded as the ignoble end of Lever's spectrum of total involvement, then it also gained from the altruistic end. Typically, he thought about the social implications of working as an artist and he endowed a fund for the Royal Academy so that needy members or their widows might be provided with a pension in old age.

When the hot holiday lassitude of August 1914 was shattered by the declaration of war on Germany, Port Sunlight was as shocked as the rest of the country, and its subsequent patriotic response was equally overwhelming. The Reservists and Territorials, of which there were nearly five hundred working for Lever Brothers, were the first to go, packing their kit-bags and reporting to their units in the very first days of August. Then many more men from the Village joined the crowds queueing at the recruiting offices in Liverpool, and from the Port Sunlight section of the St John Ambulance Brigade a body of nineteen men volunteered for medical service and were sent off to the south of England to be attached to Army units preparing to leave for France.

The M.P. for Wirral undertook to raise a new battalion, and posters were displayed in the Works calling on men to enrol in the Gladstone Hall. The makeshift recruiting centre was besieged with volunteers, of whom over seven hundred were accepted for immediate service in the Wirral Battalion of the Cheshire Regiment. Lever announced that the wives of all married volunteers, and any dependants of single men, would receive regular payments from the Company to supplement the men's Army pay to the level of their usual wages.

On the first Sunday in September a farewell service attended by the men and their families was held in the Auditorium, and they were addressed by Lever. Early the next morning they went off by train to Chester, where they formed up outside the station and, with Lever at the head, marched through the City to the Castle, where he handed them over to the General, who declared that the Army was,[5] 'indebted to Sir William Lever and his colleagues for the splendid example they have set to all employers of labour, and, when I see this fine body of young men, I have no fear whatever as to the result of the war.' By evening the Port Sunlight contingent was on its way to Salisbury Plain to start its training with Kitchener's Army.

Writing a few days later to his son, now Vice-Chairman of Lever Brothers, Lever said,[6] 'your suggestion as to co-partnership is a most excellent one. I had purposed always to do some thing on the point of co-partnership for those men at the Front. I think we had better not make any pronouncement on the subject, as it would be read by strangers as a bait to induce the men to recruit. The men are recruiting without any inducement and therefore it is hardly fair to them to make any announcement at present. When they return from the Front, victorious conquering heroes, then will be the time to put forward your suggestion which is a most excellent one. There is no need for you to return home on Tuesday unless you wish to do so. . . .'

Lever's connection with the Wirral Battalion did not lapse when he stepped aside from the head of the Port Sunlight seven hundred at the gates of Chester Castle. When the men arrived on Salisbury Plain with thousands upon thousands of others from all over Britain, they found that the Army organisation had been quite unable to cope with the enormous numbers of recruits enlisted. They were not only hopelessly deficient in weapons, vehicles, and other fighting equipment but they were short of uniform, and even mugs, plates, and other mess traps. Unlike the other bewildered and uncomfortable citizen-soldiers, however, the Wirral Battalion had Lever watching their interests. He at once had cutlery and kitchen utensils sent to them from the dining-halls at Port Sunlight, and he chivvied the authorities about all aspects of their welfare. He visited the men in camp several times to discover exactly what their needs were, and went personally to the War Office, or sent his son, to make representations about matters from the supply of ground-sheets to the advisability of the Battalion joining the Third Army rather than the Second so that they should get more adequate training before going to the Front.

The Battalion went out to France in September 1915 and for over two years took part in some of the most intense fighting on the Somme and in the Ypres salient. By February 1918 they had suffered such severe casualties – well over two thousand – that the Battalion's identity was effectively destroyed, it was pointless to send in any more replacements and the survivors were dispersed among other fighting units. Altogether during the War over four thousand men from Lever Brothers and its associated companies served in the armed forces, and of these over five hundred were killed.

Lever himself, well over sixty when the War broke out, was on this ground alone ineligible for military service. But he joined the Port Sunlight section of the Birkenhead and District Volunteer Training Corps, one of many such units which were formed all over the country in 1914 from men ineligible for active service who nevertheless were trained for home defence and other emergencies. Lever's career as a private in the unit did not last more than a month or two, but during that time he readily submitted – in a squad of managers, clerks, and workmen – to being drilled by one of the office commissionaires who was a former regimental sergeant-major. Very soon the demands upon the business in war-time, and his membership of a number of newly created official advisory or executive bodies, meant that Lever had to withdraw from the unit. But late in the War, when such volunteers were more formally organised by the War Department into a Volunteer Force, he was created an honorary lieutenant-colonel of the Port Sunlight contingent. In this quasi-military force Lever thus held only two ranks – the lowest and the highest – and these would have been the only ranks which he would have thought appropriate to a man of his position.

Of the committees outside the soap industry to which Lever was appointed during the War, one in particular made very heavy demands upon his time. This was the Central Control Board (Liquor Traffic), set up by Lloyd George when he was Minister for Munitions, for the purpose of 'controlling the sale and supply of intoxicating liquor in naval, military, munition or transport areas, where such control should be found expedient for the successful prosecution of the war'.[7] The Board, appointed under the Defence of the Realm Act (Dora) was given wide powers of inspection and enquiry, and their task was to recommend to the Minister, and hence to the War Cabinet, regulations to be applied under the Act to the sale of drink. Under the chairmanship of Lord D'Abernon, there were about a dozen members of the Board, including Neville Chamberlain, Waldorf Astor, Philip Snowden, and J. H. Thomas. There were over a hundred meetings of the full Board, and many other meetings of sub-committees. Lever sat on the sub-committee concerned with the provision of canteen facilities for workers. This and other duties for the Board involved him in visits, often lasting several days, to the principal centres of war production and military concentration all over the country.

Companies in the armament and shipbuilding industries were asked what restrictions on drinking they would like to see applied in their own areas in order to improve production and safety in factories and shipyards. Often there would be proposals for the closing of public houses near factories, and then Board members would have to investigate the matter closely and make recommendations. More generally, on a national scale, the Board was responsible for introducing restricted licensing hours – 12 to 2.30 p.m. and 6 to 9 p.m. – the reduction in the proof strength of spirits and the restriction of their sale for consumption 'off the premises', the banning of drinks 'on the slate' or any other form of credit sale, and the introduction of the 'no treating' rule. At the request of the War Cabinet they also considered whether orders should be enforced for 'the manufacture and supply of intoxicating liquor to be acquired by the State'. When the State did take over all liquor sales in Carlisle and Gretna, Lever, who was no lover of nationalisation, was moved to favourable comment on the improved efficiency which resulted from the elimination of the previous very high level of competition.

The Board, and Lord D'Abernon in particular, were especially well satisfied with their introduction into Britain of the no treating order – so distasteful to homesick Rupert Brooke in pre-war Germany. In a minute to the Minister, the Board said of the no treating order that it 'to a great extent put an end to practices which are unreservedly admitted to be harmful, and ought not to be allowed to revive. The habit of a group of several persons going into a public house and each in turn standing drinks to all the others, the habit of treating any chance acquaintance found in or outside the premises – a direct encouragement to the loafer and sponger – and the practice of treating men in uniform even though complete strangers, all lead directly to insobriety and extravagance and in some ways constitute a tyrannical system from which many are glad to be relieved. . . . However much, therefore, in certain respects the Order may appear to interfere with social habits, the Board venture to think that . . . it has the support of wide and well-informed public opinion. . . .'

There was another wide and equally well-founded public sentiment; a suspicion that some members of the Board, in particular Lord D'Abernon, were choosing to overlook the nature of the original directive to the Board that 'national efficiency for war purposes and not social reform was the object of their mission'. As soon as the War was over the public expected the restrictions to be removed. On 18 November 1918 the Minister of Munitions, Winston Churchill, sympathetic perhaps about the possible effects of unwelcome teetotalism, wrote to the Board with a copy of an intelligence report prepared for the War Cabinet, 'You may be interested in the enclosed excerpt from today's Secret Report on Labour Unrest. It refers to the North Western District, that is Liverpool etc.'

The report dealt with opinion among Shop Stewards. 'The Shop Stewards also state that it is nearly time the ridiculous "no treating" Order is abolished. They say most of them know how to dodge it at the local pubs, but the moment a stranger or a policeman in plain clothes comes in, they have to act like a lot of criminals and they are getting tired of it. They contend that the big man can take his pals to an hotel and stand them a bottle of wine, and it is nearly time they are allowed to stand a pal a glass of beer. They had put up with it because they had been told it was necessary, but this tale wouldn't wash now. They say that the British tradesman is not a Bolshevik or a boozer and he wants to be treated as a man, and governed by men, not fanatics. If he is not he may do extreme things. They are moderate men and they want their glass of beer under the conditions they had it before the war, otherwise there will be trouble for Lord D'Abernon, whom they describe as a bigot, and the sort of man who would incite the workers to revolt.'

Much the same sentiments were expressed more publicly in the Press[8] and in due course the country was rid of the no treating order, but the afternoon drink in a public place is still no longer part of the respectable British way of life.

Lever's contribution to the war effort had the comprehensive range that characterised his attitude to any of his major interests. The direct welfare of the Wirral Battalion and other servicemen from Port Sunlight, and his demanding work on the Liquor Board for the improved efficiency of the munitions industry, were only a fraction of the extra tasks he took on. He was a member of a War Office committee, formed to control the contract prices paid for certain non-military stores, and later called the Navy and Army Canteen Committee. He gave Cedar

Lawn – the house across the disputed footpath from The Hill at Hampstead Heath – for use as a hospital, and a large part of Thornton Manor was converted to form a privately maintained Red Cross Hospital for about fifty patients with his daughter-in-law as Commandant. He contributed generously to war charities and Government War Loans as a natural extension of the benevolent use he had always made of his money. He had made some notable cash contributions – such as ten thousand pounds to the Congregational movement[9] – to a wide variety of causes, and the five thousand pounds to Lloyd George's Land Campaign Fund was not his only gift in that direction. A letter[10] from 10 Downing Street in 1917 to Miss Stevenson comments that 'your manoeuvre had helped them to raise £1000 from [Lever].'

But in preference to a simple cash donation Lever favoured a form of benefaction in which he gave much of his time to a worthy cause: advising, planning, obtaining official co-operation, and giving the project a starting boost or helping it over a difficult patch with the gift of land, buildings, or some other facilities. Any cause which managed so to engage his support was most fortunate. The 'Star and Garter Home for Disabled Soldiers, Sailors, and Airmen' was such a cause, which took much of his attention during the War. He became a treasurer of the 'Star and Garter' in 1915 immediately after the hotel of that name at Richmond had been presented to the Red Cross. The hotel was demolished and more suitable buildings put up, to which Lever made a considerable contribution by way of cash and furniture, and he also gave valuable advice based on his experience in planning and erecting buildings, including a hospital, at Port Sunlight. As treasurer he was a great fund-raiser, able to lead the way himself at any charity sale in aid of the Home. He received from the Queen at Buckingham Palace a cheque for £150,000 collected for the fund by the women of the Empire, and at the end of the War when the Navy and Army Canteen Board found itself with surplus funds he was able to persuade the authorities to divert £100,000 of that surplus into the 'Star and Garter' account.

Many a man over sixty would have considered the war charities, the welfare work, and the Government committees to be a large enough stint even in wartime. But to Samuel Smiles's faithful disciple, who by five-thirty most mornings had already done his exercises and taken a cold bath, these were but subsidiary activities to the running of his business. Like most of his countrymen Lever did not foresee in 1914 that this was to be a war quite unlike those which had previously roused the patriotic sentiment of a British people, hitherto largely unaffected by the fighting, while a small professional army spilt its blood overseas. 'Over by Christmas' was the confident cry, and Lever's own attitude at the start was very much that of 'business as usual during alterations'.

Lever's concept of business as usual brought him swiftly into conflict with those responsible for enforcing the Allied blockade of Germany. He recognised and grudgingly accepted that the Lever Brothers Company in Austria, and in Germany where there was a very large factory at Mannheim, would not be allowed to deliver their profits to England. Indeed he managed to get permission from both sides to sell the German company, the final payment being deferred until after the War. But Lever then went on to propose to the British Government that he should be allowed to continue to export soap to territories now occupied by the enemy. Even if some of this soap did get sent on to Germany, he said,[11] 'it would make the Germans clean but it would not make them better fighters. . . . I do not feel that life in the trenches or the battlefield, notwithstanding constant washings, can be affected very much by the question of what soap is issued, whether good soap from England or poor soap from Germany.' Furthermore, Lever, desperate for any excuse to avoid loss of trade, declared that the less soap the Germans needed to make for themselves, the less glycerine would there be for explosives.

The British Government rejected this spurious reasoning and soon gave him a lesson in war priorities. In 1915 they commandeered all the glycerine stocks in the country at a much lower price than Lever thought reasonable, and in 1916 the soap-makers were suddenly told that they must double their glycerine output because of the grave shortage of explosives. Lever had to change his tune and tell his managers to step up the boiling and if necessary regard the sale of soap as 'a secondary consideration, the production of glycerine being the main consideration'.

Such State interference became more obtrusive, inevitably perhaps in view of the importance of glycerine in making explosives, and the fact that most of the soap industry's raw materials had to be shipped into Britain through the hunting U-boat packs. Under the circumstances Lever accepted the need for more and more State control as the War went on. Some aspects of the arrangements suited Lever well, but he was not a complaisant committee member, and senior civil servants on the various organising boards and committees were badly put out by his assumption of direct access to the Minister. The ultimate extension of State control to the replacement of individual brands by a standard soap, and its rationing to the public, struck at two of Lever's most cherished commercial principles. More welcome was the Government suggestion that Lever should manufacture margarine to alleviate the shortage of edible fats. It was a most significant move which brought the Company into competition with the Dutch – the principal makers of margarine – and profoundly influenced its long-term future. Lever Brothers' margarine was given the name 'Plate' and at first, in 1915, it was unprofitable and unpalatable, but by the end of the War the Company had become one of the largest and most important margarine producers in the United Kingdom.

The margarine project might have been a new one but the problem in the early stages was the very old one of getting the formula right, for the first batches tasted very strongly of vegetable oil. The production of the extra glycerine also raised old problems, to which Lever supplied old solutions. His fears that sales of the extra soap produced would be 'only of secondary consideration' were not justified. In the event the extra soap produced was snapped up by the public, and Lever Brothers had to boil soap in vats put into any buildings they could press into service, and even had to put collars round the existing vats to increase their capacity. For Lever this all-out production drive was reminiscent of the early days making Sunlight at Warrington. The effort was not to meet the Government glycerine target but to satisfy the soaring demand from British housewives whose husbands were bringing home fat wage packets from munition factories where the wives themselves, and daughters too, were often also employed. Lever was delighted at this expansion of the soap market which had appeared for some time to be saturated. But although this bigger market augured well for the post-war future of Lever Brothers, the upheaval in wages which was its principal cause carried the seeds of the first serious industrial troubles at Port Sunlight.

Not all the difficulties were old ones, although the price and scarcity of raw materials were, as always, chronic problems. Getting the raw materials from West Africa to Britain was a particularly expensive business with the shipping trade largely in the hands of the Elder Dempster line, and freight charges high. Lever's reaction was predictable: in 1916 he set up his own shipping organisation by bringing the Company's steamer from the Solomons and buying the six cargo boats of a small Manchester shipping firm. Two other vessels were built specially to Lever Brothers' order. Four ships out of this little fleet of nine were sunk by U-boats.

On land, too, the Company was suffering from the enemy. The factory near Brussels was captured by the Germans, but not before discreet sabotage by the British Works manager and some of the Belgian staff had made the glycerine plant largely ineffective. The Works manager, who spoke fluent French and Flemish, disappeared long enough to grow a beard, and then came back in the guise of a Belgian employee, and, until the Germans left, he was able to arrange that the glycerine production was minimal.[12] The other factory captured by the Germans was at Lille. The U.S. Vice-Consul there, technically a neutral, brought messages to Lever from the local, Italian chairman of Lever Brothers. Mr Macchi, the manager, was able to let Lever know[13] how production was running and to reveal that the Germans had commandeered a large amount of glycerine found at the Works. Macchi had, however, been able to conceal some stocks of glycerine from them. This was not only dangerous but must have been very difficult since there were a thousand soldiers billeted inside the Works which had been made a key position in the German defences against an expected Allied attack on Lille. Hopes that this would not be a frontal assault with heavy shelling were not realised. Sadly, Macchi's home was destroyed by shell-fire a few months later while he and his wife sheltered in the cellar, and this experience was thought to have been responsible for his death shortly afterwards.

For everyone on the Home Front during the War the banalities of domestic life continued despite the bloodshed and the valour just across the sea. Sometimes the dull little tasks seemed especially poignant because they were on behalf of men at the Front in a violent other-world. Lever wrote in 1916,[14] 'I may say I have had a mutiny in the domestic staff at the Hill because I laid down the rule that we must eat Plate margarine. I have not heard whether it has subsided, but I had to interview the whole staff in the dining-room yesterday morning before leaving. Several of the maids have told the Housekeeper that they would rather leave than eat the margarine, and of course I have to insist upon the margarine being eaten. I have not heard of any maids leaving but, of course, it is a little early yet for me to have heard.'

Up in Cheshire the problem was with duck on the lake at Thornton Manor. Lever wrote to his son,[15] 'There are a great number which will not fly and many of them must be generations old. Old ducks, by not getting up to fly, influence younger birds to do the same. The result is that you have vast quantities of duck which consume hundredweights of food and give no sport in return. . . . It seems wrong to be thinking of this in wartime but if not dealt with now it will only become a greater problem later. . . . to be feeding fat old ducks which yield no food in return is not "war economy"!' Correspondence about the cunning old duck who had mastered the sporting rules continued, sometimes by telegram, until in 1917 the village policeman brought the matter to an end by declaring that the tame swans on the lake might be fed, but not the wild duck, which, Lever decided, must therefore be shot.

In 1916 Lever attended a meeting at the Royal Institute of British Architects about designs for war memorials. He wrote to his son that two designs were in stained glass and he suggested that this idea[16] might be adapted 'to make a war Memorial for each home in Port Sunlight that has lost a son or a father in the war. I do not think it need cost very much if we were to produce the glass transparency in paper . . . the whole of the transparency except the name of the fallen hero could be printed . . . and then we could at Port Sunlight put the individual name of the fallen hero on one or more of the transparencies for the individual homes. I think we ought to then fasten them on some window, at the relatives' suggestion, of the house in which the hero had lived which would be a perpetual reminder of him. . . . The cost of this would come out of the War Memorial fund. I suggest this, not because there would be any difficulty with the expense which need not be heavy, but because it would make it more their own memorial when it was subscribed for as part of the funds of the general memorial scheme.' Lever's unsympathetic critics might use a phrase or two here, out of context, to reinforce their antipathy, but, in fact, this private letter to his own son shows well his genuine admiration for the best of 'his' people, the restless activity of his mind seeking ways to further the cause of all connected with Port Sunlight, and an appreciation of the independent spirit which shuns the demeaning taint of charity.

In June 1917 Lever was raised to the Peerage and took his seat in the House of Lords at the end of July. The Prime Minister, Lloyd George, was the principal guest at a celebration dinner, given for the new Peer by Lord Beaverbrook, and attended by Bonar Law, Winston Churchill, F. E. Smith, and Lord Reading (Rufus Isaacs). A few months later Lloyd George and Beaverbrook sought to use Leverhulme as the 'front man' for the purchase of the *Daily Chronicle*,[17] to be made into the mouthpiece of the Coalition Liberals. The purchase money, ostensibly coming from Leverhulme and one other, was actually to be provided by Beaverbrook, a declared Tory. This particular shady manoeuvre came to nothing, and when Leverhulme was questioned about it later his deafness appeared to present an impenetrable barrier to enquiry and he said he had never heard of the scheme.

Lord Leverhulme of Bolton-le-Moors, as he now became, was delighted with the honour and welcomed the opportunity of a platform in Parliament where he could on occasion put forward his views on industrial and social reform and seek to influence the Government. He did not wish or expect to form part of that Government, and he would undoubtedly have been cramped and frustrated as a junior Minister. But such a post was unlikely to be offered to him, at any rate by Lloyd George, who was probably correct in believing that he could not work in co-operation with other men.[18] In choosing his title Leverhulme brought together the names of himself, his wife, and Bolton, their birthplace and the scene of their happy youth. Even in this matter he managed to attract controversy. The College of Heralds looked with disfavour upon the unprecedented compounding of husband's and wife's name in such a title. But the new Peer was not one to be intimidated by Heralds, and after a few weeks of brisk argument the style and title were recorded in the form he wished.

A little over a month later Leverhulme was able to show Lloyd George some concrete appreciation of his Peerage when the Prime Minister stayed at Thornton Manor. He brought a large party including Mrs Lloyd George and his younger daughter, and among his office staff were Frances Stevenson and Philip Kerr, his personal assistant so disliked by the Foreign Office. Kerr arrived separately in a rather shabby suit, carrying his own case, and was directed to the back door by the butler who took him for Lloyd George's valet.[19] The Prime Minister stayed five days, no doubt glad of the change after his unavailing efforts to dissuade Haig from mounting the Third Battle of Ypres which was now dragging to muddy disaster at Passchendaele. Inevitably, while staying at the Manor, Lloyd George visited Port Sunlight, addressing the workers there and thus completing a hat-trick of visiting Prime Ministers.

But the principal official purpose of Lloyd George's visit was to attend the Royal National Eisteddfod of Wales which was held in Birkenhead in 1917. Leverhulme had been invited to preside over the function, and he delivered a characteristically well-prepared speech in which he noted that at one time the Wirral had been 'as Welsh as Carnarvon', and made an early public reference to the Six-Hour Day which was an industrial reform he would have dearly liked to bring about.

# 12

# *Capital and labour*

Towards the end of the War Stanley Unwin, then a young man in his father's publishing house, was sent for by Lord Leverhulme, handed a huge pile of pamphlets and leaflets, and told to make a book of them.[1]

Whenever Leverhulme made a speech which he considered to be of some importance he had copies printed and young Unwin could see at a glance that the material was highly repetitious. With some diffidence he told Leverhulme, 'You can't print this as it stands, it will need editing.'

'Aye,' he replied with a good Lancashire accent, 'that's what I want you to do.'

As he left the interview carrying with difficulty his mass of raw material, Unwin was told that in making his proposition about publication he should 'remember I shall want a lot of copies'. He was also told to name his fee for editing the work, and ever afterwards regretted that he only asked twenty-five pounds. He does seem to have been singularly unfortunate in his financial relations with his millionaire author, for he records that on one occasion he unaccountably had a Leverhulme cheque for half a crown returned to him marked 'no assets'.

The book was brought out in 1918 and published separately in the United States, the first sentence of the Editor's Foreword stating, with reticence and understandable licence, 'When Lord Leverhulme gave me permission to reprint in book form a collection of his Addresses, I had no conception of the mass of material from which I should be called upon to make a selection.'

The Addresses selected were delivered over a period of some twenty years to audiences as different – or perhaps as similar – as the Institute of Directors and the Liverpool Trades and Labour Council, the Port Sunlight Men's Meeting and the Royal Society of Arts. The views advanced by Leverhulme covered wide areas of industrial efficiency and social welfare, which he regarded as complementary. The two principal topics, dealt with exhaustively in their own right and mentioned repeatedly in the discussion of other subjects, were Co-Partnership and the Six-Hour Day. In Viscount Haldane's introduction to the book he suggested that Leverhulme was trying to 'better the condition of both soul and body', and certainly his concept of the Six-Hour Day, although rooted in a rigorous analysis of factory efficiency, had almost as much to do with the heart and spirit as with dividends and wage packets.

Leverhulme believed that during the War it had been well established, in munition and other factories where the task was simple and repetitive, that longer hours resulted in a lower output of poorer quality. He looked forward to the immediate post-war period when there would be an enormously increased demand 'to replenish stocks that have been allowed to run down, both for our home and export trade, and as we have the machinery available . . . which hitherto in most industries has been run for only 48 hours per week, a solution of this one of our difficulties can be best and most readily found by working our machinery for more hours and our men and women for fewer hours. We must have a six-hour working day for men and women, and by means of six-hour shifts . . . we must work our machinery twelve, eighteen, or twenty-four hours per day. . . . You can only increase wealth by increasing production. You can only increase wages by increased investment of capital in machinery, resulting in increased production and reduced cost. You can only increase production on the basis of increased consumption. . . . The way to make people increase consumption is by increasing leisure. Increases of consumption also depend on increases in wages and reduced costs, so that wages are not only larger in coin, but in purchasing power. All this means the raising of the standard of living on sound and healthy lines. . . . The Six-Hour Day has an intimate bearing on these ideals. It does not mean a loafer's paradise. . . . From fourteen years of age to seventy years of age is a long lifespan, and if you consider the conditions of attending, for eight hours a day, the same automatic machinery and following the same routine, with its continual deadly, monotonous round of toil, those of us whose employment is varied will realize how this bites into the soul of a man or woman and tends to corrode it. . . . Of all welfare work in factories, a proper apportionment of the time is the one that will yield the best results, and is the problem most pressing for solution. . . . We can get into a working day of six hours all the work we are capable of when that work is monotonous. . . . The Six-Hour Day is already a most urgent and much-needed condition of working hours in all industries where women and girls are employed. It must be remembered that a large proportion of women engaged in industries, whether married or single, have, unlike their fathers and brothers, some housework to do as well as their work in industrial employment. And these hours of housework and the resulting fatigue must be remembered when considering their hours of work in the factory, workshop, or office. . . . I believe . . . that the workmen of this country – I have endeavoured to practise it in my own limited way – have as much right to an artistic home, a comfortable home in a garden, with all the amenities of life, as their employer. . . . What use is it talking to a workman about a nice artistic home . . . when he only comes home to sleep and to rest for the next day, leaves early, and his only time at home is an occasional Sunday? You won't raise a taste for an artistic home under these conditions. Art flourishes only where there is leisure . . . reduced hours of labour are essential for an increased demand. . . . We shall . . . be able to pay for six hours work at least the same . . . as we pay for eight, because labour will be capable of as much work in six as in eight hours. . . . The human element working two shifts of six hours each, the mechanical element working twelve hours, or more, we shall have two funds created, one for reducing the price of the article and another for increasing the wages on the top of the reduction of hours.'

Leverhulme's argument for the Six-Hour Day was a composite of views formed in a lifetime of social and industrial pioneering. Opponents pointed out, what he already knew well, that there were important industries, agriculture for instance, in which his argument was not applicable. He had no illusions about the speed with which his scheme might be taken up: 'the adoption simultaneously, in all industries of the United Kingdom, of a six-hour working day is absolutely impossible and impracticable. As with the acorn that produces the British oak, the growth of the six-hour day movement will be slow, but none the less sure.'

Confident that the working classes would one day achieve the Six-Hour-day, Leverhulme speculated about the way in which the new leisure might be employed. Joviality gets little priority with social prophets, who are inclined to promise an abundance of nourishment with never a feast day. If H. G. Wells could conjure up a Modern Utopia of unwelcome asceticism it is hardly surprising that Leverhulme should look to self-improvement rather than self-indulgence to fill the future leisure hours.

Shift workers on the Six-Hour-day would have mornings or afternoons free for compulsory State training. Boys and girls between fourteen and eighteen would spend two hours each working day in higher grade education and physical training. Those between eighteen and twenty-four would spend two hours a day on technical and higher education such as is only provided in the universities, plus the inevitable physical training. Between twenty-four and thirty the time would be spent on military training and preparation for National Service. 'After thirty years of age the citizen would have completed his period of compulsory attendance under State Regulations, and would be fully equipped by education and training for all the duties of citizenship, and might reasonably be trusted to make, as did St Paul, but in his own way, his own voluntary contribution to social advancement and betterment.'

It was an old man's chilly millennium and it never dawned, even at Port Sunlight where the prophet could usually call the tune. As early as 1919, when even the most precocious acorn would barely have had time to sprout, Leverhulme had given up. He wrote to his son,[2] 'Can we do anything with regard to the payment of wages of co-partners and others through banks. Our annual meeting will be coming along. If I have to report that we have failed with our six-hour day scheme I should not want also to report that we have failed with regard to payment through banks.'

As the War drew towards its end and thoughts turned to 'a land fit for heroes', it became clear that ideas and standards uprooted and scattered by the years of turmoil and destruction would not settle back into the old pre-war pattern. Authority, privilege, and the established order were everywhere questioned, and industrial unrest became common. In September 1918 there was a strike of most electricians in the Merseyside area over the employment of a non-union foreman in a munition factory at Aintree. The matter was settled by the man joining the union, and the Ministry of Munitions gave an undertaking that there would be 'no victimisation'. Some time later Lever Brothers electricians, who had supported the union's call for a 'sympathetic' strike during the dispute, complained that at the next distribution of co-partnership certificates they received reduced allocations, in some cases nothing at all. Leverhulme, of course, told the union that awards of co-partnership certificates could be varied at his discretion.

Lord Citrine was at this time the first full-time secretary of the Electrical Trades Union in the Liverpool–Birkenhead district. He described[3] how he went with a small deputation to Port Sunlight and met some of the managers and directors headed by Leverhulme, a 'sprightly, fresh-complexioned fellow, small of stature but sturdy, and usually wore a grey suit and top hat and, on occasions, a fancy waistcoat. He had keen restless eyes and would have attracted notice in most places'. At the meeting Leverhulme at once took up the running: 'he spoke in a conversational tone, and his discourse was so closely reasoned that he almost convinced me. When at length Leverhulme asked me whether I wished to say anything I started to controvert much of what he had said. I had scarcely begun before he butted in with an appropriate anecdote or an objection to counter my argument. It was all done courteously and indeed affably, but the result was that the interview finished with my feeling that I had been completely defeated on every material point.'

Citrine and his party left, but at the bottom of the stairs he remembered that he had not asked for a copy of the shorthand notes of the meeting. He hurried back upstairs, knocked on the office door, and entered. 'Standing in line at the top of the room like a squad of recruits were the directors and officials. Leverhulme was walking across the front of them with his head down and his hands clasped behind his back. The directors could see me but Leverhulme couldn't until he reached the end of his traverse and turned to go the other way. Then he looked at me for a few seconds with a scowling face, flushed with anger.' Citrine apologised for the intrusion and explained that he wanted a copy of the notes of the meeting. Leverhulme at once gave instructions that he was to be supplied with a transcript and Citrine departed once more, amazed at this glimpse of Leverhulme's relationship with his senior colleagues, and wondering what was the subject of the tirade against them.

The dispute about co-partnership and the electricians dragged on and was clearly of fundamental concern to the Trade Union movement generally. Leverhulme agreed that there should be a full enquiry, under the chairmanship of the Secretary of the General Federation of Trade Unions, into the Port Sunlight Co-Partnership scheme and its effect on industrial relations and Trade Unionism. Some weeks after the enquiry had ended Citrine was invited to discuss the findings at a meeting chaired by Leverhulme. Citrine decided that this time he would not allow himself to be out-manoeuvred as he had been at their last meeting. This time he would be the one to dictate the tone of the discussion, so knowing of Leverhulme's uncertain temper he deliberately tried to upset him. As soon as the meeting started Citrine complained about the girl who was taking notes: clerical workers at Port Sunlight were on strike and he refused to take any part in the proceedings until the girl, who was a Lever Brothers employee, was removed and replaced by a shorthand writer from an agency. This opening row set the tone for an ill-tempered wrangling confrontation between Citrine and Leverhulme, with the latter first denying and then admitting that he had personally invited Citrine by letter. Then Leverhulme declared inadmissible the enquiry's finding that 'co-partnership and trade unionism at Lever Brothers are incompatible'. He said that it was only included in the report because of an error by one of his directors, when in fact it was the unanimous conclusion of all members of the enquiry. Citrine was well pleased with his chosen tactics, satisfied that on this occasion he had more than held his own with Leverhulme.

When he received the notes of the meeting he was amused to find that all the angry controversy had been edited out. Citrine concluded, 'In spite of everything I liked Leverhulme, martinet though I knew him to be. He was undoubtedly sincere in his efforts to make life better for his work-people. . . . He was ready at one stage to introduce, entirely of his own free will, a six-hour day. . . . This offer was made to the trade unions at a time when fifty-three hours a week, or even more, were common in many industries. I have no doubt whatever that he would have established this far-reaching reform but for the attitude of some of the trade unions, who declined the proposal because it conflicted with their rules.'

Leverhulme's maiden speech in the House of Lords in June 1918 was against a Bill to Introduce a Decimal System of Coinage. He was in favour of decimal money but disagreed with the Bill's proposal to retain the pound and sub-divide it, introducing at the bottom of the scale a new coin worth 20 per cent more than the old penny. Leverhulme took the grocer's view that the halfpenny was the fundamental unit in the domestic economy of the great mass of people in the country. He would retain it as the basis of a decimal system, making a hundred halfpennies a 'Royal', and abolishing 'the parvenu sovereign which had only come into use since 1817'.

His second speech in the Lords, in February 1919, was during a debate on 'Industrial Unrest'. It was in complete contrast to the stylised gloom of previous speakers and it got the House by the ears, surprising the Peers with ideas about industrial relations which they found novel, encouraging, and, on the whole, to their taste.

'On the subject of strikes, let us consider what a strike is. There is no commodity bought and sold between any two individuals without a small strike taking place. I cannot see how we could with advantage attempt to deprive a body of men of the right to use this means, common to all of us, in connection with the only article that they have to sell, namely, their labour. And it would seem to me, therefore, that we must bear patiently with this state of affairs at the present time.

'Do you not think that we have been rather teaching the lesson that a scarcity of labour has brought advantages through the operation of strikes, that a plentiful supply of labour has not brought; and have we not taught that by means of strikes wages have been advanced, and that where no strike has taken place salaries have not been advanced? I think it is deplorable that it should be so, but that is the position. . . . I venture to say that at the present time there is a deep-rooted suspicion between employers and employed which ought not to exist. I think it rises entirely from misunderstanding.

'The workman is not to be kept running as a machine by satisfying his wants. Every fresh aspiration of the workman that we grant to-day will lift him higher and give him fresh aspiration to-morrow, and so we shall always have what we call labour unrest if we are to be a healthy community. . . .

'While the War has been going on, wages have, rightly and properly, advanced by over 100 per cent, but if instead of that 100 per cent increase, labour had received the whole of the profits made in all the industries of the country, the rise in wages would not have been 30 shillings a week but well under a pound a week. These are facts that I want our workers to understand. If we are to prevent strikes it is not for us to say to the worker that he shall not have the same right as other citizens to demand as high a price as the market can give for his labour, but it is our duty to see that the worker is properly acquainted with the conditions under which he works and the effect upon industry of every rise of wages.

'Why should we not recognise that it is a right and proper human aspiration for a workman to desire an increase in wages? Those who, like myself, have been born and bred in a Lancashire manufacturing town, have listened, between five and half-past in the morning, whilst lying in bed, to the patter of the clogs of people going down the street on the way to the mills, and have heard the same patter between five and six o'clock in the evening when the work-people have come back. Some of you, like myself, may remember the condition of the workers in the late fifties, when, amongst male operatives, you could only see two patterns of legs – the knock-kneed and the bow-legged. . . . When there was a reduction in the long hours, we were told that the industries of the country would be ruined. A member of your Lordships'

House, the late Lord Shaftesbury, brought forward "in another place" the question of the age at which child labour should enter mills, and it was raised. Instead of our industries being ruined they were more prosperous than ever, as we all know.

'Cannot we put our heads together and say to our workmen: "You want more wages and shorter hours; then let us see if we cannot work so that you can have both. The key to the position is that if we shorten hours and increase wages we must reduce the cost of production. If we do not reduce it, then you, as the workers, will find, however much your wages have gone up, that their purchasing power is reduced". . . .

'I believe that if we admit that the British workman is as fine a type as there is in the world . . . and we then set our minds to try if we cannot satisfy his natural and right ambition for an improved social position . . . discussing as partners what road we shall take, then I believe that on those lines, and working in that way, we shall find that the bogy of strikes will be shorn of all its terrors. We shall then find that a strike will be merely a prelude to consideration of the situation; and that quickly and readily we shall not only raise ourselves as a producing nation . . . but that here in England the price of commodities will come down, and in this process, we shall have taken the only course that will enable us to discharge our heavy load of debt.'

When Leverhulme sat down there was applause of a length and intensity rarely heard in the House of Lords, and he subsequently received many personal congratulations, including a note from Lord Curzon reading,[4] 'It is a matter of common consent that you delivered one of the finest speeches that has been heard for years.'

Much of what Leverhulme said would have found favour outside the House of Lords, and many of the ideas were sound and far-sighted, perhaps too far-sighted for practical politics. But when he declared that if all the profits had been shared among the workers they would have got a pound a week rise instead of thirty shillings, his reasoning was spurious – they would surely have got a pound *extra*, making two pounds ten shillings in all – and even if the distributed profits correctly calculated had only come to a few pence per employee it would still have been a barren argument. The profits if shared by the multitude of employees might only come to a few pence, but when divided by the comparatively small number of shareholders the answer was different, and if account was taken, as it was in reality, of the number of shares held by just a few rich men then the rewards became staggeringly disproportionate. However numerically sound, it is pointless to say that the rich man's castle split into flats among his employees would only give each worker a home the size of a cake of soap. The poor man at the gate still sees a castle, and justifiable envy pays no heed to meaningless arithmetic.

A speech on Industrial Unrest by a Liberal millionaire in the House of Lords might seem unreal, but in Leverhulme's case it was possible to follow him to the hurly-burly of picketing and union bargaining and so compare theory and practice.

Most of the workers at Port Sunlight during the War joined the National Warehouse and General Workers Union, but some of the clerical staff later left that union to join a new one, for clerks only, called the Liverpool Shipping Clerks Guild. In 1920 both organisations were seeking increased pay for the clerks and they were told by Leverhulme to come to some agreement between themselves and then meet him to negotiate a settlement. But the Union claimed that they, and not the Guild, were the only true representatives of the clerical workers and that they should therefore negotiate on behalf of all the clerks. This claim was not accepted by either the Guild or Leverhulme and so the Union called out its members: first the clerks only, and then the factory workers, too, so that there were thousands on strike at Port Sunlight. Members of the Guild continued to work and so, too, did scores of others. The Union declared that the Guild was black-legging but said that their pickets were using no violence in spite of large numbers crossing their lines to go into work. The women and girls on strike from the Factory were not exactly tranquil. They gathered at the Works entrance and any clerks going in were pelted with the contents of dinner bags. The local paper's report[5] is a little difficult to take literally: 'Custards, pies, and sandwiches flew through the air or were jammed down the clerical collars, but fortunately all kept a fairly even temper.'

At the height of the trouble a notice[6] approved by Leverhulme appeared in the Works and Village. It was headed 'Stoppage of

Work' and read, 'Until an agreement has been arrived at between these two Unions every effort will be made to find employment for those who turn in to work. The Directors are determined during the Strike and afterwards to stand by all Employees who remain loyal to the Company.' This was by any standards a provocative gesture and, although it suggested consideration for non-strikers rather than victimisation for strikers, it might easily have been put up by the most reactionary of employers. Yet during a wage dispute, at another time quite close to this, Leverhulme had appeared at his most liberal.[7]

This dispute also concerned office staff and the case had gone to arbitration. But the clerks were not satisfied with the award made and furthermore they felt that their case had not got a fair hearing. They wanted to take the matter further but found that there was no appeal allowed. A meeting was called at Port Sunlight attended by Leverhulme, a Trade Union representative, and many of the clerks. Leverhulme challenged the Trade Union official to show him any wage rate in Port Sunlight which was lower than that paid for corresponding work elsewhere in the district. There was a certain amount of cut and thrust between them, Leverhulme managing to refute most of the cases put forward, without preparation by the official, but agreeing that one case appeared to justify a rise. Then addressing the meeting on the main issue Leverhulme told them that since they were apparently not entitled to any legal appeal they could set up their own appeal committee and he would abide by the findings, whatever the wage rate proposed. The only condition he laid down concerned the constitution of the appeal committee. He said that it should be made up of both men and women, all of whom must be co-partners, which meant they had all served the Company at least five years. In addition he decreed that none of the members should be a Foreman, or a Manager, or in any way connected with the Board of Directors.

Such a flamboyant gesture, so attractive to Leverhulme, could hardly have been made anywhere but at Port Sunlight, and was unlikely to advance the cause of worker participation in industry generally. Leverhulme, in any case, did not believe that factory workers could, without long training, contribute usefully to decision-making at Board level. 'There is,' he wrote,[8] 'a great desire, and not an unreasonable desire, and certainly a healthy desire, on the part of the workman to take some share in the control of the factory he works in, and it is a desire that should be encouraged; but we cannot take a rank-and-file worker out of the factory today and put him on the Board of Directors and expect that he will be able to give valuable help and assistance. He must be trained; we have all had to be trained.'

Lever made a start with the training of young people at Port Sunlight by arranging for boys and girls from the office to go to evening classes at the Company's expense until they were eighteen years old. But he was not satisfied with this, and in 1917 he set up a more ambitious scheme in the Company's own Staff Training College. Young people attended the College in the firm's time – not when they were tired after a day's work – and received instruction in accountancy and business studies, languages, chemistry and engineering, physical education, and other subjects thought appropriate to their jobs. Attendance was compulsory for factory boys and girls between fourteen and sixteen, for boys in skilled trades until the end of their apprenticeship, and for office juniors from fourteen to eighteen. Although this training scheme only operated within his own 'kingdom' at Port Sunlight, Leverhulme hoped that it might be the forerunner of a Government-sponsored system of further education and training eventually operating nationally in association with the Six-Hour Day.

At about the same time as he set up his Staff Training College Leverhulme bought himself another kingdom closer in concept, perhaps, to his Congo concession than to Port Sunlight. The new land he acquired was in the Western Islands of Scotland, where he intended to revolutionise the life of what he considered to be a deprived community by the application of his strongly held social principles and proven business methods.

Lewis and Harris, joined by a narrow strip of land, are really one large island although usually spoken of separately. They are in the Outer Hebrides, north of Skye, and separated from the north-west coast of Scotland by the thirty miles of unfriendly water of the North Minch. It is about sixty miles from the Butt of Lewis in the north to Leverburgh at the south end of Harris, and the land is about twenty-five miles across at the widest part of Lewis: altogether an area of about a thousand square miles of which Lewis occupies about three-quarters.

In 1918 the total population was about forty thousand, over three thousand of whom were concentrated in the only town, Stornoway, situated in the east coast of Lewis with a good harbour for the fishing fleet. The land is inhospitable to man, bleak, wet, and windy, a treeless waste of peat-bog, moor, rugged highlands, streams and lochs. What little arable land there is yields poorly and the grass is rarely rich enough for farm cattle. The principal economic asset of Lewis when Leverhulme came there was the fishing. Any prosperity the people had ever known had come from the sea, yet the majority of them were obsessed with the ownership of land: miserable crofts of a few acres.

After the Jacobite rebellion had greatly weakened the clan system the ownership of land in the Highlands and Islands of Scotland tended to pass into the hands of lairds who were often absent in the South, leaving the management of their estates to factors. The crofters supported a poor standard of life by growing hay, oats, barley, and potatoes on the five or six acres which they rented. The crofter and his family lived in a crude stone and earth house with turf roof and smoky peat fire. The few animals they possessed shared this shelter with them. The first blow to this already pitiable life-style was the discovery in the late eighteenth century that sheep could be farmed on the moorland. Sheep farmers could pay much higher rents than the crofters so the lairds and their factors began the wholesale evictions and burning of the crofters' houses which were carried out with such brutality in the mid-1800s. The evicted crofter might put up a shelter on some poorer piece of land than that which he had been thrown off, or he might emigrate. Many chose the latter course and official policy was to encourage it with assisted passages. Resentment against the enclosure of crofts to make sheep farms burned fiercely throughout the Highlands and Islands fed by nationalist propaganda against 'foreign' landlords who sacrificed land and people to the sheep – and later to the deer, when the renting of sporting rights became very lucrative. Eventually, when the agitation had raised fears of revolution, the Government set up a

Crofters' Commission in 1883 to investigate the problem. They reported that in one part of Lewis twenty-four groups of crofts – 'townships' – had been cleared to make way for more than ten thousand sheep, and the crofters and their families sent to America or pushed into other less favourable parts of Lewis already over-crowded and even less fertile.

Following the Commission report, an Act of Parliament in 1886 gave security of tenure to the crofters, allowing them to pass on the tenancy to their heir, and forbidding eviction unless they neglected the land or failed to pay the rent. But this was of no help to those already deprived of a holding by previous evictions. In 1887, following raids by some such men, who attempted to take back croft land that had earlier been made into sheep farms, Marines were sent to the Island to restore peace. The Government-sponsored schemes to encourage emigration were poorly supported, and in 1911 Parliament passed an Act empowering them to compel landowners to sell farmland to the Department of Agriculture to be broken up and rented as crofts. Little use was made of this Act in Lewis, and by the 1914–18 War there were over three thousand crofts on Lewis, but on half of these there was an illegal squatter as well as the tenant. Furthermore there were many men away at the War who expected a croft on their return, and the Government – or at least its individual Ministers – let it be understood that the returning ex-servicemen could expect land when they were demobilised.

When Leverhulme bought Lewis he knew what a struggle he would have with the natural environment. He would, too, have expected difficulties in winning the people over to his schemes, but he was unlikely to have guessed that history and emotion would so have scarred their minds that they were crippled by an obsession to rent – not even to own – a piece of land too small to support them. It was particularly unfortunate for him that this congenital ailment was about to flare up violently.

In October 1917 Leverhulme spent a week in Lewis and Harris exploring the country thoroughly by motor-car. The last time he had been there was thirty-three years before, on holiday with his young wife. He formally took possession of Lewis in the summer of 1918, adding the ownership of Harris in 1919. It was a Saturday night in June 1918 when he returned to Lewis as Proprietor. The boat was not due at Stornoway until late, but the quay was decorated, a banner read 'Welcome to Your Island Home', crowds turned out to see him, and a pipe-band stood by to play a greeting. But there was a strangely ominous twist to the ceremony. The boat came alongside just after midnight and with the arrival of the Sabbath the pipe-band departed and the ceremonial too. It was proper that Leverhulme should now be given a quiet Sabbath greeting and the full ceremony deferred a day or two. When at last he replied to the formal address of welcome he did so at length, ending his speech,[9] 'We will work on business lines, and we will have nothing to do with philanthropy. We will be able to look each other in the face, and you will be able to say to me, "We thank you for nothing but the opportunity you have given us."' He was conscious as he said this that he too was being given an opportunity: the challenge of a new Kingdom entirely his own at a time when the single-handed control of his Company was slipping away from him. It was a challenge to organise a total community and bring prosperity to a land with which he was sentimentally linked by that holiday long ago. At the very least the island was the biggest garden he had ever tackled.

He stayed in Lewis all the summer of 1918. Through July, August, and September he was in Lews Castle planning roads and bridges all over the island, a new town scheme for Stornoway, and elaborate modernisation of the Castle itself and improvements to the grounds. It was a long time to be away from the Company headquarters and communications were not good. He wrote to his son at Port Sunlight,[10] 'The experiment in sending me coded telegrams is not a success. Telegrams in code arrive here so mutilated that after a day's work on them a correct translation is not possible.'

He still received parcels of mail with copies of Company correspondence, and he was prepared to give advice, and question decisions, even on trivial matters and often by telegram. But there was some evidence that the non-industrial affairs of the people of Port Sunlight were no longer at the centre of his thoughts. His son wrote to him in July 1918 to give him the address of the 2nd Volunteer Battalion of the Cheshire Regiment in camp at Fleetwood, and to suggest that as their Honorary Commandant he should send them a telegram of good wishes, regretting that he would be unable to visit them. He also suggested that to save time he would send, on behalf of his father, a box of cigars for the officers' mess. Leverhulme hastily agreed to the suggestions, only questioning whether the number of cigars was sufficient, to which his son replied that what he had in mind was a gesture of goodwill rather than 'keeping the officers in smokes for the duration of the camp'. Leverhulme continued, 'In addition I am sending about twenty boxes of twenty-five kippers each for the non-commissioned officers and men. . . . These are real Stornoway kippers and are made by one of the firms who will be joining with us in developing Lewis fisheries, so that I can vouch for the quality. . . . Salmon are too elusive for me to depend upon. . . . The keeper asked me if he might put a net at the mouth of one of the rivers in Stornoway harbour which would make it a certainty to get some salmon. But I preferred not to adopt this means as it is obvious that fishing in this way for our own requirements would give the impression that netting salmon at the mouth of rivers was something that could be done by others. . . . I would have been pleased to have sent salmon to the officers in addition to the cigars but, as you understand, they are too uncertain.' Leverhulme's response was, as always, generous – showing an appreciation of the equivalent military ranks of domestic fish which is perhaps not valid today – but it may not have been without significance that he should have had to be reminded of his responsibilities to the Port Sunlight Volunteers.

That Leverhulme, during the War and after it, did not play as large a part in public affairs as might have been expected was due in part to the demands made upon his time by business affairs and by his own reforming work in industrial relations and housing, which almost constituted a private ministry of social service. But, in addition, his increasing deafness after his return from the Congo in 1913 made it impossible for him to sustain for any length of time the conversational give and take of committee work, for which in any case he had a certain aversion, not to say contempt. As a man of swift decision and action he looked upon the long boring process of discussion, negotiation, concession,

Sir William and Lady Lever, 1913

King George V at Port Sunlight

Lord Leverhulme in 1919

Leverhulme with children at Port Sunlight

Leverhulme with Lloyd George at Port Sunlight

Leverhulme at Lady Lever Gallery

and recommendation much as a football crowd regards a gym display before the Cup Final. But he enjoyed the more ceremonial of public duties, and two pleased him particularly because of their association with his native roots: he was High Sheriff of Lancashire from 1917 to 1918, and Mayor of Bolton from 1918 to 1919.

Bolton had always been an object of Leverhulme's nostalgic affection and he made many gifts to his native town. The great park at Rivington, subject of litigation with Liverpool Corporation, had been intended as such a gift, but in the end had benefited the people of Bolton in a roundabout fashion, and he later gave them another park, named after him. He bought the house called Hall i' th' Wood in which Samuel Crompton perfected his 'mule' and thus revolutionised cotton spinning. Leverhulme had this very old house carefully restored and filled with furniture and household goods of the sixteenth and seventeenth century to make a public museum of early Lancashire domestic life and a memorial to Crompton, whose invention contributed so much to Bolton's nineteenth-century prosperity, and who received little recognition in his own lifetime. Leverhulme had been associated with his brother in the gift to Bolton of a fine church in memory of their father and mother, and he had formed, and supported for the twenty-odd years of its existence, the Bolton Court and Alley Concerts Society, modelled on a similar organisation in Liverpool, which provided brass band performances, concerts, and other entertainments in the poorer districts of the town. Leverhulme's principal benefaction to his home-town was probably the long series of gifts he made to Bolton Grammar School – not his old school: he had attended the Church Institute – and the Girls High School. The old Grammar School, founded in the sixteenth century, was rebuilt by one Robert Lever in 1641, and included in its articles was a clause saying that anyone of the blood and name of Lever living in Bolton should, if fitted, be made a Governor of the school if there was a vacancy. Two and a half centuries later, that clause brought a handsome dividend when William Lever was appointed Governor in 1898. He gave buildings and a swimming pool to the school, but most important was his establishment of a Trust of Lever Brothers shares which in 1920 gave an annual income of twenty thousand pounds to Bolton

School: formed by amalgamating the boys' and girls' schools. His most ambitious scheme for Bolton, a complete replanning of the Town Centre based on a study by the Town Planning Department of Liverpool University, was discussed for several years but never came to fruition, the Corporation's more cautious alternative plan being adopted instead.

When Leverhulme became Mayor of Bolton in the autumn of 1918 he was determined that business commitments and his new venture in Scotland should not prevent him giving good service to his birthplace. His daughter-in-law acted as Mayoress at public functions, and he managed to take the chair at every monthly meeting of the full Council. He followed the work of the committees, and he made a serious contribution to the restructuring of a complex and unwieldy local rating system. Almost his first official function, and certainly his most pleasant one, was to preside over the celebration of peace and give a Victory Ball in Bolton Town Hall.

Leverhulme presided over similar celebrations at Port Sunlight, and welcoming dinners when the soldiers and sailors came home. Showing rather disturbing foresight, he had, early in 1916, discussed with a leading sculptor a war memorial for Port Sunlight, believing that the best men would be swamped with work as soon as the War was over. He felt strongly that such a memorial should be a work of art created solely to honour the dead and that it would then always be such a reminder, whereas the original significance of a more functional creation like a village hall might eventually be overlooked. The memorial, a group of bronze figures, was unveiled just before Christmas 1921 by two Lever Brothers employees, one blinded on the Somme and the other a V.C. In his speech Leverhulme suggested that in the coming New Year they all consecrate themselves[11] 'to the nobler task of restoring peace and good will, love and friendship, trade and commerce with all peoples – with our former enemies no less than with our sorely tried and true and trusted Allies.'

The euphoric madness that burst out in Britain after the War shook the commercial world as convulsively as the worlds of fashion and entertainment. Near insatiable consumer demand after wartime deprivation encouraged the growth of all kinds of business, and wartime profits were available to finance expansion and new ventures. Released from discipline and restriction, and free at last from the fear of sudden death, most people were hell-bent on returning to the things they had done before the War, when they did so they intended to pursue them without pre-war inhibitions. Leverhulme was no exception, save perhaps for the scale of his imprudence. He had unfinished business left over from before the War – left over, indeed, from 1906. He wanted the control of those soap firms that had so far evaded the Lever Brothers net: Crosfield's, Gossage's, Knight's and some smaller firms – everything except the powerful and untouchable C.W.S. By 1920 these last citadels of the private soap industry were his, and he controlled nearly two-thirds of British production. It was a development which attracted the attention of the Beveridge Committee on Trusts, and a Government enquiry on the costs and profits of Lever Brothers' operations eventually decided that the price of household soap must be reduced by twopence, to nine-pence a pound. Leverhulme had argued his case pointing to the great cost and complexity of his Company's activities beyond the simple making and selling of soap, but the committee was not prepared to take the view that soap prices should support tropical ventures no matter how great their promise of commercial, or even political, benefits in the long run.

To buy out the remainder of the private soap industry, and thereby settle some old scores, Lever had paid a very high price. He had in nearly every case made the directors of the companies he took over an offer which was 'too good to refuse'. Leverhulme was dedicated to the practice of business and not to its cash rewards, and he had always believed that the business drive of the less totally dedicated was vulnerable to monetary considerations. He believed that Ordinary shareholders, content with a good dividend and unwilling to jeopardise it, would resist promising but risky business ventures. For this reason he had kept the Ordinary shares in his own hands and issued Preference shares, with fixed dividends, to the public. He was applying the same principle when he persuaded his competitors to exchange their business interests for his cash.

Leverhulme was nearly seventy, the size and complexity of the

Company's interest meant that the Board of Directors had to assume more and more authority, and the purchase of Lewis carried a hint of withdrawal. Having won the battle of the British soap industry, there were two fundamental Company activities which he wanted to see moving strongly in the right direction into the post-war world. These were the old struggle to get a fair grip on world production of raw materials and the plan to repeat in the new margarine industry all that he had accomplished with soap. As well as buying British soap firms, Leverhulme extended his interests in the milling of oil-bearing seeds, he bought the Southern Whaling and Sealing Company which operated in the Antarctic, he bought an interest in Philippine coconut oil. If the rest of the world was on a spending spree so too was Leverhulme, and in 1919 he increased the authorised capital of Lever Brothers from forty to a hundred million pounds.

Of all the items on Leverhulme's expensive post-war shopping list, the most important and costly was the Niger Company of West Africa. His interests in this area up to this time were confined to the MacIver Company which he had bought in 1910 to give him a trading foothold there, and the factories for the production of palm-oil in Nigeria and Sierra Leone. These were relatively small, and so far unprofitable, enterprises: the Niger Company was on an altogether larger scale.

In 1885, at the Berlin Conference which divided Africa among the Great Powers, the British claim to a sphere of influence in Nigeria was based largely upon the fact that the trade in that area was already almost wholly in the hands of Britain through the National Africa Company set up by George Goldie. In 1886 the British Government declared Southern Nigeria a Protectorate and granted the company a charter under the title of the Royal Niger Company. The Royal Niger Company was to govern and preserve order and gradually to abolish slavery in the region. To cover the costs of this administration the Company could levy certain custom duties and it was given a free hand with trading except that it was not permitted to exercise a monopoly. Other European traders inevitably complained of monopoly, and native traders within the Company's area believed that their profits were reduced. The Company's posts near the boundaries of its territory had to contend with legal and illegal commercial tactics by native traders across the border, whose competitive sense was keen to the point of burning down the Company trading posts and eating the officials. In 1900 the British Government assumed administrative control and the Company's role became exclusively commercial under the new name of the Niger Company, a flourishing concern which made a quarter of a million pounds a year profit during the War.

In 1919 the Board of Lever Brothers probably first became aware that an approach might be welcomed by the Niger Company. In January 1920 Levers told their broker that they were likely to go ahead with the purchase of the Company and that they would need something over seven million pounds in cash. A decision was required in a matter of days, and in Leverhulme's absence, but with his complete subsequent approval, the Board completed the deal, agreeing to a price of over eight million pounds to be paid in July 1920, until which time the Niger directors would continue in control of their Company's affairs.

This was a slightly unusual arrangement, but what was even more remarkable was the fact that in the rush of the negotiations there had been no careful examination of the accounts of the Niger Company, and furthermore that the Lever Brothers Board had no certain knowledge of where they were going to raise this large amount of cash. The situation deteriorated abruptly when it was discovered that the Niger Company had a two million pound overdraft, and when a disastrous 50 per cent fall in the price of raw materials coincided with the five-month period during which the Niger directors exercised control of their Company's affairs without financial responsibility for their decisions. Lever Brothers' broker, after a very stormy interview with Leverhulme, declined to underwrite any part of the required capital. Leverhulme had to go himself into the money market and with considerable difficulty raised the eight million pounds to buy the Niger Company, but the process strained his credit to the limit, and it still left the two million pound overdraft which he managed to stave off until the end of the year. But Leverhulme's policy of expansion and acquisition caused disquiet among the bankers holding the overdraft, and early in 1921 they threatened that if it were not paid off they proposed to issue a writ for the liquidation of the Niger Company, an action which might have initiated a catastrophic chain of events for Lever Brothers at a time of particular economic difficulty for all large businesses. This indignity and danger was only avoided by a brilliant piece of business negotiation brought off by Cooper, an accountant called in by Leverhulme from a firm he had used for many years. Cooper negotiated a loan from Barclay's Bank, the security for which was an issue of Debenture stock held by the bank. This was a fundamental departure from Leverhulme's financial principles, but he had no choice in the matter. Payment of the interest on the Debentures was a prime charge on the Company's funds, and as owner of this large block of stock the bank now had a certain say in the affairs of Lever Brothers – a most significant curb of Leverhulme's autocratic control.

In these dark financial days of 1920 Leverhulme decided to try once more to get a portrait of himself which would in his opinion do him justice. It was a frustrating quest for one whose self-satisfaction was coupled with an unnatural sensitivity to criticism, but who nevertheless had a perceptive advertiser's eye, well used to putting a price on the flattering unreality of the chocolate box. He was caught between sycophant and shaving mirror.

His almost automatic attachment to what was judged best in the established order of things made it almost inevitable that he should go to Augustus John, then at the height of his fame if not his powers. The artist had embarked upon painting portraits which, between the wars, caused him such restless dissatisfaction, and of which he wrote to Rothenstein that he was 'dying to get through with them and tackle other things'.[12]

In the summer of 1920 Leverhulme appeared for his first sitting in John's Chelsea studio, explaining that he could spare little time, and that he was an almost impossible subject to which no artist had done justice. John experienced none of the blocks which later kept him picking unhappily at Lord D'Abernon's portrait for five years. The work proceeded briskly and the artist expressed great satisfaction with Leverhulme's finished portrait. The sitter, however, was not so pleased. The eyes, nose, and mouth were not his, he declared, at which John offered him brushes and palette. But the two men parted with less rancour than disappointment, the portrait was sent off to Rivington, a week later the cheque reached Chelsea, and this might have been the end of an unsatisfactory little incident of small importance or interest. Leverhulme had not got the portrait he hoped for, but this was no great surprise to him. John got no praise which he would have liked, but a good fee which he needed and which was the principal reason for undertaking the work.

Leverhulme's private feelings were however deeper than disappointment. To a friend he wrote that the portrait was 'chastening' and 'humbling to pride'.[13] He had hoped somehow to see displayed not his appearance but his aspirations, whereas John's fine portrait showed the nature which was the source of those aspirations, and the physical effects of a lifetime of pursuing them. The shaving mirror can be forgiven because its criticism is private and impersonal, a mere reflection like the face itself, but Leverhulme felt himself to be wounded by John's study. He made up his mind that without making any fuss he would ensure that it was never seen by his family, friends, or the public.

When the portrait was delivered to Rivington, Leverhulme himself opened the packing case and cut out of the framed portrait a piece rather more than a foot square containing the head and face. This he folded and placed in the back of his safe, leaving the remainder of the picture in its frame in the packing case with a label in his own handwriting: 'Remainder of a portrait by Augustus John.'

Unfortunately for Leverhulme's plan to keep the matter dark, his housekeeper came across the case, which carried the artist's name and address, and it was sent back to Chelsea where it lay like a time-bomb in the studio while John was away on holiday in Wales.

When John returned to Chelsea and discovered the mutilated picture in his studio he was furious. Nevertheless the letter he wrote to Leverhulme on 30 September 1920[14] was reasonably restrained and ended, 'I am intensely anxious to have your Lordship's explanation of this, the grossest insult I have ever received in the course of my career. I am glad to say I had the portrait photographed before delivering it to you, and I propose to give it and the subsequent treatment at your hands the widest publicity.'

Leverhulme's reply was conciliatory and he explained that he had intended to take the whole canvas from the frame and put it in his safe. He had not reckoned on the internal shelves and partitions and had therefore decided to put away only the head 'which is the important part of the portrait'. He went on to say, 'As far as my knowledge goes, the portrait is my copyright, and cannot be published, notwithstanding the fact that you have a photograph of it, without my consent, but in any case I feel sure we are both of us far too good friends that you would wish to do anything that would annoy me, and I certainly have no intention to do anything that would annoy yourself.'

John, not unreasonably, expressed some surprise that Leverhulme had intended to keep the portrait in his safe, particularly as he had complained at an earlier sitting that the canvas chosen was too small. This seems to add weight to the conclusion that Leverhulme decided to suppress the portrait when he saw it completed and for that reason he had it sent to Rivington, where he then found that the safe would only accommodate a small part of the canvas. There was some argument by letter about the ownership of the copyright which, as the law then stood, remained in the hands of the artist unless the terms of the commission expressedly gave it to the buyer. Leverhulme then drew upon his own artistic knowledge and experience: 'I do not really feel that you can claim any greater certainty of pleasing clients than Reynolds or Rembrandt or any other of the world's greatest artists.

'You will find that when a Reynolds portrait comes up at Christies', and a letter can be produced from the sitter objecting to something in the portrait, it gives an added value in the eyes of some purchasers, and it is well known that the world's greatest masterpieces were not considered by the sitters to be exact portraits. I believe it is on record that Romney replied to a criticism of this kind that he did not guarantee works of art – or words to that effect. Surely your position cannot make you immune from the previous experiences of all the world's greatest artists. . . .'

Answering this letter point by point John noted that Lord Leverhulme's chief anxiety in the affair hinged on the possibility of publication of the photograph of the picture which he had seen fit to destroy. The artist pointed out that even if sitters had not considered the world's greatest masterpieces to be exact portraits, all the same the masterpieces had survived intact. 'The mutilation of a work of art is unjustifiable, even if the mutilator happens to be the owner of the picture.' This seems to be an unexceptionable statement, but it is an interesting one to have been made by an artist who, by his own account, had once destroyed a newly completed portrait of the Earl of Athlone, in the presence of the sitter, because, 'Suddenly I couldn't bear it.'

The correspondence had been kept private although John had talked of the matter to friends and had shown some of them what he called 'Lord Leverhulme's Watch-chain', the headless remains of the portrait. But the *Daily Express* got hold of the story and ran it on 8 October 1920 without revealing the names of the 'Famous Peer and Great Artist'. Reporters discovered John spending the week-end at Broadstairs as the guest of Lady Tredegar and he was persuaded to allow the *Express* to publish the full text of the letters which had passed between him and Leverhulme.

There was a public outcry, much of it in terms of the conflict between the philistine, millionaire soap-maker and the sensitive genius. This simplified to the point of absurdity the personalities of a hard-headed philanthropist who had assembled one of the world's greatest collections of art treasure, and a waning artist idolised by a raffish self-styled *avant-garde*, who painted portraits to keep the domestic pot bubbling.

In his autobiography[15] John wrote that when the story of the Leverhulme portrait was published, 'with photographs of the work, before and after treatment. Telegrams and cables now began to pour in from artistic bodies all over the world, including if not China and Peru, certainly Japan and the U.S.A. Public demonstrations also took place. The students of the London Art Schools united in organizing a procession to Hyde Park, bearing aloft a gigantic replica of the celebrated soap-boiler's torso, the head being absent: this was accompanied by eloquent expressions of indignation, scorn and ridicule.

'In Italy they went further. A twenty-four hour strike was called, involving everyone connected with the painting industry, including models, colour-men and frame-makers. A colossal effigy entitled "IL LE-VER-HUL-ME" was constructed of soap and tallow, paraded through the streets of Florence, and ceremoniously burnt in the Piazza dei Signori, after which the demonstrators, reforming, proceeded to the Battisteria where a wreath was solemnly laid on the altar of St. John. . . .'

Contemporary photographs[16] suggest that in the London demonstrations any hint of temperamental artistic abandon was heavily overlaid with British respectability. It was an orderly procession, led by a brass band and escorted by constables walking alongside. A large banner several yards square showed a portly figure of Leverhulme with a quiff, and the legend 'What's the matter with it?' A smaller, kinder picture of John was also carried aloft. After the burning of the effigy – inscribed 'Lord Leave-a-hole' – the procession went to the National Gallery and left Leverhulme's caricature outside before going on, one hopes, to revels more appropriate to student celebrations of Guy Fawkes Day than the dull and somewhat contrived affair that had occupied the afternoon.

Although the students from the Slade, John's old Art School, had chosen Leverhulme to be their guy, *The Times*[17] reported that in London the favourite guy appeared to be 'Pussyfoot', the temperance advocate, 'though the ex-Kaiser was not entirely overlooked'.

The *Manchester Guardian* declared, 'the bottom of the case is that there is something in a work of art which, in the higher equity as distinct from the law, you can not buy.' But neither John nor Leverhulme chose to seek the opinion of the Courts, and the matter was forgotten until a remarkable and pleasant sequel some years later.

Some time after Leverhulme died his grandson, now the third Viscount, discovered the head of the Augustus John portrait folded in the back of a safe at Thornton Manor. He had never seen it before – indeed any mention of the portrait within the family circle was forbidden by his grandfather. The portrait head was framed and put on display at the Manor and in due course brought to the attention of Sir Gerald Kelly of the Royal Academy. At Kelly's suggestion the Viscount, with some misgivings about the effect of a letter signed Leverhulme, wrote to John to ask if by chance he still had the rest of the picture. The response was a charming letter from John saying that, far from being bitter enemies, he and Leverhulme had parted friends. John promised to look for the 'body' but nothing more was heard.

When the Royal Academy's Augustus John retrospective exhibition of 1950 was mooted, Kelly asked the third Viscount Leverhulme if he would lend the 'head' which was duly put on exhibition. John saw it at the opening and went home and, with his wife, searched his studio and found the 'body' which was taken to the Academy. A Dr J. Hell did a swift transplant operation in time for the whole portrait to be displayed before the exhibition closed. After the exhibition was over the restorer completed his work at leisure and, as Kelly remarked, 'with Hellish ingenuity'.

The whole portrait (*frontispiece*) now hangs in Thornton Manor, the home of the third Viscount, who recalls that Augustus John added a final pleasant touch to what had superficially seemed a cantankerous business by insisting on paying the bill for the restoration, which neither legally nor morally could possibly have been his duty. Two very dissimilar men – each talented, aggressive, and sensitive, in different manners – had met, clashed, and gone their ways bearing no grudges.

It is not especially remarkable for a sitter to wish to hide his portrait. When Augustus John painted Montague Norman, the banker refused to hang the picture in his home or at the Bank of England, and only after his death was it displayed. In the case of the Leverhulme portrait, chance and the efforts of the sitter's family eventually revealed the strange story of its disappearance and rescued it from oblivion. There is, perhaps, a parallel in Sutherland's portrait of Winston Churchill, who did not disguise his dislike of the picture, which seems, at least for the time being, to have vanished.

When Leverhulme asked that the Augustus John portrait be sent to The Bungalow at Rivington it was almost certainly not his original intention.[18] The limited wall space there was filled with tapestry, embroidery, and engravings, but there were no large oil paintings. He may possibly have wanted it for Lews Castle in Stornoway, but it is more likely – or at least the speculation is more tempting – that he wanted a fine commanding portrait for the Company so that when his actual attendances at headquarters became rarer and eventually ceased altogether, his presence would still be apparent. In 1921 the Company headquarters moved from Port Sunlight to Lever House in London, as befitted its now enormous international prestige and importance. It was a time of change from the old order: the Captain had moved north from his old position of total command on the Bridge at Port Sunlight, and now the control itself had moved away from the model Factory and Village in the Wirral to London, where it was exercised by the Board of Directors, now committed to paying some attention to the bankers who were major Debenture holders.

# 13

# *Western Isles*

The purchase of the Niger Company shook the financial stability of Lever Brothers, initiated fundamental changes in its control, and might easily have brought the Company to disaster. Leverhulme's share of the blame for the scandalously irresponsible conduct of the negotiations lay principally in the attitude of mind he had induced over the years in his Board of Directors. They stood in considerable fear of his displeasure, and knew that the certain way to incur it was to muff a chance of making Lever Brothers bigger and more powerful. He himself was abroad and took little or no part in the negotiations, while his directors were hustled by the Niger Company's hints about other buyers, and haunted by a knowledge of their own Chairman's consuming desire for expansion. They were too little conditioned to major responsibility, and unfamiliar with making a critical analysis to justify a personal decision. When they signed the contract with the Niger Company early in 1920 and received Lever's cable – 'Congratulations. Price high but suicidal if we had let opportunity lapse' – the directors must have heaved a sigh of relief and been confirmed in the dangerous view that expansion, whatever the conditions, was the key to favour and success in the Lever Brothers organisation.

As the truly disastrous nature of the transaction gradually became revealed in 1920 and 1921, Leverhulme castigated his directors in private for their incompetence. In public, he attacked the Niger Company board, who, during the months they remained in control after the deal was completed, tried to support prices by buying raw materials in a falling market when they were already heavily over-stocked. But Leverhulme was quite clear about his public duty as Chairman. He wrote to his son, who was Vice-Chairman, about the forthcoming annual general meeting of the newly acquired Niger Company,[1] 'Mr Cooper is strongly of the opinion that there will be a great number of dissatisfied shareholders present when they see that the reserve fund has disappeared and there is a balance of loss of over eight hundred thousand pounds, and that questions are certain to be asked. Under these circumstances I think that I would like to take the chair myself so that you may be spared having to deal with these shareholders. I shall be very pleased to act in any way as you may wish. . . . It is not only the questions that might be asked in connection with the Niger Company but questions that might be asked in connection with Lever Brothers as affected by the losses of the Niger Company.'

It is not altogether surprising to see the hint of deference to his son, who regularly deputised for him at board meetings. More significant is the nature of the reference to Cooper, who, since rescuing the Company from the financial quicksands of the Niger affair, had played an increasingly positive role in the affairs of Lever Brothers, probably, it is suggested,[2] at the recommendation of the banker Debenture holders. He was soon to take a formal directorship and then move on to higher things.

Leverhulme had been preparing for withdrawal from the principal role in Lever Brothers for some time, but not perhaps as completely or as quickly as the Board would have wished. The Niger fiasco had loosened his grip faster than he planned, and in a manner which he disliked. He therefore threw himself all the more vigorously into his personal scheme for the Isle of Lewis, where he would once more be in sole command. When he had first looked for a project for his 'retirement' he had almost bought a very large estate in the Midlands. But there a certain amount of development had already taken place and he eventually decided against it when the opportunity arose for him to get hold of Lewis, where not only was there a castle and estate to be worked upon but also the prospect of starting again from scratch on an entirely new business adventure. His plans for the future prosperity of the Island centred upon the application of modern science and his own business skills to establishing a large and thriving fishing industry. He made this clear in his reply to the address of welcome he received, delayed a few days by the Sabbath, when he first came to Lewis as Proprietor.

Traditionally, the mainstay of the Lewis fishing industry was the herring, which was of particularly high quality in the Minch, the stretch of water between the Island and the mainland of Scotland. During the spring and summer months many scores of drifters came and based themselves on Stornoway. This fleet, which followed the herring shoals on their regular migration around to the East Coast of Scotland and England, was supported on shore by thousands of tough Scottish fish-lassies who gutted the herring and packed them with salt in barrels for export to Germany and Eastern Europe. When the herring fleet moved on from Stornoway, the local drifters and hundreds of local girls went with it. With the loss during the War of the European market for salt herring, the fish had been packed in ice for sale in British shops as fresh herring, and there had been some growth in curing the fish to produce kippers and bloaters. But Stornoway's future as a herring port was not assured. Although it had a good harbour, well placed for the fishing grounds, its remoteness meant additional transport costs for ice, fuel, boxes, and anything else that had to be imported, and also for the landed fish which was almost all sent to the mainland. Furthermore, the lack of facilities and entertainment ashore, made Stornoway unattractive to the visiting crews, while Sabbath restrictions – on sailing, fishing, or landing – meant that drifters, which were normally at sea for something like eighteen hours, might have their operations affected on two, or even three, days of the week.

Catches of fish other than herring were small: a trivial amount of shell-fish, mostly lobster, and an amount of cod, haddock, and other white fish, which was about one-tenth of the value of the herring catch. The white fish catch, although small, was significant for the future because it was achieved almost entirely by local in-shore fishermen using long lines from small boats, whereas a rich harvest was gathered further out in the Minch by deep trawlers operating from other Scottish ports.

When Leverhulme came to Lewis the fishing was suffering from the withdrawal of many men, and some vessels, for war service with the naval reserve. It would not be enough, though, simply to return to pre-war standards. Leverhulme intended that post-war Stornoway should be improved and enlarged to attract landings of fish from visiting vessels to supplement catches made by local boats and his own fleet of modern drifters and trawlers. There would be an ice-making factory at Stornoway, and cargo vessels with refrigerated holds to take the fresh fish to a depot on the mainland at Fleetwood, Lancashire, which was well placed to serve the industrial towns of the north of England. To deal with the regular problem of the glut of fish, Leverhulme enlarged the herring-curing facilities in Lewis, built a canning factory, and installed plant to make fish-cakes, fish-paste, glue, animal feed, and fertiliser, from the offal and from certain fish, like dogfish, which were not normally served at table. He provided similar facilities at Fleetwood, where he also had experiments performed which might have put the kitchen clock forward a generation if he had not been dissatisfied with the performance of the pilot plant for the production of quick-frozen fish. These were all parts of a plan to be put into immediate operation, while further ahead he talked of providing aircraft to find herring shoals for the fleet, and of radio communications between harbour, fishing vessels, and spotting plane. As far as possible he would export from the Island a minimum of salt fish in barrels, which commanded a very low price. Instead he would get as much as possible of his catches into the shops as high-priced fresh fish, and anything in excess of the market demand he would can or cure, and sell as opportunity arose later of a good price. The last drop of profitability would be squeezed out by the plant which processed offal, trimmings, and unmarketable species.

To operate this well-engineered commercial system Leverhulme needed steady, reliable workers. If the people of Lewis would give him six days' honest work week after week regularly through the year, he would take them out of the poverty of the crofter's stinking hut, away from the grinding struggle to survive, to a life of comfortable security, with water in the tap and money in the pocket to buy things for home and family.

Stornoway, the capital, was a busy little town with banks, shops, hotels, and many offices and warehouses connected with the fishing and the tweed industry. The inhabitants, mostly bi-lingual in Gaelic and English, were used to steady work and might have been well suited to employment in Leverhulme's new organisation, but they already had work, and their living standards were well above those of the crofters. It was the crofters and the squatters in the predominantly Gaelic-speaking countryside away from Stornoway who were the targets of Leverhulme's drive for social reform, and from them he hoped to recruit his labour force. If they worked for him, his scheme would prosper and they would gain a civilised standard of living. The proposition had a misleading simplicity, like offering jobs as road-sweepers to a colony of meths drinkers: the condition of meths drinker makes change the uphill choice. Not that the crofters of Lewis were meths drinkers, although many of them were often the better, or the worse, for a mug or two of whisky.

The crofter was a man of varied employment who had to decide each day what was the most important work to be done. This independent life gave him self-confidence and an agility of mind in his own interest that outsiders were surprised to find in one who lived in such squalid conditions, working at unpleasant, difficult, and dangerous tasks, occasionally relieved by periods of brutish indolence. The fundamental components of his existence were his house, his plot of land, and his boat. He ploughed and sowed his six acres, and harvested vegetables and grain for his family, and for the animals who got what grazing they could on the communal moorland at the back of the group of crofts, or township. Sometimes the women of the crofts would take the animals off in the summer, for weeks at a time, to remote moorland pastures, or 'shielings'. Several families might share a rough shelter built there, taking turns to guard the animals and to work at the spinning-wheel and the milk churn that would be taken with them. A fine summer shieling, shared by the women and some of the younger children, was a time of refreshment, and an affectionate legend in Island memory like hop-picking to the cockney. The man of the croft was as likely to be found a mile off-shore in his boat as tilling the land. During the spring and summer, using long lines with many hooks, he caught white fish for his family and for sale locally, he tended a few lobster pots, and he dug the land and sowed his crops. He was likely to go off for several weeks at a time during the peaks of the herring season as an extra deckhand with the drifters, but he would always be back on the croft in the late summer for the harvest. His wife was no stranger to the heaviest of the tasks, and she also worked at the hand loom, producing tweed from wool which was usually carded, spun, and dyed in Stornoway, although in Leverhulme's time many of the crofters in Lewis and Harris still spun and dyed their own thread.

The economy of the croft, almost as diverse as that of Lever Brothers, did not appeal to Leverhulme. The crofter, selling any white fish or cloth he had in excess of his family's needs, reminded Leverhulme too strongly of the native of British West Africa, who, with his hand mill, would prepare enough palm-oil to satisfy the needs of his family, and then might gather a little extra palm fruit and bring it in to the trading post and sell it to Lever Brothers' agents.

Leverhulme's projects were not of a scale to use casual labour or the excess fish after a family's need was satisfied. He needed full-time workers all the year round, and his needs were incompatible with the crofting system. He proposed to provide such an attractive alternative that crofters would voluntarily forsake their miserable holdings, and those others, now demanding land, would end their agitation. He would not evict anyone who wanted to stay, but he would do nothing to encourage crofting: he would not, for instance, finance the repair of the crofters' boats neglected during the War, nor would he provide money for engines to make them more efficient. When he was known to favour an end to crofting, and when he was pouring money elsewhere into Lewis so generously, the mere fact of not subsidising crofting was regarded by some as a positive act of ill-will.

To support his fishing industries Leverhulme needed new roads and bridges to communicate with the subsidiary fishing ports and canning factories, etc., which he intended to build in parts of the Island other than Stornoway. For the crofters and others who would come to work full-time in his factories and fishing boats he needed good houses. For Stornoway itself, his plan, which would eventually involve knocking down much of the existing town, was strongly reminiscent of Port Sunlight, with wide avenues, imposing public buildings, and spacious factories, offices, and warehouses.

It was 1919 before building on Lewis got seriously under way. McAlpine's were the main contractors and employment was provided for many local men on roadbuilding and other labouring work. The first Leverhulme money began to appear in Lewis pockets. The Stornoway houses were two-storied, stone-built, and all had bathrooms. In the country the cottages to replace the croft houses were bungalows with living-room, three bedrooms, kitchen, and bathroom. The roofs were of felt and board, covered with corrugated iron, and the outside walls were peat set in wooden frames. The strangely low standard of the building style and material – poor, that is, compared with the new Stornoway houses, but palatial compared with the old croft house – was because it was intended that the people should do the building themselves, in housing associations under the supervision of an expert provided free by Leverhulme, who would allow individuals to make changes, like stone walls, if they could afford the material and manage the work. Leverhulme was prepared to advance as a loan all but about fifty pounds of the price, and each house had a quarter-acre allotment of land for vegetables.

With plans made and work started on the social and industrial building to support his development of the fishing, Leverhulme now looked to the far end of the commercial chain and bought the best fishmonger shop in most of Britain's big towns, to provide an outlet for his product. All the shops were refitted to a standard pattern of high quality and their previous owners installed as managers. Looking back to previous business successes, as he always did, Leverhulme sought a name for his new fishery business and for the product which he hoped would have the same success as Sunlight. After turning over in his mind many names including Silvascale, Island Deep, and Wavecrest, he asked the trade-mark expert at Port Sunlight to investigate whether it was possible to register Mac as a trade name. So Leverhulme's fishing fleet in Lewis was known as the MacLine Company, and the fish shops in the main streets of Britain became Mac Fisheries. The first was opened in February 1919 and within two or three years there were nearly four hundred. The Mac Fisheries Company developed with enormous speed and success, buying fish from all the big ports, because Lewis could satisfy only a tiny fraction of its requirements. With Leverhulme in command, growth and takeover were inevitably key policies of the Company. In a very short time this new enterprise had embraced Wall's, the ice-cream and sausage manufacturer, several firms specialising in different sections of the fish trade, and companies owning and operating fishing fleets. None of these companies had any specific connection with Lewis, which had now produced a truly national food group, although this meant little more to the Island than an assured market for its fish, because all the capital, and hence the profits and capital appreciation, belonged to Leverhulme.

It would have been very convenient if Leverhulme could have built his roads, and houses, and factories, and bought his fishing fleet, before the War was over, so that crofters, and in particular the returning ex-servicemen, could have seen his schemes alongside the old system and made their choice. He was undoubtedly inspired to take on the Lewis project by motives similar to those which had prompted his Port Sunlight venture, and his great success in Cheshire gave him hope, indeed confidence, that he could solve some of the major problems of the Western Isles. There were, however, certain fundamental differences between the two projects which made the social problems to be overcome in Lewis much more severe.

When Port Sunlight was put up beside a muddy, desolate Mersey creek there was no question of the destruction of cherished building or landscape, nor did the factory and village threaten anybody's way of life. The Port Sunlight population was drawn from the very large communities of Birkenhead and Liverpool. Merseysiders who disliked the way Lever organised the lives of his workers need hardly be aware of the existence of the Lever Brothers works a few miles away. But the Leverhulme plans for Lewis would alter the appearance of the Island and affect almost everyone's life. Those who for any reason opposed the plans would be an ever-present disgruntled group putting the blame for the alteration in their lives on those who co-operated with

Leverhulme, and inclined to suggest that in doing so they had betrayed the traditions of the Islands and the sacrifices of their forefathers.

Leverhulme was famous and Lewis was small: it was impossible for him to come to the Island and get anything significant done without publicity. Consequently the debate about his scheme began before he had anything to show which might win over the doubters. All he could do was to try to sell himself to the Islanders, and he went to considerable trouble to do so. He made anything the excuse for entertainment at Lews Castle in the early days of his Proprietorship: dances, garden parties, and dinners, with the guests mostly from Stornoway. They were lively gatherings, with Leverhulme managing to guide them towards a series of set pieces – toasts, anecdotes, jokes, even recitations and songs – rather than conversational exchanges which his deafness made so difficult. A visitor described an evening entertainment at the Castle,[3] 'His management of the mixed elements in the party was a masterpiece. He seemed to exercise a sort of mesmeric power over his guests, that bent them readily but unconsciously to his will. . . . There was music, dancing, and some very good singing – in English and Gaelic – and much merriment.' Some of the girls present teased Leverhulme, calling on him to sing 'the bathing song', which had slightly risqué words that he was known to have by heart. 'He pretended to be shocked . . . then with dramatic suddenness he agreed. "Very well; if you insist, I shall sing a song – and I shall sing the bathing song." He couldn't sing; he could only croak. And that versatile little man croaked heartily through a song which would make an Irish navvy blush. As *encore*, in the Irish dialect, he gave an excellent recitation, displaying real humour and histrionic ability of a high order.'

The crofters were rarely invited to these parties at the Castle – Leverhulme thought they would be overawed – but if one called for any reason he was always treated with great consideration. Leverhulme went out to the country townships, talking slowly in English to the assembled crofters. He remembered to use correct Scottish names and titles, and often made a joke or two about being English, although he was careful not to make the common mistake of being more Scottish than the Scots. He struck just the right note by adding to his wardrobe, when he came to Scotland, no more than an overcoat and plus-four suit in Island tweed. Leverhulme's campaign to commend himself to the Islanders during his first months there was very successful, but he had nothing to show that could convince the people of the material benefits of his plans. He tried to make up for this deficiency by sending parties from Lewis to look over Port Sunlight. They travelled in style, but to most of them the place was like some fictional civilisation, and they usually returned with no other effect than the confirmation of whatever were their original prejudices, for or against Leverhulme's ideas.

From June 1918, when Leverhulme was welcomed as the new owner of Lewis, until March 1919 was a honeymoon period. He went through all his party tricks in a systematic campaign to make himself personally attractive to the Islanders and to convince them of the worth of the plans he had for their future together. For their part they responded to his advances, accepting the small frivolous gifts he offered and wondering about the realities of the new life that lay ahead, excited and a little timid because it seemed likely to be very different from that which they had been used to for so long. Both sides were experienced enough not to be too starry-eyed about the future, expecting that they would each have to change some established attitudes, but feeling that any such give and take would turn out to be well worth while. What neither side foresaw was that a third party – a mutual friend, perhaps, but more devoted to the Islanders than to Leverhulme – would complicate their relationship. This third party was the Politician, a composite of Robert Munro, the Secretary of State for Scotland; Donald Murray, the Member for the Western Isles; and a number of supporting characters including most of the House of Commons, passionately anxious to redress past oppression of the Highlanders who had now so recently served with outstanding bravery in the War.

The 1911 Small Landholders Act had given the Scottish Secretary, on behalf of the Government, the power to acquire by compulsory purchase certain farms in the Highlands and Islands in order that they might be broken up to provide more crofts. The designation of the farms covered by the Act and the compensation to be awarded were matters of some complexity. In 1913, before Leverhulme's advent, four farms on Lewis had been scheduled for take-over, but the move had been opposed by the Proprietor at that time, and with the outbreak of war it was left in abeyance. If the matter was put on one side officially, it was certainly not forgotten by would-be crofters away in the Forces, or by supporters of the Highland League which was politically dedicated to land reform. A Leading Seaman on active service wrote to the *Stornoway Gazette*[4] saying that in the matter of their reinstatement on crofts 'all Lewismen can now plainly see that they have been quiet too long'. It was an action and a sentiment that would have earned the sailor at least the reputation of 'trouble maker' if it had been reported to his ship. Less vulnerable activists at home could publicise strong, even extreme, views, and bolster their case by referring to those away fighting:[5] 'our brave lads shall not be compelled for want of land to emigrate again', and[6] 'is there a landlord in the British Empire who could grudge them the soil which they so bravely defended from the savage and brutal Huns?' Such strong views as these, expressed in 1917, evoked a response from the Government. The Lord Advocate stated with remarkable firmness, in Inverness,[7] 'We are entitled to expect that the land question in the Highlands should be settled for once and for all . . . everyone is agreed that the people of the Highlands must be placed in possession of the soil.' The Lewis Crofters Association in 1917 put up to Robert Munro, the Secretary for Scotland, a proposal that the whole of Lewis should be bought by the Government and entirely devoted to a settlement for crofters and fishermen. Munro informed the Association through their M.P. that he was considering the suggestion. But, if Munro had any serious intention of embarking on a course which would be so politically and administratively difficult, he was thwarted when Leverhulme bought the Island in 1918.

In the summer of 1918 the Scottish Office first proposed to Leverhulme that under the Small Landholders Act, the Board of Agriculture should take possession of certain of his farms and create something fewer than a hundred and fifty crofts. It was unfortunate that, with both sides genuinely seeking the welfare of the Island, there should have been the hint of a row at the very start of the negotiations. The official sent to Lews Castle by the Scottish Office to discuss the proposals rubbed Leverhulme up the wrong way by adopting an aggressive attitude. It was a serious mistake, but perhaps understandable. If, like so many Scottish politicians and officials, he was sensitive about the undeniably heartless behaviour of English landlords towards the Highlands in the past, he might well have felt that his long journey to Lewis with his plans was pandering unnecessarily to a rich Sassenach whose consent was not needed before his farms were taken. Furthermore, there is no record of the attitude adopted by Leverhulme at the meeting, although another official recorded an impression of his first encounter with Leverhulme under similar circumstances a little later in the negotiations:[8] 'At very first glance one would put him down as rather insignificant, but that impression was extremely short-lived. Charm, tact, decision, power, radiated from the man's every word, look, and gesture. I had never met a man who was so obviously a megalomaniac and accustomed to having his own way. . . .'

At the General Election in December 1918 a reorganisation of constituency boundaries meant that for the first time the Western Isles returned its own member. There were three candidates: one standing as 'Labour and Highland League' polled just over eight hundred votes, while the other two candidates got over three thousand votes each. The Lloyd George Coalition Liberal candidate was a London shipping-line owner who had Leverhulme's private encouragement, and the Independent Liberal was Donald Murray, the Medical Officer of Health for Lewis who had been born on the Island. All three candidates publicly supported the policy of breaking up the farms to provide crofts. Murray was elected with a majority of nearly four hundred over the other Liberal and, although he had not spoken against Leverhulme's plans during the election campaign, he subsequently did them much harm. Most people at the time of the election had no thought of any incompatibility between Leverhulme's schemes and the provision of more crofts. This was certainly Munro's view when he discussed the matter further with Leverhulme, who, however, maintained that the economic difficulties of the Western Isles could be solved by his scheme, whereas to provide a few hundred more crofts on Lewis would be like giving a hungry donkey one oat. His old disenchantment with the inertia of Parliamentary processes was reawakened, and he was convinced that the only sensible course in Lewis was to abandon the futile land reform legislation so laboriously enacted at Westminster, leaving him to get on briskly and single-handed with revitalising the Western Isles.

By the beginning of 1919 the positions taken up by those involved were fairly well defined. Munro, himself a Highlander, knew and shared the special feelings of the people about the reinstatement of the crofts. As a politician he believed that all parties supported the land reform recommendations which, since the Crofters Commission in 1884, had gradually acquired more legal force with the passage of various Acts of Parliament. He saw no reason why Lewis should not have Leverhulme's industrial schemes as well as more crofts. He knew, too, that if crofts were not provided he would, as Secretary for Scotland, attract harsh criticism in the Commons, the Cabinet, and the country.

Leverhulme – although this was not yet public knowledge – saw the croft system as a millstone round the neck of the Island's economic past, and had no intention that it should cripple the future. In his arguments, still private, with the Secretary for Scotland, he produced two major points. He claimed that the farms were essential to supplying the needs of the community, particularly milk, under his new plan. He stuck pigheadedly to the point that Lewis must not import milk from the mainland, when, in fact, this would have been of little significance, particularly with the great increase in shipping traffic which his schemes would bring about. A much more telling second point was that the proposed break-up of the Lewis farms would only provide a fraction of the number of crofts demanded, and that all the land in the Islands would still not satisfy the cry for more and bigger crofts. Whatever his stated reasons, he refused to believe that the hopelessly inefficient croft system could exist alongside his own streamlined commercial operation. Once his scheme was running he believed the crofts would be deserted by men and women wanting the higher standard of living he would provide. Meanwhile, however, although he would tolerate the existing crofts, he would certainly not do anything to increase their number.

The Islanders saw as yet no cause to take sides. They wanted Leverhulme to go ahead with his scheme and they expected that, as a demonstrably generous man concerned with the good of the people, he would create more crofts. The soldiers and sailors away from home had not been exposed to the charms of Leverhulme's studied self-promotion in 1918, but they too expected crofts and a bright future in the new schemes. For many of them, safe at last after the bloodiest of wars, their bright new future was snuffed out just as they were about to set foot again on the soil which had such a special meaning for them.

On New Year's Eve 1918, five hundred of the men from the Islands left Kyle of Lochalsh to cross the Minch for demobilisation leave and a return to their families and the way of peace. To get this large number home in time for New Year's Day the Admiralty arranged for H.M. Yacht *Iolare* to assist the regular mailboat by carrying the naval contingent, some two hundred and sixty men. She sailed late in the evening into a rising gale, but the storm could not quench the gaiety of the midnight celebrations on board. Just before two in the morning they sighted the lights of Stornoway and got their kit and their presents together, ready to go ashore to greet families and friends waiting in scores at the harbour. By an error of judgment a vital alteration of course was too long delayed and the vessel struck rocks just east of the harbour. Almost at once she listed heavily and started to settle with huge seas breaking over her. But so close was she to the shore that many men jumped for it, confident of struggling across the ten yards or so of heaving water between them and safety. Most drowned, or were smashed to death on the rocks, while just a mile away the crowd at the harbour waited for their men, unaware that anything was amiss until the stunning appearance of a few half-drowned men gasping out the news and calling for a rescue party. Little could be done because the sea had already started to break the vessel apart. In all, two hundred and six men died, their bodies being thrown up on to the shore to be identified and mourned by families with party food and drink untasted in their homes.

The people of Lewis drew together in their misery as they had so often done in the past. Leverhulme expressed his condolences and generously supported the relief fund. But, for all the success of his campaign to introduce himself to the Islanders, the tragedy set him apart from them and all he could be was a sympathetic stranger. The economic and social problems were for a time immersed in the misery. But the spring was coming and sowing had to be done.

In the first days of March 1919 men invaded the Island farms, drove off the farmers' animals, broke down boundary walls, and staked out six-acre plots. The 'raids' had begun – they were, said the men, a demonstration against the Government and its slowness, and they confidently expected Leverhulme's approval and support.

The raiding spread rapidly all over Lewis, and by the summer sixteen out of the twenty-two farms on the Island had been affected. The raiders were surprised when Leverhulme made it clear that he disapproved totally of their law-breaking and asked them to leave the farms. Some did, but others put up shelters for their families on the stolen plots. Meanwhile, opposition to the raiders was expressed in many quarters when it was learned that the Proprietor was against them. Leverhulme took no legal action against the men who remained in occupation of the farms after he had asked them to leave. He was unwilling to prosecute ex-servicemen, however misguided, who were trying to secure homes for their families, and he was far from sure that such legal action would have been successful when there was considerable support for the raiders within the Island, and even more from highly vocal politicians on the mainland. He travelled round Lewis addressing gatherings of raiders and others, trying to persuade them that their future lay with him and not the old, failed crofting system. At one such meeting in the open air there were nearly a thousand present, and he was cheered as he left. But he may have been misled by such cordiality. Many of the Islanders felt a loyalty to him as Proprietor; they liked what they regarded as his rich eccentricity; they awaited his new schemes with interest and the hope of profit. He made a good and amusing speech so they cheered him, but they did not lightly cast away old ideas, and they would still probably support crofting. Unequivocal support for Leverhulme was strongest in Stornoway, while the Free Church, worried perhaps about an industrial Sabbath, studiedly omitted to condemn the raiding. The Highland Land League openly approved the raiding and supplied money to the raiders. If there was some doubt about the extent of genuine support for Leverhulme in Lewis and Harris there was almost unanimous criticism of him elsewhere. The House of Commons, perhaps naturally, allowed themselves to be guided by the new Member for the Western Isles. But Murray was personally dedicated to land reform, and his commitments at Westminster kept him too long away from his remote constituency. He was not able to perceive the extent of local feeling for Leverhulme which therefore went unrepresented in the House. Leverhulme was particularly hurt by the criticism of him, even from his own party, during the Scottish Estimates debate in August 1919. The Liberal member for Montrose accused him of 'taking upon himself to tell these people . . . that their future lives are to be guided along lines laid down, not by themselves . . . but according to the dictates of a successful soap-boiler who happened to buy up that island'. Meanwhile, when the Proprietor landed at Stornoway within days of this debate he was greeted by cheering crowds and fireworks. Munro, under some political pressure, insisted that he must pursue the break-up of the farms, and Leverhulme's attitude towards him hardened. He now asked for ten years' postponement of further land reform in Lewis and Harris to give him time to prove his scheme. He supported the request with a threat that a continuation of the current official policy would probably lead to him abandoning his schemes. On this note – but with work forging ahead on factories, power-house, gas works, houses, and roads – Leverhulme, in November 1919, left for the United States, while in London the directors of his company negotiated the Niger deal, which would cripple Lever Brothers financially for several years.

When Leverhulme returned early in 1920 he found that there had been more raiding on Lewis and he went up to see what he could do. By now he was aware of the serious financial problem facing Lever Brothers, who had to raise a very large sum in cash in the next few months to pay for the Niger Company. It suited his purse, and it suited his mood at the time, to make a punitive gesture which saved him something over ten thousand pounds a year, equivalent in capital to a small but significant fraction of the money needed by Lever Brothers. He announced that he intended in future to concentrate his efforts on Stornoway and on Harris, and that all work in the country areas of Lewis would be abandoned.

His plans for Harris were not so elaborate as those for Lewis and they went ahead more smoothly. The southern island – or southern part of the joint island – had a smaller and more scattered population, and there were no large farms to attract raiders. Because Leverhulme had bought Harris a little later than Lewis his plans had been correspondingly delayed and both he and the local population had been able to profit from the mistakes in the north. The men of Harris had a certain neighbourly antagonism towards Lewis and were prepared to put themselves out to attract to the south the Proprietor's interest, favour, and subsidy. He in his turn made it quite clear what he expected, and at a meeting at Obbe he meticulously obtained the agreement of the people of Harris on a number of points of co-operation. Included in the public promises was the abandonment of raiding, a ten-year ban on seeking more crofts, and even the option of clearing crofts if necessary as long as alternative land was provided at Leverhulme's expense. All these points were put repeatedly to the meeting and translated into Gaelic so that there was no room for misunderstanding. The somewhat wary atmosphere at the meeting was a little mellowed when it was proposed that Obbe should be renamed Leverburgh as more fitting for the new port that would be built there. In mentioning this to Munro, Leverhulme gave the impression that after the enthusiastic meeting the residents had quite independently approached him with a request so to use his name. There is, however, some evidence that he may have helped the idea forward by suggesting that the port should be renamed after one of the earlier Proprietors. The official change of name in 1920 was, at any rate, made on the petition of the crofters to the Postmaster General.

The termination of Leverhulme's schemes in Lewis, apart from Stornoway, hardened the resolve of the raiders not to budge.

Leverhulme took legal action against them after appeals to them by his local agent had been ignored. By April 1920, when he himself was away from Britain on one of his frequent journeys abroad, he had the necessary legal powers to have raiders committed to prison, and many people on Lewis wished to see him do so. But, in an interview with Leverhulme's representative, the Secretary of State for Scotland, Munro, asked that the men should not be committed to prison and pointed out that if this happened then as Secretary for Scotland he had the power to order their release. Munro and Leverhulme gave accounts of this incident which differed slightly, but enough to reflect a certain discredit on one or the other of them depending upon which version is accepted. Indisputable are the facts that Leverhulme did not have the raiders committed to prison, and that he was furiously angry. He was on his way back from South Africa, and had his representative come out to the Canary Isles to meet his ship and explain the position to him fully. From there he cabled orders that legal proceedings against the raiders should be dropped, that no further materials were to be shipped to Stornoway, and that all work of his on Lewis was to cease except to make unfinished buildings weatherproof.

The announcement caused astonishment and uproar in Lewis. Leverhulme's attitude that it had been forced upon him by the intransigence of the Secretary for Scotland was widely accepted, and when he visited the Island in June 1920 he was once more greeted by thousands of cheering people on the quay at Stornoway. It is noteworthy that July 1920 was the deadline for paying the cash for the Niger Company, and once again, as with the earlier partial shut-down on Lewis, economic difficulty was one more factor determining his decision, in addition to the angry response of a frustrated man, and the sharp eye for an astute manoeuvre in what had now become a personal battle with Munro.

He swiftly consolidated his position in this battle by making a concession and agreeing to release some important farms on the west coast for crofts. Then he stated simply, publicly, and frequently, that all he now wanted before resuming his public works in Lewis was a ten-year guarantee of freedom from Scottish Office interference: that is, Munro must not take his farms nor must he hint at rescinding any punishment imposed on raiders in the law courts. Support for Leverhulme and murmuring against the Scottish Office and the Government now grew to such an extent that Munro mentioned the matter in Cabinet and asked Lloyd George whether, in spite of an imminent coal strike, he might have permission to[9] 'visit Lewis and endeavour to compose the differences between Leverhulme and ex-service raiders, as a result of which he has stopped schemes in Lewis which were bringing in four thousand pounds a week (or nearly) to the island'.

It was agreed that Munro should go to Lewis as soon as possible, but before he could do so his wife died and the visit was undertaken instead by the Lord Advocate, who was not a Cabinet Minister but was even more dedicated than Munro to land reform. This official visit in October 1920 did not materially change the situation. Any local sympathy with the raiders was being eroded in spite of – perhaps to some extent because of – supporters outside the Island, including some left-wing extremists. At the end of December 1920, at meetings throughout Lewis called for the purpose, votes of confidence were taken on Leverhulme's proposals, and resolutions were put promising abstinence from raiding for ten years. In most cases the votes were unanimous, and overall there was probably 99 per cent support for Leverhulme.

Munro asked to see the Prime Minister to discuss the matter, which he described as[10] 'vital and urgent', and in January 1921 he wrote to Leverhulme and conceded defeat: as long as the development schemes proceeded, the Scottish Office would take no more land for crofts.

With victory won over Munro and the Scottish Office, Leverhulme should have been able to re-focus on the main issue of rehabilitating Lewis. A great effort now, with a massive injection of cash into the Island, would bring things rapidly to the point where there would be results to show, most raiding would fade away in the face of public opinion, and the remainder would be stamped out by legal action. But just at this crucial time Leverhulme was rigidly locked in the financial difficulties of Lever Brothers and the Niger Company, there were threats of liquidation in the air, his own bankers were refusing to advance him money on overdraft, and he could not realise capital for fear of almost certainly upsetting the precariously poised financial credibility of his Company. There was no triumphant surge forward of Lewis affairs – instead came a huge reduction by Leverhulme in his private expenditure, including an end to improvements at the Castle and a cutback in staff. He made a small and ineffectual gesture of starting some public work in April 1921, but Leverhulme's grand scheme for Lewis was now firmly directed downhill to oblivion. In May all work stopped, he withdrew his representative from the Island, and cancelled all the summer invitations to Lews Castle. On August 31st in a speech at Stornoway he formally admitted that the slump in world trade would prevent any resumption of the work during 1921.

As soon as he read the reports of Leverhulme's speech Munro was on to him in a flash. He sent him a letter dated 3 September 1921, by hand, to his home at Hampstead, saying that he now considered himself relieved of any undertaking given previously, and that he proposed to put in hand,[11] 'a generous measure of land settlement'. There was no riposte Leverhulme could make other than to accept and say that this would of course make it impossible for him, or anyone else, to develop the Island. In a petulant, dismissive phrase he told Munro that he should get on at once with the resettlement of all the land on all the big farms, and that he would not stand in his way. There was here, just the seed in his mind of a final gesture yet to come, which would combine in a remarkable fashion altruistic public benefaction and bloody-minded personal vindictiveness.

The winter of 1921 brought severe unemployment to Great Britain and acute distress to Lewis. That winter, and all through 1922, many hundreds of young men and a few girls completed their arrangements to emigrate. The first three hundred went to Canada in the spring of 1923 on board a liner which called specially at Stornoway and took them all away in one batch. During this sad period Leverhulme made one or two empty gestures towards a future when he might take up again his work in Lewis, but such little serious effort as he could manage was directed towards Harris, where Borve Lodge now became his residence when he visited the Western Isles. In October 1922

Leverhulme with Harry Lauder

Port Harcourt, departure 1924

Leverhulme houses at Stornoway

Munro lost his place as Secretary for Scotland when the Conservatives took office.

In November 1922 Leverhulme's elevation to a Viscountcy in Lloyd George's resignation Honours List precipitated an unedifying squabble that paraded in a trivial charade some of the attitudes which had contributed to the real tragedy in Lewis. Leverhulme felt sentimentally attached to the Western Isles, even after his disappointments there, as he did to Bolton, his native town and part of his Baronial title. He now proposed to adopt the style 'Viscount Leverhulme of the Western Isles', and there was an outcry that this would be offensive because it was so close to 'Lord of the Isles', a royal title of great significance in Scottish history. Most of the people who actually lived on Lewis and Harris were pleased that he chose to include them in his title, but Gaelic Societies on the mainland felt the insult keenly and complained widely and loudly. Scotland's independence was declared to be affronted because Lyon King at Arms had not been properly consulted by the College of Heralds. Hairs were split and feathers ruffled, but the Sovereign had approved the title and no one took any official action to change it.

On 3 September 1923, two years to the day after Munro's letter which signalled the end of the Lewis venture, Leverhulme addressed the Stornoway Council and the Lewis District Council at a meeting which he had asked should be specially convened on that date. His audience gathered expectantly with much speculation about what they would hear, but no one came near guessing what a stunning effect his speech would have. He told them that he intended to leave Lewis and that he wanted to retain no part of it. All the crofters could have as a gift the freehold of their land, and the rest of the property – Castle, farms, sporting rights and lodges – would be vested in Trusts on behalf of the people of the town of Stornoway and the country districts of Lewis. He gave them a month to accept his offer and left the hall, saying privately to a friend[12] that this was one of the two saddest days of his life, the other being the day he lost his dear wife.

It took a little while for the raiders, and the extremists of the Highland Land League, and the administrators of the Scottish Office, and the departed Munro, to realise that this magnificent gesture had struck the head off the highly evolved body of land resettlement agitation in the Islands. Leverhulme told them to take the land and make their system work. The crofters, the Lewis District Committee and the Scottish Office examined the gift, considered the implications of owning and running the property, and shied terrified away. Only Stornoway, always on Leverhulme's side, accepted the gift, set up the Trust, and to a large extent made it work for the benefit of the town.

Left with so much of the Island he no longer wanted, Leverhulme sold off as much as he could, many of the buyers being interested principally in the shooting and fishing.

It was a truly Pyrrhic victory for him. His enemies had been forced to admit that they would rather welcome the reviled sporting landlords than themselves own the land they had campaigned for; but the Leverhulme plan for a prosperous Lewis was totally in ruins.

The poet and author Louis MacNeice who spoke no Gaelic and lived in London, visited the Islands in the 1930s and described the complex nature of the inhabitants with affection, unblinded by sentiment, in a book[13] which included 'The Ballad of Lord Leverhulme', from which the following verses are taken:

Lord Leverhulme was a grocer's son,
He learned to sell when he was young,
And all the tunes that he could play
Was 'Advertising makes it pay' –
    Over the hills and across the skies,
    By God it pays to advertise.

. . . . . . .

Nearing seventy Lever said,
'Just one more coup before I'm dead:
I'll help those lame dogs over their stiles,
I'll stamp my name on the Western Isles.'

. . . . . . .

Lever started the heavenly climb,
He went up the stairs two at a time.
St. Peter said, 'Make room, make room,
Here comes Viscount Leverhulme.'

St. Peter said, 'Don't be cross with me
But this is a mere formality;
Have you any failure to confess?'
And Lever truthfully answered, 'Yes.

I left my programme incomplete,
The Western Islands had me beat.'
St. Peter said, 'I'm not surprised;
To tackle Lewis was ill-advised.

. . . . . . .

The Scottish Islands are a rotten deal,
Those Celts are terribly difficile;
We find them unwilling to pull their weight
When we let them in at the Golden Gate.

They've no team spirit, they won't take part
In our study circles and community art
And at garden parties they won't concur
In speaking English – which is de rigeur.

. . . . . . .

So welcome now to the realms divine
And sign your name on the dotted line.
You'll find the life up here a spree
For Heaven is a joint-stock company.'

. . . . . . .

But far below in the Western Seas
The moors were quiet in the Hebrides,
The crofters gossiped in Gaelic speech
And the waves crept over the lonely beach.

More than anything else, the drying up of Leverhulme's financial resources at the crucial moment caused the failure in Lewis. Even this might only have delayed the project if the past intolerant behaviour of the factions towards each other had not ruled out any chance of them waiting patiently for better days. Much of the intolerance was on Leverhulme's side, particularly towards what he thought was the visionless bumbling of officials. Towards his opponents among the people of Lewis he showed not so much intolerance as impatient disbelief at the way they failed to make up their minds. He did not believe that their characters and aspirations were complex. In another context (p. 82) he had specifically chosen the Scotsman as an example of a hard practical man without imagination. Such a man should instantly have recognised the material advantages he was being offered, and realised that the croft kept him from giving his full attention to a proper job of work. Much the same might have been said of observing the Sabbath or drinking whisky, and Leverhulme could not see that to persuade the traditional Lewisman to give up any of these activities would require a long wooing. If his only objective had been to make Lewis a profitable industrial unit he might have succeeded by importing labour, like a modern oil man. But Leverhulme wanted to change – too quickly – the people as well as the economy, and this was the root of his personal failure.

When Leverhulme's wife died in 1913 he had tried to blunt the edge of bereavement by making his third journey round the world, with a close family party. Now, at the 'second saddest' time of his life, he made his fourth round-the-world voyage. He was away from the autumn of 1923 to the spring of 1924. Different members of the Company travelled with him for different parts of the journey, but two men accompanied him all the way: D'Arcy Cooper, now the Vice-Chairman of Lever Brothers, and Jonathan Simpson, the companion of Leverhulme's childhood and youth, and still a close friend in old age.

Cooper's influence on the Company was growing rapidly since his rescue act over the financing of the Niger deal and the discharge in the nick of time of the two million pound hidden overdraft. Leverhulme liked and admired him, and was happy enough to be easing responsibility on to someone who had already saved the Company from disaster. The number and variety of enterprises in the Lever Brothers stable was now very large, and Cooper was kept busy unravelling the tangled reigns of authority which once had led to a single pair of hands. He was converting the administrative structure of the Company as comprehensively as Leverhulme himself would have tackled a house or estate. Not only was he changing the business style from one-man grocery to multi-function international, but he was also looking to the financial foundations which had become a matter of some public concern now that Lever Brothers had grown so large. The published accounts of the Company and its associates were complex and obscure, sometimes deliberately so. Profit figures and dividends were boosted by the sale of assets, the Chairman issued certain shares to himself at below market price and sold them at a profit. The *Investors Chronicle* commented,[14] 'Obviously if you own all the shares in any Company you can call the value of them what you like. But the prudent man would be slow in valuing his own investments to offset definite loss in one direction by theoretical gains in another.' The justification of such cavalier financial manipulation on the grounds that Leverhulme controlled all the Ordinary shares had become more and more unconvincing since these now represented less than one-twentieth of the issued capital, and the Preference shareholders thus bore a considerable element of the risk.

With the withdrawal from Lewis and all its schemes, Leverhulme had more time to concern himself again with the affairs of Lever Brothers. This development was not altogether welcome to Cooper and his fellow directors, who had been inclined to feel that the Chairman's extravagances in the Western Isles, although singularly ill-timed in such a difficult financial period, had the merit of keeping him away from some of the discussions about reorganisation and future policy, which consequently were considerably less fraught with tension and anxiety than they might have been. A further result of the failure in Lewis was that Lever Brothers acquired a number of extra interests which Leverhulme now saw fit to sell to the Company: Mac Fisheries with its subsidiaries including Wall's ice-cream and sausages, and another large food company which had belonged to Angus Watson, an old friend and ex-employee who had done well in business on his own account with 'Skipper' sardines his most famous product. However unwelcome the administrative complications of adding these and other food groups to the Company, the acquisitions turned out to have great importance in the future development of the great Lever combine.

By the early 1920s, with Leverhulme over seventy and beginning to retire from full command, things had changed at Port Sunlight. Boom and expansion had given way to slump, and it was no longer the apple of an ever-watchful Chairman's eye. He still took a considerable part in the discussion of labour problems in the Works, and indeed some of his contributions were violently expressed to the Board when he disagreed with their proposals. In some cases such violence appeared to be incited not so much by a particular decision as by general frustration and anger at changing times and conditions, which sometimes caused him to flounder among unfamiliar problems and unpalatable solutions.

The general recession in trade induced a world trend towards the shutting down of factories and the limitation of production. Leverhulme regarded this as probably the most distasteful and reprehensible business policy short of defrauding the public of their money. Although he resisted any curtailment of activity, he had to accept that Port Sunlight did not need, and could not afford to retain, all its employees – something over eight thousand. New techniques and higher efficiency had improved production over the previous few years, and the public demand could now be satisfied with many hundred fewer employees. It stuck in Leverhulme's gullet that the result of efficiency was to be unemployment, and when he was no longer able to sustain his resistance to the cuts he stubbornly shifted his ground to the way in which the dismissals would be carried out.

It was unfortunate that the first cuts – affecting a thousand people – were scheduled to be made soon after the big strike which had arisen out of a dispute between two unions at Port Sunlight (p. 178). Leverhulme insisted that no employee who had been 'loyal' to the Company during the strike should be dismissed. His son pointed out that not to strike was not necessarily to be loyal, since some unions had not called out their members. To confine dismissals to those who had struck would be to violate the fundamental Trade Union principle of no victimisation, to say nothing of some of Leverhulme's own stated views about the right to strike. The Chairman raged and stormed, but in the end the dismissals were made without the loyalty test, and with pensions and cash payments which were generous by the standards of the time. Soon afterwards wages at Port Sunlight were cut, as they were throughout British industry. Leverhulme was proud that his rates were still above the union level, and he introduced some modest unemployment and sickness benefits within the Company. But these were pathetic tatters compared with the grand benevolent flourishes of the old days, and he had no imaginative scheme ready for the new conditions.

There was in 1922 a dispute concerning the introduction of a Two Shift System which led to the Home Secretary receiving a Trade Union delegation complaining about the hardship it inflicted upon the workers.[15] The early shift started at 6 a.m. and there was a special train to Port Sunlight which left Birkenhead at 5.10 a.m. But since the Liverpool tramcars did not start running until 5 a.m. some people, including women and young girls, were having to leave home at 4 a.m. and walk through the dark streets to the Mersey ferry, subject to 'all the great danger of molestation in a cosmopolitan seaport town'. Before the system was put into operation, three hundred and eighty girls in the Dry Soap Factory were asked by their supervisor whether they were prepared to work shifts. Only half a dozen were in favour, and when this was reported to the works manager in the morning it was said that the proposal would be dropped. But that afternoon 'the new manager from America' stated that two hundred girls would be dismissed if they did not agree to try the system for a six-week period. After four weeks, when there was a ballot about continuing the shift work, the girls were required to write their tally numbers on their voting papers.

These were the sort of complaints that could not have arisen if Leverhulme had been following the affairs of Port Sunlight with his old enthusiasm, but if by some mischance anything like this had occurred in the old days then the complaints would have been heard and settled in the Chairman's office, not in Whitehall.

The cuts of the bleak 1920s seemed very remote from the warmth and promise of the big Co-Partners meetings in the old Auditorium, yet, though the times were hard and jobs scarce, labour conditions had moved forward. In the half-century of Leverhulme's working life many of his own employees had progressed, from homes of such poverty that improvement was the only aim, to an undreamed-of standard of living which they feared to lose. Leverhulme became increasingly aware that fear could motivate as strongly as reward, perhaps more strongly than small reward. In 1923 he considered the causes of the increased efficiency of Lever Brothers and decided that it was[16] 'not the fact of any increased bonus, but the fact that we had begun to comb out inefficient men. We have been combing out inefficient men, and too highly paid men, elderly men, and men past their work. . . . I am confident that this has produced a state of "fear" in the minds of the remainder . . . and it is this, in my opinion, which has been the cause of the improved efficiency results achieved today.' He himself had never known personal financial deprivation; but he had always felt keenly the fear of failure, and as Chairman of Lever Brothers he had particularly dreaded having to come empty-handed to the shareholders at the Company annual meeting. Once or twice in the past the Ordinary Dividend had only been saved by financial manoeuvres that were not to everyone's taste. But in these crisis days there was a serious probability of real financial disaster, and Leverhulme recognised his own motivation when explaining why in the 1920s he was driving himself – and others – harder than ever:[17] 'if I must be perfectly candid with myself I am convinced that it has been the gnawing fear in my heart that Lever Brothers would have to pass their dividends. I had placed myself in this position by accepting money from all classes of investors, including widows, spinsters, clergymen, and others – all subscribers for Lever Brothers shares from the confidence that they had in the business and myself, and that these might possibly have to forgo their dividends which would mean probably curtailment of what they depended upon for their day-to-day food, clothing, rent, etc. Candidly, this has been my great "fear", and this is what has caused me to get up at 4.30 in the morning.'

In 1921 a quite unexpected competitor caused considerable alarm to Lever Brothers. A number of British seed-crushing mills and oil refineries had been in loose combination since the turn of the century and, under the title of British Oil and Cake Mills, they had grown greatly in strength during the War and had entered the margarine trade. In 1921 they formed the British Soap Company and put on the market 'New Pin', a direct competitor to Sunlight, aggressively promoted with extensive and striking advertising and a very lavish gift scheme. There was close similarity between the methods of Lever Brothers and those of the British Oil and Cake Mills, particularly in their diversification policy and the way in which they went about building up trade in the soap business. Their success was considerable and Lever Brothers felt themselves threatened not only by the loss of custom but also by the possibility of a revival of the extremely expensive gift wars of the pre-1914 era. In 1924 negotiations started between Lever Brothers and the British Soap Company to bring the gift scheme to an end. But, under Leverhulme's influence, the scope of the bargaining was dramatically enlarged. The whole of the British Oil and Cake Mills passed into the hands of Lever Brothers, the gift scheme ceased, 'New Pin' was allowed to fade away, and a vast new interest in milling and refining was acquired by the Lever combine.

This was Leverhulme operating with all his old business confidence and enterprise. In personal affairs, too, he retained his old bite. He commissioned Sir William Orpen to paint a full-length portrait of him in his robes as Mayor of Bolton, and the picture was completed and presented by Leverhulme to the Corporation of Bolton in the late summer of 1921. So soon after the enjoyable scandal of the row with Augustus John, the newspapers and their public were delighted to discover that Leverhulme and Orpen were in dispute about the price to be paid for the portrait. They had agreed upon a fee of three thousand pounds for a full-length portrait of the subject standing. The delivered picture showed him seated, and was therefore, Leverhulme calculated, only a three-quarters portrait and not to be charged at the full rate. Before the matter was settled without too much ill-feeling there was a quite disproportionate amount of public and private comment and correspondence. In a Third Leader, *The Times* commented[18] rather acidly that 'The British public is often accused of indifference to art, but unjustly. It has a curious, irrelevant interest in art as a commodity, the price of which is incalculable.'

Leverhulme's own greatest contribution to public art, the Lady Lever Art Gallery at Port Sunlight, was officially opened in December 1922. He had given much time to every aspect of this project, from the design of the building to the arrangement of the exhibits which were many of the very best items from his own huge collection. The Derby shepherd and shepherdess, which had started it all in Wigan, were given a prominent place. So, too, was a Napoleon room, containing furniture from Malmaison, a death mask of the Emperor, and a number of his personal possessions. Whether Leverhulme considered the furniture to be ornamental in a room dedicated to Napoleon or Napoleon to provide a handy theme for a fine collection of furniture is open to conjecture. No detail of the gallery that might be improved by his personal attention was ignored, however small. He supervised the craftsmen preparing the plaster decoration for the Adam room, specifying exactly the colour shades he thought correct. When one or two small objects were stolen during opening hours he suggested that several of the widows living in Port Sunlight would be glad to earn a little extra money by sitting with their knitting in the gallery for a few hours a week as a deterrent to pilfering.

In the 1920s, especially after the closing of Lews Castle, Leverhulme's social life was centred on The Hill, his house at Hampstead, where his sister acted as hostess for him. A neighbour told how cheerfully Leverhulme welcomed visitors, especially children, in spite of the deafness which sometimes only allowed him to catch an isolated sentence or two;[19] 'but the effort was too great for long social intercourse and the company soon preferred to listen to the flow of excellent pointed stories that would often pour from him in increasing stream. . . . That was when he was in the mood. At other times he would remain quite silent absorbed by his own cheerful thoughts. . . . I remember attending a great dinner party at his Hampstead house. Lord Leverhulme sat in a large solitary chair at the head of the table and his sister, who was equally deaf, at the other end. He was silent throughout the dinner but his smile bathed us in a pleasant radiance. It had the effect of gracious speech, and suddenly over the dessert he really spoke, "It is a great advantage to be deaf," he said, beaming on us all, "because you can't hear anything that is said against you." We all hastened to protest that we were far removed from such a crime, but he heard nothing and having spoken he lapsed again into a prolonged silence of smiles. Then once again he broke the silence, "Another advantage of being deaf," he said, "is in business. You can form your own plans and need not listen to anyone's advice." Again he smiled and went silent.'

His disability did not prevent him from entertaining on a large scale, and he developed the trick of making set speeches and stories take the place of conversation, so that he appeared to be playing a part in the talk. On occasion he might rise at the end of each course and propose a toast with a brief speech. His similar technique in handling public political meetings sometimes brought discomfiture to his chairman. After delivering a provocative speech he might walk off the platform saying he would not be able to hear questions, and leaving the unfortunate chairman alone to 'face the tigers'.

Leverhulme became extremely fond of dancing in his late sixties, and he had a fine ballroom built at The Hill where he often invited a few young people specially for the dancing which took place after dinner. He was rather concerned that this interest might be thought frivolous in a man of his age. He told his son,[20] 'the explanation is simply this: I spend the day entirely surrounded by men, and I don't want to spend my evenings also in ponderous conversation with men. I like to have a few young friends about me whom I can chaff. It keeps my mind young, and prevents me becoming dull and heavy.'

Leverhulme was in his office at Lever House very frequently, and when he was away he corresponded regularly with his son about the business, not necessarily the most important affairs of the Company but often smaller matters which he understood well and which particularly interested him. Advertising was such a topic. In July 1922 he wrote[21] to his son agreeing that they might advertise in *John Bull* now that Horatio Bottomley was no longer associated with the paper. Father and son were also in agreement[22] about the advertising value of sky-writing. Lever Brothers had spent a thousand pounds on twenty-five flights, mostly over seaside holiday towns, where VIM or LUX was the word written in smoke in the sky. Leverhulme felt that the principal value of such stunts was in the newspaper publicity they attracted, but felt that this particular one was not worth continuing. On a rather different scale of advertising Leverhulme was pleased to be able to tell his son that Lutyens had invited him to provide miniature tablets of Sunlight for Queen Mary's Doll's House, but he regretted that there seemed little prospect of getting their margarine in. Occasionally Leverhulme's own projects would come into the correspondence and he was delighted to report favourably on the first season's herring fishing from Leverburgh in the summer of 1924.

There was one matter on which father and son were not in agreement. Despite the wishes and advice of family, friends, and doctors, Leverhulme was absolutely determined to visit Africa in the winter of 1924. Those who argued against it knew that this would be no retirement cruise in the sunshine for a seventy-three-year-old but a punishing journey taking in rough and unhealthy country, with every available hour occupied by some task or discussion. Each meeting or excursion or inspection would be taken at such speed and intensity that all present would be exhausted, except Leverhulme, who would move on to tackle the next job and to wear out a fresh set of managers and officials. In the face of all the opposition Leverhulme declared that he would still go to Africa if the way were lined with machine-guns and mines. In Africa were the best and the worst of his great commercial–social enterprises and he wanted, therefore, to inspect each of them.

Les Huileries du Congo Belge had prospered and brought increasing profit to the Company, while Leverhulme's social ideas had enormously raised the material standards of a native population long used to starvation, squalor, and disease. Seven mills now processed sixty thousand tons of palm fruit and kernels every year and produced ten thousand tons of oil. Seventeen thousand natives and two hundred Europeans were employed. A thousand kilometres of road had been built, and a railway seventy kilometres long, while the Company's river fleet had nineteen steamers and over seventy barges. There were ten hospitals, three large schools, and, for the natives, five hundred brick houses, soon to be increased to twelve hundred. Indeed such was the prosperous momentum of the Congo project that most of these figures would go up by half in the next year or two. The success was now clear to all, and Leverhulme enjoyed the interested enquiries and congratulations of King Albert and the Belgian Government who had given him virtually a free hand in this enormous tropical colony. In contrast, his parallel venture in the British colonies in West Africa had been a failure, entirely due in Leverhulme's opinion to the pedestrian incompetence of the Colonial Office and the British civil servants in West Africa.

Leverhulme was well pleased with what he found in the Congo in October 1924. He wrote in his diary,[23] 'What a change in 12 years! I see visibly great change in appearance but there is even a greater improvement and advance in both white and black members of the staff.' He did not however think that the black man was yet ready for management responsibility as the natives had not acquired organising ability even in limited areas such as the wooding stations which provided fuel for river steamers.[24] 'One can always tell a white man's wooding station by the ample stocks of wood. It takes a white man to organise a wooding station.' There were flaws in his own organisation of course. He wrote[25] of a white employee as 'a good man, reported however to flog the natives, which is illegal and must be stopped if the case'. In one area he was not satisfied with the medical facilities which were shared with a Railway Company:[26] 'This system works badly and cannot continue. We must have a doctor and at once. Our concession requires it and humanity demands it without delay.' More philosophically, he reflected on a visit to Sunday Service at the Baptist Mission in Kinshasa where the congregation was exclusively white, the negroes being obliged to attend at a different time. Apparently the Coast negroes had requested to be allowed to attend the 'white' service, and had been asked if they would then be willing for the Congo negroes also to attend with them. The reply was 'No'. Recording all this in his diary[27] Leverhulme concluded, 'What will heaven be like?'

As he left the Congo Leverhulme wrote home,[28] 'Although we were all greatly impressed with what had been done, we have really only begun to scratch the soil. . . . we are all full of enthusiasm and confidence in the future of our Belgian Concessions.' It was with very different feelings that he approached the next stage of his journey, a visit to British West Africa. The trouble in West Africa was Colonial Office policy on land tenure, although in Leverhulme's view this was run a close second by Sir Hugh Clifford, a Colonial civil servant and Governor.

As far back as 1908 Lever Brothers had commenced their bid for palm-oil concessions in British West Africa. Almost at once they had on the one hand been suspected by competitors of being unduly favoured by the Colonial Office, and on the other hand been suspected by the Colonial Office of wanting to get possession of the natives' land and exploit it unscrupulously. The Colonial Office policy was that the freehold of land in the Colonies must not be purchased by British companies. Lever Brothers wanted freeholds to protect the capital they would have to invest, but the best deal they could get was a twenty-year concession to operate in certain areas. The concession gave them the exclusive right of erecting mills in these areas to extract oil from palm fruit and kernels bought from the natives.

It was at this stage that Clifford began to display his rather truculent opposition to instructions from the Colonial Office, and became a symbol to Leverhulme of unintelligent and ill-natured obstruction. In a despatch to the Secretary of State from Government House, Accra, Clifford reported that he had delayed the passage of the Palm Oil Bill through the Legislative Council because he did not believe that certain aspects had been sufficiently considered. In particular he did not approve of Lever Brothers being given the monopoly of erecting mills in their concession areas because the natives might eventually acquire sufficient money to do this themselves.[29] 'If . . . all land is to be recognized as the property of the natives, and if Government is to restrict its interference with land to such regulation of its management as may be dictated by a higher appreciation of the common interest than is possessed by the native landowners, I can see no justification for introducing legislation one of the effects of which will be to prohibit native landowners from adopting improved methods for treating their own produce. Yet such, I submit, is the nature of the Palm Oil Bill now before the Legislative Council. . . . In the event of it being held that the objection now raised to the principle of the Bill is not valid, I shall be greatly obliged if you will instruct me as to the line of argument whereby it is to be met.'

The Secretary of State, Harcourt, pointed out that there was no reason why natives should not combine together and be granted concessions under the Ordinance. He went on,[30] 'I trust that, in view of these considerations you will be able to induce the Unofficial Members to reconsider their opposition to the Ordinance, but, if not, it must be carried by the use of the official vote, as I cannot withdraw from my pledge to Messrs Lever to pass the Ordinance substantially in the form which it has now taken.'

But Clifford was not one to lie down at the first intimation of defeat. He replied at once,[31] 'I need not say that it is with the utmost reluctance that I again enter upon a discussion of the question, but I must crave your patience for a further hearing because it appears to me that a principle of great moment is involved. . . .' He needed to crave patience, for his despatch was of tremendous length, but to no avail. The Bill was passed but the battle was far from finished.

Incorporated in the detailed conditions of the concessions was a rule that all particulars of the operations carried out by concessionaires must be made available, in confidence, to the Governor so that he might decide whether it was in the interests of the Colony that further similar concessions should be granted. Leverhulme wrote privately to the Secretary of State[32] expressing his anxiety: 'it is obvious that if, on receipt of this information, the Governor considers that we have not, in his opinion, by that time attained sufficient success our so-called concessions will be terminated. If, on the other hand, he considers we have made a success, he will make like grants to our competitors who have risked nothing, but, on the contrary, have taken the wise precaution of waiting the result of our experiment. . . . I consider that this Ordinance and Rule 9 constitute a most harsh and arbitrary dealing with us, practically before the ink is dry on the signatures to the so-called concession.'

The letter did the trick, and orders went out from Whitehall for the rule to be repealed. It was something of a moral victory for Leverhulme, but the whole affair had turned him against any further major investment in British West Africa, where the constant obstruction contrasted so strongly with the free hand he had in the Congo where he had made great progress.

After the War the dismal performance in British West Africa and the obvious success of the Congo enterprise seemed to Leverhulme to make redundant any further argument about the relative merits of his approach, and that of the Colonial Office administrators, to improving the lot of the African native. But with the purchase of the Niger Company in 1920 Lever Brothers acquired substantial new trading interests in British West Africa and Leverhulme came again into conflict with Clifford, now Governor of Nigeria. The new argument was about fiscal policy, in particular the imposition of duties to replace the revenue lost when liquor imports were banned in response to a League of Nations recommendation. For Leverhulme the attack on the new duties was no more than the exercise of pressure to secure a commercial advantage. Clifford, for his part, was doing no more than defend an *ad hoc* set of taxes improvised to replace revenue unexpectedly lost. No principles were at stake, but there was pride and antipathy. In Leverhulme's public speeches he often returned to the old theme of misguided land policy: 'Europe will not agree that the British people should straddle all the hundreds of thousands of acres of tropical land, capable of producing cotton . . . and other products, under some bureaucratic and autocratic form of Government, which, ostrich-like, buries its head in the sand and refuses to see the march of progress. Crown colonies, under the policy which prevails, have become a collection of tin tents. Substantial buildings can only be erected on freehold property.' Leverhulme did not forbear to mention Clifford by name in his speeches, and Clifford replied publicly with what Leverhulme called[33] 'a torrent of undignified abuse'. When Leverhulme was visiting Lagos in 1925 at the end of his African tour he was officially entertained by Clifford at Government House, and in return invited Clifford to dine with him in his yacht. With maximum offensiveness and publicity Clifford refused the invitation, thereby causing considerable Press comment in Africa and Britain.

The post-war quarrel between the two men, a silly, old men's feud, publicly conducted, was in Leverhulme's case rooted in his lifelong contempt for bureaucracy. His inability to manage officials showed up in the Western Isles and in Africa, and in both these instances he abandoned one place, with some show of petulance, and moved elsewhere. He ignored British West Africa in his building and development, and made a brilliant success of the project in the Congo, regarding this as one in the eye for Clifford and the Colonial Office. He left Lewis and moved to Harris, expecting there to bring off a success that would be one in the eye for Munro and the Scottish Office. Leverhulme thought the bureaucrats were stupid, and they thought he was 'too clever by half'. Each party was jealous of the special power wielded by the other, and neither seemed to believe that the other might be motivated by high principles.

On 15 March 1925 Leverhulme arrived back in London from Africa and closed his special diary with the words 'Home Sweet Home'. It was indeed a sweet homecoming, for in the next few weeks he attended the annual general meetings of his big companies, Lever Brothers, The Niger Company, and Les Huileries du Congo Belge. To each audience he was able to report better progress and bigger profits. 'The great hindrance to the more rapid recovery of the world's stability,' he declared, 'is that all the nations are suffering from a surplus of politics and a shortage of production.' In Brussels he showed the film of his African Journey to King Albert and Crown Prince Leopold, and dined with the King and Queen at the Palace.

His last public speech was in Bolton, to a large audience of children at the Sunday School attached to the Congregational Church which he had presented to his native town. He returned to London by the sleeper train on the Sunday night. On the Monday he had a chill which developed into pneumonia, and on 7 May 1925 he died. His body lay in state at the Lady Lever Art Gallery and many hundreds filed past the coffin before he was buried by the side of his wife in the crusader-style tomb, which he had designed for them, at Christ Church, Port Sunlight. That so many of the people of the Village should have chosen to pay him this last respect would have pleased him. His paramount regard was for himself and for the extensions of himself in his family, the small group of friends of his childhood, and the firm of Lever Brothers. But as his sympathies stretched out from this central core they were not smoothly attenuated. Instead, like a freak sound wave, they left a dead space close at hand and reappeared, diminished but still strong, at some distance. To the lowly and the eminent he was always devoted and loyal. It was his equals – those who felt entitled to challenge his opinion or thwart his intentions – who were most likely to see the brutal side of his face and find themselves cynically used or violently abused. For the King, or Gladstone, or Lloyd George, he was quite prepared to sit up and beg, round up sheep, or dig a few truffles. For Labour, for his work-people, he had a conscientious regard, attending to their education and welfare as one of them might have devoted himself to the training of a promising and well-loved whippet.

As soon as he died the Board of Lever Brothers gave orders for all development on Harris to stop, and so Leverhulme's scheme for the Western Isles perished with almost nothing achieved there. Other schemes, still hardly more than ideas – for instance, a centre at Grosvenor House for the encouragement of the arts – never lived at all. The Leverhulme Trust, which provides funds to research workers in science, medicine, social services, etc., only came into being after his death.

Of all the things which Leverhulme left behind, three are quite outstanding: Port Sunlight, the Lady Lever Art Collection, and the Unilever Corporation itself. He had great admiration for what he called the ability to 'organise an idea', and these three achievements show to what an extent he possessed this talent himself. Where the control of a project was entirely in his hands there usually remains a fine memorial. But the value of his contribution is less certain when he had to rely on other men to pick up and carry forward his ideas. Yet the quality of some of those ideas, expressed long ago, shines out from the pages of old journals like a gold coin in a box of rusty trinkets.

Strangely for a man so devoted to advertising, he was least successful when he tried to change people's attitudes and behaviour. He could create Port Sunlight on an empty marsh, but he failed to rebuild Stornoway or Bolton; he could sell soap but not the Six-Hour Day. He had learned early to knock on doors and discover exactly how customers used his soap, but with less tangible things he did not have the same success in discovering the secrets of the minds of those he wished to influence. To promote his Six-Hour Day he mostly addressed employers' associations, apparently believing that it was in their power to impose a shift system. It was rather like advertising Sunlight only in *The Lady*. Co-partnership did not have the results he had expected, and, for all his efforts to make it into something big, he did not see that an infinitesimal share in the firm would not alter an employee's attitude to work. To use his own term, there is a threshold for self-interest to be effective.

Perhaps a disciple of Samuel Smiles, with every moment of every day planned and usefully employed, expects significant results to appear with greater speed and regularity than is ever possible in human relations. Yet perhaps Smiles might have said that any man's life would be well spent if he could say at the end that he had made a success of his work, whatever it was; that he had produced something of his own which was an example and an inspiration to others; and that he had helped others to do the same in their own way. By these standards, with his case represented today by the Unilever Corporation, Port Sunlight, and the Leverhulme Trust, then William Hesketh Lever, Baron Leverhulme of Bolton-le-Moors, Viscount Leverhulme of the Western Isles, was faithful to his upbringing and he used his life well.

# *Notes and Sources*

Principal published sources:
Viscount Leverhulme, by his son (Allen & Unwin, 1927 (VL)
History of the Unilever Company, by Wilson (Cassell, 1954) (Hist.)

Principal private sources:
Archives at Unilever House (U.H.A.)
Archives at Port Sunlight (P.S.A.)

### *1. Bolton*

1 *Bolton District Congregationalist*, April 1893.

### *5. The Village*

1 V.L.

### *6. Soap combine*

1 *Pall Mall Gazette*, 18 July 1889.
2 To W.H.L., 23 June 1915, U.H.A.
3 *The Lancashire Grocer.*
4 Hist.
5 Grahame to Lever, 18 October 1906, V.L.
6 Lever to Grahame, 19 October 1906, *ibid.*
7 *House of Northcliffe* by Paul Ferris (Weidenfeld & Nicolson, 1971).
8 *F.E.* by Birkenhead (Eyre & Spottiswoode, 1959).
9 *Life of Lord Carson* by Marjoribanks (Gollancz, 1932).
10 *Northcliffe* by Pound & Harmsworth (Cassell, 1959).

[11] Hist.
[12] *Truth*, July 1907.
[13] *Northcliffe* by Pound & Harmsworth.
[14] *Ibid.*
[15] 15 May 1902, U.H.A.
[16] 4 July 1905, U.H.A.
[17] 1 March 1905, U.H.A.
[18] Diary, 1892.
[19] (Simpkin, Marshall, & Co., 1893).
[20] Birkenhead, 1894 speech.
[21] 10 May 1923, U.H.A.

## *7. The House of Commons*

[1] 27 April 1906; *The Times*, 28 April 1906.
[2] *Parl. Debates*, 4th Series, Vol. 156, p. 343.
[3] *Portraits of the New Century* by Raymond (Benn, 1928).
[4] *Daily Telegraph*, 23 July 1907.
[5] Hist.
[6] 1901, Hist.
[7] 20 July 1915, U.H.A.
[8] H. Fricke to L., presumed 5 January 1910, U.H.A.
[9] L. to Fricke, 7 January 1910, U.H.A.
[10] L. to W.H.L., 11 August 1915, U.H.A.
[11] *Birkenhead News*, 22 November 1909.
[12] 19 October 1909, U.H.A.
[13] 10 January 1910, U.H.A.
[14] L. to Crowther, 26 November 1909, U.H.A.
[15] U.H.A.
[16] *Report on Profit Sharing & Labour Co-Partnership in the U.K.* (Board of Trade, 1912).
[17] *Quarterly Review*, Vol. 219, 1913.
[18] *Ibid.*
[19] Address to Institute of Directors, 17 June 1913, U.H.A.

## *8. South Sea Islands*

[1] *Black Man's Burden* by Morel (National Labour Press, 1920).
[2] *Life of George Cadbury* by Gardiner (Cassell, 1923).

[3] Public Record Office, Colonial Office Papers 881/13, Australian 206, Confidential.

[4] Public Record Office, Colonial Office Confidential Papers 881/11/192.

[5] Public Record Office, Confidential Papers 881/13, Australia 213.

[6] V.L.

### *9. The Congo*

[1] 11 December 1903, Cd. Paper 1933 of 1904.

[2] *The Black Man's Burden.*

[3] *Ibid.*

[4] Cd. Paper 6561, Serial 1, 6 July 1908.

### *10. Isolation*

[1] 4 April 1911 to F. W. Brock, U.H.A.

[2] Hist.

[3] *Enterprise in Soap and Chemicals* by Musson (Manchester University Press, 1965).

[4] Hist.

[5] *Times Law Report*, 24 May 1913.

[6] V.L.

[7] G.L.C. Archives.

[8] Spender, *Contemporary Review*, Vol. 127, 1925.

[9] 26 March 1913. Published in *The Times*, 29 March 1913.

[10] 27 March 1913. *Ibid.*

[11] Colonial Office Command Paper.

[12] *The Times*, 9 July 1913.

[13] V.L.

[14] P.S.A.

### *11. The Lady Lever art gallery*

[1] 5 October 1913, Beaverbrook Library, Lloyd George Papers, C2/3/14.

[2] *Ibid.*, 22 October 1913, C/10/1/58.

[3] 1910, V.L.

[4] 14 February 1916, Lever Art Gallery Archive.

[5] V.L.

[6] 11 September 1914, U.H.A.

[7] Public Record Office, War Cabinet Confidential Paper, HO 185, 229 *et seq.*

[8] E.g. *Morning Advertiser*, 31 October 1918, and *Yorkshire Post*, 29 October 1918.

[9] *The Times*, 23 February 1911.

[10] Sutherland to Stevenson, 19 September 1917, Beaverbrook Library, Lloyd George Papers, F/93/2/3.

[11] Hist.

[12] V.L.

[13] L. to W.H.L., 26 March 1915, U.H.A.

[14] Hist.

[15] 20 February 1916, U.H.A.

[16] 18 July 1916, U.H.A.

[17] *Beaverbrook* by A. J. P. Taylor (Hamish Hamilton, 1972).

[18] Hist.

[19] *The Years that are Past* by Frances Lloyd George.

## 12. *Capital and labour*

[1] *The Truth about Publishing* by Stanley Unwin (Allen and Unwin).

[2] 22 September 1919, U.H.A.

[3] *Men and Work* by Citrine (Hutchinson, 1964).

[4] V.L.

[5] *Liverpool Daily Post & Mercury*, 11 June 1920.

[6] P.S.A.

[7] P.S.A.

[8] *Six-Hour Day* by Leverhulme (Allen & Unwin, 1918).

[9] V.L.

[10] 31 July 1915, U.H.A.

[11] V.L.

[12] Augustus John to Wm. Rothenstein, 6 May 1929. *Augustus John* Vol. I by Michael Holroyd (Heinemann, 1974).

[13] Leverhulme to Wilson Barret, Blumenfeld Papers, Beaverbrook Library.

[14] Correspondence, Leverhulme to John, *Daily Express*, 15 October 1920.

[15] *Chiaroscuro* by Augustus John (Jonathan Cape, 1954).

[16] *Illustrated London News*, 13 November 1920.

[17] 6 November 1920.
[18] V.L.

## 13. *Western Isles*

[1] 16 June 1922, U.H.A.
[2] Hist.
[3] *Highland Journey* by Colin MacDonald (Moray Press, 1943).
[4] 16 March 1917.
[5] *Stornoway Gazette*, 2 February 1917.
[6] 19 December 1917. *Lord of Isles* by Nicolson (Weidenfeld and Nicolson 1960).
[7] 11 October 1917. Ibid.
[8] *Highland Journey* by Colin MacDonald.
[9] 13 September 1920, Beaverbrook Library, L.G. paper, F/1/7/50.
[10] 7 January 1921, *ibid.*
[11] 3 September 1921, Scottish Office Records.
[12] *Lord of Isles.*
[13] *I Crossed the Minch* by Louis MacNeice (Longmans, 1938).
[14] 1920, Hist.
[15] T.U.C. Library, HD 5110.
[16] Hist.
[17] Hist.
[18] 23 September 1921.
[19] Spender, *Contemporary Review*, Vol. 127, 1925.
[20] V.L.
[21] 3 July 1922, U.H.A.
[22] 18 July 1922, U.H.A.
[23] 17 October 1924, U.H.A.
[24] 18 October 1924, U.H.A.
[25] 28 November 1924, U.H.A.
[26] 18 November 1924, U.H.A.
[27] 30 November 1924, U.H.A.
[28] Hist.
[29] Colonial Office Paper, CO 879/115/1023.
[30] *Ibid.*
[31] *Ibid.*
[32] *Ibid.*
[33] *The Times*, 12 April 1924.

# Index

# Paranın Psikolojisi

**PARANIN PSİKOLOJİSİ**
MORGAN HOUSEL


Sertifika No: 44921

Eylül 2023

ISBN 978-605-74006-5-9



Dizi Editörü
**Hakan Feyyat**

Çeviri
**Canan Feyyat**

Grafik Uyarlama
**Aydın Tibet**

Yayın Koordinatörü
**Tuğba Atamtürk**

Ofset Hazırlık
**Scala Yayıncılık**

Baskı
**Egem Basım Yayın San. ve Tic. Ltd. Şti.**
Gümüşsuyu Mah. Odin İş Merkezi
B Blok Kat: 2 No: 436 Topkapı - İstanbul
Sertifika No: 43624

Scala Yayıncılık
İstiklal Cad. Han Geçidi Sok. 116-3B
Galatasaray Beyoğlu - 34430 İstanbul
Tel: (0212) 251 51 26
Faks: (0212) 245 28 43
e-mail: scala@scalakitapci.com

İnternet satış
**scalakitapci.com**

# Paranın Psikolojisi

SERVET, AÇGÖZLÜLÜK VE MUTLULUK ÜZERİNE
SONSUZA DEK DEĞİŞMEYECEK DERSLER

MORGAN HOUSEL

Çeviri
CANAN FEYYAT

SCALA
YAYINCILIK

Beni eğiten ebeveynlerime,
Bana rehberlik eden Gretchen'e
Bana esin veren Miles ve Reese'e

# İÇİNDEKİLER

*Dâhi, etrafındaki herkes aklını kaybederken ortalama şeyler yapan kişidir.*

– Napolyon

*Dünya, hiç kimsenin asla gözlemleyemeyeceği bariz şeylerle doludur.*

– Sherlock Holmes

# SUNUŞ

Davranışsal ekonomiye ve onun bir alt dalı olan davranışsal finansa ilişkin bilimsel çalışmaların ortaya koyduğu bulgular, finansal kararlarda insan faktörünün rolüne ve etkisine dair açıklayıcı ve ikna edici kanıtlar getirdikçe "paranın psikolojisi" olarak tanımlanan kavram da hızla öne çıktı. Özellikle 2008 küresel finans krizinden sonra, "paranın psikolojisi"ne odaklanan araştırmalar, istatistiksel çalışmalar ve deneyler ivme kazanırken, bu alandaki makalelere ve kitaplara yönelik ilgi giderek arttı.

Bugün geleneksel-klasik ekonomi teorisini savunan çok sayıda ekonomist ve akademisyen finansın matematik temelli bir alan olduğunu kabul ederken, hem genel olarak yatırımcı camiasının psikolojisini anlamanın, hem de kendi bireysel psikolojimizi daha iyi tanımanın sağlayacağı getirileri de denkleme dahil etmek gerektiğini vurguluyor.

Özellikle de 2008 krizi sonrasında yayınlanmış çok sayıda tez çalışması, makale ve kitap da aynı şekilde bu anafikirden yola çıkıyor. Hatta dünyanın birçok ülkesinde Paranın Psikolojisi başlığıyla yayınlanmış farklı kitaplar var. Bu yayınların hepsi de sonuçta, finansal kararlarımızın bizi biz yapan karakter özelliklerimizle, duygularımızla, hem kişisel hem de toplum olarak kolektif deneyimlerimizle şekillendiğini açıklamayı amaçlıyor.

Bu nedenle de, az sonra okuyacağınız kitabın içeriğine geçmeden önce bir soruyla başlamak istiyorum: Morgan Housel'ın kaleme aldığı Paranın Psikolojisi, şu ana kadar yayınlandığı bütün ülkelerde milyonlarca okura ulaşmış olması, tanınmış ekonomistlerden övgüler alması, yatırım ve finansla ilgisi olsun veya olmasın herkese tavsiye edilmesi için nasıl bir fark yaratmış olabilir?

Her şeyden önce, Warren Buffett, Charlie Munger, Howard Marks, Daniel Kahneman, Richard Thaler geleneğinden gelen Morgan Housel bu kitapta okura hakikaten başarılı bir bileşim sunuyor. Birincisi, davranışsal finansın bugüne kadar ortaya koyduğu teorileri, bulguları ve karmaşık kavramları, finansal kararlarımızı etkileyen önyargı ve yanlı davranış eğilimlerini ekonomist bakış açısıyla ele alıyor. İkincisi, bütün bunları yatırımcı arka planıyla süzgeçten geçirerek, bilimsel çalışmalar ve istatistiklerle desteklenen pratik çıkarımlar sunuyor. Üçüncüsü, Wall Street Journal'ın ödüllü finans yazarı olarak, ele aldığı her konuyu, uzak ve yakın tarihten gerçek hikâyeler ve anekdotlarla beslediği sürükleyici ve kolay kavranabilen anlatılara çevirebiliyor.

Paranın Psikolojisi, adının da gayet açık ortaya koyduğu gibi finans ve yatırımın hisse seçimi ve portföy oluşumu gibi teknik yönlerine ya da değerleme ve analiz yöntemlerine değil, finansal kararlarımıza yön veren tutum ve zihniyetin arkasındaki psikolojiye ışık tutuyor. Kitapta yer alan 20 bölümün her biri kendi içinde bir mesaj iletirken, ortak tema ve anafikir, yatırım getirilerini optimize eden makineler değil insan olduğumuza, finansal başarımızı eğitim ve bilgi arka planından çok, parasal kararlardaki davranışlarımızı biçimlendiren psikolojimizin belirlediğine odaklanıyor.

Housel kitabın başında, yedi milyar insan ve sonsuz hareketli parçadan oluşan bir oyunda "tek ve eşsiz olduğunuz" önermesinden yola çıkıyor. "Farklı kuşaklardan gelen, farklı gelir düzeylerine sahip olan, farklı ebeveynlerce yetiştirilen, dünyanın farklı yerlerinde, farklı ekonomilerin içine doğmuş farklı teşvikler içeren farklı iş piyasalarını deneyimleyen ve şans seviyeleri farklı olan insanların çok farklı dersler öğrendiklerini" hatırlatarak öz-farkındalığa vurgu yapıyor.

Dünyaya bakışımızın kişi olarak kendimize özgü benzersiz yaşam deneyimleriyle şekillendiğine, fakat bu deneyimlerin nesiller boyunca evrilen kolektif insan deneyiminin sadece küçük bir kısmını yansıttığına, dolayısıyla da sınırlı kaldığına işaret ediyor. Bu sınırlı deneyiminin parasal kararlarımızı, finansa, yatırıma ve tasarrufa bakışımızı ve hatta algımızı hangi açılardan ve nasıl etkileyip yönlendirebildiğini, hangi hatalara ve önyargılara yol açabildiğini ortaya koyuyor.

Kısacası, herkesin dünyaya bakışının biraz eksik olduğunu, fakat o boşlukları doldurmak için eksiksiz bir anlatı oluşturduğumuzu vurguluyor. İnsanların para konusunda verdikleri her kararın, o sırada sahip oldukları bilgileri alıp dünyanın işleyişiyle ilgili kendilerine özgü zihinsel modelin içine yerleştirmeleriyle gerekçelendirildiğine dikkat çekiyor.

Her bölümün konusunu ve iletmek istediği mesajları tek tek yorumlayan uzun bir sunuş yazısı, öz-farkındalığa vurgu yapan bu kitabın hem kurgusuna hem de amacına ters düşebilir. Housel'ın kitapta işaret ettiği gibi "Mutluluk, sonuç eksi beklentilerdir" görüşünden yola çıkarak, yorumu siz okurlara bırakıyorum.

Ancak genel olarak değerlendirirsek, Morgan Housel bizi finansal kararlarımıza ve genel olarak bakış açımıza yön veren eğilimlerimiz, yani "paramızın psikolojisi" üzerinde düşünmeye davet ediyor.

Yatırım ve tasarruflarda bileşiklenmenin kaldıraç etkisini anlatırken, bir varlığa büyümesi için yıllar verilebildiğinde sonucun nasıl değiştiğini Warren Buffett ve Jim Simons örnekleriyle, ayrıca varsayımsal kişilerin yıllar içindeki getirilerini karşılaştırarak açıklıyor.

Herkesin zaman içinde kaçınılmaz olarak deneyimlediği öngörülemeyen iniş-çıkışları atlatabilmek için dayanıklılığın kilit önem taşıdığını vurguluyor. Ayakta kalma zihniyetini gerçek dünyada uygulamanın "paranızın psikolojisiyle" ilişkisine, servet üretmek ile serveti elde tutmanın farklı beceriler gerektirdiğine dikkat çekiyor.

Ayrıca genellikle gözden kaçan bir şeyin altını çiziyor: Finansal kararlar alırken duygularınızı tamamen bir kenara bırakacak kadar soğukkanlı bir şekilde rasyonel olmayı hedeflemeyin. Oldukça makûl olmayı hedefleyin, o kadar. Makûl daha gerçekçidir ve uzun vadede o fikre bağlı kalma şansınız daha yüksektir, ki para yönetiminde en çok önem taşıyan şey de budur.

Biz Inveo Portföy olarak, yatırımcılarımızın uzun vadeli finansal hedeflerine ulaşmalarına yardımcı olmak için aktif portföy yönetimi ile değer katma misyonumuzu hayata geçirirken, özel portföy yönetiminin "kişisel"liği konusunda bu kitaptan çok şey öğrenebileceğimizi düşünüyoruz. Aynı zamanda, finansal okuryazarlığa katkı çabalarımızda hedeflerimizi gerçekleştirme yönünde buradaki önerilerin hepimiz için fayda yaratacağına inanıyoruz.

Morgan Housel'ın kaleme aldığı Paranın Psikolojisi esas olarak, finansal kararlar alırken veya kararlarınızı analiz ederken kendinizi iyi tanıyıp eğilimlerinizin farkına varmanızın önemine ve bu öz-farkındalık sayesinde zihninizin, düşüncelerinizin ve iradenizin gücünden faydalanabileceğinize dikkat çekiyor. İster finans ve yatırımdan, ister genel anlamda hayattan bahsediyor olalım, güçlü ve zayıf yönlerimizi, algılarımızı ve eğilimlerimizi doğru tanımlamadıkça, kendimizi geliştirmekte ve amaçlarımıza ulaşmakta zorlanacağımızı yadsıyamayız.

Housel biz sektör profesyonellerinin de, kendi sektörümüzü ve iş yapış yöntemlerimizi değerlendirmek üzere çarpıcı ve kışkırtıcı bir saptama ile yüzleşmemizi istiyor: "Son yirmi yılda finans sektörü en iyi üniversitelerden gelen, en zeki beyinleri topladı. Bundan on yıl önce finans mühendisliği Princeton Mühendislik Fakültesi'nin en popüler bölümüydü. Peki bunun bizleri daha iyi yatırımcı yaptığına dair herhangi bir kanıt var mı? Ben hiç görmedim."

Morgan Housel, akıcı bir üslubun yanında zengin öykü ve anekdotlarla süslediği bu kitabında, biz yatırım yönetimi profesyonellerine de farklı bir kapı açıyor. Genel olarak, somut rakamlar ve testlerin sağladığı veriler ile değerlendirdiğimiz yatırımcılarımıza, biraz farklı gözlüklerle bakmamızı öneriyor: "Finansta da tıpta da uyulması gereken bazı temel ilkeler olduğu doğrudur; ancak önemli finansal kararlar hesap tablolarına veya ders kitaplarına bakarak alınmaz. Sofrada alınır. Genellikle de amaç, getirileri en üst düzeye çıkarmak değil, bir eşi veya çocuğu hayal kırıklığına uğratma olasılığını en aza indirmektir. Bu tür şeyleri tablolarda, grafiklerde veya formüllerde özetlemek zordur ve kişiden kişiye büyük farklılıklar gösterir. Biri için işe yarayan bir çözüm, bir başkası için sonuç vermeyebilir."

Tüm dünyada büyük ilgi gören bu kitabın finans ve yatırımla ilgili olsun veya olmasın, herkes için faydalı çıkarımlar içerdiğini düşünüyoruz.

Morgan Housel'e, kitabı Türk okurlarla buluşturan Scala Yayıncılık ekibine, titiz çevirisi için Canan Feyyat'a ve bu çabada emeği geçen herkese ayrı ayrı teşekkür ederiz.

Keyifli okumalar,

**Halim Çun**
**Inveo Portföy, Genel Müdür**

## GİRİŞ

# Yeryüzündeki En Büyük Gösteri

Üniversite yıllarımı Los Angeles'ta güzel bir otelde çalışarak geçirdim.

Sık sık gelen konuklardan biri teknoloji sektöründe üst düzey yöneticiydi. Yirmili yaşlarında Wi-Fi yönlendiricilerdeki önemli bileşenlerden birini tasarlayarak patentini almıştı. Birkaç şirket kurmuş ve satmıştı. Müthiş başarılıydı.

Fakat parayla, güvensizlik ile çocuksu bir aptallığın karışımı olarak tanımlayabileceğim türden bir ilişkisi vardı.

Desteyle para taşırdı; yüz dolarlık banknotlardan oluşan birkaç santim kalınlığındaki para destesini görmek isteyen herkese, görmek istemeyenlerin de çoğuna gösterirdi. Genellikle içkili olduğunda, üstelik hiç gereği yokken, zenginliğiyle açık açık ve yüksek sesle böbürlenirdi.

Bir gün iş arkadaşlarımdan birinin eline birkaç bin dolar tutuşturup "Caddenin sonundaki kuyumcuya git ve bana 1000 dolarlık altın sikke al," demişti.

Bir saat sonra, altınlarını eline alan teknoloji yöneticisi, arkadaşlarıyla birlikte Pasifik Okyanusu'na bakan bir rıhtımda toplanmıştı. Sonra da altınları denize atmaya, taş kaydırır gibi kaydırmaya ve kahkahalar atarak, hangisinin altınının daha ileri gittiği konusunda tartışmaya başlamışlardı. Sırf eğlence olsun diye.

Aynı adam birkaç gün sonra otelin restoranında bir lambayı patlattı. Yöneticilerden biri lambanın 500 dolar değerinde olduğunu ve yerine yenisini koyması gerektiğini söyledi.

Teknoloji yöneticisi inanmamış bir ifadeyle "Beş yüz dolar mı istiyorsun?" diye sordu ve cebinden bir tomar para çıkararak yöneticinin eline tutuşturdu. "Al sana 5000 dolar. Şimdi gözümün önünden çekil. Bir daha da beni böyle aşağılama!" dedi.

Bu tutumunun ne kadar sürdüğünü merak ederseniz, yanıt "uzun değil." Sıfırı tükettiğini ben yıllar sonra öğrendim.

Bu kitabın ana fikri, paranızı iyi kullanmanızın ne kadar zeki olduğunuzla pek ilgisi olmadığı; buna karşılık nasıl davrandığınızla yakından ilgili olduğu önermesine dayanıyor.

Dahası, davranışı öğretmek zor; gerçekten zeki insanlara bile.

Duygularının kontrolünü kaybeden bir dahi finansal açıdan tam bir felaket olabilir. Tam tersi de doğrudur. Hiçbir finansal eğitimi olmayan sıradan insanlar, zekânın formal ölçütleriyle hiç ilgisi olmayan bir avuç davranışsal beceriye sahip olmaları halinde varlıklı olabilirler.

---

Wikipedia'daki en sevdiğim yazılardan biri şöyle başlıyor: Ronald James Read Amerikalı hayırsever, yatırımcı, hademe ve benzin istasyonu görevlisiydi."

Ronald Read, Vermont'un kırsal kesiminde dünyaya gelmişti. Ailesinde lise bitiren ilk kişi oydu; üstelik okula her gün otostopla gidip gelirdi.

Ronald Read'i tanıyanların onun hakkında söyleyebileceği pek bir şey yoktu. Bütün bildikleri, sade ve sıradan bir yaşamı olduğuydu.

Read 25 yıl boyunca bir benzin istasyonunda arabalara bakım yapmış, sonra da 17 yıl boyunca JCPenny'de* yerleri süpürmüştü. Otuz sekiz yaşındayken 12,000 dolara iki yatak odalı bir ev almış ve ömrünün geri kalanını orada geçirmişti. Elli yaşında dul kalmış, bir daha da evlenmemişti. Bir arkadaşı, en büyük hobisinin odun kesmek olduğunu anımsıyor.

Read 2014 yılında, 92 yaşında öldü. Ve işte o zaman, kırsalda yaşayan alçakgönüllü hademe, uluslararası basının manşetlerine çıktı.

2014 yılında 2,813,503 Amerikalı öldü. Bunların 4000'den azının, vefat ettikleri dönemdeki net varlığı 8 milyon doların üzerindeydi. Ronald Read, onlardan biriydi.

Bir zamanların hademesi vasiyetnamesinde üvey çocuklarına 2 milyon dolar, yaşadığı yerdeki hastaneye ve kütüphaneye de 6 milyon doların üzerinde para bırakmıştı.

Read'i tanıyanlar şaşıp kalmıştı. Bütün bu parayı nereden bulmuştu?

Sonunda işin içinde önemli bir sır olmadığı anlaşıldı. Read ne piyango kazanmıştı ne de birinden miras kalmıştı. Elinden geldiğince her kuruşunu biriktirmiş ve blue chip şirketlerin hisselerine** yatırım yapmıştı. Sonra da on yıllar boyunca, birikimleri 8 milyon doları aşıncaya kadar beklemişti.

---

* JCPenney: ABD'de 49 eyalette ve Porto Riko'da 840 lokasyonda hizmet veren mağazalar zinciridir. Geleneksel ürünleri satmanın yanı sıra, JCPenney mağazaları içinde Fine Jewelry, Salon by InStyle ve Sephora'ya ayrılmış bölümler de vardır. (ÇN)

** Blue Chip Şirket: Yüksek işlem hacmine sahip olan ve kârını her yıl düzenli olarak yatırımcılarıyla paylaşan şirketler. Öz varlık kârlılığını istikrarlı olarak artır-

İşte böyle. Hademelikten hayırseverliğe.

Ronald Read'in ölümünden birkaç ay önce, Richard adlı bir adam da haberlerdeydi.

Richard Fuscone, Ronald Read'de olmayan her şeye sahipti. Harvard mezunuydu, işletme yüksek lisansı vardı; Merrill Lynch'te üst düzey yöneticiydi ve hayırseverliğe yönelmek için 40'lı yaşlarında emekliye ayrıldığında, finans alanında başarılı bir kariyer yapmıştı. Merrill Lynch eski CEO'su David Komansky, Fuscone'nin "iş dünyasındaki bilgeliğini, liderlik yeteneklerini, sağlam muhakemesini ve dürüstlüğünü" övmüştü.[1] İş dünyası dergisi Crain's, bir dönem onu "40 yaş altındaki en başarılı 40 iş insanı" listesine dahil etmişti.[2]

Fakat sonra, altın sikkelerle taş kaydırmaca oynayan teknoloji yöneticisi gibi, Fuscone için de her şey tuzla buz olmuştu.

Fuscone 2000'li yılların ortalarında, Connecticut'ın Greenwich kasabasındaki onbir banyolu, iki asansörlü, iki havuzlu, yedi garajlı 1675 metrekarelik evini genişletmek için büyük miktarda borçlandı; evin aylık bakım gideri 90,000 doların üzerindeydi.

Sonra, 2008 yılında finansal kriz vurdu.

Kriz herkesi vurdu. Ama görünüşe göre Fuscone'yi toz duman etmişti. Yüksek miktarda borcu ve varlıklarının likit olmaması nedeniyle iflasa başvurdu. 2008 yılında iflas mahkemesindeki yargıca "halen hiçbir gelirim" yok dediği iddia ediliyor.

Önce Palm Beach'teki evi haciz edildi.

2014 yılında, sıra Greenwich'teki malikâneye geldi.

---

mayı başarırlar. İşlem hacminin yüksekliği sayesinde likittirler. Volatiliteleri düşüktür ve istikrarlı getiri sağlarlar. (ÇN.)

Ronald Read'in servetini bağışlamasından beş ay önce, Fuscone'nin malikânesi hacizle satışa çıkarıldı; konukların "evin içindeki kapalı havuzun kenarında verilen yemek ve dans davetlerinin heyacanını dün gibi anımsadığı" malikâne, sigorta şirketinin biçtiği değerin yüzde 75 altında bir fiyata satıldı.[3]

Ronald Read sabırlıydı; Richard Fuscone açgözlüydü. İkisi arasındaki muazzam eğitim ve deneyim farkını ortadan kaldıran da sadece bu olmuştu.

Her ne kadar iyi bir tavsiye olsa da, buradan çıkarılacak ders, daha çok Ronald gibi olmak ve Richard'a benzememek değil.

Bu hikâyelerin büyüleyici yanı, finans bağlamında son derece özgün olmaları.

Üniversite diploması, eğitimi, arkaplanı, formal deneyimi ve bağlantıları olmayan biri, en iyi eğitimi almış, en iyi şekilde kendini geliştirmiş ve en iyi bağlantılara sahip biri karşısında bu kadar üstün performansı başka hangi alanda gösterebilir?

Ben bulmakta zorlanıyorum.

Ronald Read'in Harvard eğitimli bir cerrahtan daha iyi kalp nakli yapabileceğini düşünmek imkânsız. Ya da en iyi mimarlardan daha üstün bir gökdelen tasarımı gerçekleştirebileceğini. Bir hademenin dünyanın en iyi nükleer mühendislerinden üstün performans gösterdiğine dair bir hikâyeyi de hiçbir zaman duymayacağız.

Fakat yatırım alanında bu tür hikâyeler oluyor.

Ronald Read'in Richard Fuscone ile bir arada varlık gösterebilmesi gerçeğinin iki açıklaması var. Birincisi, finansal sonuçların zekâ ve çabadan bağımsız olarak, şanstan kaynaklandığı söylenebilir. Bu bir ölçüde doğrudur ve kitapta ayrıntılı olarak tartışacağız. İkinci açıklaması ise (ki ben daha yaygın olduğunu düşünüyorum) finansal başarının zor bir bilim olmamasıdır. Finansal başarı, nasıl davrandığınızın ne bildiğinizden daha önemli olduğu, insana özgü kişisel beceri ve niteliklerden biridir.

Ben para bağlamındaki bu kişiye özgü, insani becerilere* paranın psikolojisi diyorum. Bu kitabın amacı, kısa hikâyelerden yararlanarak sizleri, kişiye özgü nitelik ve becerilerin paranın teknik yönünden daha önemli olduğuna ikna etmek. Bunu da Read'den Fuscone'ye kadar herkesin ve ikisi arasında kalanların daha iyi finansal kararlar almasına yardımcı olacak şekilde yapacağım.

Benim deneyimlerim, kişiye özgü bu beceri ve niteliklerin büyük ölçüde hafife alındığını gösteriyor.

Finans, daha çok bir formüle veri girdiğiniz ve o formülün size ne yapacağınızı söylediği matematik temelli bir alan olarak öğretiliyor ve bütün yapmanız gerekenin bu olduğu varsayılıyor.

Eğer maaşınızın yüzde 10'unu tasarrufa ayırıyorsanız ve altı aylık acil durum fonunuz varsa, kişisel finans bağlamında bu doğru.

Faiz oranları ile değerlemeler arasındaki tarihsel korelasyonları biliyorsanız, yatırım bağlamında da doğru.

Finanstan sorumlu genel müdürün sermayenin net maliyetini ölçebildiği kurumsal finans bağlamında da doğru.

Bunların hiçbiri kötü veya yanlış değil. Mesele şu ki, ne yaptığınızı bilmeniz, o şeyi yapmaya çalışırken kafanızın içinde olanlar konusunda size hiçbir şey söylemez.

---

* Yazar burada "soft skills" terimini kullanıyor. Belirli bir mesleğe veya disipline bağlı olmayan, kişinin kendine özgü kişilik özellikleriyle şekillenen bu beceri ve nitelikler, Türkçe'de insani beceri ya da beşeri beceri olarak da tanımlanıyor; veya kimi kaynaklarda "soft beceri" olarak geçiyor. (ÇN.)

Siz ister ilgilenin ister ilgilenmeyin, iki konu herkesi etkiler: Sağlık ve para.

Sağlık sektörü modern bilimin zaferidir; ömür beklentisi dünya genelinde yükselmiştir. Doktorların insan vücudunun işleyişiyle ilgili eski fikirlerinin yerini bilimsel keşifler almıştır ve bu sayede de neredeyse herkes daha sağlıklı.

Para sektörü -yatırım, kişisel finans, iş planlama- ise başka bir hikâye.

Son yirmi yılda finans sektörü en iyi üniversitelerden gelen, en zeki beyinleri topladı. Bundan on yıl önce finans mühendisliği Princeton Mühendislik Fakültesi'nin en popüler bölümüydü. Peki bunun bizleri daha iyi yatırımcı yaptığına dair herhangi bir kanıt var mı?

Ben hiç görmedim.

Yıllar boyunca toplum olarak gerçekleştirdiğimiz kolektif denemelerle ve hatalarımızla, nasıl daha iyi çiftçi, daha iyi tesisatçı ve daha ileri kimyager olabileceğimizi öğrendik. Fakat deneme ve yanılma, bize kişisel finans bağlamında daha iyi olmayı öğretti mi? Eskisinden daha az mı borca gömülüyoruz? Kara günler için birikim yapmaya daha mı meyilliyiz? Emekliliğe hazırlanıyor muyuz? Paranın mutluluğumuzu nasıl etkilediği veya etkilemediği konusunda gerçekçi görüşlerimiz var mı?

Ben önemli bir kanıt görmedim.

Kanımca bunun en önemli nedeni, para konusunda fiziğe çok benzer şekillerde (kurallar ve yasalarla) düşünüyoruz ve öyle öğretiliyoruz; buna karşılık psikolojik yönden (duygular ve nüanslarla) yeterince düşünmüyoruz ve o şekilde yetiştirilmiyoruz.

Ve bu da bana, hem önemli hem de büyüleyici geliyor.

Para her yerde, hepimizi etkiliyor ve çoğumuzun kafasını karıştırıyor. Para konusunda herkes biraz farklı düşünüyor. Para bize risk, güven, mutluluk gibi yaşamın birçok alanına dair dersler sunuyor. Pek az şey, insanların davranış şeklini açıklama bağlamında paradan daha güçlü bir büyüteç sunabilir. Ve bu, yeryüzündeki en büyük gösterilerden biridir.

Paranın psikolojisine ilişkin benim kendi değerlendirmelerim, bu konuda on yılı aşkın bir süre boyunca yazdıklarımla şekillendi. Finans alanında yazmaya 2008 yılında başladım. Finansal krizin ve 80 yılın en kötü ekonomik durgunluğunun başlangıcıydı.

Olmakta olanları yazabilmek için, önce neler olmakta olduğunu anlamak istedim. Fakat finansal krizden sonra öğrendiğim ilk şey, bırakın yapılması gerekenleri, neler olduğunu ve bunların niçin olduğunu kimsenin tam olarak açıklayamayacağını görmek oldu. Her iyi açıklamanın, aynı ölçüde ikna edici çürütmesi vardı.

Mühendisler bir köprünün çökme nedenini belirleyebilirler; çünkü belli bir alana, belli bir oranda güç uygulanması halinde o alanın çökeceği konusunda fikir birliği vardır. Fizik tartışmaya açık değildir. Yasalarla yönetilir. Finans ise farklıdır. İnsanların davranışlarıyla yönetilir. Üstelik benim davranışım bana mantıklı gelebilir, fakat size çılgınca görünebilir.

Finansal krizi inceledikçe ve o konuda yazdıkça, bu olayı finansın merceğiyle değil, psikoloji ve tarih merceğiyle daha iyi açıklayabileceğimizi çok daha net gördüm.

İnsanların kendilerini niçin borca gömdüklerini kavramak için faiz oranlarını incelemeniz gerekmiyor; hırsın, açgözlülüğün, güvensizliğin ve iyimserliğin tarihini incelemeniz gerek.

Yatırımcıların bir ayı piyasasının* en alt seviyesinde niçin satışa geçtiklerini anlamak için gelecekteki beklenen getirilerin matematiği üzerinde çalışmanız gerekmiyor; ailenize bakıp da yatırımlarınızın onların geleceğini tehlikeye atıp atmadığını sorgulayarak endişelendiğiniz zaman yaşayacağınız üzüntüyü düşünmeniz gerekiyor.

Voltaire'in şu gözlemini severim: "Tarih hiçbir zaman tekrar etmez; insanlar ise her zaman kendini tekrar eder." Bu gözlem parayla ilgili davranışımıza çok iyi uyuyor.

2018 yılında, insanları para konusunda etkilediğini gördüğüm en önemli 20 hata, ön yargı ve kötü davranış nedenini ana hatlarıyla anlatan bir rapor yazdım. Raporun başlığı Paranın Psikolojisi idi ve bir milyondan fazla insan okudu. Bu kitapta konuyu daha derinlemesine ele aldım. Rapordaki bazı kısa pasajlara, burada da aynen yer verdim.

Bu kitapta yer alan 20 bölümün her biri, paranın psikolojisinin en önemli yönleri olduğunu düşündüğüm, çoğu kez de mantığa ve genel kanıya ters düşen olguları anlatıyor. Her bölüm ortak bir tema etrafında gelişiyor; fakat her birinin kendine özgü bir konusu var ve birbirinden bağımsız olarak okunabilir.

Uzun bir kitap değil. Rica ederim... teşekküre ne gerek var? Çoğu okur başladığı kitabı bitiremiyor; çünkü bence, tek bir konu için 300 sayfalık açıklama gerekmiyor. Okumaktan vazgeçeceğiniz uzun bir konu yerine, 20 kısa başlık altında anlatmayı uygun gördüm.

Hadi başlayalım.

---

* Ayı Piyasası (Bear Market): Piyasanın karamsar ve fiyatlardaki ana trendin düşüş yönünde olduğu dönem. Tersi, yani piyasanın iyimser ve fiyatlardaki ana trendin yükseliş yönünde olduğu piyasalar da Boğa Piyasası olarak bilinir. (ÇN)

# 1

# Hiç Kimse Çılgın Değildir

Para ile ilgili kişisel deneyimlerinizin belki yüzde 0.00000001'i dünyada olanlarla bağlantılı olabilir; buna karşılık, dünyanın işleyişine ilişkin düşünce biçiminizin yüzde 80'i kişisel deneyimlerinizle şekillenebilir.

İZNİNİZLE BİR PROBLEMDEN söz etmek isterim. Sözünü edeceğim problem, paranızı nasıl kullandığınız konusunda kendinizi daha iyi hissetmenizi ve başkalarının paralarını nasıl kullandığı konusunda daha az yargılayıcı olmanızı sağlayabilir.

İnsanlar parayla bazı çılgınca şeyler yaparlar. Fakat kimse çılgın değildir.

Mesele şudur: Farklı kuşaklardan gelen, farklı gelir düzeylerine sahip olan, farklı ebevenlerce yetiştirilen, dünyanın farklı yerlerinde, farklı ekonomilerin içine doğmuş bulunan, farklı teşvikler içeren farklı iş piyasalarını deneyimleyen ve şans seviyeleri farklı olan insanlar, çok farklı dersler öğrenirler.

Her birimizin dünyanın işleyişine dair kendimize özgü, benzersiz bir deneyimimiz vardır. Ayrıca deneyimlediğimiz şeyler, ikinci elden öğrendiklerimizden daha zorlayıcıdır. Böylece hepimiz -siz, ben, herkes- hayatımız boyunca paranın işleyişi konusunda kişiden kişiye müthiş değişiklik gösteren bir dizi görüş edinir ve onlara bağlanırız. Size çılgınca görünen bir şey, bana mantıklı gelebilir.

Yoksulluk içinde büyümüş olan birinin risk ve ödüle dair düşüncesi, zengin bir bankacının çocuğunun denese de kavrayamayacağı kadar farklıdır.

Yüksek enflasyon döneminde büyümüş biri, fiyatların istikrarlı seyrettiği dönemde büyümüş birinin hiç de yaşamak zorunda olmadığı bir şey deneyimlemiştir.

Büyük Buhran* sırasında herşeyini kaybetmiş bir hisse senedi broker'ı, 1990'ların sonlarındaki görkemli dönemi yaşayan teknoloji sektörü çalışanlarının aklına hayaline gelmeyecek bir şey deneyimlemiştir.

Otuz yıldır ekonomik durgunluk görmemiş olan Avustralyalı, hiçbir Amerikalının yaşamadığı bir şey deneyimlemiştir.

Bu örnekler böyle devam edip gider. Deneyimlerin listesi sonsuzdur.

Siz para konusunda benim bilmediğim şeyler bilirsiniz; ben de sizin bilmediklerinizi. Hayatınız boyunca benden farklı inançlar, amaçlar ve öngörülerle karşılaşır, onları deneyimlersiniz. Bunun nedeni birimizin diğerinden daha akıllı ya da bilgili olması değildir. Farklı ve ikna ediciliği de bir o kadar güçlü deneyimlerle biçimlenmiş olan farklı yaşamlar sürdüğümüz için böyledir.

Para ile ilgili kişisel deneyimlerinizin belki yüzde 0.00000001'i dünyada olan bitenlerle bağlantılı olabilir; buna karşılık, dünyanın işleyişine ilişkin düşünce biçiminizin yüzde 80'i kişisel deneyimlerinizle şekillenebilir. Bu nedenle, aynı zekâ düzeyindeki insanlar ekonomik durgunlukların nasıl ve niçin olduğu, paranızla ne yapmanız, neye öncelik vermeniz, ne kadar risk almanız gerektiği konusunda ve bunun gibi birçok şeyde aynı görüşte olmayabilir.

Frederick Lewis Allen 1930'ların Amerikasını konu alan kitabında, Büyük Buhran'ın "milyonlarca Amerikalıyı ömürlerinin sonuna dek derinden etkilediğini ve yaşamlarına damga vurduğunu" yazıyor. Fakat bir dizi farklı deneyim

---

* Büyük Buhran: Ekim 1929'da ABD'de borsanın çöküşüyle başlayan, sonrasında da dünyaya yayılan ekonomik bunalım dönemi. Büyük Bunalım, Büyük Depresyon ve Büyük Çöküş olarak da bilinir. (ÇN.)

söz konusuydu. John Fitzgerald Kennedy 25 yıl sonra, başkanlık seçimleri için yürüttüğü kampanya sırasında, Büyük Buhran'dan neler anımsadığını soran bir gazeteciye şu yanıtı vermişti:

> Büyük Buhran konusunda ilk elden bilgi sahibi değilim. Ailem dünyanın en büyük servetlerinden birine sahipti ve o dönemde eskisinden de varlıklıydık. Daha büyük evlerimiz, daha çok hizmetlimiz vardı ve daha çok seyahat ediyorduk. Doğrudan gördüğüm tek şey, babamın sırf iş vermek için, karınlarını doyurabilsinler diye fazladan bahçıvan tutmasıydı. Harvard'da ders olarak okuyuncaya kadar Büyük Buhran hakkında gerçek anlamda bilgi sahibi değildim.

Bu konu, 1960 seçimlerinin ana gündem maddelerinden biriydi. İnsanlar, son kuşağın en büyük ekonomik hadisesini bilmeyen birinin nasıl olup da ekonominin başına geçirilebileceğini düşünüyordu. JFK bunu, birçok açıdan, ikinci Dünya Savaşı deneyimiyle aştı. İkinci Dünya Savaşı bir önceki kuşağın en yaygın deneyimiydi ve bu da JFK'nin en büyük rakibi Hubert Humphrey'de olmayan bir şeydi.

Bizim için zorluk şudur: Eğitim ve ileri görüşlülük, düzeyi ne olursa olsun, hiçbir zaman belirsizlik ve korkunun gücünü gerçek anlamda yaşatamaz.

Büyük Buhran sırasında herşeyini kaybetmenin nasıl bir şey olduğunu yazılıp çizilenlerden okuyabilirim. Fakat bunu bizzat deneyimlemiş olanların izlerini taşıdığı duygusal yaralar bende yok. Ve bunu yaşamış olanlar, benim gibi birinin hisse senedi sahibi olmak gibi şeylerden niçin memnuniyet duyduğunu anlayamaz. Dünyayı farklı merceklerden görürüz.

Hesap tabloları hisse senedi piyasalarındaki büyük düşüşlerin tarihsel sıklığını modelleyebilir. Fakat insanın eve gelip çocuklarının yüzüne baktığında, onların yaşamlarını etkileyecek bir hata yapıp yapmadığından endişelenme duygusunu modelleyemezler. Tarihi okuyup incelemek, size bir şeyler anladığınız duygusunu verir. Ancak bir şeyi yaşayıncaya ve sonuçlarını bizzat hissedinceye kadar, davranışınızı değiştirmenize yetecek kadar anlamayabilirsiniz.

Hepimiz dünyanın nasıl işlediğini bildiğimizi düşünürüz. Fakat hepimiz, onun yalnızca ince bir dilimini deneyimlemişizdir.

Yatırımcı Michael Batnick'in dediği gibi "Bazı dersleri anlamak için deneyimlemek gerekir." Hepimiz, farklı biçimlerde, bu gerçeğin kurbanlarıyız.

---

Ulusal Ekonomik Araştırmalar Dairesi'nde (National Bureau of Economic Research) görevli iki ekonomist Ulrike Malmendier ile Stefan Nagel, 2006 yılında Tüketici Finansmanı Anketi'nin 50 yılını derinlemesine inceleyerek, Amerikalıların paralarını nasıl kullandığı konusunda ayrıntılı bir çalışma gerçekleştirdi.[4]

Teoride, insanların yatırım kararlarını, amaçları doğrultusunda ve önlerindeki yatırım seçeneklerinin karakteristik özellikleri temelinde alması gerekir.

Fakat insanlar böyle yapmıyor.

Malmendier-Nagel ikilisinin çalışması, insanların ömür boyu yatırım kararlarının büyük ölçüde, kendi kuşaklarından yatırımcıların deneyimlerine, özellikle de yetişkinlik yaşamlarının başlarındaki deneyimlere bağlı olduğunu gösteriyor.

Bu araştırmaya göre, yüksek enflasyon ortamında büyüyenler, yaşamlarının ilerleyen dönemlerinde tahvillere, düşük enflasyon ortamında büyümüş kişilere oranla daha az para yatırmışlar. Hisse senedi piyasasının güçlü olduğu dönemde büyüyenler, hisselerin zayıf olduğu dönemde büyümüş kişilere oranla, yaşamlarının ilerleyen dönemlerinde paralarının daha büyük bir kısmını hisse senetlerine yatırmış.

Malmendier ve Nagel şöyle yazıyor: "Bulgularımız, bireysel yatırımcıların risk alma isteğinin, kişisel hikâyelerine bağlı olduğuna işaret ediyor."

Yani zekâ, eğitim veya gelişmişlik meselesi değil. Sadece saçma sapan bir şans yüzünden nerede ve ne zaman doğmak kısmet olmuşsa…

*Financial Times* gazetesi 2019 yılında ünlü tahvil yöneticisi Bill Gross ile bir söyleşi yapmıştı. Söyleşide şöyle bir ifade yer alıyordu: "Gross on yıl önce veya sonra doğmuş olsa, muhtemelen bugün olduğu yerde olmayacağını kabul ediyor." Gross'un kariyeri, neredeyse mükemmel bir şekilde, faiz oranlarında yaşanan ve tahvil fiyatlarının yükselmesini getiren kuşaksal çöküşe denk gelmişti. Bu tür bir şey yalnızca karşınıza çıkan fırsatları etkilemekle kalmıyor; o fırsatlar hakkındaki düşüncenizi de etkiliyor. Gross için tahviller, servet üretme makineleriydi. Yüksek enflasyon ortamında büyüyen ve bunun acısını çekmiş olan babasının kuşağı ise, tahvilleri pekalâ servet öğütücüsü olarak görebilir.

İnsanların paraya ilişkin deneyimleri arasındaki farklar, birbirine oldukça benzer olduğunu düşünebileceğiniz durumlarda bile hiç küçük değil.

Hisse senetlerini ele alalım. 1970 yılında doğmuş biriyseniz, ergenlik döneminizde ve 20'li yaşlarınızda S&P 500 Endeksi enflasyona uyarlı olarak neredeyse 10 kat yükselmişti. Bu muhteşem bir getiri. 1950 yılında doğmuş olsanız, ergenlik döneminizde ve 20'li yaşlarınızda enflasyona uyarlı piyasa, kelimenin gerçek anlamıyla kıpırdamamış olacaktı. Doğum yılları nedeniyle şans eseri ayrılmış olan bu iki grup insan, hayatları boyunca hisse senedi piyasasının işleyişi konusunda tamamen farklı bir bakış açısına sahip olacaktı:

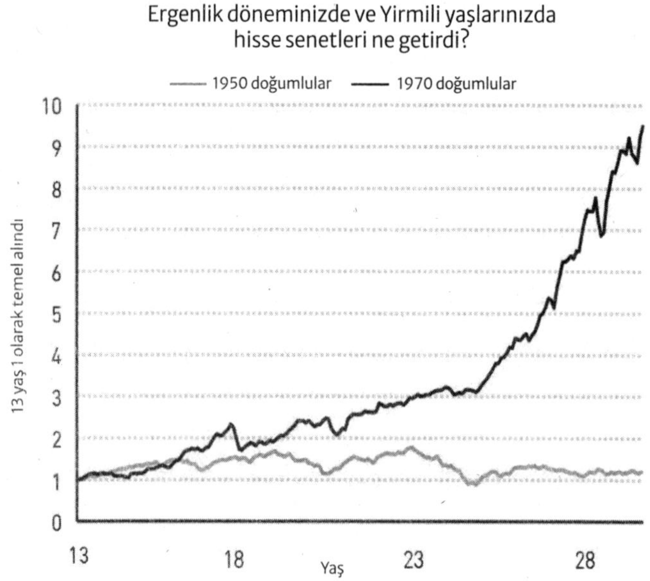


Ya da enflasyona bakalım. 1960'ların Amerikası'nda doğmuş olsanız, ergenlik döneminizde ve yirmili yaşlarınızda -yani ekonominin işleyişine dair bilgilerinizin temelini geliştirdiğiniz, etkilenmeye açık olduğunuz gençlik yıllarınızda- enflasyon, fiyatları üç kat yükseltmiş olacaktı. Bu, çok şey anlamına geliyor. Benzin kuyruklarını ve maaşların ay sonunu getirmeye güçlükle yettiği günleri hatırlayacaktınız. Fakat 1990 yılında doğmuşsanız,

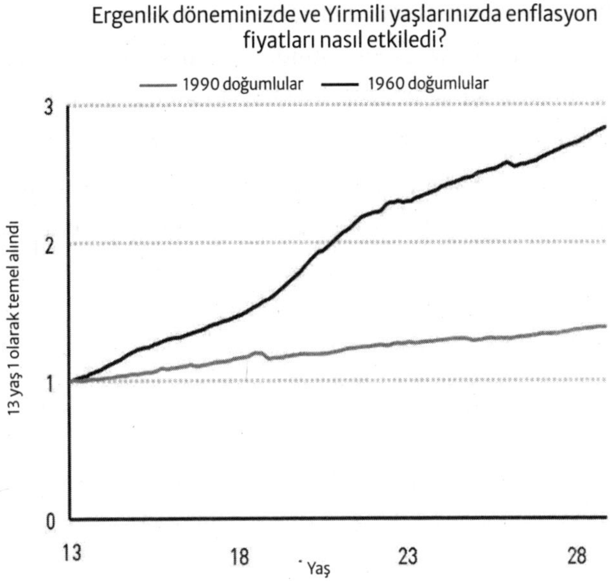


enflasyon şu ana kadarki hayatınız boyunca o kadar düşük oldu ki, böyle bir şey muhtemelen aklınızdan bile geçmez.

Kasım 2009'da Amerika genelinde işsizlik oranı yaklaşık yüzde 10 idi. Fakat 16-19 yaş grubundaki lise mezunu olmayan Afrika kökenli Amerikalı erkekler arasındaki işsizlik oranı yüzde 49'du. Buna karşılık 45 yaş üstü ve üniversite mezunu Beyaz kadınlar arasındaki işsizlik oranı yüzde 4'tü.

İkinci Dünya Savaşı sırasında Almanya ve Japonya'nın yerel hisse senedi piyasaları yerle bir oldu. İki ülke de bombardıman altındaydı. Savaş sona erdiğinde, Alman çiftçiler ülkenin vatandaşları için günde yalnızca 1000 kalorilik gıda üretiyordu. ABD ile karşılaştırırsak, Amerikan hisse senedi piyasası 1941 yılı ile 1945 sonu arasındaki dönemde iki katından fazla yükseldi ve neredeyse 20 yılın en güçlü ekonomisi hüküm sürüyordu.

Bu iki gruptaki insanların hayatlarının geri kalan kısmında enflasyon konusunda aynı şeyi düşünmesini kimse bekleyemez. Ya da hisse senedi piyasaları konusunda... Ya da işsizlik konusunda... Ya da genel olarak para konusunda.

Bu iki gruptaki insanların finansal bilgiye aynı tepkiyi vermesini de kimse bekleyemez. Hiç kimse, aynı teşvik ve motivasyon unsurlarından etkilendiklerini varsayamaz.

Hiç kimse, aynı tavsiye kaynaklarına güvenmelerini bekleyemez.

Hiç kimse, neyin önemli olduğu, neye değdiği, bir sonraki süreçte neler olacağı ve önlerindeki en iyi yolun hangisi olduğu konusunda aynı fikirde olmalarını bekleyemez.

Paraya bakışları farklı dünyalarda şekillenmiştir. Ayrıca yeri gelir, para bağlamında bir grup insanın uçlarda olduğunu düşündüğü bir görüş, bir başkası için tamamen mantıklı olabilir.

*New York Times* birkaç yıl önce Tayvan'ın dev elektronik üreticisi Foxconn'daki çalışma koşullarını anlatan bir yazı yayınladı. Koşullar genel olarak acımasızdı. Bu yazıyı okuyanlar, haklı olarak üzüldü. Fakat Çinli bir işçinin yeğeninden son derece ilginç bir yanıt geldi. Yeğen, yorum bölümüne gönderdiği notta şöyle diyordu:

> Teyzem birkaç yıl Amerikalıların "terhane*" dedikleri bir yerde çalıştı. Ağır bir işti. Mesai saatleri uzun, maaşı "düşük" ve çalışma koşulları "kötü..." Peki teyzemin o fabrikalarda çalışmaya başlamadan önce ne yaptığını biliyor musunuz? Fahişelik yapıyordu.

---

* Terhane: Yazar burada ucuza, sigortasız, sağlık güvencesiz, çoğunlukla da çocuk işçi çalıştıran fabrika ya da atölyeleri tanımlayan "sweat shop" terimini kullanıyor. Genellikle Uzakdoğu ile anılan ve tekstil sektöründe faaliyet gösteren bu oluşumlar, çalışanları sömürdükleri için tepki çekiyor ve eleştiriliyor. (ÇN.)

Eski yaşam biçimiyle kıyaslandığında, teyzemin terhanede çalışması, bence olumlu bir gelişme. Şahsen ben, teyzemin birkaç dolar için şeytani bir kapitalist patron tarafından "sömürülmeyi", bedeninin birkaç kuruş için birçok erkek tarafından sömürülmesine tercih ettiğini çok iyi biliyorum.

Bu yüzden de birçok Amerikalının düşünce biçimi karşısında rahatsızlık duyuyorum. Biz Batı ile aynı olanaklara sahip değiliz. Hükümet anlamında yönetim altyapımız farklı. Ülkeler farklı. Evet, fabrikada çalışmak ağır iş. Daha iyi olabilir mi? Evet... fakat sadece Amerika'daki benzer işlerle kıyasladığınızda.

Bu sözler karsışında ne diyeceğimi bilemiyorum. Bir yanım, şiddetle karşı çıkmak istiyor. Bir yanım ise anlamak istiyor. Fakat bu örnek, esas itibarıyla, bir tarafın mantıken siyah-beyaz olması gerektiğini düşündüğü konularda, farklı deneyimlerin nasıl çok farklı görüşlere götürebileceğini gösteriyor.

İnsanların para konusunda verdikleri her karar, o sırada sahip oldukları bilgileri alıp dünyanın işleyişiyle ilgili kendilerine özgü zihinsel modelin içine yerleştirmeleriyle gerekçelendirilir.

Bu insanlar yanlış bilgilenmiş olabilir. Eksik bilgiye sahip olabilirler. Matematikte kötü olabilirler. Yozlaşmış pazarlama teknikleriyle ikna edilebilirler. Ne yaptıkları hakkında en küçük fikirleri olmayabilir. Karar ve eylemlerinin sonuçlarını yanlış değerlendirebilirler... Ah, hiç böyle yapabilirler mi?

Fakat insanların aldığı her finansal karar, o anda onlara mantıklı görünür ve kafalarının içindeki, doldurmaları gereken kutucukları doldurur. Yaptıkları şey konusunda kendilerine bir hikâye anlatırlar ve o hikâye onlara özgü, benzersiz deneyimlerle biçimlenmiştir.

Basit bir örneği, piyango biletlerini ele alalım.

Amerikalıların piyango biletlerine harcadıkları para, film, video oyunları, müzik, spor etkinlikleri ve kitap harcamalarının toplamından daha fazla.

Peki piyango biletlerini kim alıyor? Çoğunlukla yoksul insanlar.

ABD'de en alt gelir düzeyindeki haneler, piyango biletlerine yılda ortalama 412 dolar harcıyor ve bu rakam en yüksek gelir grubundakilerin dört katı. Amerikalıların yüzde 40'ı acil bir durumda 400 doları bir araya getiremiyor. Bu, şu anlama geliyor: Yılda 400 dolarlık piyango bileti alanların büyük bölümünü, acil bir durumda 400 doları bir araya getiremeyenler oluşturuyor. Kara günleri için bir kenara ayırmaları gereken parayı, büyük ikramiyeyi kazanma şansı milyonda bir olan bir şey için savuruyorlar.

Bu bana çılgınlık görünüyor. Muhtemelen size de öyle görünüyordur. Fakat ben en alt gelir grubunda değilim. Muhtemelen siz de değilsiniz. Bu nedenle de, piyango bileti alan alt gelir grubundaki insanların bilinçaltındaki muhakeme biçimini mantık çerçevesinde kavrayabilmek çoğumuz için zordur.

Yine de kendinizi biraz zorlayın ve şöyle bir şeyi hayal etmeye çalışın:

> Maaşla geçiniyoruz ve birikim yapmamız mümkün görünmüyor. Daha yüksek ücretle çalışma olanağımız da yok. Güzel tatillere çıkmaya, yeni arabalar almaya, özel sağlık sigortası yaptırmaya ve güvenli mahallelerdeki evlerde oturmaya gücümüz yetmiyor. Borç içinde kıvranmadan çocuklarımıza üniversite okutamıyoruz.

> Finans kitapları okuyan sizlerin şu anda elinde bulunan veya edinme şansının yüksek olduğu çoğu şey, bizde yok. Bizim için piyango bileti almak, sizin zaten sahip olduğunuz ve gayet doğal gördüğünüz iyi şeyleri elde edebilme bağlamında somut bir düş kurabilmenin tek yolu. Biz bir düş satın almak için para ödüyoruz ve siz o düşü zaten yaşamakta olduğunuz için bunu anlayamayabilirsiniz. Bu nedenle, sizden daha çok piyango bileti alıyoruz.

Bu tür bir mantık yürütmeyi kabul etmek zorunda değilsiniz. Parasız kalınca piyango bileti almak her şekilde kötü bir fikir. Fakat ben piyango satışlarının niçin sürmekte olduğunu bir miktar anlıyorum.

Ve bu fikir, yani "Yaptığın şey çılgınca görünüyor, fakat niçin yaptığını bir miktar anlayabiliyorum" düşüncesi, finansal kararlarımızın büyük bölümünün kökenini ortaya koyuyor.

Pek az kişi tamamen hesap tablolarına dayalı finansal kararlar alır. Bu tür kararlar genelde sofrada veya bir şirket toplantısında alınır. Ve bunlar, kişisel hayat hikâyenizin, size özgü dünya görüşünüzün, egonun, kibirin, pazarlamanın ve bazı tuhaf motivasyon unsurlarının bir araya gelerek size uygun bir anlatıya dönüştürüldüğü yerlerdir.

---

Parayla ilgili kararların neden bu kadar zor olduğunu ve niçin bu kadar çok yanlış davranış sergilendiğini açıklamaya yardımcı olan bir diğer önemli nokta da, bunun ne denli yeni bir konu olduğunu kabul etmek.

Para, uzun zamandır hayatımızda. İlk resmi para birimini, MÖ. 600 yılında, bugün Türkiye toprakları içinde yer alan Lidya'nın kralı Alyattes'in icat ettiği düşünülüyor. Fakat parasal kararların modern temeli -tasarruf ve yatırım- pratik olarak bebek denilebilecek kavramlara dayanıyor.

Örneğin, emekliliği ele alalım. 2018 yılı sonunda ABD'deki emeklilik hesaplarında 27 trilyon dolar vardı ve bu rakam, sıradan yatırımcının tasarruf ve yatırım kararlarını yönlendiren ana itkinin emeklilik olduğunu ortaya koyuyor.[5]

Fakat emeklilik hakkı kavramı bütününde, en fazla iki kuşak öncesine dayanıyor.

İkinci Dünya Savaşı öncesinde Amerikalıların büyük bölümü ölene dek çalışıyordu. Beklenti de, gerçek de buydu. Altmışbeş yaş üstü erkeklerin iş gücüne katılım oranı 1940'lara kadar yüzde 50'nin üzerindeydi:

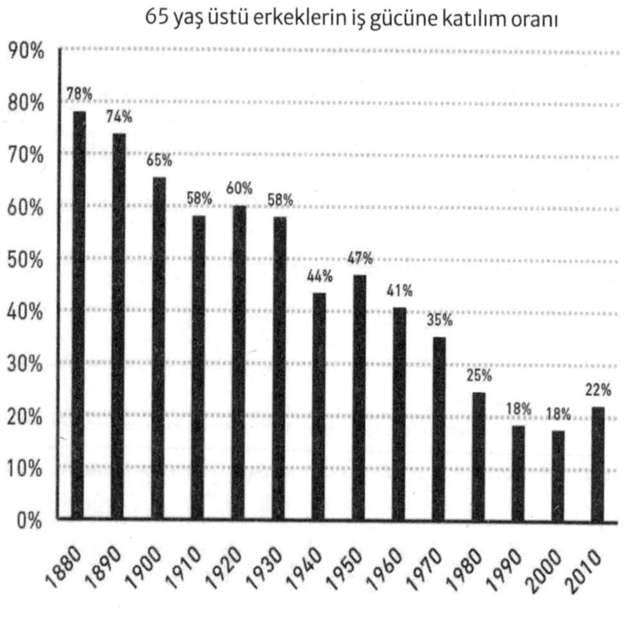

Sosyal Güvenlik yasası bunu değiştirmeyi hedefliyordu. Fakat başlangıçta sağladığı fayda ve olanaklar, doğru dürüst bir emekliliğe oldukça uzaktı. Ida May Fuller 1940 yılında ilk Sosyal Güvenlik ödeneğini aldığında, eline geçen rakam 22.54 dolardı; enflasyona uyarladığınızda 416 dolar. Enflasyona uyarlı ortalama Sosyal Güvenlik ödeneği, 1980'lere kadar aylık 1000 doların üzerine çıkmadı. 1960'ların sonuna kadar 65 yaş üstü Amerikalıların dörtte birinden fazlası Amerikan Nüfus Dairesi tarafından yoksul olarak sınıflandırılıyordu.

Toplumumuzda "Eskiden herkesin emekli aylığı vardı" şeklinde yaygın bir inanış mevcut. Fakat bu fazlasıyla abartılıyor. Employee Benefit Research Institute'a (Çalışanlara Yönelik Sosyal Yardımları Araştırma Enstitüsü) göre: "1975 yılında, 65 yaş üstü kesimin yalnızca dörtte birinin emekli aylığı vardı." O mutlu azınlık içinde, hane gelirinin yalnızca yüzde 15'i emekli aylığından geliyordu.

*New York Times* 1955 yılında, emekliye ayrılma isteğinin giderek arttığını, fakat bunu hayata geçirmedeki başarısızlığın sürmekte olduğunu yazıyordu: "Eski bir deyişle ifade edersek, herkesin dilinde emeklilik var; fakat görünen o ki, pek az kişi bu konuda bir şeyler yapıyor."[6]

Onurlu bir emekliliğin herkesin hakkı olduğu ve bu haktan herkesin yararlanması gerektiği fikri, ancak 1980'lerde yerleşebildi. O zamandan beri de, o onurlu emekliliği hak etmek için herkesin kendi parasından tasarruf ederek yatırım yapması gerektiğine dair bir beklenti gelişti.

Bunun ne kadar yeni bir fikir olduğunu yinelememe izin verin: 401(k) -ABD'de emeklilik sisteminin belkemiğini oluşturan yatırım aracı- 1978 yılına kadar hayata geçmiş değildi.

1998 yılına kadar Roth IRA* yoktu. Yani insan olsaydı, içki içme iznini henüz elde etmiş olacaktı.

Emeklilik dönemimiz için tasarruf etme ve yatırım yapma konusunda birçoğumuzun kötü olması, kimseyi şaşırtmasa gerek. Çılgın değiliz. Sadece, bu işte yeniyiz.

Aynı şey üniversite için de geçerli. 1940 yılında 25 yaş üstü lisans mezunu Amerikalıların oranı 20'de 1'in altında iken, 2015 yılında 4'te 1'e geldi.[7] Bu süre içinde, enflasyona uyarlı ortalama üniversite harcı, dört kattan fazla yükseldi.[8] Toplumu bu denli hızlı etkileyen, böylesine büyük ve önemli bir şey, başka bazı şeyleri, örneğin son 20 yılda niçin bu kadar çok sayıda insanın öğrenci kredileri konusunda yanlış kararlar aldığını açıklıyor. Onlarca yıllık birikmiş deneyim yok; öğrenmeye, ders çıkarmaya çalışmak için bile yeterince zaman geçmiş değil. Yeni yeni kanatlanıyoruz.

Geçmişi 50 yılı bulmayan endeks fonları için de aynı şey geçerli. Son 25 yılda hayatımıza giren hedge fonlar için de öyle. Gazi Yasası'nın** milyonlarca Amerikalı için borçlanmayı kolaylaştırdığı İkinci Dünya Savaşı sonrasına kadar tüketici kredileri bile yaygın kullanılmıyordu.

---

* Roth IRA: Belli bir gelir düzeyindeki kişilere açık olan bireysel emeklilik hesabıdır. 1997 yılında hayata geçirilmiş ve adını eski Delaware senatörü William Roth'dan almıştır. Roth IRA'lar ile geleneksel IRA'lar arasındaki en büyük fark, vergilendirilme biçimidir. Roth IRA sistemi, belirli koşulların yerine getirilmesi koşuluyla vergiden muaf olarak para çekmeye izin verir. (ÇN.)

** Gazi Yasası: (GI Bill) ABD'de İkinci Dünya Savaşı gazilerine, eve dönüşlerinden sonra mali ve sosyal yardım sağlamak amacıyla çıkarılan yasa. 1944 tarihli bu yasa adını, Amerikan askerinin "eğilmezliğini ve bükülmezliğini" vurgulayan Galvanized Iron (galvanize demir) teriminden alıyor. Savaşta, özellikle de İkinci Dünya Savaşı'nda çarpıştıktan sonra evlerine dönen askerler, kısaca GI olarak anılıyor. Kitap boyunca Gaziler olarak çevirdim. (ÇN.)

Köpekler 10,000 yıl önce evcilleştirildikleri halde, yabani atalarının bazı davranışlarını hâlâ koruyorlar. Biz ise, modern finansal sistemdeki 20-50 yıl arası deneyimimizle, mükemmel biçimde uyum sağlamayı ümit ediyoruz.

Olgular ve gerçeklerden çok, duygulardan etkilenen bir konu olması nedeniyle, bu durum sorun oluşturuyor. Fakat bir yandan da, para konusunda niçin her zaman doğru davranıp, yapmamız gerekeni yapmadığımızı açıklamaya yardımcı oluyor.

Hepimiz para konusunda çılgınca şeyler yapıyoruz; çünkü hepimiz bu oyunda görece yeniyiz ve size çılgınca görünen bir şey, bana mantıklı gelebilir. Fakat kimse çılgın değildir; hepimiz, kendimize özgü, benzersiz deneyimlerle, belli bir anda bize mantıklı gelen kararlar alırız.

Şimdi izninizle, Bill Gates'in nasıl zengin olduğuna dair bir hikâye anlatayım.

# 2

# Şans ve Risk

Hiçbir şey göründüğü kadar iyi veya
göründüğü kadar kötü değildir.

Şans ve risk kardeştir. İkisi de, yaşamda her sonucun bireysel çaba dışında bazı güçler tarafından yönetildiği gerçeğini ifade eder.

New York Üniversitesi (NYU) profesörü Scott Galloway, başarıyı -hem kendimizin, hem de başkalarınının başarısını- değerlendirirken hatırlamamız gereken çok önemli bir fikre işaret ediyor: "Hiçbir şey göründüğü kadar iyi veya kötü değildir."

---

Bill Gates dünyada bilgisayarı olan sayılı liselerden birinde okudu.

Seattle'ın hemen dışındaki Lakeside School'da bilgisayar olmasının çarpıcı bir hikâyesi var.

Bill Dougall İkinci Dünya Savaşı sırasında Amerikan donanmasında pilot olarak görev almıştı ve savaş sonrasında da matematik ve fen öğretmenliği yapıyordu. Microsoft'un kurucu ortağı, merhum Paul Allen'ın ifadesiyle "Yalnızca kitaplardan çalışmanın yeterli olmadığına inanan ve gerçek dünya deneyiminin önemini vurgulayan bir öğretmendi. Ayrıca da, gençlerin üniversiteye başladığında bilgisayarlar hakkında bazı şeyler bilmesi gerektiğini anlamıştı."

Dougall 1968 yılında, öğretmenlik yaptığı Lakeside School'un Anneler Kulübü'nden bir ricada bulunarak, yıllık kermes satışı gelirinden elde edilen paranın -yaklaşık 3000 dolar- General Electric'in ana terminaline bağlı Teletype 30 Model paylaşımlı bir bilgisayarın kiralanmasında kullanılmasını istedi. Gates ileride bu konudan söz ederken "Paylaşımlı sistem fikrinin henüz 1965 yılında icat edilmiş olduğunu" belirterek, "Birileri oldukça ileri görüşlüydü," ifadesini kullanacaktı. Birçok üniversitenin lisans bölümlerinde, Bill Gates'in sekizinci sınıfta erişebildiği kadar ileri bilgisayar yoktu. Ve Gates kendini bilgisayardan alamıyordu.

Bill Gates 1968 yılında sınıf arkadaşı Paul Allen ile tanıştığında 13 yaşındaydı. Allen da onun gibi okulun bilgisayarını takıntı haline getirmişti ve iyi anlaşıyorlardı.

Lakeside'ın bilgisayar etkinliği, genel ders programına dahil değildi. Bağımsız ve seçmeli bir programdı. Bill ile Paul okuldan sonraki serbest zamanlarında, haftasonları gece yarılarına kadar bilgisayar başında dilediklerini yapıyor, yaratıcılıklarını coşturuyorlardı. Kısa sürede bilgisayar kurdu olmuşlardı.

Allen yıllar sonra o günlere dair şöyle bir anısını paylaşmıştı: "Bir gece geç saatlerde yine bilgisayar başındayken, Gates bana *Fortune* dergisini göstererek 'Fortune 500 şirketlerinden birini yönetmek sence nasıl bir şey?' diye sordu. Hiçbir fikrim olmadığını söyledim. Gates de bana, 'Belki bir gün kendi bilgisayar şirketimiz olur' dedi." Microsoft'un şu andaki değeri bir trilyon doların üzerinde.

Hızlıca biraz matematik yapalım.

Birleşmiş Milletler'e göre 1968 yılında dünya genelinde orta öğrenim yaşındaki nüfus, yaklaşık 303 milyondu.

Bunun yaklaşık 18 milyonu ABD'de yaşıyordu.

Yaklaşık 270 bini Washington eyaletindeydi.

Yüz binden biraz fazlası Seattle bölgesindeydi.

Seattle'daki yüz binden biraz fazla öğrencinin yalnızca 300'ü Lakeside School'a gidiyordu.

Orta öğrenim çağındaki bir milyon öğrenciden yalnızca bir tanesinin karşısında, bilgisayar satın almak için gereken nakit ve ileri görüşlülük bileşimi vardı. Bill Gates onlardan biriydi.

Gates, bu söylediğim şeyin ifade ettiği anlam konusunda kendini kötü hissetmiyor. Okulun 2005 yılı mezuniyet töreninde yaptığı konuşmada şöyle demişti: "Lakeside olmasaydı, Microsoft olmazdı."

Gates inanılmaz zeki ve fevkalâde çalışkan, esasen inanılmaz zekâsından bile çalışkan bir insan; ayrıca, bilgisayarların geleceği konusunda, sektördeki en deneyimli yöneticilerin bile yakalayamadığı vizyonu, henüz ergenlik çağındayken geliştirmişti. Aynı zamanda da Lakeside Lisesi'ne gitmekle bir milyon kişiden önde başlangıç yapmıştı.

Şimdi izin verirseniz, Gates'in arkadaşı Kent Evans'tan söz etmek istiyorum. Evans, şansın kardeşi riskten de aynı oranda güçlü bir doz deneyimlemişti.

Microsoft'un başarısı sayesinde Bill Gates ve Paul Allen isimleri evlerimizin içine kadar girdi. Fakat onların döneminde Lakeside lisesindeki bilgisayar dâhileri ekibinin üçüncü bir üyesi daha vardı.

Kent Evans ile Bill Gates sekizinci sınıfta çok iyi arkadaş olmuşlardı. Gates'in ifadesiyle, Evans sınıfın en iyi öğrencisiydi.

Gates, *Inside Bill's Brain* (Bill'in Beyninin İçi) adlı belgeselde Kent ile yaptıkları "gülünç denecek kadar uzun telefon konuşmalarını" anımsıyor. "Kent'in telefon numarasını hâlâ biliyorum" diyor: "525-7851."

Evans da bilgisayar konusunda Gates ve Allen kadar yetenekliydi. Lakeside bir zamanlar okulun ders programını ayarlamakta zorluk çekiyordu; yüzlerce öğrencinin almış olduğu dersleri birbiriyle çakışmayacak şekilde düzenlemek hayli karmaşık bir iş. Okul yönetimi, bu sorunu çözecek bilgisayar programını yazma görevini Bill ile Kent'e -sonuçta iki çocuk- vermişti.

Paul Allen'ın tersine, Bill'in ticari zekâsı ve sonsuz hırsı Kent'te de vardı. Gates belgeselde, "Kent hep avukatlarınki gibi büyük bir çantayla dolaşırdı" diyor ve şöyle anlatıyor: "Sürekli beş veya altı yıl sonra yapacaklarımızı planlardık. CEO mu olalım? Ne tür bir etkimiz olabilir? General mi olmalıyız? Büyükelçi mi olmalıyız?" Bill ile Kent ne yapacaklarını bilmeseler de, her ne olursa olsun birlikte yapacaklarını biliyorlardı.

Gates belgeselde Kent ile olan arkadaşlığını anımsarken durgunlaşıyor.

"Birlikte çalışmaya devam edebilirdik. Eminim, üniversiteye beraber giderdik" diyor.

Kent de Gates ve Allen ile birlikte Microsoft'un kurucu ortağı olabilirdi.

Fakat Kent, liseden mezun olamadan, dağcılık yaparken bir kazada hayatını kaybetmişti.

ABD'de her yıl yaklaşık 36 kişi dağcılık yaparken yaşamını yitiriyor.[9] Lise çağında dağa tırmanırken ölme olasılığı, yaklaşık olarak milyonda bir.

Bill Gates, Lakeside Lisesi'ne girmekle milyonda bir kişinin sahip olduğu şansı deneyimlemiştir. Kent Evans, Gates ile birlikte başarmak istediklerini gerçekleştiremeyerek milyonda bir kişinin karşılaşabileceği riski deneyimlemiştir. Zıt yönlerde hareket eden aynı güçte, aynı büyüklükte iki kuvvet.

Şans ve risk, yaşamda elde edilen her sonucun bireysel çabanın dışında güçler tarafından yönetildiği gerçeğini ifade eder. Birbirlerine o kadar benzerler ki, ikisine de eşit derecede saygı göstermeden ne birine, ne de diğerine inanabilirsiniz. Her ikisi de başımıza gelir; çünkü dünya eylemlerinizin yüzde 100'ünün, sonuçlarınızın yüzde 100'ünü belirleyemeyeceği kadar karmaşıktır. Aynı güçle hareket ederler: Yedi milyar insan ve hareket halindeki sonsuz parçadan oluşan bir oyundaki tek kişisinizdir. Sizin kontrolünüz dışındaki eylemlerin rastlantısal etkisi, sonuç bağlamında, bilinçli karar ve eylemlerinizden daha önemli olabilir.

Her ikisini de hem ölçmek, hem de kabul etmek zordur; bu yüzden de çoğu kez gözden kaçırılır. Her Bill Gates'in karşısında, onun kadar yetenekli ve azimli olduğu halde yaşam ruletinin karşı tarafına denk gelmiş bir Kent Evans vardır.

Şansa ve riske gerektiği gibi saygı gösterirseniz, insanların finansal başarılarını -hem kendinizinkini, hem de başkalarınınkini- değerlendirirken, hiçbir zaman göründüğü kadar iyi veya göründüğü kadar kötü olmadığını fark edersiniz.

---

Yıllar önce Nobel ödüllü ekonomist Robert Shiller'e, "Yatırım konusunda bizim bilemeyeceğimiz ne bilmek istiyorsunuz?" diye sormuştum.

"Başarılı sonuçlarda şansın tam olarak nasıl bir rol oynadığını" diye cevap vermişti.

Bu yanıtı seviyorum; çünkü gerçekte hiç kimse, finansal başarıda şansın rolü olmadığını düşünmez. Fakat şansı nicel olarak ölçmek zor olduğundan ve insanların başarısını şansa borçlu olduğunu ima etmek kaba kaçacağından, varsayılan duruş genellikle, başarıda şans faktörünü dolaylı olarak görmezden gelmektir.

Size, "Dünyada bir milyar yatırımcı var" desem ve "tamamen rastlantısal olarak, bunlardan 10 tanesinin büyük ölçüde şans eseri milyarder olduğunu bekler miydiniz?" diye sorsam, "Tabii ki" diye yanıt verirsiniz. Fakat bu yatırımcıların kimler olduğunu -onların yüzüne- söylemenizi istesem, muhtemelen yanıt vermekten çekinirsiniz.

Öyle olduğunu bilsek bile, başkalarını değerlendirirken başarılarını şansa bağlamak sizi kıskanç ve kötü gösterir. Kendinizi değerlendirirken başarınızı şansa bağlamak ise, kabul edilemeyecek kadar moral bozucu olabilir.

Ekonomist Bhashkar Mazumder, erkek kardeşler arasında gelir düzeylerinin boy ve kilodan daha korelasyonlu olduğunu kanıtlamış bulunuyor. Siz zengin ve uzun boylu iseniz, erkek kardeşinizin de zengin ve uzun boylu olma olasılığı yüksek. Bence çoğumuz, kendi içimizde bunun doğru olduğunu biliyoruz. Aldığınız eğitimin kalitesi ve size açılan kapılar, büyük ölçüde anne ve babanızın sosyo-ekonomik durumuyla bağlantılı. Fakat siz bana zengin iki erkek kardeş bulun, ben de size bu çalışmanın bulgularının onlar için geçerli olmadığını düşünen iki erkek kardeş göstereyim.

Başarısızlığı değerlendirirken de -ki bu iflastan tutun da kişisel bir amacı gerçekleştirememeye kadar her şey olabilir- aynı hataya düşülür.

Başarısız işletmeler yeterince uğraş vermiyor mu? Kötü yatırımlar yeterince iyi düşünülmeden mi yapılıyor? Tutarsız kariyerler tembellikten mi kaynaklanıyor? Bazen, evet. Tabii ki öyle...

Fakat ne kadar? Peşinden gitmeye değen her şeyin başarılı olma olasılığı yüzde 100'ün altında; risk ise, denklemin talihsiz tarafında olduğumuzda başımıza gelen şey. Aynı şansta olduğu gibi, bir sonucun ne kadarının içerdiği riske oranla bilinçli bir karar olduğunu eleştirel bir gözle değerlendirmeye çalışırsak, mesele fazlasıyla zor, dağınık ve karmaşık bir hal alır.

Diyelim ki bir hisse senedi aldım ve beş yıl sonra olduğu yerde kaldı. Daha en başında satın almakla yanlış bir karar vermiş olmam mümkün. Para kazandırma olasılığı yüzde 80 olan iyi bir karar vermiş olup da olasılıklardaki şanssız yüzde 20'lik kesite düşmüş olmam da mümkün. Hangisi olduğunu nasıl bilirim? Hata mı yaptım, yoksa yalnızca risk gerçeğini mi deneyimliyorum?

Önceden verilmiş bazı kararların akıllıca olup olmadığını istatistiksel olarak ölçmek mümkün. Fakat gerçek dünyada, gündelik yaşamda bunu yapmayız. Kolay ama çoğu kez fazlasıyla yanlış yönlendiren basit hikâyeleri tercih ederiz.

Yatırımcılar ve şirket liderleri arasında yıllar geçirdikten sonra, başkalarının başarısızlığının genelde kötü kararlara bağlandığını, buna karşılık kişinin kendi başarısızlığının çoğu kez riskin karanlık tarafına yüklendiğini gördüm. Sizin başarısızlıklarınızı değerlendirirken büyük olasılıkla açık ve basit bir neden-sonuç hikâyesini tercih ediyorum; çünkü sizin kafanızın içinden geçenleri bilmiyorum. Bana göre en mantıklı hikâye "Kötü bir sonuç aldığınıza göre, kötü bir karar vermiş olmalısınız" şeklinde. Fakat kendimi yargılarken, geçmişteki kararlarımı haklı göstererek ve kötü sonuçları riske bağlayarak müthiş bir hikâye uydurabilirim.

İyi kararlar almış, fakat riskin talihsiz tarafını deneyimlemiş yatırımcılar *Forbes* dergisinin kapağında boy göstermez. Fakat hemen her zaman vasat, hatta belki pervasızca kararlar almış ve şansı yaver gitmiş zengin yatırımcılar *Forbes*'a kapak olur. Aynı parayla yazı-tura atmışlar, kimine yazı, kimine tura gelmiş.

Bu meselenin tehlikeli yönü şu: Hepimiz para konusunda neyin doğru, neyin yanlış olduğunu öğrenmeye çalışıyoruz.

Hangi yatırım stratejileri iyi sonuç veriyor? Hangileri vermiyor?

Nasıl zengin oluruz? Yoksul düşmekten nasıl kaçınırız?

Bu dersleri öğrenirken genellikle başarıları ve başarısızlıkları gözlemliyoruz ve kendimize "Falancanın yaptığını yap; filancanın yaptığını yapmaktan kaçın" diyoruz.

Elimizde sihirli bir değnek olsaydı, bu sonuçların ne kadarının tekrarlanabilir karar ve eylemlerden kaynaklandığını; buna karşılık bu karar ve eylemlerin iki yönden birine yönelmesinde rastlantısal risk ve şansın ne kadar rol oynadığını ve bu iki olasılığın birbirine oranını tam olarak bulabilirdik. Fakat elimizde sihirli bir değnek yok. Beyinlerimiz nüanslara bakmaya pek istekli değil ve kolay yanıtları tercih ediyor. Bu yüzden de, örnek almamız veya kaçınmamız gereken özellikleri belirlemek, sıkıntı yaratacak düzeyde zor olabiliyor.

İzninizle bir hikâye daha anlatayım. Bu hikâyemizin kahramanı da Bill Gates gibi müthiş başarılı biri; fakat başarısının yeteneğinden mi şansından mı kaynaklandığını açıkça söylemek zor.

---

Cornelius Vanderbilt yönetmekte olduğu demiryolu imparatorluğunu genişletecek bir dizi iş anlaşmasını henüz tamamlamıştır.

Danışmanlarından biri kendisine giderek, altına imza attığı her anlaşmayla yasaları çiğnediğini söyler.

Vanderbilt danışmanına bakar ve "Aman Tanrım, John…" der. "Bir demiryolunu New York Eyaleti'nin yasalarına uygun olarak yönetebileceğini düşünmüyorsun, öyle değil mi?"[10]

Bunu okuduğumda ilk düşündüğüm şey şuydu: "Bu tutumu sayesinde o kadar başarılı oldu." Vanderbilt'in döneminde yasalar demiryolları açısından elverişli değildi. O yüzden de "yasaların canı cehenneme" diyerek kendi bildiği gibi devam etmişti.

Vanderbilt müthiş başarılıydı. Böylece de yasaları göz ardı etme yaklaşımını -ki başarısında son derece önemli bir unsur olduğu herkesçe biliniyordu- bilgelik olarak görme fikri, ona çekici geliyordu. O hırçın vizyoner, hiçbir şeyin yoluna çıkmasına izin vermiyordu!

Fakat bu analiz ne kadar tehlikeli? Aklı başında hiç kimse, bile bile suç işlemeyi, iyi bir girişimcilik özelliği olarak görüp tavsiye etmez. Vanderbilt'in hikâyesinin çok farklı bittiğini hayal etmeniz hiç zor değil; yasaları çiğnediği için yaptığı iş yasa dışı ilan edildi ve genç şirketi mahkeme emriyle çökertildi.

Dolayısıyla da, burada bir sorunumuz var.

Vanderblit'i yasaları çiğnediği için coşkuyla överken, aynısını yapmış olan Enron'u hararetle eleştirebilirsiniz. Belki de kanunun kuvvetinden kaçarken birinin şansı yaver gitmiş, diğeri ise kendini riskin karanlık tarafında bulmuştu.

John D. Rockefeller için de aynı şeyi söyleyebiliriz. Sık sık yasalardaki boşluklardan yararlanması -bir yargıç şirketi için "sıradan bir hırsızdan daha iyi değil" ifadesini kullanmıştı- tarihçiler tarafından çoğu kez "kurnaz ticaret kafası" olarak tanımlanıyor. Belki de öyleydi. Fakat hikâye ne zaman değişir ve "Güncelliğini yitirmiş eski yasaların, inovasyonun yoluna çıkıp engellemesine izin vermedin" söyleminin yerini, "Suç işledin" söylemi alır? Ya da "Rockefeller bir dâhiydi, başarılarından ders almaya çalışın" söyleminin yerini, "Rockefeller bir suçludur, ticari başarısızlıklarından ders almaya çalışın"a dönmesi için hikâyenin ne kadar değişmesi gerekir? Çok az.

Vanderbilt bir zamanlar "Yasadan bana ne?" demişti. "Güç bende değil mi?"

Yaptı ve işe yaradı. Fakat bunun, çok farklı sonuçlanan bir hikâyenin son sözleri olduğunu hayal etmek gayet kolay. Cesur ile pervasız arasındaki çizgi ince olabilir. Riske ve şansa doğru faturayı kesmediğimizde de, o ince çizgi genellikle görünmez olur.

Benjamin Graham tüm zamanların en büyük yatırımcılarından biri, değer yatırımının fikir babası ve Warren Buffett'ın ilk dönemlerdeki akıl hocası olarak tanınır. Fakat Benjamin Graham'ın yatırım başarısının büyük bölümü, büyük miktarda GEICO hissesine sahip olmasından kaynaklanıyordu; ki bu da, kendisinin de kabul ettiği gibi, meşhur metinlerinde dile getirdiği çeşitlendirme kurallarının hemen hemen her birini çiğnemek anlamına geliyordu. Cesur ile pervasız arasındaki ince çizgi burada nereye düşüyor? Bilmiyorum. Graham, bonanzası* GEICO için şöyle yazmıştı: "Talih kuşu veya fevkalâde zekice bir karar; ikisini birbirinden ayırabilir miyiz?" Pek kolay olmaz.

Aynı şekilde, 2006 yılında, Yahoo!'nun şirketini satın almak için yaptığı bir milyar dolarlık teklifi geri çevirdiği için Mark Zuckerberg'in de dâhi olduğunu düşünüyoruz. Geleceği gördü ve silahlarına yapıştı. Fakat insanlar, Yahoo!'nun Microsoft'tan gelen satın alma teklifini geri çevirmesini aynı

---

* Bonanza: Aniden gelen büyük şansı, yani "talih kuşu" dediğimiz olguyu ifade eder. Fakat aynı zamanda olağanüstü büyük ve zengin maden yatağı anlamında da kullanıldığı için Bonanza olarak bırakmayı uygun gördüm. (ÇN)

hararetle eleştiriyorlar; ah şu ahmaklar, yapabiliyorken nakite geçmeliydiler! Girişimcilerin buradan çıkarması gereken ders ne? Hiçbir fikrim yok; çünkü risk ile şansı birbirinden ayırmak çok zor.

Sayısız servet (ve iflas) kaldıraç kullanmanın sonucunda gelmiştir.

En iyi (ve en kötü) yöneticiler, çalışanlarını ellerinden geldiğince sıkı çalıştırırlar.

"Müşteri her zaman haklı" ve "Müşteri ne istediğini bilmiyor" söylemlerinin ikisi de ticari bilgelik olarak kabul edilir.

"İlham verecek derecede cesur" ile "aptalca pervasızlık" arasındaki çizgi bir milimetre olabilir ve ancak sonradan görülebilir.

Şans ve risk, ikiz gibi birbirine benzer.*

Bu kolay çözülebilecek bir sorun değil. Neyin şans, neyin beceri ve neyin risk olduğunu belirlemek, parayı en iyi nasıl yöneteceğimizi öğrenmeye çalışırken karşı karşıya kaldığımız en büyük problemlerden biri.

Fakat iki şey, sizi daha iyi bir yöne yöneltebilir.

**Kimi övüp kime hayran olduğunuza dikkat edin. Kimi küçük görüp, onun gibi olmak istemediğinize dikkat edin.**

Bir başka ifadeyle, sonuçların yüzde 100'ünün gösterilen çabaya ve alınan kararlara bağlı olduğunu varsayarken dikkatli olun. Oğlum dünyaya geldikten sonra ona bir mektup yazmıştım ve mektubun bir yerinde şöyle demiştim:

---

* Yazar burada, aynı biyolojik kökenden gelmedikleri halde ikiz gibi birbirine benzeyen iki varlığı ifade eden "doppelgangers" terimini kullanıyor. (ÇN)

Bazı insanlar eğitime önem veren ailelerin bir üyesi olarak dünyaya gelirler; bazıları ise eğitime karşı ailelerin. Bazıları girişimciliği teşvik eden, gelişen ve büyüyen ekonomilerin içine doğarlar; bazıları savaş ve sefalet koşullarında dünyaya gelirler. Başarılı olmanı ve bunu hak etmeni istiyorum. Fakat bütün başarıların çok çalışmaya bağlı olmadığını ve bütün sefaletlerin de tembellikten kaynaklanmadığını anla. Kendin dahil, insanları yargılarken bunu unutma.

**Dolayısıyla da, belli bireylere ve vaka calışmalarına daha az, yaygın kalıplara ise daha çok odaklanın.**

Uçlardaki örnekleri incelemek tehlikeli olabilir; çünkü genelde uç örnekleri -milyarderleri, CEO'ları veya haberlere egemen olan büyük çaplı iflasları- inceleme eğilimi gösteririz ve içerdikleri karmaşıklık nedeniyle uç örneklerin başka durumlara uygulanabilirliği asgari düzeydedir. Sonuç ne kadar ekstrem olursa, çıkarılacak dersleri kendi yaşamınıza uygulama ihtimali o kadar düşer; çünkü sonucun, şans ve riskin aşırı uçlarından etkilenmiş olma olasılığı da bir o kadar yüksektir.

Başarı ve başarısızlığın daha yaygın kalıplarına bakarak hayata geçirilebilir çıkarımlara yaklaşırsınız. Kalıp ne kadar yaygınsa, sizin hayatınıza uygulanabilirliği de o kadar fazla olabilir. Warren Buffett'ın yatırım başarısını göstermek zordur; çünkü aldığı sonuçlar o kadar uçlarda ki, ömür boyu performansında büyük ihtimalle şansın rolü çok olmuştur ve şans güvenilir bir şekilde taklit edilebilecek bir şey değildir. Fakat Yedinci Bölüm'de göreceğimiz gibi, zamanlarını kontrol eden insanların hayatta daha mutlu olma eğilimi sergilemeleri, işinize yarayabilecek, yeterince yaygın ve genel bir gözlemdir.

Sevdiğim tarihçi Frederick Lewis Allen, kariyeri boyunca ortalama Amerikalı'nın yaşamını tanımlamaya uğraştı; nasıl yaşadıklarını, nasıl değiştiklerini, hangi işleri yaptıklarını, akşam yemeğinde ne yediklerini, vesaire. Haberlere egemen olan uç şahsiyetleri inceleyerek öğrenileceklerdense, bu tür geniş kapsamlı gözlemlerde daha yararlı dersler olduğunu düşünüyorum.

---

Bill Gates bir keresinde şöyle demişti: "Başarı kötü bir öğretmendir. Zeki insanların zihnini çelerek kaybetmeyeceklerini düşünmeye iter."

İşler aşırı derecede iyi giderken, bunun düşündüğünüz kadar iyi olmadığını anlayın. Yenilmez değilsiniz ve size başarıyı getirenin şans olduğunu kabul ediyorsanız, o halde hikâyenizi aynı hızla tersine çevirebilecek olan kuzeni riske de inanmalısınız.

Fakat aynı şey tersi için de doğru.

Başarısızlık berbat bir öğretmen olabilir; çünkü bazen, yalnızca riskin acımasız gerçeklerini düşündükleri kimi zamanlarda, zeki insanların zihnini çelerek korkunç kararlar vermiş olduklarını düşünmeye iter. Başarısızlıkla başa çıkmanın püf noktası, finansal yaşamınızı, kötü bir yatırımın ve ulaşılamamış bir finansal hedefin sizi tamamen bitirmeyeceği, böylece de olasılıklar lehinize dönünceye kadar oyunda kalmaya devam edebileceğiniz şekilde düzenlemektir.

Ancak daha da önemlisi, başarıda şansın rolünü giderek daha iyi anladıkça, riskin rolü kendimizi affetmemiz ve başarısızlıkları yargılarken anlayışa yer bırakmamız gerektiği anlamına gelir.

Şimdi, şanslarını zorlayan iki adamın hikâyesine bakalım.

# 3

# Asla Yetmez

Zengin insanlar aptalca şeyler yaptığında...

2019 YILINDA KAYBETTİĞİMİZ, Vanguard'ın kurucusu John Bogle bir keresinde, para konusunda yeterince kafa yormadığımız bir şeye ışık tutan bir hikâye anlatmıştı:

> Kurt Vonnegut, bir milyarderin Shelter Adası'nda verdiği bir davette, arkadaşı Joseph Heller ile sohbet ederken, davete ev sahipliği yapan hedge fon yöneticisinin bir günde kazandığı paranın, Heller'in müthiş popüler kitabı Madde 22'den* o güne dek elde ettiği gelirin tamamından fazla olduğunu söyler. Heller de "Evet, ama ben de onun asla yeterince sahip olamayacağı bir şeye sahibim..." yanıtını verir.
>
> *Yeterince.* Bu sözcüğün içerdiği etkili ifadeye hayran olmuştum; bunun iki nedeni vardı: Birincisi, kendi yaşamımda bana çok şey verildi; ikincisi, Joseph Heller bundan daha doğru ifade edemezdi.
>
> Günümüz toplumunun eleştirilecek unsurlarından biri, yeterli sözcüğünün, aramızdaki en zengin ve en güçlü kişilerin çoğu dahil olmak üzere bizler için ifade ettiği anlam konusunda bir sınır yok gibi görünmesi.

Bu gerçekten son derece zekice ve muazzam güçlü bir ifade.

---

* Madde 22: Bu kitabın İngilizce orijinal adı Catch-22 idi. (ÇN)

Bir şeye sahip olma bağlamında "yeterli" diyememenin tehlikelerine dair iki örnek vereyim ve bunlardan ne gibi dersler alabileceğimize bakalım.

---

Rajat Gupta, Kolkata'da doğmuş ve ergenlik çağında yetim kalmıştı. İnsanlar, hayata beyzboldaki üçüncü kaleden başlayan ayrıcalıklı bir azınlıktan söz ederler. Gupta hayatında beyzbol stadyumu bile görmemişti.

O başlangıç noktasından sonra başardıkları ve elde ettikleri ise hakikaten muazzamdı.

Gupta 40'lı yaşlarının ortasında, dünyanın en prestijli danışmanlık firması McKinsey'in CEO'suydu. 2007 yılında, Birleşmiş Milletler ve Dünya Ekonomik Forumu'nda bazı görevler üstlenmek üzere şirketten ayrıldı. Bağış ve hayırseverlik alanında Bill Gates ile bazı ortak çalışmalar yürütmeye başladı. Halka açık beş şirketin yönetim kuruluna girdi. Kolkata'nın varoşlarından gelen Gupta, kelimenin gerçek anlamıyla, o dönemin en başarılı iş insanlarından biri oldu.

Başarısı muazzam bir serveti de beraberinde getirdi. 2008 yılı itibarıyla Gupta'nın servetinin değerinin 100 milyon dolar olduğundan söz ediliyordu.[11] Bu çoğumuzun erişemeyeceği, akıl almaz bir para... O kadar büyük paranın yıllık yüzde 5 getirisi, saatte neredeyse 600 dolar üretir; üstelik her gün, 24 saat boyunca.

Gupta hayatta istediği her şeyi yapabilirdi.

Anlatılanlara bakılırsa da, istediği sadece 100 milyon dolarlık bir milyoner olmak değildi. Rajat Gupta milyarder olmak istiyordu. Üstelik bunu fena halde istiyordu.

Gupta, Goldman Sachs'ın yönetim kurulundaydı; yani çevresi dünyanın en varlıklı bazı yatırımcılarıyla sarılıydı. Bir yatırımcı özel sermaye devlerinin kazançlarından söz ederken Gupta'yı şöyle tanımlıyor: Bence o çevrede olmak istiyordu. Sonuçta orası milyarderler çevresi. Goldman, yüzlerce milyon dolarlık servete sahip olan insanların bir araya geldiği bir çevre, öyle değil mi?[12]

Doğru. Böylece Gupta bol kazançlı bir ek iş bulmuştu.

2008 yılında, Goldman Sachs finansal krizin gazabına uğradığı sırada, Warren Buffett bankanın ayakta kalabilmesine yardımcı olmak için 5 milyar dolar yatırım yapmayı düşünmüştü. Goldman'ın yönetim kurulu üyesi olması vesilesiyle, Gupta bu işlemi kamuoyundan önce öğrenmişti. Kıymetli bir bilgiydi. Goldman'ın ayakta kalıp kalmayacağı şüpheliydi ve Buffett'ın desteğinin bankanın hissesini yükselteceği kesindi.

Henüz nihai karara bağlanmamış olan bu anlaşmayı, Goldman'ın yönetim kurulu toplantısı sırasında bağlanan bir telefonla öğrenen Gupta, 16 saniye sonra telefona uzanıp Raj Rajaratnam adlı bir hedge fon yöneticini aramıştı. Bu arama kaydedilmemiş; fakat Rajaratnam, anında 175,000 adet Goldman Sachs hissesi aldığına göre, ne konuşulduğunu tahmin edersiniz. Sonuç olarak, Buffett-Goldman anlaşması saatler sonra kamuoyuna açıklandı. Goldman hissesi yükseldi. Rajaratnam hızlı bir şekilde bir milyon dolar kazandı.

Bu olay Gupta'nın bu eğilimine yönelik iddialardan yalnızca bir tanesiydi. SEC (ABD'nin Sermaye Piyasası Kurulu) Gupta'nın içeriden aldığı bilgilerle 17 milyon dolar kâr sağladığını iddia ediyor.

Kolay paraydı. Soruşturmayı yürüten savcılar içinse daha da kolay bir dava oldu.

Gupta ile Rajaratnam içeriden öğrenenlerin ticareti suçundan* cezaevine girdi; her ikisinin de kariyeri ve itibarı, geri dönülemez biçimde mahvoldu.

Şimdi de Bernie Madoff'u ele alalım. İşlediği suç herkesçe biliniyor. Madoff, Charles Ponzi'nin kendisinden sonra gelmiş geçmiş en tanınmış Ponzi düzenbazı. Suçu açığa çıkıncaya kadar, 20 yıl boyunca yatırımcıları dolandırdı; işin ironik yanı, bu düzenbazlığın da Gupta'nın hummalı faaliyetinden sadece birkaç hafta sonra ortaya çıkmış olmasıydı.

Bu olayda gözden kaçan şey, Madoff'un da, tıpkı Gupta gibi sadece bir dolandırıcı olmadığıydı. Kendisini meşhur eden Ponzi planından önce, Madoff da yasalara uygun davranan, son derece başarılı ve meşru bir iş insanıydı.

Madoff piyasa yapıcıydı, dolayısıyla da işi, hisse senedi alıcıları ile satıcılarını eşleştirmekti. Bu işte çok iyiydi. *Wall Street Journal* 1992 yılında Madoff'un piyasa yapıcı şirketini şöyle tanımlıyordu:

> Büyük Kurul'da** devasa hacimli hisse senedi işlemleri gerçekleştiren ve hayli kârlı bir menkul kıymet şirketi olan Bernard L. Madoff Investment Securities'i kurdu. Madoff'un şirketi günde ortalama 740 milyon dolarlık elektronik işlem yapıyor ve bu rakam, New York Borsası'ndaki işlemlerin yüzde 9'una karşılık geliyor. Madoff'un şirketi, son derece hızlı ve ucuza işlem gerçekleştirebiliyor; müşterilerinin emirlerini yerine getiren broker'lık firmalarına hisse başına bir peni

* İçeriden öğrenenlerin ticareti (insider trading): Kamuya açıklanmamış bilgiye dayalı ticaret. (ÇN.)

** Büyük Kurul: Big Board; New York Borsası için kullanılan bir terim. (ÇN)

ödüyor; böylece de çoğu hissenin işlem gördüğü alış ve satış fiyatları arasındaki farktan (spread'den) kâr ediyor.

Bu yazıyı hazırlayan gazeteci, henüz ortaya çıkmamış bir dolandırıcılığı yanlış aktarıyor değildi. Madoff'un yürüttüğü piyasa yapıcılık işi yasaldı. Eski çalışanlardan birinin ifadesine göre, Madoff'un şirketinin piyasa yapıcı kolu, yılda 25 ile 50 milyon dolar arasında kazanıyordu.

Bernie Madoff'un düzenbazlık yapmayan meşru şirketi, her yönüyle muazzam bir başarıydı. Dahası, onu muazzam -ve de meşru- bir şekilde servet sahibi yapmıştı.

Ama bir kez daha, işin içine düzenbazlık girmişti.

Gerek Gupta, gerekse Madoff konusunda kendimize şu soruyu sormalıyız: Yüzlerce milyon dolarlık varlığa sahip olan biri, niçin daha fazla kazanmak için böylesine gözükara davranıp her şeyini riske atar?

Ayakta kalma mücadelesi veren insanların, bulundukları o ince çizgide suç işlemeleri ayrı bir konu. Bir keresinde, Nijeryalı düzenbaz bir sanatçı *New York Times*'a yaptığı açıklamada, başkalarına zarar verdiği için kendini suçlu hissettiğini, fakat "yoksulluğun suçluluk duygusunun getirdiği acıyı insana yaşatmayacağını" söylemişti.[13]

Gupta ile Madoff'un yaptığı ise çok başka bir şey. Zaten her şeyleri vardı: Hayal edilemeyecek bir servet, prestij, güç, özgürlük. Fakat daha fazlasını istedikleri için bütün bunları bir kenara attılar.

*Yeter* duyguları yoktu.

Bunlar uç örnekler. Fakat bu davranışın kriminal olmayan versiyonları da var.

Hedge fonu Long-Term Capital Management'ta kişisel serveti onlarca, hatta yüzlerce milyon dolar olan trader'lar çalışıyordu ve servetlerinin büyük bölümünü kendi fonlarına yatırmışlardı. Sonra, daha fazlasına sahip olmak için o kadar çok risk aldılar ki, 1998 yılında, tarihin en güçlü ekonomisinin ve en büyük boğa piyasasının ortasında, her şeylerini kaybetmeyi başardılar.

Warren Buffett bunu daha sonra şöyle yorumladı:

> Sahip olmadıkları ve ihtiyaçları olmayan parayı kazanmak için sahip oldukları ve ihtiyaç duydukları şeyleri riske attılar. Bu aptallık. Bu tamamen aptallık. Sizin için önemli bir şeyi, önemli olmayan bir şey için riske atmak son derece anlamsız.
>
> Sahip olduğunuz ve ihtiyaç duyduğunuz şeyleri, sahip olmadığınız ve ihtiyaç duymadığınız şeyler için riske atmanız için hiçbir neden yok.

Son derece bariz olan, fakat bir o kadar göz ardı edilen şeylerden biri de budur.

Çok azımızın Gupta veya Madoff gibi 100 milyon doları olacak. Ancak bu kitabı okuyanların önemli bir yüzdesi, hayatlarının bir noktasında, ihtiyaç duydukları ve makûl olan her şeyi, ayrıca istediklerinin çoğunu karşılayacak bir maaş alacaklar veya buna yetecek miktarda paraya sahip olacaklar. Eğer siz de onlardan biriyseniz, birkaç şeyi unutmayın.

**1. En zor finansal beceri, hedefi yerinden oynatmamaktır.**

Bu, zor olması bir yana, aynı zamanda da en önemli becerilerden biridir. Sonuçlarla birlikte beklentiler de yükseliyorsa, daha fazlası için uğraş vermenin herhangi bir mantığı yok; çünkü, daha fazla çaba harcadıktan sonra da aynı duyguyu hissedeceksiniz. Daha fazlasına, daha çok paraya, daha çok güce, daha çok prestije sahip olmanın verdiği haz, eğer hırsı, tatmin duygusundan daha hızlı artırırsa tehlikeli olmaya başlar. Bu durumda ileri doğru atılan bir adım, hedefi iki adım ileri iter. Kendinizi geride kalmış gibi hissedersiniz ve farkı kapatıp hedefe ulaşmanın tek yolu, giderek daha fazla risk almak olur.

Modern kapitalizm iki şeyde uzmandır: Servet üretmek ve kıskançlık yaratmak. Belki de bu ikisi el ele ilerliyor; emsallerinizin önüne geçme isteği, sıkı çalışmanın yakıtı olabilir. Fakat "yeter" duygusu olmazsa, hayatın hiçbir eğlencesi kalmaz. Dedikleri gibi mutluluk, aslında sadece sonuç, eksi beklentidir.

**2. Burada sorun, sosyal kıyaslamadır.**

Yılda 500,000 dolar kazanan çaylak bir beyzbol oyuncusu düşünün. Bu gelir düzeyiyle, nereden bakarsanız bakın zengindir. Fakat diyelim ki, 430 milyon dolara 12 yıllık kontrat imzalamış olan Mike Trout ile aynı takımda oynuyor. Aralarında bir kıyaslama yaparsanız, çaylak oyuncunun hali fenadır. Şimdi de Mike Trout'u düşünün. Yılda 36 milyon dolar çılgınca bir miktar. Fakat unutmayın ki, 2018 yılının en çok kazanan ilk 10 hedge fon yöneticisi listesine girebilmek için yılda en az 340 milyon dolar kazanmanız gerekiyordu.[14] Yılda 340 milyon dolar kazanan hedge fon yöneticisi de kendini, 2018 rakamlarına göre yılda en az 770 milyon dolar kazanan ilk beş hedge fon yöneticisi ile karşılaştırır. İlk beştekiler, kendilerinden de önde olanlarla, 2018 yılında kişisel serveti 3.5 milyar dolar artan Warren Buffett gibi insanlarla karşılaştırmaya gidebilirler. Ve Buffett gibi biri de daha ileriye, 2018 yılında net değeri 24 milyar dolar yükselmiş olan Jeff Bezos'a bakabilir; bir denklem kurarsak, Bezos'un bir saatte kazandığı para "zengin" beyzbol oyuncusunun bir yıl boyunca kazandığından daha fazla.

Burada bütün mesele, sosyal kıyaslamada tavan noktasının, gerçekte hiç kimsenin erişemeyeceği kadar yüksek olmasıdır. Yani hiçbir zaman kazanılamayacak bir savaştır; ya da kazanmanın tek yolu, sizin sahip olduklarınız, çevrenizdekilerin sahip olduklarından az da olsa, elinizdekilerle yetinip böyle bir savaşa hiç girişmemektir.

Bir arkadaşım yılda bir kez Las Vegas'ı tavaf eder. Bu ziyaretlerinden birinde krupiyeye, "Siz hangi oyunları oynuyorsunuz ve hangi kumarhanelere gidiyorsunuz?" diye sormuş. Krupiye taş gibi sert bir ifadeyle şu yanıtı vermiş: "Las Vegas'ta bir kumarhanede kazanmanın tek yolu, girer girmez çıkmaktır."

Başkalarının servetine erişmeye çalışırken de tamamen aynı şey geçerli; oyunun işleyişi bu.

### 3. "Yeterli" çok az demek değildir.

"Yettiği" kadarına sahip olma fikri muhafazakârlık gibi görünebilir; fırsatı ve potansiyeli masada bırakıp gitmek olarak yorumlanabilir.

Ben bunun doğru olduğunu düşünmüyorum.

Bence "Yeterli" demek, tam tersinin -daha fazlası için doyumsuz bir açlığın- sizi pişmanlık noktasına iteceğinin farkına varmaktır.

Ne kadar yemek yiyebileceğinizi bilmenin tek yolu, mide fesadına uğrayıp hasta oluncaya kadar yemektir. Böyle bir şeyi pek az kişi dener; çünkü yemek ne kadar güzel olursa olsun, kusmak insanı bir o kadar kötü yapar. Fakat bazı nedenlerle iş dünyası ve yatırımda aynı mantık geçerli değil; çoğu kişi daha fazlası için uğraşmayı sürdürüyor ve ancak her şey mahvolduğunda ve durmak zorunda kaldığında buna son veriyor. Elbette ki, böyle bir durum kişinin işinin bozulması veya sürdüremeyeceği riskli bir yatırım gibi masum bir nedenden de kaynaklanabilir. Fakat üzerinde yaşadığımız dünyada, sonuçları ne olursa olsun her kuruşa değdiğini düşünerek çalma yoluna giden Rajat Gupta'lar ve Bernie Madoff'lar da var.

Ne var ki, her ne olursa olsun o bir kuruşa sırt çevirememek, eninde sonunda gelip sizi bulur.

### 4. Kazanç potansiyeli ne olursa olsun riske asla değmeyecek birçok şey vardır.

Rajat Gupta cezaevinden salıverildikten sonra *New York Times*'a yaptığı açıklamada yaşadıklarından bir ders aldığını söyledi:

> Hiçbir şeye -itibarınıza, başarınıza veya buna benzer hiçbir şeye- fazla bağlanmayın. Şimdi düşünüyorum da, ne önemi var? Evet, bu meselenin haksız yere itibarımı mahvettiği doğru. Fakat bu, yalnızca itibarıma çok bağlanıp önem verdiğim takdirde sıkıntı verecek bir şey.

Bu ifadeler, yaşadığı deneyimden çıkarılabilecek en kötü sonuç gibi görünüyor ve benim gördüğüm, itibarının yok olup gittiğini bilen, fakat onu umarsızca geri kazanmak isteyen bir adamın kendini haklı çıkarmaya çalışarak rahatlama çabasından başka bir şey değil.

İtibar paha biçilmezdir.

Özgürlük ve bağımsızlık paha biçilmezdir.

Aile ve dostlar paha biçilmezdir.

Sevdikleriniz tarafından sevilmek paha biçilmezdir.

Mutluluk paha biçilmezdir.

Ve bütün bunları elinizde tutmanın en iyi yolu, zamanı geldiğinde, onlara zarar verecek risklere girmekten vazgeçebilmektir. Sizin için yeterli olan noktaya geldiğinizi bilmektir.

Güzel haber şu ki, "*yeterli*" noktası oluşturmak için kullanılabilecek araç fevkalâde basit ve yukarıda saydığım paha biçilmez değerlerin hiçbirine zarar verebilecek riskler almayı gerektirmiyor.

# 4

# Bileşiklenmenin Gücünü Doğru Kavrayamamak

Warren Buffett'ın net değeri 84.5 milyar dolar olan varlıklarının 81.5 milyar doları 65'inci doğum gününden sonra geldi. Zihinlerimiz bu tür abesliklerle başa çıkabilecek şekilde oluşturulmamış.

BİR ALANDA ALINAN dersler, çoğu kez hiç ilgisi olmayan alanlar hakkında önemli şeyler öğretir. Örneğin buzul çağının bir milyar yıllık tarihini ve paramızı büyütmek için bize neler öğrettiğini ele alalım.

---

Yeryüzüne ilişkin bilimsel bilgilerimiz düşündüğümüzden daha kısa bir geçmişe dayanıyor. Dünyanın işleyişini anlamak, çoğu kez yüzeyinin hayli derinliklerini araştırmayı gerektiriyor, ki bu da yakın dönemlere kadar pek de yapamadığımız bir şey. Isaac Newton yıldızların hareketini, gezegenimize ilişkin bazı temel unsurları anlamamızdan çok önce değil, sadece birkaç yüzyıl önce hesapladı.

Bilim insanları ancak Ondokuzuncu Yüzyıl'da, yeryüzünün birkaç kez buzlarla kaplandığı konusunda görüş birliğine varabildi.[15] Aksini iddia etmek için fazlasıyla kanıt vardı. Dünyanın her yeri, daha önceki dönemlerde donmuş bir yerkürenin izlerini taşıyordu: Rastgele yerlere dağılmış devasa kayalar; ince katmanlara ayrılmış kaya yatakları. Zamanla, tek bir buzul çağı değil, üzerinde çalışıp değerlendirebileceğimiz beş ayrı buzul çağı olduğuna dair kanıtlar giderek açıklık kazandı.

Gezegenimizi dondurmak, tekrar eritmek, sonra yeniden dondurmak için muazzam miktarda enerji gerekiyordu.

Yeryüzünde (kelimenin gerçek anlamıyla yeryüzünde, yani dünyanın yüzeyinde) bu döngülere ne yol açıyor olabilirdi? Bu her ne ise, gezegenimizdeki en kuvvetli güç olmalıydı.

Öyleydi de. Fakat hiçbirimizin beklemediği bir şekilde.

Önceleri buzul çağlarının nasıl oluştuğuna dair çok sayıda teori vardı. Dahası bunlar, muazzam jeolojik etkilerini gözler önüne serecek kadar muazzam teorilerdi. Sıradağların yükseltilerinin, dünyanın rüzgârlarını iklim değişikliğine yol açacak kadar değiştirebilmiş olabileceği düşünülüyordu. Bazıları ise dünyanın doğal halinin buzul olduğunu ve bu doğal halin, bizi ısıtan büyük çaplı volkanik patlamalarla kesintiye uğradığı fikrine sıcak bakıyordu.

Ne var ki, bu teorilerin hiçbiri buzul çağlarının döngüsünü açıklayamıyordu. Sıradağların yükselişi veya bazı büyük yanardağlar tek bir buzul çağını açıklayabilirdi. Fakat bu döngünün beş kez yinelenmesini açıklayamıyordu.

1900'lerin başında Milutin Milankoviç adlı Sırp bilim insanı, Dünya'nın diğer gezegenler karşısındaki konumunu inceleyerek, bugün doğru olduğunu bildiğimiz buzul çağları teorisini ortaya koydu: Buna göre, güneşin ve ayın yerçekimsel gücü, Dünya'nın hareketini hafifçe etkilemekte ve Dünya, güneşe doğru eğilmekte. Bu döngünün bazı dönemlerinde -ki bu onbinlerce yıl sürebiliyor- Dünya'nın iki yarımküresi, normalin biraz altında veya biraz üstünde güneş ışını alıyor.

Ve işin eğlenceli kısmı da burada başlıyor.

Milankoviç'in teorisi başlangıçta, Dünya'nın yarımkürelerindeki bir eğimin, gezegenimizi buzula çevirecek kadar şiddetli kışlara yol açtığını varsayıyordu. Fakat Wladimir Köppen adlı bir Rus meteorolog, Milankoviç'in çalışmalarını daha da derinleştirerek, büyüleyici bir ayrıntı keşfetti.

Gezegenimizin buza dönüşmesinin suçlusu soğuk kışlar değil, hafif serin geçen yazlardı.

Döngü, hava bir yaz, o kış yağan karı eritecek kadar ısınmadığında başlıyor. Hafif serin geçen yaz ayları boyunca erimemiş olan buz tabanı, ertesi kış karın birikmesini kolaylaştırıyor, ki bu da hem ertesi yaz karın kalkmama olasılığını artırıyor, hem de bir sonraki kış daha da çok kar birikmesini getiriyor. Sürekli kar yağması ve kalkmayan kar tabakası, güneş ışığını daha fazla yansıtarak soğumayı şiddetlendiriyor; bu da daha fazla kar yağmasını getiriyor ve süreç böyle devam ediyor. Birkaç yüzyıl boyunca biriken mevsimsel kar yığını, muazzam bir buz tabakasına dönüşüyor ve buzul süreci başlıyor.

Tersi durumda da aynı şey oluyor. Dünyanın yörüngesinde, daha fazla güneş ışığı girmesine yol açan bir eğim meydana geldiğinde daha çok kar eriyor ve bu da izleyen yıllarda daha az ışık yansımasına yol açıyor; o durumda ısı artıyor; ısının artması, ertesi yıl daha çok kar yağmasını önlüyor ve böyle devam ediyor. Döngü bu.

Burada çarpıcı olan nokta, koşullardaki görece küçük bir değişiklikten böylesine büyük bir şeyin ortaya çıkması. Serin geçen bir yazdan kalan ve o dönemde kimsenin önemsemediği ince bir kar tabakasıyla başlıyorsunuz ve sonra, jeolojik anlamda göz açıp kapayıncaya kadar kısa bir sürede, yeryüzünün tamamı kilometrelerce kalınlıkta buz tabakasıyla kaplanıyor. Buz bilimci Gwen Shultz'un ifade ettiği gibi, "Buz tabakalarının oluşmasını mutlaka yağan kar miktarıyla ilişkilendirmek gerekmiyor; asıl önemli nokta, karın erimeyip yeryüzünde kalmış olması."

Buzul çağlarından çıkarabileceğimiz en önemli ders şu: Müthiş sonuçlar elde etmek için müthiş bir güce sahip olmanız gerekmiyor.

Bir şey bileşerek büyüyorsa -küçük bir büyüme gelecekteki büyüme için yakıt oluşturuyorsa- küçük bir başlangıç temeli o denli olağanüstü sonuçlara yol açabilir ki, mantığa meydan okuyormuş gibi görünür. Neyin mümkün olduğunu, büyümenin nereden geldiğini ve neye yol açabileceğini hafife almanız mantığa aykırı olabilir.

Para konusunda da böyledir.

---

Warren Buffett'ın servetini nasıl oluşturduğuna dair 2000'den fazla kitap yazılmıştır. Bunların birçoğu harika kitaplardır. Fakat pek azı, basit bir gerçeğe yeterince değinir: Buffett'ın serveti yalnızca iyi bir yatırımcı olmasından değil, kelimenin gerçek anlamıyla çocukluğundan beri iyi bir yatırımcı olmasından kaynaklanmıştır.

Bu satırları yazdığım sırada Warren Buffett'ın varlıklarının net değeri 84.5 milyar dolardı. Bunun 84.2 milyar doları 50'inci doğum gününden sonra birikmişti; 81.5 milyar doları, 60'lı yaşlarının ortalarında, Sosyal Güvenlik sistemi kapsamında emekliliği hak ettiği dönemde gelmişti.

Warren Buffett fenomen bir yatırımcıdır. Fakat başarısının tamamını yatırım dehasına bağlarsanız, kilit bir noktayı kaçırırsınız. Başarısının gerçek anlamda anahtarı, bir yüzyılın dörtte üçü boyunca, yaklaşık 75 yıl fenomen yatırımcı olmasıdır. Yatırım yapmaya 30'lu yaşlarında başlasaydı ve 60'lı yaşlarında emekli olmayı seçseydi, çok az kişi adını duymuş olabilirdi.

Küçük bir fikir jimnastiği yapalım.

Buffett ciddi anlamda yatırım yapmaya başladığında 10 yaşındaydı. Otuz yaşına geldiğinde servetinin net değeri 1 milyar dolar, enflasyona uyarlanmış haliyle de 9.3 milyon dolardı.[16]

Peki ya Buffett daha normal bir insan olsaydı, gençliğini ve 20'li yaşlarını dünyayı keşfederek, tutkusunu bularak geçirseydi ve de 30 yaşına geldiğinde net değeri, diyelim ki 25,000 dolar olsaydı?

Ya da diyelim ki, o olağanüstü yıllık yatırım getirilerini elde etmeyi sürdürseydi (yıllık yüzde 22), fakat 60 yaşına geldiğinde, golf oynamak ve torunlarıyla vakit geçirmek için yatırım işini bırakıp kendini emekli etseydi?

O zaman bugünkü net değeri kabaca ne kadar olurdu?

84.5 milyar dolar olmazdı.

11.9 milyon dolar olurdu.

Şu andaki net değerinin yüzde 99.9 altında.

Warren Buffett'ın finansal başarısının tamamını, ergenlik yıllarında inşa ettiği finansal temele ve yaşlılık yıllarında sürdürdüğü uzun ömürlülüğe bağlamak çok doğru olabilir.

Yeteneği yatırım, fakat sırrı zamandır.

Bileşiklenme* işte böyle işler.

Bunu bir de şöyle düşünün. Evet, Buffett tüm zamanların en zengin yatırımcısı. Fakat şu anda en "büyük" yatırımcı Buffett değil, en azından yıllık ortalama getirilerle ölçülüğünde.

Renaissance Technologies adlı hedge fonun başındaki Jim Simons 1988 yılından bu yana yıllık yüzde 66 oranında getiri üretti. Bu rekora yaklaşan kimse yok. Az önce gördüğümüz

* Bileşiklenme (compounding): Bileşerek bütünleşme, büyüme, birikme, çoğalma, toplanma. (ÇN.)

gibi, Buffett yıllık bazda kabaca yüzde 22, yani Simons'ın üçte biri kadar bir miktara ulaştı.

Bu satırları yazdığım sırada Simons'ın varlıklarının net değeri 21 milyar dolardı. Simons'ın serveti -söz ettiğimiz rakamların ışığında kulağa ne kadar saçma geldiğini biliyorum ama- Buffett'ın yüzde 25'i kadar.

Simons daha iyi bir yatırımcıysa, aradaki bu yüzde 75'lik fark neden? Çünkü Simons, 50 yaşına gelene dek yatırım işinde atacağı doğru adımı bulamadı. Simons'ın yatırım alanında geçirdiği zaman, Buffett'ın servetini topladığı zamanın yarısından daha az. Eğer James Simons yüzde 66 yıllık getirileri, Buffett gibi 70 yıllık bir zaman aralığında elde etseydi, serveti -lütfen nefesinizi tutun- altmış üç kentilyon dokuz yüz katrilyon yedi yüz seksen bir trilyon yedi yüz seksen milyar yedi yüz kırk sekiz milyon yüz altmış bin dolar olurdu.

Bunlar pratikte mümkün olamayacak kadar komik rakamlar. Mesele şu ki, büyüme varsayımlarında küçük gibi görünen değişiklikler, komik ve pratikte mümkün olmayan rakamları getirebilir.

Dolayısıyla da, bir şeyin neden bu kadar güçlü hale geldiğini -bir buzul çağının niçin oluştuğunu veya Warren Buffett'ın neden bu kadar zengin olduğunu- araştırırken, başarının temel itici güçlerini genellikle gözden kaçırırız.

Pek çok insanın şöyle dediğini duyarım: Bileşik faiz tablosunu görmek -ya da birikim yapmaya 30'larınızda değil de 20'li yaşlarda başladığınızda emeklilik birikiminizin ne kadar daha büyük olacağına dair hikâyelerden birini duymak- hayatımı değiştirdi. Fakat muhtemelen değiştirmedi. Bileşik faiz tablosunu görmenin veya o hikâyelerden birini duymanın yaptığı şey muhtemelen, onları şaşırtmaktı; çünkü sonuçlar sezgisel olarak doğru görünmüyordu. Doğrusal düşünme, üstel düşünmeden çok daha sezgiseldir. Sizden 8+8+8+8+8+8+8+8+8'i aklınızdan toplamanızı istesem, birkaç saniye içinde yapabilirsiniz (72'dir). Fakat 8×8×8×8×8×8×8×8×8'yi ezbere hesaplayın desem, kafanız patlar (134,217,728'dir).

IBM, 1950'lerde 3.5 megabitlik bir sabit sürücü yaptı. 1960'lara gelindiğinde birkaç düzine megabite çıkıldı. 1970'lerde IBM'in Winchester sürücüsünün saklama alanı 70 megabitti. Sonra sürücülerin boyutları katlanarak küçülürken, saklama alanları giderek büyüdü. 1990'ların başında tipik bir PC'nin saklama alanı 200-500 megabitti. Ve sonra... *booom*... her şey patladı.

1999: 6 gigabitlik sabit sürücüsüyle Apple'ın iMac'i geldi.

2003: Power Mac'te 120 gig'e çıkıldı.

2006: Yeni iMac'te 250 gig'e çıkıldı.

2011: 4 terabitlik ilk sabit sürücü;

2017: 60 terabitlik sabit sürücüler;

2019: 100 terabitlik sabit sürücüler geldi.

Bütün bunları bir araya getirirsek: 1950 yılından 1990'a kadar saklama alanında 296 megabit kazandık. 1990'dan bugüne kadar ise 100 milyon megabit kazandık.

1950'lerde teknoloji konusunda iyimser görüşte biri olsaydınız, saklama alanının 1000 kat büyüyeceğini tahmin etmiş olabilirdiniz. Oldukça coşkulu bir iyimser olsaydınız, belki 10,000 kat büyüyeceğini söylerdiniz. Buna karşılık, pek az kişi "Benim ömrüm sürecince 30 milyon kat büyüyecek" diyebilirdi. Fakat, öyle oldu.

Bileşerek bütünleşmenin mantık dışı doğası, en zekilerimizin bile, bu olgunun gücünü gözden kaçırmasına neden olabilir. Bill Gates, 2004 yılında yeni Gmail'i eleştirdi ve insanların bir gigabit saklama alanına ihtiyaç duyacak olmasına şaşırdığını ifade etti. Yazar Steven Levy şöyle yazıyor: "En ileri teknolojiler konusunda böylesine güncel olmasına rağmen, muhafaza edilmesi gereken bir emtia olan saklama alanı konusundaki zihniyeti hâlâ eski paradigmaya dayanıyordu." Bazı şeylerin ne kadar hızlı büyüyebileceğine asla alışamazsınız.

Buradaki tehlike, bileşme/bileşiklenme olgusunu sezgisel olarak kavrayamadığımız zaman, içerdiği potansiyeli genellikle görmezden gelmemiz ve sorunları başka yollarla çözmeye odaklanmamızdır. Fazla düşündüğümüzden değil, bileşiklenmenin içerdiği potansiyeli nadiren oturup düşündüğümüz için böyle yaparız.

Buffett'ın başarısının altını çizen 2000 kitabın hiçbirinin başlığı "*Bu Adam 75 Yıldır Aralıksız Yatırım Yapıyor*" değil. Oysa başarısının büyük bölümünde kilit unsurun bu olduğunu biliyoruz. Sadece, sezgisel olmadığı için bu matematiğe kafamızın basması zor.

Ekonomik döngülere, alım-satım stratejilerine ve sektörlere dair çok sayıda kitap var. Ama en önemli ve en güçlü kitabın adı "*Kapa çeneni ve Bekle*" olmalı. Uzun vadeli ekonomik büyüme grafiğini içeren tek sayfalık bir kitap.

Bu kıssadan çıkarılabilecek hisse, hayal kırıklığı yaratan alım-satım işlemlerinin, kötü stratejilerin ve başarılı yatırım girişimlerinin çoğunun sorumlusunun, bileşiklenmenin mantık dışılığı olabileceğini anlayabilmektir.

Öğrendikleri ve yaptıkları şeylerde en yüksek yatırım getirilerini elde etmek için bütün çabalarıyla uğraş verdikleri için insanları suçlayamazsınız. Sezgisel olarak, zengin olmanın en iyi yolu bu gibi görünüyor.

Ancak iyi yatırım, mutlaka en yüksek getiriyi elde etme meselesi değildir; çünkü en yüksek getiriler, tekrarlanamayan tek seferlik isabetli atışlar olma eğilimindedir. İyi yatırım, sebatla sürdüreceğiniz ve çok uzun bir süre boyunca tekrarlanabilecek oldukça iyi getiriler elde etme meselesidir. Bileşiklenme, işte o zaman coşar.

Bunun tersi -elinizde tutamayacağınız devasa getiriler elde etmek- bazı trajik hikâyelere yol açar. Bunları da izleyen bölümde anlatacağım.

# 5

# Varlıklı Olmak Mı? Varlıklı Kalmak Mı?

İyi yatırım, mutlaka iyi kararlar almaya bağlı değildir. İşleri sürekli olarak berbat etmeme meselesidir.

ZENGİN OLMANIN MİLYON tane yolu ve bunu nasıl yapacağınızı anlatan bol miktarda kitap olduğu doğru.

Fakat varlıklı kalmanın tek yolu var: Bir miktar tutumluluk ile bir miktar paranoyanın bileşiminden oluşan kıvamında bir karışım.

Ve bu, yeterince tartışmadığımız bir konu.

Birbirini hiç tanımayan, fakat neredeyse bir yüzyıl önce ilginç bir şekilde yolları kesişen iki yatırımcının hikâyesiyle hızlı bir giriş yapalım.

---

Jesse Livermore, zamanının en büyük hisse senedi trader'ıydı. 1877 doğumlu Livermore, çoğu insan böyle bir şeyin varlığından bile habersizken profesyonel trader olmuştu. Otuz yaşına geldiğinde, servetinin enflasyona uyarlı değeri 100 milyon dolardı.

Jesse Livermore 1929'da zaten dünyanın en tanınmış yatırımcılarından biriydi. O yıl Büyük Buhran'ı başlatan borsa çöküşü, Jesse Livermore adını tarihe kazıdı.

1929 Ekimi'nin son haftasında, ileride Kara Pazartesi, Kara Salı ve Kara Perşembe olarak adlandırılacak olan üç gün içinde, hisse senedi piyasası üçte birden fazla değer kaybetti.

Livermore 29 Ekim günü eve döndüğünde, eşi Dorothy en kötüsünden korkuyordu. Wall Street spekülatörlerinin intihar ettiğine dair haberler New York'a yayılmaktaydı. Eşi ve çocukları Jesse'yi gözyaşları içinde karşıladılar; kayınvalidesi o kadar perişandı ki çığlıklar atarak başka bir odaya saklanmıştı.

Biyografi yazarı Tom Rubython'a göre, Jesse birkaç dakika öylece durup şaşkın şaşkın etrafına bakmış; kafasını toplayıp da olup bitenleri anlayıncaya kadar tek kelime etmemişti.

Sonrasında da müthiş haberi ailesine vermişti: Şansı ve dâhiyane bir hareketi sayesinde, piyasada kısa pozisyon almış, düşecek olan hisselere oynamıştı.

"Mahvolmadık mı yani?" diye sormuştu Dorothy.

"Hayır sevgilim..." demişti Jesse. "Bugüne kadarki en iyi işlem günümü geçirdim; inanılmaz zenginiz ve ne istersek yapabiliriz."

Dorothy doğruca annesine koşup rahatlamasını söylemişti.

Jesse Livermore bir gün içinde 3 milyar doların üzerinde para kazanmıştı.

Borsa tarihinin en kötü haftalarından birinde, dünyanın en zengin adamlarından biri olmuştu.

Livermore ailesi bu akıl almaz başarıyı kutlarken, bir başka adam, çaresizlik içinde New York sokaklarını arşınlamaktaydı.

Abraham Germansky multimilyoner bir emlak geliştiricisiydi; 1920'lerde servet kazanmıştı. Kükreyen 1920'lerin sonlarında, ekonomi patlamaktayken, o da hemen her başarılı New Yorklu'nun yaptığını yaparak, yükselişteki hisse senedi piyasasında çok büyük bahislere girmişti.

26 Ekim 1929 günü *New York Times* Germansky'nin trajik sonunu anlatan iki paragraflık bir haber yayınladı:

> Bayan Abraham Germansky dün sabah, Broadway'deki 225 no'lu binada faaliyet gösteren avukatı Bernard H. Sandler'i, Mount Vernon'dan arayarak Perşembe

> sabahından beri kayıp olan kocasını bulmasına yardımcı olmasını istedi. Sandler, Doğu Yakasında emlak işletmeciliği yapan 50 yaşındaki Germansky'nin hisse senetlerinde büyük çaplı yatırımı olduğunu söyledi.
>
> Bayan Germansky'nin Sandler'e verdiği bilgiye göre, bir arkadaşı, kocasını Perşembe günü geç saatlerde Wall Street'te, borsanın yakınlarında görmüştü.
>
> Bu şahsın Bayan Germansky'e söylediğine göre, kocası Broadway'e doğru yürürken elindeki fiyat şeridini parçalayarak kaldırıma saçıyordu.

Ve bildiğimiz kadarıyla, Abraham Germansky'nin sonu buydu.

Burada bir çelişki var.

Ekim 1929 çöküşü Jesse Livermore'u dünyanın en zengin adamlarından biri yaptı. Abraham Germansky'yi ise mahvetti, belki de canını aldı.

Ancak izleyen dört yılı hızla ileri sararsanız hikâyelerin yolları tekrar kesişir.

1929'daki zaferinden sonra, aşırı derecede özgüven geliştiren Livermore, giderek daha büyük bahislere girdi. Borçlarının artmasıyla çok yara aldı ve sonunda her şeyini borsada kaybetti.

1933'te sıfırı tüketti ve bunun utancıyla iki gün ortadan kayboldu. Eşi onu bulmak için harekete geçti. New York Times 1933'te, "1100 Park Avenue'de oturan borsa trader'ı Jesse L. Livermore kayıp ve dün öğleden sonra saat 3'ten beri görülmedi" diye yazıyordu.

Livermore döndü, ama önündeki yol artık belliydi. Bir zaman sonra canına kıydı.

Zamanlama farklı olsa da, Germansky ile Livermore bir karakter özelliğini paylaşıyorlardı: İkisi de servet sahibi olma konusunda çok iyiydiler, buna karşılık serveti elde tutma konusunda aynı oranda kötüydüler.

"Servet sahibi" olmak kendinize uyarlayacağınız bir sözcük olmasa bile, bu gözlemden çıkarılan dersler, her gelir seviyesindeki herkes için geçerlidir.

Parayı elde etmek bir şeydir. Onu elde tutmak ise başka bir şeydir.

---

Para konusunda başarıyı tek bir kelimeyle özetlemem gerekirse, "ayakta kalmak" derim.

Altıncı Bölüm'de göreceğimiz gibi, halka açık hale gelecek kadar başarılı olan şirketlerin yüzde 40'ı, zaman içinde değerinin tamamını fiilen kaybetti. Forbes 400'ün en zengin Amerikalılar listesinde, ölüm veya başka bir aile üyesine para transferi dışında nedenlerle gerçekleşen 10 yıllık değişim oranı ortalamada yüzde 20 civarında.[17]

Kapitalizm zordur. Ancak bunun bir nedeni, para kazanmanın ve parayı elde tutmanın iki farklı beceri olmasıdır.

Para kazanmak risk almayı, iyimser olmayı ve kendinizi ortaya koymayı gerektirir.

Ancak parayı elde tutmak, risk almanın tam tersini gerektirir. Alçakgönüllü olmayı ve elde ettiğiniz şeyin aynı hızla sizden geri alınabileceğinden korkmayı gerektirir. Tutumlu olmayı ve elde ettiklerinizin en azından bir kısmının şansa bağlanabileceğini kabul etmeyi gerektirir; bu nedenle de geçmişteki başarının sonsuza dek tekrarlanacağına güvenilemez.

Charlie Rose, Sequoia Capital'in başındaki milyarder Michael Moritz'e, Sequoia'nın niçin bu kadar başarılı olduğunu sormuş. Moritz, bazı girişim sermayesi şirketlerinin beş veya on yıl boyunca başarı gösterdiğini, ancak Sequoia'nın 40 yıldır başarılı olduğunu belirterek, uzun ömürlülüğe değinmiş. Rose neden böyle diye sormuş ve konuşma söyle devam etmiş:

> Moritz: Sanırım, başarısız olmaktan her zaman korktuk.
>
> Rose: Gerçekten mi? Yani korku, öyle mi? Yalnızca paranoidler mi ayakta kalır?
>
> Moritz: Bu söylediğinizde gerçek payı çok büyük... Biz yarının dün gibi olmayacağını varsayıyoruz. Başarılarımıza güvenip yan gelip yatamayız. Halimizden memnun olamayız. Dünün başarısının yarının iyi şansına dönüşeceğini varsayamayız.

İşte yine, ayakta kalma meselesi.

"Büyüme" veya "beyin" veya "içgörü" meselesi değil. En büyük farkı yaratan şey, pes etmeden veya vazgeçmeye zorlanmadan uzun süre ortalıkta kalabilmek. İster yatırımda, ister kariyerinizde, ister sahibi olduğunuz işletmede, stratejinizin temel taşı bu olmalı.

Ayakta kalma zihniyetinin para bağlamında bu kadar önemli olmasının iki nedeni var.

Bunlardan biri bariz: Sıfırı tüketmeyi göze alabilecek türden kazanımlar pek az görülür.

Diğeri ise, Dördüncü Bölüm'de gördüğümüz gibi, bileşiklenmenin mantığa aykırı matematiğidir.

Bileşiklendirme, yalnızca bir varlığa büyümesi için yıllar verilebiliyorsa işe yarar. Meşe ağacı dikmek gibidir: Bir yıllık büyüme asla fazla ilerleme göstermez; 10 yıl anlamlı bir fark geliştirebilir ve 50 yıl kesinlikle olağanüstü bir şey yaratabilir. Ancak bu olağanüstü büyümeyi elde etmek ve sürdürmek, herkesin zaman içinde kaçınılmaz olarak deneyimlediği bütün o öngörülemeyen iniş-çıkışlardan kurtulmayı gerektirir.

Buffett'ın yatırım getirilerini nasıl elde ettiğini, en iyi şirketleri, en ucuz hisse senetlerini, en iyi yöneticileri nasıl bulduğunu anlamaya çalışmak için yıllarca uğraşmamız gerekebilir. Bu zor. Fakat o kadar zor olmayan ama eşit önemde başka bir şey yapabilir ve Buffett'ın neleri yapmadığına odaklanabiliriz.

Borca sürüklenmedi.

Yaşadığı 14 ekonomik durgunluk sırasında paniklemedi ve satmadı.

Ticari itibarını lekelemedi. Tek bir stratejiye, tek bir dünya görüşüne veya geçici bir eğilime yapışıp kalmadı.

Başkalarının parasına bel bağlamadı (yatırımları, halka açık bir şirket aracılığıyla yönetmek, yatırımcıların sermayelerini geri çekemeyecekleri anlamına geliyordu). Kendini ateşe atmadı, işi bırakmadı veya emekli olmadı.

Ayakta kaldı. Ayakta kalmak ona uzun ömürlülük verdi. Ve uzun ömürlülük -10 yaşından en az 89 yaşına kadar sürekli yatırım yapmak- bileşiklendirmenin harika bir şekilde işlemesini sağlayan şeydir. Bu tek nokta, onun başarısını tanımlamadaki en önemli unsurdur.

Ne demek istediğimi gösterebilmem için Rick Guerin'in hikâyesini dinlemelisiniz.

Warren Buffett-Charlie Munger ikilisinin yatırımcı olarak ortaklığını muhtemelen duymuşsunuzdur. Oysa 40 yıl önce grubun bir üyesi daha vardı: Rick Guerin.

Warren, Charlie ve Rick birlikte yatırım yapıyorlardı, şirket yöneticileriyle birlikte görüşüyorlardı. Sonra Rick, en azından Buffett ve Munger'ın başarısına kıyasla diyelim, ortalıktan kayboldu. Yatırımcı Mohnish Pabrai bir keresinde Buffett'a, Rick'e ne olduğunu sormuş. Mohnish, o gün aralarında geçen konuşmayı şöyle anımsıyor:

> [Warren] şöyle dedi: "Charlie ile ben inanılmaz varlıklı olacağımızı biliyorduk. Varlıklı olmak için acelemiz yoktu; olacağını biliyorduk. Rick de bizim kadar akıllıydı, fakat acele ediyordu."
>
> Sonuçta olay şuydu: 1973-1974 krizinde Rick kaldıraç kullanmıştı. O iki yıl içinde hisse senedi piyasası neredeyse yüzde 70 düşünce de teminat kapatma çağrıları almaya başlamıştı. Böylece Berkshire'daki hissesini, adedi 40 doların altında bir fiyat karşılığında Warren'a satmıştı. Warren bana "Rick'in Berkshire'daki hissesini ben aldım" dedi. Fakat aslına bakarsanız, Rick kaldıraçlı olduğu için satmak zorunda kalmıştı.[18]

Charlie, Warren ve Rick'in varlık edinme konusundaki yetenekleri eşitti. Fakat Warren ile Charlie'de bu yeteneğin yanında, varlıklı kalma becerisi de vardı. Ki, zaman içinde en çok önemli beceri budur.

Nassim Taleb bunu şöyle ifade ediyor: "Bir 'üstünlüğünüzün' olması ve ayakta kalmak iki farklı şeydir: Birincisi, ikincisini gerektirir. Yıkıma uğramaktan kaçınmalısınız. Ne pahasına olursa olsun."

---

Ayakta kalma zihniyetini gerçek dünyada uygulamak, üç şeyin değerini bilmeyi gerektirir.

1. **Büyük getiriler istemekten çok, finansal anlamda çökertilemez olmak istiyorum. Ve eğer çökertilemez olursam, esasen çok büyük getiriler elde edeceğimi düşünüyorum; çünkü, bileşiklenme olgusunun harikalar yaratmasını görebilecek kadar uzun süre dayanabileceğim.**

Boğa piyasalarında hiç kimse nakit tutmak istemez. Herkes değeri hayli yükselmekte olan varlıklara sahip olmanın peşindedir. Boğa piyasası sırasında nakit tutarken muhafazakâr görünürsünüz ve öyle hissedersiniz; çünkü iyi kâğıtlara sahip olmamakla ne kadar çok getiriden vazgeçtiğinizin gayet farkındasınızdır. Diyelim ki nakit yüzde 1 kazanıyor ve hisse senetleri yılda yüzde 10 getiri sağlıyor. Aradaki bu yüzde 9'luk fark, sizi her gün kemirir.

Ancak elinizdeki nakit, bir ayı piyasası sırasında hisselerinizi satmak zorunda kalmanızı engelliyorsa, o nakitten kazandığınız gerçek getiri yılda yüzde 1 değildir; bunun katları olabilir, çünkü yaşam boyu getiriler açısından düşündüğünüzde, çaresizlik içinde yapılacak zamansız bir hisse senedi satışını önlemek, düzinelerce "büyük kazananı" seçmekten daha fazlasını getirir.

Bileşiklendirme, büyük getiriler elde etmeye dayanmaz. Sadece en uzun süre boyunca kesintisiz sürdürülen iyi getiriler -özellikle kaos ve geniş çaplı tahribat dönemlerinde- her zaman kazanacaktır.

**2. Planlama önemlidir; fakat her planın en önemli kısmı, planın plana göre gitmeyeceğini planlamaktır.**

Ne mi diyorum? Siz plan yaparsınız, Tanrı güler. Finans ve yatırımda planlama çok önemlidir, çünkü mevcut eylemlerinizin makûl sınırlar içinde olup olmadığını görmenizi sağlar. Ancak her türden planın pek azı, gerçek dünyayla karşılaştığında ayakta kalır. Önümüzdeki 20 yıl içindeki gelirinizi, tasarruf oranınızı ve piyasa getirilerinizi öngörüyorsanız, son 20 yılda kimsenin öngöremediği bütün o büyük hadiseleri düşünün: 11 Eylül; konut patlaması ve sonrasında yaklaşık 10 milyon Amerikalının evlerini kaybetmesine yol açan çöküş; neredeyse dokuz milyon insanın işini kaybetmesine neden olan finansal kriz; ardından hisse senedi piyasalarındaki rekor ralli ve ben bu satırları yazdığım sırada dünyayı sarsan koronavirüs.

Planlar, ancak gerçeklikten sağlam çıkabildikleri takdirde faydalıdır. Ve bilinmeyenlerle dolu bir gelecek, herkesin gerçeğidir.

İyi bir plan, bu söylediklerimin doğru olmadığı beklentisiyle yola çıkmaz; bu gerçeği kucaklar ve hataya yer bırakmaya ağırlık verir. Bir planın belirli unsurlarının gerçekleşmesine ne kadar çok ihtiyaç duyarsanız, finansal hayatınız o denli kırılgan hale gelir. Tasarruf oranınızda hataya yeterince yer bırakırsanız, mesela "Piyasa önümüzdeki 30 yıl içinde yılda yüzde 8 verirse harika olur; ancak yılda yalnızca yüzde 4 verse de benim için iyidir" diyebilirseniz, planınız o kadar değerli hale gelir.

Birçok girişim yanlış olduğundan değil, her şeyin "tamamen" doğru olmasını gerektiren bir durumda "büyük ölçüde" doğru olduğu için başarısız olur. Hata payı -genellikle güvenlik marjı olarak tanımlanır- finansın en az kıymet verilen güçlerinden biridir. Hata payı bırakmak, birçok şekilde olabilir: Tutumlu bir bütçe, esnek düşünce ve esnek bir zaman çizelgesi, yani bir dizi sonuç karşısında mutlu bir şekilde yaşamanızı sağlayacak her şey.

Bu, muhafazakâr olmaktan farklı bir şeydir. Güvenlik marjı, belirli bir risk düzeyinde ayakta kalma şansınızı artırarak, başarı şansını yükseltmek demektir. Sihri şudur: Güvenlik marjınız ne kadar yüksekse, olumlu sonuç alma bağlamında gereksindiğiniz üstünlük avantajı o kadar küçük olur.

### 3. Dengeli bir kişilik, yani geleceğe iyimser bakmak, fakat o geleceğe ulaşmanızı engelleyecek şeyler hakkında paranoid düşünmek hayati önem taşır.

İyimserlik genellikle, işlerin iyi gideceği inancı olarak tanımlanır. Ama bu, eksik bir tanım. Makûl düzeyde iyimserlik, olasılıkların lehinize olduğuna ve arada muazzam sıkıntılar yaşansa bile, zaman içinde her şeyin dengelenerek iyi bir sonuca ulaşacağına duyulan inançtır. Aslında geleceğe giden yolun büyük sıkıntılarla dolu olacağını *bilirsiniz*. Uzun vadeli büyüme eğrisinin sağa doğru yukarı yönlü olduğu konusunda iyimser olabilirsiniz; ancak, şimdi ve o zaman arasındaki yolun kara mayınlarıyla dolu olduğundan ve her zaman böyle olacağından da aynı derecede emin olabilirsiniz. Bu ikisi, birbirini dışlayan şeyler değildir.

Bir şeyin kısa vadede berbatken, uzun vadede kazanabileceği fikri, içgüdüsel olarak kabul edeceğiniz bir şey değildir; fakat hayatta birçok şey böyle işler. Yirmi yaşındaki ortalama bir insan muhtemelen, iki yaşındayken beyninde bulunan sinaps bağlantılarının kabaca yarısını kaybetmiş olur. Ancak 20 yaşındaki ortalama bir çocuk, iki yaşındaki ortalama bir çocuktan çok daha zekidir. İlerleme boyunca yıkım mümkündür, fakat aynı zamanda da fazlalıklardan kurtulmanın etkili bir yoludur.

Anne/baba olduğunuzu ve çocuğunuzun beyninin içini görebildiğinizi hayal edin. Her sabah çocuğunuzun kafasındaki sinaptik bağlantıların azaldığını görüyorsunuz. Panikliyorsunuz! "Olamaz, burada kayıp ve yıkım var. Müdahale edilmesi gerek. Doktora göstermeliyiz!" diyorsunuz. Fakat böyle yapmazsınız. Tanık olduğunuz şey, büyümenin normal seyridir.

Ekonomiler, piyasalar ve kariyerler de genellikle benzer bir yol izler; kayıplarla birlikte büyürler.

Amerikan ekonomisinin son 170 yıldaki performansına bir göz atalım:

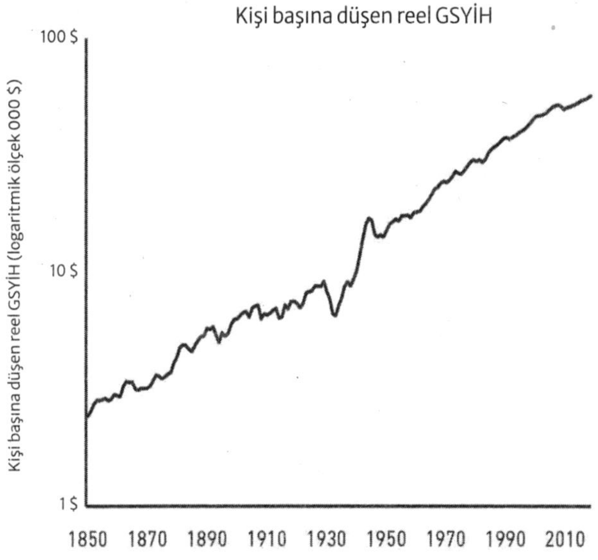


Grafik böyle söylüyor. Fakat bu dönem boyunca neler olduğunu biliyor musunuz? Nereden başlasak...

- Dokuz büyük savaşta, toplam 1.3 milyon Amerikalı hayatını kaybetti.
- Kurulan şirketlerin kabaca yüzde 99.9'u iflas etti.
- Dört ABD başkanı suikast sonucu öldürüldü.
- Tek bir yıl içinde 675,000 Amerikalı grip salgını yüzünden öldü.
- Otuz ayrı doğal afet yaşandı; bunların her biri, en az 400 Amerikalının hayatına mal oldu.
- Toplamda 33 ayrı ekonomik durgunluk dönemi yaşandı ve bunların toplamı 48 yıl sürdü.
- Bu durgunluklardan herhangi birini öngören tahminci sayısı sıfıra yakın.
- Hisse senedi piyasalarında en az 102 kez, bir önceki en yüksek seviyeden yüzde 10'un üzerinde düşüş yaşandı.
- Hisse senetleri en az 12 kez değerinin üçte birini kaybetti.
- Yıllık enflasyon 20 ayrı yılda yüzde 7'yi aştı.
- Google'a göre, "ekonomik karamsarlık" sözcüğü gazetelerde en az 29,000 kez geçti.

Bu 170 yılda yaşam standardımız 20 kat artmasına rağmen, karamsarlık duymamıza yol açacak somut nedenlerimizin olmadığı bir gün bile geçmedi.

Aynı anda hem paranoid hem de iyimser olabilen bir zihniyeti sürdürmek zordur; çünkü, olayları siyah-beyaz görmek, nüansları kabul etmekten daha az çaba ister. Ayrıca uzun vadeli iyimserlikten yararlanacak kadar uzun süre ayakta kalabilmeniz için kısa vadeli paranoya gerekir.

Jesse Livermore bunu zor yoldan çözmüştü.

İyi zamanları, kötü zamanların sonu olarak görmüştü. Varlıklı olmak, ona hep varlıklı kalacağını ve yenilmez olduğunu hissettirmişti. Neredeyse her şeyini kaybettikten sonra ise şöyle düşünmüştü:

> Bazen düşünüyorum da, bir spekülatörün kibirlenmemek için neleri yapmaması gerektiğini öğrenme karşılılığında ödeyebileceği hiçbir bedel yüksek sayılmamalı. Zeki adamları yıkıma uğratan büyük darbelerin büyük çoğunluğunun çıkış noktası kibirlenip şişinme olabilir.

"Bu pahalı bir hastalık" demiş Livermore. "Herkes için, her yerde pahalı bir hastalık."

İzleyen bölümde, zorluklara ve şanssızlıklara rağmen büyümeyi kavramanın ne kadar güç olabileceğini başka bir yönden ele alacağız.

# 6

# Yazı Geldi, Siz Kazandınız

Zamanın yarısında yanılsanız bile servet oluşturabilirsiniz.

*Otuz yıldır bu işle uğraşıyorum. Bence bu işin basit matematiği, bazı projelerin sonuç vermesi, bazılarının ise vermemesi. İkisini de zorlamak için bir sebep yok. Bir sonrakine geçersiniz, olur biter.*

– Brad Pitt'in Screen Actors Guild Ödülü töreninde yaptığı konuşmadan

HEİNZ BERGGRUEN 1936 yılında Nazi Almanyasından kaçtı. Amerika'ya yerleşerek, UC Berkeley'de edebiyat okudu.

Hakkında anlatılanların çoğuna göre, gençliğinde özellikle umut vaat eden biri değildi. Ancak 1990'lara gelindiğinde Berggruen, neresinden bakarsanız bakın, tüm zamanların en başarılı sanat tacirlerinden biriydi.

Berggruen 2000 yılında Picasso, Braque, Klee, ve Matisse'nin eserlerinden oluşan devasa koleksiyonunun bir kısmını, 100 milyon euro'nun üzerinde bir fiyata Alman hükümetine sattı. Almanlar için bu alım öyle bir kelepirdi ki, bağış olduğunu düşünmüşlerdi. Koleksiyonun özel piyasadaki değeri bir milyar doların oldukça üzerindeydi.

Bir insanın çok sayıda baş yapıt toplayabilmesi, şaşırtıcı. Sanat olabildiğince öznel bir alan. Bir insan, üstelik daha yaşamının başında, yüzyılın en çok rağbet gören eserlerine ileride neler olabileceğini nasıl öngörebilirdi?

"Beceri" diyebilirsiniz.

"Şans" diyebilirsiniz.

Fakat yatırım şirketi Horizon Research'ün bununla ilgili üçüncü bir açıklaması var. Hem de yatırımcıları yakından ilgilendiren bir açıklama.

Şirketin araştırma raporunda, "Büyük yatırımcıların çok miktarda sanat eseri satın aldığı" belirtiliyor.[19] Rapor şöyle devam ediyor: "Bu koleksiyonların bir bölümünün büyük yatırımlar olduğu ortaya çıktı ve bunlar, portföyün toplam getirisinin, en iyilerin getirisine yakınsamasını sağlamak için yeterince uzun bir süre elde tutuldu. Hepsi bu."

Büyük sanat tacirleri endeks fonları gibi çalışıyorlardı. Alabilecekleri her şeyi satın alıyorlardı. Dahası, beğendikleri parçaları değil, portföyler halinde alım yapıyorlardı. Sonra da oturup, onların arasından birkaç tane kazanan çıkmasını bekliyorlardı.

Hepsi bu.

Berggruen gibi birinin hayatı boyunca edindiği eserlerin yüzde 99'u pek değerli çıkmayabilir. Ama diğer yüzde 1'in Picasso gibi birinin işi olduğu anlaşılırsa, bu çok da önemli olmaz. Berggruen gibiler çoğu zaman yanılabilir, buna rağmen sonunda şaşırtıcı derecede haklı çıkabilirler.

İş ve yatırım dünyasında pek çok şey bu şekilde işler. Sonuçların büyük bölümünü az sayıda birkaç hadisenin biçimlendirdiği finans alanında, uzun kuyrukların -bir sonuç dağılımının en uzak uçları- muazzam etkisi vardır.

Bununla başa çıkmak, işin matematiğini anlasanız bile zor olabilir. Bir yatırımcının zamanın yarısında yanılıp, yine de bir servet kazanması içgüdüsel olarak mantıklı bulacağımız bir şey değil. Bu da, birçok şeyin başarısız olmasının ne kadar normal olduğunu hafife aldığımız anlamına gelir. Ayrıca, böyle olduğunda da aşırı tepki vermemize yol açar.

---

*Steamboat Willie* (Buharlı Gemi Willie) filmi, Walt Disney'i animatör olarak tanımlamıştı. Şirket olarak başarısı ise bambaşka hikâye. Disney'in ilk stüdyosu iflas etmişti. Filmlerinin yapımı korkunç derecede pahalıydı ve aşırı koşullarda finanse ediliyordu. Disney 1930'ların ortalarında 400'den fazla çizgi film üretmişti. Çoğu kısaydı, çoğu izleyiciler tarafından sevildi ve çoğu da bir servet batırdı.

Fakat *Pamuk Prenses ve Yedi Cüceler* her şeyi değiştirdi. 1938'in ilk altı ayında kazandığı 8 milyon dolar, şirketin o güne dek kazandıklarının tamamından yüksekti. Bu kazanç, Disney Stüdyoları'nı dönüştürdü. Şirketin tüm borçları ödendi. Kilit çalışanlara, belli bir süre şirkette kalmaları karşılığında ikramiye verildi. Şirket, halen bulunduğu Burbank'ta son teknolojiyle donatılmış yeni bir stüdyo satın aldı. Bir Oscar ödülü, Walt'ı ünlüden müthiş ünlüye dönüştürdü. 1938 yılına dek birkaç yüz saatlik film çekmişlerdi. Ama şirketin işi açısından önemli olan tek şey, 83 dakikalık *Pamuk Prenses*'ti.

Dev boyutlu, kârlı, ünlü veya etkili olan her şey, bir kuyruk olayının sonucudur -binde bir, hatta milyonda bir meydana gelen bir hadise-. Ve bizler, en çok da dev boyutlu, kârlı, ünlü veya etkili şeylere ilgi gösteririz. İlgi gösterdiğimiz şeylerin çoğu bir kuyruğun sonucu olduğunda da, ne kadar nadir ve güçlü olduklarını hafife almak kolaydır.

Kuyruk güdümlü bazı sektörler bellidir. Örneğin, girişim sermayesi sektörü. Bir girişim sermayesi şirketi 50 yatırım yaparsa, büyük olasılıkla bunlardan yarısının başarısız olmasını, 10'unun oldukça iyi olmasını, bir veya ikisinin ise fon getirisinin yüzde 100'ünü sağlayan "bonanza" olmasını bekler. Correlation Ventures adlı yatırım şirketi bir dönem rakamları en küçük ayrıntısına kadar incelemişti.[20] 2004 yılından 2014'e kadar yaptıkları 21,000'in üzerinde girişim sermayesi finansmanından elde ettikleri sonuç şöyleydi:

Yatırımların yüzde 65'inde para kaybetmişlerdi.

Yüzde iki buçuğu, 10 ila 20 kat arasında kazandırmıştı.

Yüzde biri, 20 kattan fazla getiri sağlamıştı.

Yüzde yarımı -21,000 şirketten yaklaşık 100 tanesi- 50 kat veya daha fazla kazanmıştı. Sektörün getirilerinin çoğunluğu, işte buradan geliyordu.

Girişim sermayesi işi zaten o yüzden bu kadar riskli, diye düşünebilirsiniz. Ayrıca girişim sermayesi yatırımı yapan herkes, riskli olduğunu bilir. Sonuçta çoğu start-up şirket başarısız oluyor ve dünya, sadece birkaç mega başarıya izin verecek kadar nazik.

Daha güvenli, daha öngörülebilir ve daha istikrarlı getiri istiyorsanız, halka açık büyük şirketlere yatırım yaparsınız.

Ya da öyle düşünebilirsiniz.

Unutmayın, *her şeyi* kuyruklar yönlendirir.

Halka açık büyük şirketlerin hisselerinin zaman içindeki başarı dağılımı, girişim sermayesi sektöründen çok farklı değildir.

Halka açık şirket hisselerinin çoğu işe yaramaz; küçük bir kısmı iyi iş yapar ve içlerinden bir avuç şirketin hissesi, piyasa getirilerinin çoğunluğunu oluşturan "olağanüstü kazananlar" haline gelir.

J.P. Morgan Asset Management, halka açık şirketleri bir araya getiren büyük ve geniş kapsamlı bir endeks olan Russell 3000 Endeksi'nin 1980 yılından bu yana ürettiği getirilerin dağılımını yayınlamıştı.[21]

Bu rapora göre, Russell 3000 endeksindeki tüm hisselerin yüzde 40'ı, en az yüzde 70 değer kaybetmişti ve bu süre içinde bir daha iyileşmemişti.

Esasen, endeksin getirilerinin tamamı, en az iki standart sapma farkla daha iyi performans gösteren yüzde 7'lik kesitten gelmişti.

Böyle bir şeyi girişim sermayesi yatırımlarından bekleyebilirsiniz. Ama çeşitlendirilmiş, sıkıcı bir endekste de olan buydu.

Halka açık çoğu şirketin bu şekilde darbe almadığı sektör yoktur. Halka açık teknoloji ve telekom şirketlerinin yarısından fazlası, yarıdan fazla değer kaybeder ve asla iyileşemez. Hatta kamu hizmetleri sektöründe iflas oranı 10'da 1'in üstündedir.

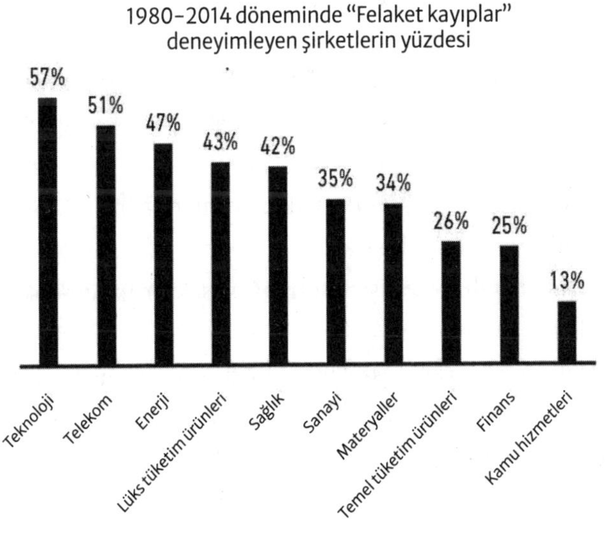

Burada ilginç olan nokta şu: Halka açık bir şirket haline gelmek ve Russell 3000'e dahil olmak için belli bir başarı düzeyine ulaşmış olmanız gerekir. Bunlar, bir anda ortaya çıkan start-up şirketler değil, köklü ve oturmuş kurumlardır. Fakat yine de, çoğunun ömrü nesillerle değil, yıllarla ölçülür.

Bir zamanlar Russell 3000 Endeksi'nde yer alan Carolco'yu örnek verelim.

İlk üç *Rambo* filmini, *Terminatör 2*, *Temel İçgüdü* ve *Gerçeğe Çağrı** dahil olmak üzere 1980'lerin ve 1990'ların en büyük filmlerinden bazılarını Carolco üretti.

Şirket 1987 yılında halka açıldı. Birbiri ardına muazzam başarılara imza attı. 1991 yılında yarım milyar dolar kazanç elde etti ve piyasa değeri 400 milyon dolardı; bu, o zamanlar, özellikle de bir film stüdyosu için büyük paraydı.

Ve sonra iflas etti.

Gişe rekorları kıran işler durdu; büyük bütçeli birkaç proje ellerinde patladı ve 1990'ların ortalarında Carolco tarih oldu. 1996'da iflas etti.

Böylece hisseler sıfırı boyladı. Geçmiş olsun. Korkunç bir kayıp. Fakat aynı zamanda da, halka açık 10 şirketten 4'ünün zaman içinde yaşadığı bir deneyim. Bence Carolco'nun hikâyesi benzersiz olduğu için değil, yaygın olduğu için anlatılmaya değer.

Ama hikâyenin asıl önemli kısmı şu: Russell 3000 Endeksi, 1980 yılından bu yana 73 katın üstünde artış gösterdi. Bu, muhteşem bir getiri. Başarının ta kendisi.

---

* Gerçeğe Çağrı: 1990 yılında Paul Verhoeven tarafından çekilen bu bilim-kurgu filminin İngilizce orijinal adı Total Recall idi. 2084 yılında geçen filmin başrollerini Arnold Schwarzenegger ile Sharon Stone oynamıştı. (ÇN)

Endeksteki şirketlerin yüzde 40'ı fiilen başarısız oldu. Ancak, son derece iyi performans gösterenlerin yüzde 7'si, işe yaramaz olanları dengeleme anlamında fazlasıyla yeterliydi. Tıpkı Heinz Berggruen gibi... ama Picasso ve Matisse yerine, bu kez Microsoft ve Walmart gibilerin sayesinde.

Birkaç şirket, piyasa getirisinin büyük bölümünü sağlamakla kalmıyor, aynı zamanda bu birkaç şirkette daha da fazla kuyruk hadisesi gelişiyor.

2018 yılında S&P 500'ün getirilerinin yüzde 6'sı Amazon'dan geldi. Üstelik Amazon'un büyümesi neredeyse tamamen, Fire Phone'dan seyahat acentelerine kadar yüzlerce ürünü deneyen bir şirketin kuyruk hadiseleri olan Prime ve Amazon Web Servislerinden kaynaklanıyordu.

Yine 2018'de S&P 500 endeksindeki getirilerin neredeyse yüzde 7'si Apple kaynaklıydı. Dahası bu da ağırlıklı olarak, teknoloji ürünleri dünyasında kuyrukların kuyruğu olan iPhone'dan geliyordu.

Peki bu şirketlerde kimler çalışıyor? Google'ın işe alımlarda kabul oranı yüzde 0.2.[22] Facebook'un yüzde 0.1.[23] Apple'ın ise yaklaşık yüzde 2.0.[24] Dolayısıyla, kuyruklu getirileri artıran bu kuyruklu projelerde çalışan kişilerin de kuyruklu kariyerleri var.

Çoğu sonucu az sayıda birkaç şeyin oluşturup belirlediği fikri, yalnızca yatırım portföyünüzdeki şirketler için geçerli değildir. Aynı zamanda yatırımcı olarak kendi davranışınızın da önemli bir parçasıdır.

Napolyon askeri dehayı, "Etrafındaki herkes aklını kaybederken ortalama şeyler yapabilen kişi" olarak tanımlamış.

Yatırımda da öyledir.

Çoğu finansal tavsiye bugünle ilgilidir. Şu anda ne yapmalısınız ve bugün hangi hisseler alım için iyi görünüyor?

Oysa çoğu zaman, bugün o kadar da önemli değildir. Bir yatırımcı olarak yaşamınızın akışı boyunca, bugün, yarın veya gelecek hafta vereceğiniz kararlar, etraftaki herkesin çıldırdığı az sayıda günde -muhtemelen zamanın yüzde birinde veya daha azında- ne yaptığınız kadar önemli olmayacaktır.

1900 yılından 2019'a kadar her ay bir dolar biriktirdiğimizi varsayarsak, nasıl bir sonuç almış olacağımıza bakalım.

Bu bir doları her ay, piyasada koşullar ne olursa olsun, Amerikan hisse senetlerine yatırmış bir yatırımcı hayal edelim. Ekonomistlerin ufukta ekonomik durgunluk göründüğünü veya yeni bir ayı piyasasının yaklaştığını haykırdığı dönemlerde bile, her ay o bir doları hisse senetlerine yatırmış olsun.

Bu yatırımcıya Sue adını verelim.

Ama belki de, ekonomik durgunluklar sırasında yatırım yapmak bizi ürkütüyor. Bu yüzden de, ekonominin durgunlukta olmadığı dönemlerde bir dolarımızı borsaya yatırıyoruz; durgunlukta olduğu dönemlerde her şeyi elden çıkarıp, bir doları nakit olarak biriktiriyoruz; durgunluk sona erdiğinde de her şeyi borsaya geri yatırıyoruz.

Bu yatırımcıya da Jim diyelim.

Ya da belki, durgunluğun bizi korkutması birkaç ay alıyor; ayrıca yeniden güven duymamız ve piyasalara geri dönmemiz de zaman istiyor. Böylece durgunluk dönemleri dışında her ay bir dolarımızı hisse senetlerine yatırıyoruz; durgunluk başladıktan altı ay sonra hepsini satıyoruz ve durgunluğun sona ermesinden altı ay sonra yine hisse senedi piyasalarına giriyoruz.

Onun adı da Tom olsun.

Bu üç yatırımcı zaman içinde ne kadar para kazanır?

Sue 435,551 dolarla çıkar.

Jim 257,386 dolar yapar.

Tom'un ise 234,476 doları olur.

Sue açık ara kazanır.

1900 ile 2019 yılları arasında 1428 ay vardı. Bunların 300'den biraz fazlası ekonomik durgunluk dönemindeydi. Böylece Sue, ekonominin durgunlukta veya durgunluğa yakın olduğu yüzde 22'lik zaman diliminde sakinliğini koruyarak, Jim veya Tom'dan neredeyse dörtte üç oranında daha fazla paranın sahibi oldu.

Daha yeni bir örnek de verebiliriz: Yaşam boyu getirileriniz açısından düşünürsek, 2008 yılı sonları ile 2009 başları arasındaki birkaç ay boyunca yatırımcı olarak nasıl davrandığınız, muhtemelen 2000 yılından 2008'e kadar yapmış olduğunuz her şeyden daha etkiliydi.

Pilotlar arasında eski bir espri vardır. Yaptıkları işin, arada bir "terör" anlarıyla kesintiye uğraması dışında saatler süren can sıkıntısı olduğunu söylerler. Aslında yatırım işinde de öyledir. Bir yatırımcı olarak başarınız, seyir kontrolüne harcadığınız yıllarla değil, araya giren "terör" anlarına nasıl tepki verdiğinizle belirlenecektir.

Bence, "Etrafındaki herkes çıldırdığında ortalama şeyler yapabilen erkek ya da kadın" ifadesi, yatırım dehasının iyi bir tanımıdır.

Her şeyi kuyruklar yönlendirir.

---

İş dünyasında, yatırım alanında ve finansta her şeyi kuyrukların yönlendirdiğini kabul ettiğinizde, birçok şeyin ters gitmesinin, bozulmasının, başarısız olmasının ve düşmesinin normal olduğunu fark edersiniz.

İyi bir hisse senedi seçicisi iseniz, belki de zamanın yarısında haklı çıkacaksınızdır.

İyi bir iş lideriyseniz, ürün ve strateji fikirlerinizin belki yarısı işe yarayabilecektir.

İyi bir yatırımcıysanız, belki birçok yıl orta karar geçecek ve çoğu kötü olacaktır.

İyi bir çalışansanız, belki birkaç girişim ve denemeden sonra doğru alanda, doğru şirketi bulacaksınızdır.

Tabii eğer iyiyseniz.

Peter Lynch, zamanımızın en iyi yatırımcılarından biridir; bir keresinde şöyle demişti: "Bir işte harikaysanız, 10 defasından 6'sında haklı çıkarsınız."

Her daim mükemmel olmanız gereken alanlar var. Örneğin, uçak uçurmak. Sonra, hemen her zaman en azından oldukça iyi olmayı isteyeceğiniz alanlar var. Restoran şefi, diyelim.

Yatırım, iş dünyası ve finans, bu alanlar gibi değildir.

Hem yatırımcılardan hem de girişimcilerden öğrendiğim şeylerden biri, hiç kimsenin her zaman iyi kararlar vermediğidir. En etkileyici insanlar, çoğu kez de uygulamaya koydukları korkunç fikirlerle doludur.

Amazon'u örnek alalım. Büyük bir şirkette başarısız bir ürün lansmanının normal ve iyi bir şey olacağını düşünmek mantıklı değil. Mantıksal olarak, CEO'nun hissedarlardan özür dilemesi gerektiğini düşünürsünüz. Ancak Amazon'un CEO'su Jeff Bezos, Fire Phone'un feci lansmanından kısa bir süre sonra şöyle dedi:

> Bunun büyük bir başarısızlık olduğunu düşünüyorsanız, şu anda çok daha büyük başarısızlıklar üzerinde çalışıyoruz. Şaka yapmıyorum. Bunlardan bazılarının yanında, Fire Phone küçücük bir darbe gibi kalacak.

Amazon'un Fire Phone'da çok para kaybetmesi sorun değildir; çünkü Amazon Web Hizmetleri gibi on milyarlarca dolar kazanan bir şey, bunu dengeleyecektir. Kuyruklar imdada yetişecektir.

Netflix CEO'su Reed Hastings bir keresinde şirketinin büyük bütçeli birkaç prodüksiyonu iptal ettiğini duyurmuştu. Ve bu konudaki tepkisini şöyle dile getirmişti:

> Şu anda isabet oranımız yüksek. İçerik ekibini bu konuda her zaman zorluyorum. Daha fazla risk almalıyız. Daha çılgın şeyler denemelisiniz; çünkü genel anlamda daha yüksek bir iptal oranımız olmalı.

Bu sözler, hezeyan belirtisi ya da sorumsuzluk değildir. Kuyrukların başarıyı nasıl yönlendirdiğini akıllıca kabul etmektir. Böylece her Amazon Prime veya *Orange is The New Black*'e karşılık "iş yapmayan" bazı projeler olacağını kesinlikle bilirsiniz.

Bunun sezgisel mantık yürütme biçimi olmamasının bir nedeni, çoğu alanda, kuyruk başarısı gösteren bir ürünün yolunu açan kayıpları değil, yalnızca bitmiş ürünü görmemizdir.

Televizyonda gördüğüm Chris Rock harika espriler yapan, kusursuz bir komedyen. Her yıl düzinelerce küçük kulüpte sahne alan Chris Rock ise, fena değil. Bu, tasarım gereği böyle. Hiçbir komedi dehası, hangi esprilerin iyi sonuç vereceğini önceden bilecek kadar akıllı değildir. Her büyük komedyen, elindeki malzemeyi büyük gösteri mekânlarında sergilemeden önce küçük kulüplerde test eder. Rock'a bir keresinde küçük kulüpleri özleyip özlemediği sormuşlar. Şu cevabı vermiş:

> Bir turneye çıktığım zaman, doğrudan doğruya büyük arenalarda başlamış olmuyorum. Mesela, bu son

turneden önce, New Brunswick'te Stres Fabrikası denen yerde performans sergiledim. Turneye hazılık sürecinde yaklaşık 40-50 gösteri yaptım.

Bir gazete Rock'ın bu küçük kulüplerdeki gösterilerini anlatan bir yazı yayınlamıştı. Yazıya göre, Rock not aldığı sayfaları karıştırıyordu ve elindeki malzemeler üzerinde epey uğraşıyordu. Bir sahnenin ortasında durup, "Bu esprilerden bazılarını kısaltmam lazım" diyordu. Yani Netflix'te benim gördüğüm iyi espriler, yüzlerce girişim sonucunda oluşmuş bir evrenden çıkan kuyruklardır.

Yatırım alanında da benzer bir şey olur. Warren Buffett'ın net değerini veya ortalama yıllık getirisini bulmak kolaydır. Hatta en iyi, en dikkate değer yatırımlarını bulmak da kolaydır. Hepsi ortada, herkese açık ve insanların konuştuğu şeyler.

Buna karşılık kariyeri boyunca yaptığı her yatırımı bilmek daha zor. Kimse başarısız seçimlerinden, girdiği kötü işlerden, kötü alımlarından bahsetmiyor. Oysa onlar da Buffett'ın hikâyesinin büyük bir parçası. Kuyruk güdümlü getirilerin diğer tarafı.

Warren Buffett, Berkshire Hathaway'in 2013 yılındaki hissedarlar toplantısında konuşurken, hayatı boyunca 400 ila 500 hisseye sahip olduğunu ve parasının çoğunu bunların 10 tanesinden kazandığını söylemişti. Charlie Munger da şöyle devam etmişti: "Berkshire'ın en iyi yatırımlarından sadece birkaçını çıkarırsanız, uzun vadeli performans sicili oldukça ortalamadır."

Bir rol modelin başarılarına özel önem verdiğimiz zaman kazanımlarının, eylemlerinin küçük bir yüzdesinden geldiğini gözden kaçırırız. Bu durum, kendi yaşadığımız başarısızlıklar, kayıplar ve aksilikler karşısında, yanlış bir şey yapıyormuşuz gibi hissetmemize yol açar. Ancak, nasıl ki ustalar sıklıkla yanılıyorsa, biz de yanılabiliriz ya da çok doğru düşünmemiş olabiliriz. Onlar sizden *daha çok* doğru düşünmüş ve *daha çok* haklı çıkmış olabilirler; fakat onlar da sizin kadar sık yanılabilirler.

George Soros bir keresinde "Önemli olan haklı veya haksız olmanız değil; haklı olduğunuzda ne kadar para kazandığınız ve haksız olduğunuzda ne kadar kaybettiğinizdir" demişti. Zamanın yarısında yanılabilir, ama yine de bir servet kazanabilirsiniz.

---

Galaksimizde 100 milyar gezegen var ve bildiğimiz kadarıyla, bunlardan yalnızca bir tanesinde akıllı yaşam mevcut.

Bu kitabı okuyor olmanız, hayal edebileceğiniz en uzun kuyruğun sonucu.

Bence bu mutlu olunacak bir şey. Şimdi, paranın sizi nasıl daha da mutlu edebileceğine bakalım.

# 7
# Özgürlük

Zamanınızı kontrol etmek,
paranın ödediği en yüksek kâr payıdır.

ZENGİNLİĞİN EN YÜKSEK hali, her sabah uyanıp "Bugün ne istersem yapabilirim" diyebilmektir.

İnsanlar kendilerini mutlu etmek için daha zengin olmak isterler. Mutluluk karmaşık bir konudur, çünkü herkes farklıdır. Ancak mutluluğun ortak bir paydası -evrensel düzeyde bir neşe ve sevinç yakıtı- varsa, o da insanların hayatlarını kontrol etmek istemeleridir.

İstediğinizi, istediğiniz zaman, istediğiniz kişiyle, istediğiniz sürece yapabilme yeteneğine paha biçilemez. Bu, paranın ödediği en yüksek kâr payıdır.

---

Angus Campbell, Michigan Üniversitesi'nde psikologdu. 1910 yılında doğmuştu ve araştırmaları, psikolojinin ağırlıklı olarak depresyon, anksiyete, şizofreni gibi insanları aşağı çeken bozukluklara odaklandığı bir çağda gerçekleşmişti.

Campbell, insanları neyin mutlu ettiğini bilmek istiyordu. 1981 tarihli *The Sense of Wellbeing in America* (Amerika'da Mutluluk Duygusu) adlı kitabı, insanların genellikle birçok psikoloğun varsaydığından daha mutlu olduğuna işaret ederek başlıyor. Ama Campbell'e göre, bazıları bunu, net bir şekilde diğerlerinden daha iyi başarıyor. Yine Campbell'e göre, mutlu olmayı başaran insanlar mutlaka gelire, coğrafyaya veya eğitim düzeyine göre gruplandırılamaz; çünkü, bu kategorilerin her birindeki pek çok kişi kronik olarak mutsuz.

Campbell mutluluğun en güçlü ortak paydasının basit olduğunu söylüyor ve bunu şöyle özetliyor:

> Kişinin yaşamının kontrolünü elinde tuttuğu yönünde güçlü bir duyguya sahip olması, hayata dair dikkate aldığımız nesnel koşulların hepsinden çok daha güvenilir bir yordayıcıdır.

Maaşınızdan daha çok. Evinizin büyüklüğünden daha çok. İşinizin prestijinden daha çok. İstediğinizi, istediğiniz zaman, istediğiniz insanlarla yapmayı kontrol edebilmek, insanları mutlu eden en genel ve en yaygın yaşam tarzı değişkenidir.

Paranın en büyük içsel değeri -ki bunun çok kıymetli bir değer olduğunu söylemek abartı olmaz- "zamanınızı kontrol etme yeteneği"dir. Harcanmamış varlıklardan gelen ve istediğiniz şeyi, istediğiniz zaman yapabilme anlamında size daha fazla kontrol sağlayan bağımsızlık ve özerklik düzeyini, yavaş yavaş elde edebilmektir.

Az miktarda servet, hasta olduğunuzda bankadaki hesabınızı bozmadan birkaç gün ücretsiz izin kullanabilmek anlamına gelir. Böyle bir imkânınız yoksa, onu elde etmek sizin için çok büyük bir şeydir.

Bunun biraz üstü, işten çıkarılmanız halinde bulduğunuz ilk işe girmek zorunda kalmak yerine, iyi bir işin karşınıza çıkmasını bekleyebilecek durumda olmak anlamına gelir. Bu, hayat değiştirici olabilir.

Acil durumlar için altı aylık bir yedek akçe, patronunuzdan korkmamak anlamına gelir; çünkü yeni bir iş bulmanız biraz zaman alsa bile mahvolmayacağınızı bilirsiniz.

Bunun üstü, ücreti daha düşük, ama çalışma saatleri daha esnek olan bir işe girebilme olanağı anlamına gelir. Daha kısa sürede gidip gelebileceğiniz bir iş de olabilir. Veya acil bir hastalık durumunda, tedavinin getireceği ek maddi yük konusunda endişelenmenizi gerektirmeyecek bir iş anlamına gelebilir.

Bunun da üstü, koşulların oluşmasını beklemek zorunda olmak yerine, istediğiniz zaman emekli olabilme yeteneğidir.

Paranızı zaman ve seçenek (opsiyon) satın almak için kullanmak, yaşam tarzı anlamında, pek az lüks ürünün rekabet edebileceği türden bir avantajdır.

Üniversite yıllarım boyunca yatırım bankacısı olmak istiyordum. Bunun tek bir nedeni vardı: Çok para kazanıyorlardı. Tek motivasyonum buydu ve bunu başarınca daha mutlu olacağımdan yüzde 100 emindim. Üniversitedeki ilk yılımda Los Angeles'taki bir yatırım bankasında yaz stajı yaptım ve bu staja kabul edilmekle kariyer piyangosunu kazandığımı düşünüyordum.

Bütün istediğim buydu.

İşteki ilk günümde yatırım bankacılarının neden çok para kazandığını anladım: İnsanların kaldırabileceğini düşündüğümden daha uzun ve daha kontrollü saatler boyunca çalışıyorlardı. Aslında, çoğu bununla başa çıkamıyor.

Gece yarısından önce eve gitmek lüks olarak görülüyordu ve ofiste bir söz vardı: "Cumartesi günü işe gelmezsen, Pazar günü geri dönmeye hiç zahmet etme." Bu iş entelektüel açıdan teşvik ediciydi, iyi para ödüyordu ve kendimi önemli hissettiyordu. Ama uyanık olduğum her saniye, patronumun taleplerinin kölesi olmuştum ve bu da, o stajı hayatımın en sefil deneyimlerinden birine dönüştürmeye yetti. Dört aylık bir stajdı. Bir ay dayanabildim.

Bırakma kararımın en zor yanı, işi çok seviyor olmamdı. Ayrıca sıkı çalışmayı kendim istiyordum. Ne var ki, kontrol edemediğiniz bir program dahilinde sevdiğiniz bir şeyi yapmak, nefret ettiğiniz bir şeyi yapmakla aynı şeyi hissettirebiliyor.

Bu duygunun bir adı var. Psikologlar reaktans, yani karşıt tepki diyorlar. Pennsylvania Üniversitesi pazarlama profesörlerinden Jonah Berger de çok iyi özetlemiş:

> İnsanlar kontrolün kendilerinde olduğunu, yani sürücü koltuğunda oturduklarını hissetmekten hoşlanıyorlar. Onlara bir şey yaptırmaya çalıştığımızda, kendilerini güçsüz hissediyorlar. Seçimi kendilerinin değil bizim yaptığımızı düşünüyorlar. Bu yüzden de, başlangıçta memnuniyetle kabul etmişlerse bile, sonrasında hayır diyorlar veya başka bir şey yapıyorlar.[25]

Bu görüşün ne kadar doğru olduğunu kabul ettiğinizde, parayı, istediğiniz şeyi, istediğiniz zaman, istediğiniz kişiyle, istediğiniz yerde, istediğiniz süre boyunca yapabilmenizi sağlayan bir hayata doğrultup hizalamanın, inanılmaz getirisi olduğunu fark ediyorsunuz.

Başarılı girişimci Derek Sivers, nasıl zengin olduğunu soran bir arkadaşına verdiği cevabı ve aralarında geçen konuşmayı şöyle yazıya dökmüştü:

> Manhattan'ın merkezinde yılda 20 bin dolar -yaklaşık asgari ücret- ödeyen bir gündüz işim vardı. Hiçbir zaman dışarıda yemek yemedim ve asla taksiye binmedim. Ayda 1800 dolar kazanıyordum ve yaşam maliyetim aylık 1000 dolar civarındaydı. İki yıl boyunca bu şekilde yaşayarak 12,000 dolar biriktirdim. O dönemde 22 yaşındaydım.

Fikrimce, 12,000 dolar biriktirdiğimde işimi bırakıp tam zamanlı müzisyen olabilirdim. Geçim masraflarımı karşılamak için ayda birkaç konser işi alabileceğimi biliyordum. Yani özgürdüm. Böylece bir ay sonra işimden ayrıldım ve bir daha hiç işe girmedim.

Sözümü bitirdiğimde, arkadaşım daha fazlasını anlatmamı istedi. Hayır dedim, hepsi bu. Arkadaşım "*Peki ya şirketini sattığında?*" diye üsteledi.

Hayır dedim, *şirketi satmam* hayatımda büyük bir fark yaratmadı. Bankada daha fazla param vardı, o kadar. Fark, ben 22 yaşındayken oldu.[26]

---

Amerika Birleşik Devletleri dünya tarihinin en zengin ülkesi. Ancak bugün vatandaşlarının ortalamada, gelir ve refah düzeyinin çok daha düşük olduğu - hatta ortalama düzeyde ve enflasyona uyarlı olarak bile- 1950'lerdekinden daha mutlu olduğuna dair pek az kanıt var. 2019 yılında 140 ülkeden 150,000 kişinin dahil olduğu Gallup anketine katılan Amerikalıların yaklaşık yüzde 45'i bir gün önce "çok endişeli" hissettiğini söylemişti.[27] Küresel ortalama yüzde 39'du. Ankete katılan Amerikalıların yüzde 55'i bir gün önce "çok stresli" hissettiğini dile getirmişti. Dünyanın geri kalanında ise, katılımcıların yüzde yüzde 35'i bu yanıtı vermişti.

Burada mesele kısmen, daha büyük ve daha iyi şeyler satın almak için daha büyük paralar harcıyor olmamız. Fakat zamanımız üzerindeki kontrolümüzden de ödün vermiş bulunuyoruz. En iyi durumda, bu iki şey birbirini sıfırlar.

1955 yılında ortalama bir ailenin enflasyona uyarlı geliri 29,000 dolardı.[28] 2019 yılında ise bu rakam, 62,000 doların biraz üzerindeydi. Bu serveti, 1950'lerin Amerikasında, ortalama bir ailenin bile anlamakta zorlanacağı bir yaşam sürmek için kullandık. 1950'de 90 metre kare olan ortalama Amerikan evi, 2018'de 225 metrekareye çıktı. Şimdi ortalama bir Amerikan evinin, sakinlerinden daha fazla banyosu var. Arabalarımız daha hızlı ve daha verimli, televizyonlarımız daha ucuz ve daha net gösteriyor.

Öte yandan, bizim zamanımıza kadar gerçekleşen gelişmeler, pek de ilerlemeye benzemiyor. Üstelik bu en çok da, bugün çoğumuzun yapmakta olduğu işin türünden kaynaklanıyor.

John D. Rockefeller, tüm zamanların en başarılı iş insanlarından biriydi. Ayrıca zamanının çoğunu yalnız geçiren bir münzeviydi. Nadiren konuşurdu, bilerek kendini ulaşılmaz kılardı ve dikkatini çekebildiğiniz ender zamanlarda da sessiz kalırdı.

Rockefeller ile ara sıra iki çift laf etmişliği olan bir rafineri işçisi, bir keresinde şöyle demişti: "Kendisi tek kelime etmeden arkasına yaslanıp oturur ve başkaları konuşşun diye bekler."

Rockefeller toplantılarda niçin sessiz durduğu sorulduğunda, çoğu kez bir şiir okuyarak yanıt verirdi:

> Bir meşe ağacında yaşlı ve bilge bir baykuş yaşardı,
> Ne kadar çok görürse o kadar az konuşur,
> Ne kadar az konuşursa, o kadar çok işitirdi,
> Neden bizler de o yaşlı ve bilge baykuş gibi değiliz?

Rockefeller tuhaf bir adamdı. Ama bugün on milyonlarca işçinin yararlandığı bir şey keşfetti.

Rockefeller'in işi kuyu açmak, trenleri yüklemek veya varil taşımak değildi. Düşünmek ve doğru kararlar vermekti. Rockefeller'ın ürettiği -sevkiyata hazır- ürün elleriyle, hatta sözleriyle yaptığı şey değildi. Kafasının içinde anlayıp çözdüğü şeydi. Demek ki zamanının ve enerjisinin çoğunu oraya harcıyordu. Günün büyük bölümünde, çoğu kişinin eğlenmeye/dinlenmeye ayırdığı veya boş vakit olarak gördüğü zamanlarda sessizce oturmasına rağmen, zihni sürekli çalışıyor, problemlere çözüm düşünüyordu.

Bu, onun zamanında görülmedik bir şeydi. Rockefeller dönemindeki işlerin neredeyse tamamı, ellerinizle bir şeyler yapmayı gerektiriyordu. Ekonomist Robert Gordon'a göre, 1870 yılında işlerin yüzde 46'sı tarımda, yüzde 35'i de zanaat veya imalattaydı. Çok az meslek, çalışanların beynine dayanıyordu. Siz düşünmezdiniz; çalışırdınız, aralıksız çalışırdınız ve yaptığınız iş gözle görülür, elle tutulur bir şeydi.

Bugün, bu tersine döndü.

Artık, işlerin yüzde 38'i "yöneticiler, memurlar ve profesyoneller" kategorisinde yer alıyor. Bunlar, karar vermeye dayalı işler. Diğer yüzde 41'i ise, genellikle eylemlerimiz kadar düşüncelerimize de dayanan hizmet sektöründe.

Çoğumuz, 1950'lerin tipik bir imalat işçisinden ziyade Rockefeller'a daha yakın görünen işlerde çalışıyoruz; bu da günümüzün, gong çalıp da fabrikadan çıktığımızda bitmediği anlamına geliyor. Kafamızın içinde sürekli çalışıyoruz, böylece de iş hiç bitmeyecekmiş gibi geliyor.

İşiniz araba yapmaksa, montaj hattında olmadığınızda yapabileceğiniz pek bir şey yoktur. İşten çıkarken aletlerinizi fabrikada bırakırsınız. Ancak işiniz bir pazarlama kampanyası oluşturmaksa -düşünceye ve karar vermeye dayalı bir iş- aletiniz, sizi asla terk etmeyen kafanızdır. İşe gidip gelirken, akşam yemeğini hazırlarken, çocuklarınızı uyuturken veya sabahın üçünde stres içinde uyanıp projenizi düşünüyor olabilirsiniz.

1950'ye göre birkaç saat daha az çalışıyor olabilirsiniz. Ama 7/24 çalışıyormuşsunuz gibi gelir.

*Atlantic* dergisinden Derek Thompson bir keresinde bunu şöyle tanımlamıştı:

> Yirmibirinci Yüzyıl'ın çalışma ekipmanı taşınabilir bir cihazsa, bu modern fabrikanın esasen bir mekân olmadığı anlamına geliyor. Fabrika, günün kendisi. Bilgisayar çağı, üretkenlik araçlarını ofisten bağımsızlaştırdı. Çoğu bilgi çalışanı -ki dizüstü bilgisayarları ve akıllı telefonları, esasen çok amaçlı ve taşınabilir medya makineleridir- teorik olarak öğleden sonra saat ikide merkez ofiste, sabaha karşı ikide Tokyo'da WeWork'ten kiralanmış ofiste veya gece yarısı kanepede üretken olabilir.[29]

Önceki nesillere kıyasla, zamanımız üzerindeki kontrolümüz azaldı. Ve zamanımızı kontrol edebilmek, mutluluğu etkileyen kilit bir etken olduğuna göre, ortalamada eskisinden daha zengin olduğumuz halde, insanların kendilerini daha mutlu hissetmemelerine şaşırmamalıyız.

Peki bu konuda ne yapıyoruz?

Bu kolay çözülecek bir problem değil; çünkü herkes farklı. Fakat bu yönde atılabilecek ilk adım, neyin aşağı yukarı herkesi mutlu ettiğini ve neyin etmediğini görüp kabul etmektir.

Gerontolog Karl Pillemer, *30 Lessons for Living* (Yaşamak için 30 Ders) adlı kitabı için ileri yaşta 1000 Amerikalıyla görüşmüş ve bu kişilerin onlarca yıllık yaşam deneyiminden öğrendikleri en önemli dersleri incelemiş. Pillemer şöyle yazıyor:

> Hiç kimse -bin kişiden biri bile- mutlu olmak için istediğiniz şeyleri satın alabilecek kadar para kazanmanız

gerektiğini, bunun için de elinizden geldiğince çok çalışmak durumunda olduğunuzu söylemedi.

Hiç kimse -bir kişi bile- en az çevrenizdeki insanlar kadar varlıklı olmanın önem taşıdığını ve onlardan daha fazlasına sahip olmanın gerçek anlamda başarı olduğunu söylemedi.

Hiç kimse -bir kişi bile- işinizi, gelecekte arzu ettiğiniz kazanç gücüne göre seçmeniz gerektiğini söylemedi.

Bu insanlar nitelikli arkadaşlıklara, kendilerinden daha büyük bir şeyin parçası olmaya ve çocuklarıyla kaliteli, yapılandırılmamış zaman geçirmek gibi şeylere değer veriyorlardı. Pillemer'in ifadesiyle, "Çocuklarınız paranızı (veya paranızın satın aldıklarını) sizi istedikleri kadar istemiyorlar; böyle bir şeyle uzaktan yakından alâkaları yok. Onlar, gayet net bir şekilde, sizi yanlarında istiyorlar."

İşte size her şeyi yaşamış olanlardan bir alıntı: Zamanınızı kontrol etmek, paranın ödediği en yüksek kâr payıdır.

Şimdi, paranın ödediği en düşük kâr payına dair kısa bir bölüme geçelim.

# 8

# Araba Paradoksundaki Adam

Hiç kimse, sahip olduklarınızdan
sizin kadar etkilenmez.

OTOPARK GÖREVLİSİ OLMANIN en iyi yanı, kaldırımlara yanaşan en havalı arabaları sürmekti. Konuklar Ferrari'ler, Lamborghini'ler, Rolls-Royce'lar, ne kadar aristokrat otomobil varsa onlarla gelirlerdi.

Öyle bir arabaya sahip olmak benim de hayalimdi; çünkü başkalarına son derece güçlü bir sinyal gönderdiklerini düşünüyordum (aslında sanıyordum). Başardın. Akıllısın. Zenginsin. Zevklisin. Önemlisin. *Bakın bana.*

İşin ironik yanı, ben onlara, yani o arabaların sürücülerine pek bakmazdım.

Güzel bir araba kullanan birini gördüğünüzde nadiren, "Vay canına, şu arabayı kullanan adam pek havalı" diye düşünürsünüz. Bunun yerine "Vay canına, o araba benim olsaydı ne hava atardım!" türünden bir düşünce geçer aklınızdan. Bilinçaltı ya da değil, insanlar böyle düşünür.

Burada bir paradoks var: İnsanlar genelde, zenginliğin başkalarına "beğenme ve hayranlık duyma" sinyali vermesini isteme eğilimindedir. Ama gerçekte o diğer insanlar, zenginliğin gıpta edilecek veya hayranlık duyulacak bir şey olduğunu düşünmediklerinden değil, sizin zenginliğinizi kendi beğenilme ve hayranlık görme arzuları için bir ölçüt olarak kullandıklarından, genellikle size hayran olmayı pas geçerler.

Oğlumun doğumundan sonra ona yazdığım mektupta şöyle demiştim: "Pahalı bir araba, lüks bir saat ve çok büyük bir ev istediğini düşünebilirsin. Ama şunu söyleyeyim, öyle olmuyor. Aslında diğer insanların sana saygı ve hayranlık duymasını istiyorsun ve de pahalı şeylere sahip olmanın bunu getireceğini düşünüyorsun. Oysa bu hemen hemen hiçbir zaman böyle olmuyor; özellikle de, sana saygı ve hayranlık duymalarını istediğin insanlar bağlamında hiç böyle değil."

Bunu otopark görevlisi olarak çalıştığım dönemde, Ferrari'leriyle otele gelen ve benim onlara aval aval bakışımı izleyerek kaldırıma yanaşan bütün o insanlar hakkında düşünmeye başladığımda öğrendim. Gittikleri her yerde insanlar onlara aval aval bakmalı ve eminim ki bunu seviyorlar. Eminim ki, kendilerine hayranlık duyulduğunu düşünüyorlar.

Ama onları umursamadığımı, hatta fark etmediğimi biliyorlar mıydı? Benim sadece arabaya aval aval baktığımı ve kendimi sürücü koltuğunda hayal ettiğimi biliyorlar mıydı?

Arabadan etkilenen benim -muhtemelen daha birçok kişinin- aslında onları, yani sürücüyü bir an bile aklından geçirmediğini fark etmeden, kendilerine hayranlık duyulmasını istedikleri için mi Ferrari almışlardı?

Aynı fikir, büyük evlerde yaşayanlar için de geçerli mi? Neredeyse kesin.

Peki ya takılar ve kıyafetler? Evet.

Varlıklı olmaya çalışmaktan vazgeçin demiyorum. Hatta lüks arabalardan. İkisini de severim.

Burada savunduğum görüş, insanların genellikle başkalarından saygı görmeyi ve beğenilmeyi arzuladığının; fakat aynı zamanda da, parayı lüks şeyler satın almak için kullanmanın, size düşündüğünüzden daha az şey getirebileceğinin ayrımına varıp kabul etmektir. Hedefiniz saygı ve hayranlıksa, onu nasıl ve nerede aradığınıza dikkat etmeniz gerekir.

Alçakgönüllülük, nezaket ve empati, beygir gücünün asla veremeyeceği kadar saygınlık getirir.

Ferrarilerle ilgili konuşacaklarımız bitmedi.

İzleyen bölümde hızlı araba paradoksuyla ilgili yeni bir hikâye bekliyor.

# 9

# Servet, Sizin Görmediklerinizdir

İnsanlara ne kadar çok paranız olduğunu göstermek için para harcamak, paranızı azaltmanın en hızlı yoludur.

PARA KONUSUNDA BİRÇOK ironi var. Bunlardan önemli bir tanesi de şu: Servet, sizin görmediklerinizdir.

Otopark görevlisi olarak çalıştığım dönem, yani 2000'li yılların ortaları, Los Angeles'ta maddi görünümün oksijen hariç diğer her şeyden önce geldiği zamanlardı.

Etrafta dolaşan bir Ferrari görürseniz, içgüdüsel olarak arabanın sahibinin zengin olduğunu varsayabilirsiniz, sürücüye pek dikkat etmeseniz bile.

Ama bu insanlardan bazılarını tanıdıkça, her zaman böyle olmadığını anladım. Birçoğu, maaşlarının büyük bir yüzdesini altlarındaki arabaya harcayan, vasat düzeyde başarılı insanlardı.

Örneğin, burada Roger diyeceğimiz bir adam hatırlıyorum. Aşağı yukarı benim yaşımdaydı. Roger'ın ne iş yaptığı hakkında hiçbir fikrim yoktu. Ama insanların bazı varsayımlarda bulunmasına yetecek bir Porsche kullanıyordu.

Sonra bir gün, Roger eski bir Honda ile geldi. Ertesi hafta ve sonraki hafta da öyle.

"Sizin Porsche'ye ne oldu?" diye sordum. Kredi ödemesini yerine getiremediği için geri alındığını söyledi. Utancın zerresi yoktu. Sanki maçın bir sonraki devresini anlatıyormuş gibi rahattı. Onun hakkında yapmış olabileceğiniz varsayımların hepsi yanlıştı. Los Angeles, Rogers'larla dolu.

100,000 dolarlık araba kullanan biri servet sahibi olabilir. Ancak servetine dair elinizdeki tek veri, o arabayı almadan önce sahip olduğu servetin, şimdi 100,000 dolar eksildiğidir (ya da borcunun 100,000 dolar daha artmış olduğudur). Hakkında bildiğiniz tek şey budur.

Zenginliği gördüklerimizle yargılama eğilimindeyiz, çünkü önümüzdeki bilgi bu. İnsanların banka hesaplarını veya aracı kurumlardaki hesaplarını göremeyiz. Bu yüzden de finansal başarıyı ölçerken dış görünüşe göre değerlendiririz. Arabalar. Evler. Instagram fotoğrafları.

Modern kapitalizm, sevilip yüceltilen bir sektörde/endüstride insanların "mış gibi yapmasına" yardımcı oluyor.

Ama gerçek şu ki, servet sizin görmediklerinizdir.

Servet, satın alınmamış güzel arabalardır. Satın alınmamış elmaslardır. Takılmamış saatler, giyilmemiş kıyafetlerdir ve birinci mevkiye yükselmeye sırt çevirmektir. Servet henüz, gördüğünüz şeylere dönüştürülmemiş olan finansal varlıklardır.

Servet hakkında böyle düşünmeyiz, çünkü göremediğimiz şeyleri bağlamlaştıramayız.

Şarkıcı Rihanna yaptığı aşırı harcamalar nedeniyle iflasa yakın bir noktaya gelmiş ve bu yüzden de mali danışmanına dava açmıştı. Danışmanın tepkisi şu olmuştu: "Ona bu şeylere para harcarsa, sonunda beş parasız ve aldığı bütün o şeylerle kalacağını söylemek, gerçekten de gerekli miydi?"[30]

Gülebilirsiniz ve lütfen gülün. Ama yanıt, evet... İnsanlara bunun söylenmesi gerekiyor. Çoğu insan milyoner olmak istediğini söylediğinde, aslında "Bir milyon dolar harcamak istiyorum" demek istiyor olabilir. Ve bu, kelimenin tam anlamıyla, milyoner olmanın tam tersidir.

Yatırımcı Bill Mann bir keresinde şöyle yazmıştı: "Zengin hissetmenin en hızlı yolu, gerçekten güzel şeylere çok para harcamaktır. Ama zengin olmanın yolu, olan paranızı harcamak, olmayanı harcamamaktır. Gerçekten bu kadar basit."[31]

Bu mükemmel bir tavsiye; ancak kanımca yeteri kadar ileri götürülmemiş olabilir. Servet sahibi olmanın tek yolu, elinizdeki parayı harcamamaktır. Bu servet yapmanın tek yolu olduğu gibi, servetin de tek tanımıdır.

*Zengin* ile varlıklı arasındaki farkı tanımlarken dikkatli olmalıyız. Bu, anlambilimin ötesinde bir şeydir. Aradaki farkı bilmemek, parayla ilgili sayısız kötü kararın kaynağıdır.

*Zenginlik*, gelir sahibi olmakla ilgili bir konudur. Yüz bin dolarlık arabayı kullanan kişinin zengin olduğu hemen hemen kesindir; çünkü o arabayı borçla almış olsanız bile, aylık ödemeleri gerçekleştirebilecek gelire sahipsinizdir. Büyük evlerde yaşayanlar da öyle. Zengin insanları fark etmek zor değil. Genellikle de tanınmak için ellerinden geleni yaparlar.

Ama *varlık*, saklıdır. Harcanmamış gelirdir. Varlık, daha sonra satın alınacak bir şey için bugün elinizde olan opsiyondur. Değeri ise size opsiyonlar (seçenekler), esneklik ve bir gün, şu andakinden daha fazlasını satın alabilecek büyümeyi sunmasıdır.

Diyet ve egzersizden yola çıkarak, bu konuda faydalı bir benzetme yapabiliriz. Kilo vermek zordur; hatta yoğun bir egzersiz programıyla bu işe girişenleri bile zorlar. Bill Bryson, *The Body* (Beden) adlı kitabında bunun nedenini şöyle açıklıyor:

> Amerika'da yapılan bir araştırma, insanların, bir antrenman sırasında yaktıkları kalori miktarını dört kat fazla tahmin ettiklerini ortaya koyuyor. Ayrıca sonrasında ortalama olarak, yaktıkları kalorinin iki katı kadar daha fazla kalori tüketmekteler... Gerçek şu

ki, yoğun bir egzersizin ardından çok yemek yiyerek, o egzersizi hızla sıfırlayabilirsiniz ve çoğumuz böyle yapıyoruz.

Egzersiz, zengin olmak gibidir. "Görevimi yaptım ve şimdi kendime mükellef bir yemek ısmarlamayı hak ediyorum" diye düşünürsünüz. Servet, bu ödül yemeğini geri çevirir ve aslında, net kalori yakar. Bu zordur ve öz-denetim gerektirir. Ancak yapabildikleriniz ile yapmayı seçtikleriniz arasında, zaman içinde size geri dönen bir fark yaratır.

Birçoğumuz için sorun, zengin rol modelleri bulmanın kolay olmasıdır. Varlıklı, yani servet sahibi insanları bulmak daha zordur; çünkü başarıları, tanım gereği daha gizlidir.

Elbette, bir şeylere çok para harcayan servet sahibi insanlar da var. Ancak bu durumlarda bile servetlerini değil, zenginliklerini görüyoruz. Almayı seçtikleri arabaları ve belki de çocuklarını göndermeyi seçtikleri okulları görüyoruz. Tasarruflarını, emeklilik hesaplarını veya yatırım portföylerini görmüyoruz. Aldıkları evleri görüyoruz, biraz esneseler alabilecekleri evleri değil.

Buradaki tehlike, bence çoğu insanın derinlerde bir yerde servet sahibi olmak istemesi. Henüz harcanmamış finansal varlıkların verebileceği özgürlüğü ve esnekliği istiyorlar. Ama "paraya sahip olmak, para harcamaktır" fikri o kadar içimize işlemiş ki, aslında servet sahibi olmanın gerektirdiği kısıtlamayı göremiyoruz. Göremediğimiz için de, öğrenmemiz zor.

İnsanlar taklit ederek öğrenmede iyidir. Ancak servetin gizli doğası, başkalarını taklit etmeyi ve onlardan öğrenmeyi zorlaştırır. Ronald Read, ölümünden sonra birçok insanın finansal rol modeli oldu. Medyada göklere çıkarıldı ve sosyal medyada sevildi. Ama hayattayken kimsenin finansal rol modeli değildi; çünkü servetinin her kuruşu, onu tanıyanlardan bile gizliydi.

Büyük yazarların eserlerini okuyamıyorsanız, yazmayı öğrenmenin ne kadar zor olacağını bir düşünün. Kimden ilham alırdınız? Kime hayran olurdunuz? Kimin ince püf noktalarını ve ipuçlarını takip ederdiniz? Bu, zor olan bir şeyi daha da zorlaştırır. Göremediklerinizden öğrenmek zordur. Ve bu da, birçok kişinin servet oluşturmasının neden çok zor olduğunu açıklamaya yardımcı olur.

Dünya hem alçakgönüllü görünüp de varlıklı olan, hem de iflasın kıyısında yaşadığı halde zengin görünen insanlarla dolu. Başkalarının başarısını çabuk değerlendirirken ve kendi hedeflerinizi belirlerken bunu aklınızda bulundurun.

---

Servet harcamadığınız bir şeyse, o halde neye yarar? Pekalâ... izin verin, sizi birikim yapmaya ikna edeyim.

# 10
# Para Biriktirin

Kontrol edebildiğiniz tek faktör,
önemli olan pek az şeyden birini üretiyor.
Ne harika...

İZİN VERİN, SİZİ birikim yapmaya ikna edeyim.

Pek uzun sürmez.

Ama ne garip, değil mi?

İnsanların para biriktirmeleri için ikna edilmeleri mi gerek?

Benim gözlemim, evet... Çoğu öyle.

Belli bir gelir düzeyini aşmış insanlar üç gruba ayrılır: Birikim yapanlar, biriktirebileceğini düşünmeyenler ve biriktirmesi gerektiğini düşünenler.

Anlatacaklarım, son iki grup için.

---

**İlk fikir basit ama gözden kaçırması kolay bir şeye dayanıyor: Servet oluşturmanın gelirinizle veya yatırım getirilerinizle çok ilgisi yoktur; buna karşılık tasarruf oranınızla yakından ilgilidir.**

Verimliliğin gücüne dair kısa bir hikâye anlatayım.

1970'lerde dünyada petrol tükeniyor gibiydi. Bunu hesaplamak zor değildi: Küresel ekonomi çok fazla petrol kullanıyordu; dünya ekonomisi büyüyordu ve çıkarabildiğimiz petrol miktarı buna ayak uyduramıyordu.

Çok şükür, petrolümüz bitmedi. Ama bunun nedeni sadece, daha çok petrol bulmamız ya da petrolü yerin altından çıkarmakta daha iyi olmamız değildi.

Petrol krizini aşmamızın en büyük nedeni, enerji tüketiminde eskisinden daha verimli arabalar üretmeye, fabrikalar ve evler inşa etmeye başlamamız oldu. Amerika Birleşik Devletleri'nin bugün GSYİH'daki her bir dolar başına enerji tüketimi, 1950 yılına kıyasla yüzde 60 daha düşük.[32] Yollardaki bütün araçların kilometre başına benzin tüketimi, 1975'ten bu yana iki katına çıktı. 1989 Ford Taurus'un (sedan) 100 kilometrede benzin tüketimi 1.30 litre. 2019 Chevy Suburban (saçma derecede büyük SUV) ise 100 kilometrede 1.29 litre benzin yakıyor.

Dünya "enerji servetini" sahip olduğu enerjiyi artırarak değil, gereksindiği enerjiyi azaltarak büyüttü. ABD'de petrol ve gaz üretimi 1975 yılından bu yana yüzde 65 artarken, enerji tasarrufu ve verimlilik bu enerjiyle yapabileceklerimizi ikiye katladı. Dolayısıyla, hangisinin daha önemli olduğunu görmek kolay.

Burada önemli olan nokta, daha fazla enerji bulmanın büyük ölçüde kontrolümüz dışında ve belirsizliklerle kaplı olmasıdır; çünkü doğru jeoloji, coğrafya, hava durumu ve jeopolitik koşulların bir araya gelmesiyle oluşan kaygan bir zemine dayanır. Ancak enerjiyi daha verimli kullanmak, büyük ölçüde bizim kontrolümüzde olan bir şey. Daha küçük bir otomobil satın almak veya bisiklete binmek, bize bağlı bir karar ve verimliliği artırma şansı yüzde 100.

Aynı şey paramız için de geçerli.

Yatırım getirileri sizi zengin edebilir. Ancak bir yatırım stratejisinin işe yarayıp yaramayacağı, yararsa bunun ne kadar süreceği ve piyasaların bu konuda size yardımcı olup olmayacağı her zaman şüphelidir. Sonuçlar, belirsizlikle kaplıdır.

Kişisel birikimler ve tutumluluk -finansta tasarruf ve verimlilik- para denkleminin daha çok sizin denetiminizde bulunan unsurlarıdır ve gelecekte de bugünkü kadar etkili olma şansı yüzde 100'dür.

Varlık (servet) oluşturmayı daha fazla para veya büyük yatırım getirileri gerektirecek bir şey olarak görüyorsanız, 1970'lerin enerji krizindeki felaket tellalları kadar karamsar olabilirsiniz. Önünüzdeki yol, zor ve kontrolünüz dışında görünebilir.

Kendi tutumluluğunuz ve verimliliğinizden güç aldığınızı düşünüyorsanız, kader yolu daha açık olur.

Servet esasen, elinize geçeni harcadıktan sonra biriken artıklardır. Ayrıca geliriniz yüksek olmasa da servet oluşturabileceğinize, buna karşılık yüksek bir tasarruf oranı olmaksızın böyle bir şansınız bulunmadığına göre, hangisinin daha önemli olduğu açıktır.

**Daha da önemlisi, servetin değeri görecedir, yani neye ihtiyacınız olduğuna bağlıdır.**

Diyelim ki, sizinle ben aynı net değere sahibiz.

Ayrıca diyelim ki, siz benden daha iyi yatırımcısınız.

Ben yıllık yüzde 8 getiri elde edebiliyorum; siz ise yılda yüzde 12 getiri üretebiliyorsunuz.

Ama ben paramı daha verimli kullanıyorum. Diyelim ki, sizin yaşam tarzınız varlıklarınız kadar hızlı büyüyüp yükselirken, sizinkinin yarısı kadar bir para benim mutlu olmama yetiyor.

Daha kötü bir yatırımcı olduğum halde, sizden daha iyi durumdayım. Daha düşük getirilere rağmen, yatırımlarımdan daha fazla fayda elde ediyorum.

Aynı şey gelir için de geçerli. Daha az parayla mutlu olmayı öğrenmek, istedikleriniz ile sahip olduklarınız arasına bir mesafe koyar; bu, maaşınız arttığında bordronuza yansıyan fark gibidir; fakat zam almaktan daha kolaydır ve daha çok sizin kontrolünüzdedir.

Yüksek tasarruf oranı, harcamalarınızın, imkânlarınızın elverdiğinden daha düşük olması anlamına gelir ve harcamalarınızın düşük olması, daha çok harcadığınız duruma göre daha çok tasarruf etmeniz demektir.

Bunu, yıllık yatırımlarda yüzde 0.1 daha yüksek performans elde etmek için ne kadar çaba ve zaman harcandığı (milyonlarca saatlik araştırma, profesyonellerin on milyarlarca dolarlık çabası) bağlamında düşünürseniz, potansiyel olarak neyin daha önemli veya peşinden gitmeye değer olduğunu görmek kolay olur.

Mali durumları, yaşam tarzlarını çok daha az çabayla yüzde iki veya üç tam puan yükseltmelerine müsait olduğu halde, getirilerine yüzde 0.01 puan daha (bir yüzdelik puanın onda birini) ekleyebilmek için haftada 80 saat didinen profesyonel yatırımcılar var.

Büyük yatırım getirileri üretmek ve yüksek maaş almak, bunları elde edebilenler için elbette muazzamdır ve bazıları başarır da. Ancak finans denkleminin bir tarafına büyük çaba harcamak, diğer tarafına ise pek çaba göstermemek, çoğu insan için fırsattır.

**Belli bir gelir düzeyini geçtikten sonra ihtiyaç duyduğunuz şey, sadece ego tatminidir.**

Herkesin temel ihtiyaçları vardır. Bunlar karşılandığında yeni bir seviyenin, rahatlık düzeyinin gerektirdiği temel ihtiyaçlar; sonrasında da hem rahatlık sunan, hem eğlenceli, hem de aydınlatıcı bir başka seviyenin temel ihtiyaçları gündeme gelir.

Ancak materyalizm düzeyini oldukça düşük tutmayıp çok fazla harcama yapmak, çoğunlukla egonun gelire yaklaştığını yansıtır; insanlara paralı olduğunuzu (veya bir zamanlar öyle olduğunu) göstermek için para harcama şeklidir.

Bunu şöyle düşünün, birikimlerinizi artırmanın en güçlü yollarından biri gelirinizi artırmak değildir. Alçakgönüllülüğünüzü artırmaktır.

Tasarrufu egonuz ile geliriniz arasına koyduğunuz mesafe olarak tanımladığınızda, yeterince iyi gelire sahip birçok insanın niçin bu kadar az tasarruf ettiğini anlarsınız. Gösteriş merakını en uç sınırlarına kadar taşımak ve aynı şeyi yapmakta olan başkalarına ayak uydurmak, içgüdülere karşı her gün mücadele vermektir.

Kişisel finansta kalıcı başarı gösteren insanlar -mutlaka yüksek gelirli olmaları gerekmez- genelde başkalarının onlar hakkında ne düşündüğünü umursamama eğilimindedirler.

**Dolayısıyla da, insanların tasarruf etme yeteneği, sandıklarından çok daha fazla kendi kontrollerindedir.**

Birikim, daha az harcamakla elde edilir.

Daha azını arzu ediyorsanız, daha az harcayabilirsiniz.

Ve başkalarının sizin hakkınızda ne düşündüğünü daha az umursarsanız, daha azını arzularsınız.

Bu kitapta sık sık belirttiğim gibi, para finanstan çok psikolojiye dayanır.

**Ayrıca birikim yapmak için belli bir nedeninizin olması gerekmez.**

Bazı insanlar bir evin veya yeni bir arabanın peşinatını ödemek ya da emeklilik döneminde kullanmak üzere belli bir fon oluşturmak için para biriktirir.

Bu elbette, harika.

Ancak tasarruf etmek için belirli bir şeyi satın almak gibi bir hedefinizin olması gerekmez.

Sırf tasarruf etmek için tasarruf edebilirsiniz. Aslında hakikaten öyle yapmalısınız. Herkes öyle yapmalı.

Yalnızca belli bir amaç için tasarruf etmek, öngörülebilir bir dünyada mantıklıdır. Ne var ki, bizimkisi öyle bir dünya değil. Tasarruf, hayatın kaçınılmaz bir yeteneğine, sizi olabilecek en kötü anda, korkunç bir sürprizle karşı karşıya bırakma kabiliyetine karşı hedge yapmak, yani kendinizi korumaya almaktır.

Harcama hedefinden bağımsız olarak tasarruf etmenin bir başka faydası da Yedinci Bölüm'de ele aldığımız şey, yani zamanınızın kontrolünü elinizde tutmaktır.

Paranın satın aldığı elle tutulur, somut şeyleri herkes bilir. Elle tutulur olmayanları anlamak zordur, bu yüzden de genelde fark edilmez. Ancak paranın elle tutulur olmayan faydaları, tasarruflarımızın bariz hedefleri olan somut şeylerden çok daha değerli olabilir ve sizi onlardan çok daha mutlu edebilir.

Harcama hedefi olmayan tasarruflar size seçenekler ve esneklik sunar, bekleme ve atılım yapma fırsatı verir. Düşünmek için zaman sağlar. Rotanızı kendi şartlarınızla değiştirmenize izin verir.

Her küçük birikim, gelecekte başkasına ait olacak olan bir noktayı alıp kendinize vermek gibidir.

**Zamanınız üzerindeki bu esneklik ve kontrol yeteneği, servetin görünmeyen getirilerindendir.**

Bankadaki nakitin size kariyer değiştirme, erken emekli olma veya endişeden kurtulma seçeneği sunma bağlamında getirisi nedir?

Hesaplanamaz, diyebilirim.

İki şekilde hesaplanamaz. O kadar büyük ve önemli ki, ona bir fiyat biçemeyiz. Ama aynı zamanda kelimenin gerçek anlamıyla da hesaplanamaz -faiz oranlarını ölçtüğümüz gibi ölçemeyiz- ve ölçemediklerimizi genelde gözden kaçırma eğilimindeyiz.

Zamanınızı kontrol edemediğinizde, yolunuza çıkan her türlü şanssızlığı kabul etmek zorunda kalırsınız. Ancak esnekliğiniz varsa, oturup düşünmenize gerek kalmaksızın fırsatların kucağınıza düşmesini bekleyecek zamanınız olur. Bu, tasarruflarınızın içerdiği gizli getirilerden biridir.

Bankada yüzde sıfır faiz getiren tasarruflar, size daha düşük maaşla ama daha fazla amaç veren bir işe girme esnekliğini; ya da o esnekliğe sahip olmayanlar çaresiz kaldığında gelişecek olan yatırım fırsatlarını bekleme esnekliğini sağlarsa, aslında olağanüstü getiri üretebilir.

**Ve bu gizli getiri giderek daha çok önem kazanmakta.**

Dünya eskiden hiper yereldi. Tarihçi Robert Gordon'a göre, sadece 100 yıl kadar önce Amerikalıların yüzde 75'inin ne telefonu vardı, ne de düzenli posta hizmeti alabiliyorlardı. Bu, rekabeti hiper yerel hale getirdi. Ortalama zekâya sahip bir işçi, kasabanın en iyisi olabilirdi ve başka bir kasabada yaşayan, kendisinden daha akıllı işçi ile rekabet etmek zorunda olmadığı için "en iyi" muamelesi görürdü.

Bu, artık değişti.

Hiper bağlantılı bir dünya, rekabet ettiğiniz yetenek havuzunun, şehrinizdeki yüzlerce veya binlerce kişiden, dünyanın dört bir yanındaki milyonlarca veya milyarlarca kişiye genişlemesi anlamına geliyor. Bu durum, özellikle de kas kuvvetiyle değil, beyin gücüyle alışmaya dayalı işler için geçerli: Öğretmenlik, pazarlama, analiz, danışmanlık, muhasebe, programlama, gazetecilik alanlarında ve hatta tıpta, küresel yetenek havuzlarındaki rekabet giderek artıyor. Dijitalleşme küresel sınırları ortadan kaldırdıkça, girişim sermayedarı Marc Andreesen'in dediği gibi "yazılım, dünyayı yedikçe" daha çok alan bu kategoriye girecek.

Rakiplerinizin kapsamı genişledikçe sormanız gereken soru şu olur: "Nasıl öne çıkarım?"

Bu soruya "Ben zekiyim" karşılığını vermek, giderek daha kötü bir yanıt oluyor; çünkü dünyada zeki insan çok. Her yıl yaklaşık 600 kişi SAT * sınavında tam puan alıyor. Ayrıca 7000 kişi de bunların birkaç puan gerisinden geliyor. Küreselleşmiş ve "kazanan her şeyi alır" düzeninde işleyen bir dünyada, bu tür insanlar giderek sizin doğrudan rakipleriniz oluyor.

Bizimki kadar bağlantılı hale gelen bir dünyada zekâ, bel bağlanabilecek bir avantaj değil.

Ama esneklik, öyle.

Zekânın aşırı rekabetçi olduğu ve birçok teknik becerinin otomatize hale geldiği bir dünyada, rekabet avantajları, iletişim, empati ve belki de en önemlisi, esneklik gibi kişisel ve incelikli becerilere dayanıyor.

Esnekliğiniz varsa, gerek kariyeriniz, gerekse yatırımlarınız anlamında karşınıza çıkacak iyi fırsatları bekleyebilirsiniz. Gerektiğinde yeni bir beceri öğrenme şansınız daha yüksek olur. Sizin yapamayacağınız şeyleri yapabilen rakiplere yetişme

* SAT sınavı: ABD'de üniversiteye giriş sınavı. Amerikalı öğrencilere ve ABD'de eğitim almak isteyen herkese açık olan SAT sınavları yıl boyunca, genelllikle de 2 ayda bir uygulanır. Sınavlarda herhangi bir katılım sınırlaması yoktur ve alınan sonuçlar 2 yıl süreyle geçerlidir. (ÇN)

bağlamında duyduğunuz aciliyet hissi azalır; buna karşılık tutkunuzu ve sevdiğiniz alanı kendi temponuzla bulma açısından daha fazla hareket alanınız olur. Yeni bir rutin, daha yavaş bir tempo bulabilir ve hayata farklı bakış açılarından bakabilirsiniz.

Çoğu kişi yapamazken bunları yapabilme yeteneği, zekânın artık sürdürülebilir bir avantaj olmadığı bir dünyada, sizi diğerlerinden farklı kılacak birkaç şeyden biridir.

Zamanınız ve seçenekleriniz üzerinde daha fazla kontrole sahip olmak, dünyanın en değerli para birimlerinden biri haline gelmekte.

İşte bu yüzden, daha çok insan tasarruf edebilir ve etmelidir.

Peki başka ne yapmaları gerek, biliyor musunuz? Bu kadar rasyonel olmaya çalışmaktan vazgeçmek. Size nedenini söyleyeyim.

# 11

# Makûl> Rasyonel

Çoğunlukla makûl olmak,
duyguları tamamen bir kenara bırakıp
rasyonel olmaya çalışmaktan
daha iyi sonuç verir.

SİZ BİR HESAP tablosu değilsiniz. İnsansınız, her şeyi berbat etmiş, duygusal bir insan.

Bunu çözmem biraz zaman aldı; ama kafama dank ettiğinde de finansın en önemli yönlerinden biri olduğunu anladım. Ayrıca genellikle gözden kaçan bir şeyi beraberinde getiriyor: Finansal kararlar alırken, duygularınızı tamamen bir kenara bırakacak kadar soğukkanlı bir şekilde rasyonel olmayı hedeflemeyin. Oldukça makûl olmayı hedefleyin, o kadar. Makûl daha gerçekçidir ve uzun vadede o fikre bağlı kalma şansınız daha yüksektir, ki para yönetiminde en çok önem taşıyan şey de budur.

Ne demek istediğimi göstermek için frengiyi sıtmayla tedavi etmeye çalışan bir adamın hikâyesini anlatayım.

---

Ondokuzuncu Yüzyıl psikiyatristi Julius Wagner-Jauregg iki benzersiz beceriye sahipti: Kalıpları tanımakta iyiydi ve başkalarının "çılgınca" gördüğü şeyleri adeta "cesurca" bulurdu.

Uzmanlık alanı, ciddi derecede nörosifilis hastalarıydı ve o dönemde frengi, tedavisi olmayan ölümcül bir hastalıktı. Zaman içinde bir kalıp görmeye başladı: İlgisiz bir hastalık nedeniyle uzun süre ateşlenmek gibi ek bir talihsizlik daha yaşayan frengi hastaları, genelde iyileşme eğilimi gösteriyordu.

Wagner-Jauregg bunun aslında yüzyıllardır varolan, fakat doktorların pek iyi anlayamadığı bir önseziden kaynaklandığını düşünüyordu: Vücudun enfeksiyonla savaşmasında ateş de rol oynuyordu.

Böylece mantıklı olan sonuca vardı.

Wagner-Jauregg, 1900'lerin başlarında, hastalarına frengiyi öldürecek kadar güçlü, buna karşılık ateşi tetikleyecek kadar düşük dozda tifo, sıtma ve çiçek hastalığı enjekte etmeye başladı. Bu, kulağa geldiği kadar (gerçekten de) tehlikeli bir şeydi. Hastalarından bazıları bu tedavi yüzünden öldü. Sonunda sıtmanın zayıf bir versiyonuna karar verdi; çünkü birkaç gün boyunca kemikleri titreten ateşten sonra, hastasına kinin vererek etkili bir şekilde karşı müdahalede bulunabilirdi.

Bazı trajik deneme-yanılmalardan sonra, deneyi işe yaradı. Wagner-Jauregg "sıtma terapisi" ile tedavi edilen 10 frengi hastasından 6'sının iyileştiğini, buna karşılık 10 hastadan 3'ünün kendi haline bırakıldığını bildirdi. 1927'de Nobel Tıp Ödülü'nü kazandı. Nobel kurumu bugün onunla ilgili şöyle diyor: "Wagner-Jauregg'in kariyeri boyunca ilgilendiği ana çalışma, ateşi tetikleyerek akıl hastalıklarını tedavi etme çabasıydı."[33]

Çok şükür, günün birinde penisilin geldi ve frengi hastaları için sıtma tedavisinin yerini aldı. Ancak Wagner-Jauregg tarihte, ateşin enfeksiyonla mücadeledeki rolünü tanımakla kalmayıp, aynı zamanda bir tedavi olarak uygulayan pek az doktordan biridir.

Ateş her zaman için gizemli olduğu kadar korkutucu olmuştur. Eski Romalılar, insanları ateşten koruyan Tanrıça Febris'e taparlardı. Bir sonraki titremeyi savuşturmak umuduyla, Tanrıça Febris'i yatıştırmak için tapınaklara tılsımlar bırakılırdı.

Ama Wagner-Jauregg bir yere varmak üzereydi. Ateş rastgele ortaya çıkan bir rahatsızlık değildi. Vücudun iyileşmesine giden yolda ateşin rolü vardı. Bugün enfeksiyonla mücadelede ateşin faydasına dair daha iyi, daha bilimsel kanıtlara sahibiz. Vücut ısısındaki bir derecelik artışın, bazı virüslerin çoğalma hızını 200 kat yavaşlattığı kanıtlandı. National Institutes of Health (Ulusal Sağlık Enstitüsü) tarafından yayınlanan bir makalede "Çok sayıda araştırmacı, ateş belirtisi olan hastalarda daha iyi sonuç alındığını tespit etti" ifadesi yer alıyor.[34] Seattle Children's Hospital'ın (Seattle Çocuk Hastanesi) internet sitesinde, çocuklarının ateşi hafifçe yükseldiğinde paniğe kapılan ebeveynleri eğitmeye ayrılmış bir bölüm var ve orada şöyle deniliyor:

"Ateş, vücudun bağışıklık sistemini çalıştırır. Vücudun enfeksiyonla savaşmasına yardımcı olur. Hasta çocuklarda 37.7 ila 40 derece arasındaki normal ateş, iyi bir şeydir."[35]

Fakat bu noktada bilim bitiyor ve yerini gerçeklik alıyor.

Ateş, neredeyse tüm dünyada kötü bir şey olarak görülür. Çıktığı gibi hızla düşürmek için Tylenol gibi ilaçlarla tedavi edilir. Bir savunma mekanizması olarak milyonlarca yıllık evrimine rağmen, hiçbir ebeveyn, hiçbir hasta, birkaçı dışında hiçbir doktor ve kesinlikle hiçbir ilaç şirketi, ateşi ortadan kaldırılması gereken talihsiz bir durumdan başka bir şey olarak görmez.

Bu görüşler, bilinen bilimle uyuşmuyor. Bir çalışmada da bu apaçık belirtiliyor: "Yoğun bakım ünitesinde ateşin tedavisi yaygındır ve bu muhtemelen, kanıta dayalı uygulamadan ziyade, standart dogmayla ilişkilidir."[36] Center for the History of Medicine (Tıp Tarihi Merkezi) direktörü Howard Markel bir keresinde ateş fobisiyle ilgili şöyle demişti: "Bunlar, arkalarında yatan bulaşıcı hastalıklar kadar yaygın kültürel uygulamalardır."[37]

Peki bu neden oluyor? Ateş faydalıysa, evrensel olarak ateşle neden savaşıyoruz?

Karmaşık olduğunu düşünmüyorum: Ateş acı veriyor. Ve insanlar acı çekmek istemiyor.

Hepsi bu.

Bir doktorun amacı, sadece hastalığı tedavi etmek değildir. O hastalığı, hasta açısından makûl olan ve hastanın tolere edebileceği sınırlar içinde tedavi etmektir. Ateşin, enfeksiyonla mücadelede yan faydaları olabilir, ancak acı verir. O acıyı durdurmak için de doktora giderim. Battaniyenin altında titrerken çift kör* yöntemiyle yapılmış çalışmaları umursamam. Ateşimi durduracak bir hapınız varsa hemen verin, derim.

Enfeksiyonunuz varsa ateşinizin çıkmasını istemek rasyonel olabilir. Ama makûl değildir.

Bu felsefe -yani rasyonel olmak yerine makûl olmayı hedeflemek- insanların paralarıyla ilgili karar verirken göz önünde bulundurmaları gereken bir başka unsurdur.

---

Akademik finansın çalışma alanı, matematiksel olarak en uygun yatırım stratejilerini bulmaktır. Benim teorime göre, gerçek dünyada insanlar matematiksel olarak optimal stratejiyi

---

* Çift kör yöntemi (double-blind): Klinik çalışmalarda uygulanan bu yöntemde, kullanılan ilacın plasebo mu yoksa deneysel ilaç mı olduğunu denek de, çalışmayı yürüten hekimler de bilmez; yani ikisi de çalışmada kullanılan ilaçlara kördür. Uygulanan tedavide deneysel bir ilaç mı yoksa plasebo mu kullanıldığını bilmenin, kişinin davranışlarını etkileyebileyeceği, hatta en iyi doktor ya da hemşirelerin bile deney grubundakiler ile kontrol grubundakilere farklı davranabileceği düşünülmektedir. Araştırmacılar çift kör yöntemini uygulayarak bu olasılığa karşı önlem almayı öngörürler. (ÇN.)

istemiyorlar. Hangi strateji geceleri rahat uyumalarını sağlayacaksa, onu istiyorlar.

Harry Markowitz, risk ve getiri arasındaki matematiksel dengeyi keşfettiği için Nobel Ödülü'nü kazandı. Bir keresinde kendi parasıyla nasıl yatırım yaptığı sorulmuştu ve modellerini geliştirmeye başladığı 1950'lerdeki portföy dağılımını şöyle anlatmıştı:

> Borsa yükselirse ve ben içinde olmazsam ya da çok düşerse ve ben tamamen içinde olursam yaşayabileceğim üzüntüyü gözümün önüne getirmiştim. Amacım, gelecekteki pişmanlığımı en aza indirmekti. Bu yüzden de, koyduğum parayı tahviller ve hisse senetleri arasında 50/50 paylaştırmıştım.

Markowitz bir zaman sonra yatırım stratejisini değiştirerek, karışımı çeşitlendirmişti. Ama burada iki şey önemlidir.

Birincisi, "gelecekteki pişmanlığı en aza indirmenin" kağıt üzerinde rasyonelleştirilmesi zor, ancak gerçek hayatta gerekçelendirilmesi kolaydır. Rasyonel bir yatırımcı, sayısal gerçeklere dayalı kararlar verir. Makûl bir yatırımcı ise bunu, bir konferans salonunda, hakkında iyi düşünmelerini istediği iş arkadaşları, hayal kırıklığına uğratmak istemediği bir eş ya da kayınbiraderi, komşusu ve kendi kişisel şüpheleri gibi aptalca ama gerçekçi rakiplerin yargılamaları altında yapar. Yatırımın, tamamen finansal mercekle bakıldığında genellikle göz ardı edilen sosyal bir yönü vardır.

İkinci önemli nokta da, bunun *iyi bir şey* olmasıdır. Markowitz ile o söyleşiyi gerçekleştiren ve ona nasıl yatırım yaptığını soran gazeteci Jason Zweig daha sonra şöyle düşünmüştü:

> Benim kendi görüşüm, insanların ne rasyonel ne de irrasyonel olduğudur. İnsanız. Gereğinden fazla düşünmeyi sevmiyoruz ve dikkatimizden bitmek bilmeyen taleplerde bulunuyoruz. Bu açıdan bakıldığında, modern portföy teorisinin öncüsünün ilk portföyünü kendi araştırmalarına pek de rağbet etmeyerek oluşturmasında şaşırtıcı bir şey yok. Daha sonra düzeltmeye gitmesi de şaşırtıcı değil.[38]

Markowitz ne rasyonel, ne de irrasyoneldir. Makûldür.

Finansta genellikle gözden kaçan şey, bir şeyin teknik olarak doğru, ancak bağlamsal olarak saçma olabileceğidir.

Yale'den iki araştırmacı 2008'de, tasarruf yapan gençlerin hisse senedi satın alırken bire iki kaldıraç (kendi paralarının her bir doları için iki dolar borç) kullanarak emeklilik hesaplarını süper güçlendirmeleri gerektiğini savunan bir çalışma yayınladı. Çalışma, yatırımcıların yaşlandıkça bu kaldıracı azaltmalarını, böylece gençken ve piyasadaki çok büyük iniş-çıkışlarla baş edebilecekken daha fazla risk almalarını, yaşlandıkça daha az riske girmelerini öneriyordu.

Araştırmacılar, kaldıraç kullanımı gençken onları silip süpürmüş olsa bile (bire iki kredi kullanırsanız piyasadaki yüzde 50'lik bir düşüş elinizde hiçbir şey bırakmaz) tasarruf sahiplerinin, sıfırı tükettikleri günün ertesinde hemen toparlanıp, bir plan dahilinde hareket etmeleri ve bire iki kaldıraçla tasarruf etmeyi sürdürmeleri halinde, uzun vadede yine de daha iyi durumda olacağını gösterdiler.

Matematik kağıt üzerinde çalışır. Bu, rasyonel bir strateji. Ama neredeyse saçma derecede mantıksız.

Hiçbir normal insan, emeklilik birikiminin yüzde 100'ünün buharlaşmasını izleyip de o stratejiyi kararlılıkla sürdürecek kadar gözüpek olamaz. O işten vazgeçerler, farklı bir seçenek ararlar ve belki de mali danışmanlarını dava ederler.

Araştırmacılar, bu strateji uygulandığında "beklenen emeklilik varlığının, yaşam döngüsü fonlarına kıyasla yüzde 90 daha yüksek olduğunu" savunuyorlardı. Bunun da dedikleri kadar makûl olmadığı yüzde 100.

---

Aslında irrasyonel gibi görünen kararlardan yana olmak için rasyonel bir sebep hep vardır.

İşte size bunlardan biri: Yatırımlarınızı sevmenizi önermeme izin verin.

Bu geleneksel bir tavsiye değil. Yatırımcıların yatırımları konusunda duygusuz olduklarını iddia etmeleri neredeyse bir onur nişanıdır; çünkü bu rasyonel görünür.

Ancak stratejinize veya sahibi olduğunuz hisse senetlerine karşı duygularınızın olmaması, işler zorlaştığında onlardan uzaklaşma ihtimalinizi artırıyorsa, rasyonel düşünce gibi görünen şey sorumluluk haline gelir. Teknik olarak kusurlu da olsa stratejilerini seven makûl yatırımcıların avantajı vardır, çünkü bu stratejilere bağlı kalma olasılıkları daha yüksektir.

Bir stratejiye zayıf olduğu yıllarda bağlı kalmak performansla çok korelasyonlu olduğu gibi, finansta pek az değişken, -performansın hem miktarı, hem de belirli bir süre boyunca yakalayabilme olasılığı bağlamında- performansla bundan daha fazla korelasyonludur. Tarihsel olarak ABD piyasalarında para kazanma olasılığı bir günlük periyotlarda 50/50, bir yıllık periyotlarda yüzde 68, 10 yıllık periyotlarda yüzde 88 ve (şimdiye kadar) 20 yıllık periyotlarda yüzde 100'dür. Sizi oyunda tutan her şeyin ölçülebilir bir avantajı vardır.

"Sevdiğin şeyi yap" mottosunu daha mutlu bir yaşamın rehberi olarak görürseniz, şans kurabiyesinin içinden çıkan boş bir tavsiye gibi görünür. Ölçülebilir başarı ihtimallerini lehinize çevirmek için gereksindiğiniz dayanıklılığı sağlayan şey olarak baktığınızda ise, herhangi bir finansal stratejinin en önemli parçasının bu olması gerektiğini anlarsınız.

Önemsemediğiniz ama gelecek vaat eden bir şirkete yatırım yaparsanız, her şey yolundayken bundan keyif alabilirsiniz. Ancak akıntının yönü kaçınılmaz olarak değiştiğinde, ilgilenmediğiniz bir şey için aniden para kaybedersiniz. Bu çifte yüktür ve en az direnç göstermenin yolu, başka bir şeye geçmektir. Başlangıçta şirket hakkında tutkuluysanız -misyonunu, ürünü, ekibi, bilimi, herhangi bir şeyi seviyorsanız- para kaybettiğiniz veya şirketin yardıma ihtiyaç duyduğu kaçınılmaz iniş dönemlerinde, en azından anlamlı bir şeyin parçası olduğunuzu hissedersiniz. Bu da vazgeçip gitmenizi önlemek için gereken motivasyon olabilir.

Para konusunda rasyonel olmak yerine makûl olmanın iyi olduğu başka zamanlar da vardır.

İnsanların yaşadıkları ülkenin şirketlerine yatırım yapmayı tercih etmesini, buna karşılık gezegenin geriye kalanını, yani yüzde 95'inden de fazlasını görmezden gelmesini ifade eden, iyi belgelenmiş bir "vatan önyargısı" var. Yatırımın fiilen yabancılara para vermek olduğunu düşünmediğiniz sürece, bu rasyonel bir tutum değildir. Fakat onlara olan aşinalığınız bu yabancıları desteklemeyi sürdürmek için gereken inanç sıçramasını yapmanıza yardımcı oluyorsa, rasyoneldir.

Günlük işlem yapmak ve tekil hisse senedi seçmek, çoğu yatırımcı için rasyonel değildir; olasılıklar büyük ölçüde başarınızın aleyhinedir. Ancak bu işe, daha çeşitlendirilmiş yatırımlarınızın geri kalanını kendi haline bırakacak kadar bir heves duyuyorsanız, küçük miktarlarda olmak kaydıyla her ikisi de makûldur. Çeşitlendirilmiş fonları savunan ve çoğunlukla da bu tür fonlara yatırım yapan yatırımcı Josh Brown, niçin bireysel hisse senetlerine de sahip olduğunu bir keresinde şöyle açıklamıştı: "Bireysel hisse senetlerini, alfa [yüksek performans] üreteceğimi düşündüğüm için almıyorum. Ben sadece, hisse senetlerini seviyorum ve 20 yaşımdan beri de hep sevdim. Ayrıca para benim, istediğimi yaparım." Oldukça makûl.

Ekonominin ve borsanın yönüne ilişkin tahminlerin çoğu korkunçtur, ancak tahmin yapmak makûl bir şeydir. Sabah uyandığınızda, kendinize dönüp de geleceğin ne getireceği konusunda hiçbir fikriniz olmadığını söylemek, doğru olsa bile zordur. Yatırım işinde tahminlere göre hareket etmek tehlikelidir. Ama insanların gelecek yıl neler olacağını niçin tahmin etmeye çalıştıklarını anlıyorum. İnsanın doğası bu. Makûl.

Vanguard'ın kurucusu merhum Jack Bogle, kariyeri boyunca düşük maliyetli pasif endeks yatırımını teşvik etmek için uğraş verdi. Oğlunun aktif ve yüksek ücretli bir hedge fon ve yatırım fonu yöneticisi olarak işe girmesi, birçokları tarafından ilginç bulundu. Yüksek ücretli fonların "basit aritmetik kurallarını" ihlâl ettiğini söyleyen Bogle, kendi parasının bir kısmını oğlunun fonlarına yatırdı. Sizce bunun açıklaması nedir?

Bogle, *Wall Street Journal*'a yaptığı açıklamada "Bazı şeyleri ailevi nedenlerle yaparız" dedi. "Bu tutarlı değilse, pekalâ... hayat her zaman tutarlı değildir."[39]

Gerçekten de, hayat nadiren tutarlıdır.

# 12
# Sürpriz!

Tarih, değişimin incelenmesidir;
ironik olarak da geleceğin
yol haritası olarak kullanılır.

STANFORD PROFESÖRÜ SCOTT SAGAN bir keresinde ekonomiyi veya yatırım piyasalarını takip eden herkesin duvarına asması gereken bir şey söylemişti: "Daha önce hiç olmamış şeyler, her zaman olur."

Tarih, çoğunlukla şaşırtıcı olayların incelenmesine dayanır. Ancak genellikle, yatırımcılar ve ekonomistler tarafından geleceğe giden yolda tartışılmaz bir rehber olarak kullanılır.

İroniyi görüyor musunuz?

Buradaki problemi görüyor musunuz?

Ekonomi ve yatırım tarihi hakkında derin bir bilgiye sahip olmak akıllıcadır. Tarih, beklentilerimizi ayarlamamıza, insanların nerede hata yapma eğiliminde olduğunu araştırmamıza yardımcı olur ve neyin işe yaradığına dair kabataslak bir rehber sunar. Ancak hiçbir şekilde geleceğin yol haritası değildir.

Birçok yatırımcının içine düştüğü ve benim "tarihçileri kahin gibi görme" yanılgısı dediğim bir tuzak var: Yenilik ve değişimin ilerlemenin can damarı olduğu bir alanda, gelecekteki koşulların sinyali anlamında geçmiş verilere aşırı bel bağlamak.

Bunu yaptıkları için yatırımcıları suçlayamazsınız. Yatırımı zor bir bilim olarak görüyorsanız, geçmiş, gelecek için mükemmel bir rehber olmalı diye düşünürsünüz. Jeologlar, milyarlarca yıllık tarihsel verilere bakabilir ve dünyanın nasıl davrandığına dair bazı modeller oluşturabilirler. Meteorologlar da öyle. Ve tabii doktorlar; böbrekler 1020'de nasıl çalışıyorsa, 2020'de de aynı şekilde çalışıyor.

Ancak yatırım, zor bir bilim değildir. Zeki insanları bile gergin, açgözlü ve paranoid hale getirebilecek, ayrıca refah düzeyleri üzerinde çok büyük etkisi olacak şeyler hakkında, sınırlı bilgiyle, hatalı kararlar veren büyük bir grup insandan söz ediyoruz.

Büyük fizikçi Richard Feynman bir keresinde şöyle demişti: "Düşünsenize, elektronların duyguları olsaydı fizik ne kadar zor olurdu?" Pekalâ, yatırımcıların duyguları var. Oldukça küçük bir kesiminin diyelim. Bu nedenle, yalnızca geçmişte yaptıklarına dayanarak bir sonraki aşamada neler yapacaklarını tahmin etmek zor.

Ekonominin temel taşı, bir şeylerin zamanla değişmesidir; çünkü görünmez el, her şeyin sürekli olarak çok iyi veya çok kötü kalmasından nefret eder. Yatırımcı Bill Bonner bir keresinde Bay Piyasa'nın nasıl işlediğini şöyle anlatmıştı: "Üzerinde 'Kapitalizm İş Başında' yazan bir tişört, elinde de balyoz var." Pek az şey, çok uzun süre aynı kalır ve bu da tarihçilere kahin gibi davranamayacağımız anlamına gelir.

Parayla bağlantılı her şeyin en önemli itici gücü, insanların kendilerine anlattıkları hikâyeler ile mal ve hizmetlere yönelik tercihleridir. Bu unsurlar, genelde hareketsiz durmazlar. Kültürle ve her kuşakla birlikte değişirler. Daima değişmekteler ve hep değişecekler.

Burada kendi zihnimizde geliştirdiğimiz kandırmaca, para bağlamında o noktada bulunmuş, bunu yapmış olan kişilere aşırı hayranlık duymaktır. Belirli olayları deneyimlemek, daha sonra ne olacağını bilmenizi gerektirmez. Aslında, nadiren böyle olur; çünkü deneyim, tahmin yeteneğinden çok, aşırı özgüvene yol açar.

Yatırımcı Michael Batnick bir keresinde bunu çok iyi açıklamıştı. Çok az sayıda yatırımcının faiz oranlarında artışa hazırlıklı olduğu, çünkü bunu hiç deneyimlemediği -faiz oranlarında son büyük yükseliş dönemi neredeyse 40 yıl önce gerçekleşti- argümanı karşısında, Batnick geçmişte olanları deneyimlemenin ve hatta incelemenin önemli olmadığını, çünkü geçmişteki deneyimlerin, faiz oranları gelecekte yükseldiğinde neler olacağı konusunda rehber görevi görmeyebileceğini savunarak şöyle demişti:

> Ne yani? Mevcut faiz artırımı bir öncekine mi, yoksa ondan öncekine mi benzeyecek? Farklı varlık sınıfları benzer şekilde, aynen mi yoksa tam tersi mi davranacak?
>
> Ona bakarsanız, 1987, 2000 ve 2008 hadiseleri sırasında yatırım yapmakta olan insanlar çok farklı piyasaları deneyimlediler. Ayrıca, bu deneyimin aşırı özgüvene yol açması mümkün değil mi? Hatalı olduğunu kabul edememek? Önceki sonuçlara bağlanıp kalmak?

Yatırım geçmişine, bundan sonra olacakların rehberi bağlamında çok fazla güvendiğinizde iki tehlikeli şey olur.

**1. İbreyi en çok hareket ettiren, normalden sapmış, sıradışı hadiseleri muhtemelen kaçırırsınız.**

Tarihsel verilerdeki en önemli hadiseler, normalin büyük ölçüde dışına çıkan, rekor kıran olaylardır. Ekonomide ve borsada ibreyi hareket ettiren bunlardır. Büyük Buhran. İkinci Dünya Savaşı. Nokta-com balonu. 11 Eylül. 2000'lerin ortasında konut sektöründe yaşanan çöküş. Normalden sapmış bir avuç hadise çok büyük bir rol oynar, çünkü arkalarından gelecek olan pek çok ilgisiz olayı etkiler.

Ondokuzuncu ve Yirminci yüzyıllarda 15 milyar insan dünyaya geldi. Ancak bunlardan sadece yedi tanesi hiç var olmamış olsaydı, küresel ekonominin ve bütün dünyanın bugün ne kadar farklı olacağını hayal etmeye çalışın:

- Adolf Hilter
- Joseph Stalin
- Mao Zedong
- Gavrilo Princip
- Thomas Edison
- Bill Gates
- Martin Luther King

Bunun en anlamlı liste olduğundan bile emin değilim. Ancak bu yedi kişi bir şeylere damgasını vurmamış olsaydı, sınırlardan teknolojiye ve sosyal normlara kadar günümüz dünyasına ilişkin her şey farklı olurdu. Bunu şöyle de ifade edebiliriz: Geçen yüzyılda dünyanın aldığı yönün belki de büyük bölümünden insanların yüzde 0.00000000004'ü sorumluydu.

Aynı şey projeler, yenilikler ve olagelen hadiseler için de geçerli. Geçen yüzyılı şunlar olmadan hayal edin:

- Büyük Buhran
- İkinci Dünya Savaşı
- Manhattan Projesi
- Aşılar
- Antibiyotikler
- ARPANET
- 11 Eylül
- Sovyetler Birliği'nin çöküşü

Yirminci yüzyılda kaç proje ve olay gerçekleşti? Milyarlarca, trilyonlarca, kim bilir? Ancak yalnızca bu sekizi, dünya düzenini diğerlerinden daha büyük ölçüde etkiledi.

Kuyruk olaylarını hafife almayı kolaylaştıran şey, bir şeylerin nasıl bileşip bütünleştiğini hafife almanın gayet kolay olmasıdır. Örneğin, 11 Eylül'ün nasıl Federal Reserve'i faiz oranlarını düşürmeye yönelttiğini, bunun da konut balonunun şişmesinde pay sahibi olduğunu, bunun da finansal krizin yolunu açtığını, bunun da iş piyasasının zayıflamasını getirdiğini, bunun da on milyonlarca kişiyi üniversite eğitimi almaya yönlendirdiğini, bunun da öğrenci kredilerinde 1.6 trilyon dolarlık temerrütü ve yüzde 10.8 temerrüt oranını getirdiğini... Öğrenci kredilerindeki mevcut durumu 19 hava korsanına bağlamak, içgüdüsel olarak yapılabilecek bir şey değil; fakat normalden sapmış, sıradışı birkaç kuyruk hadisesinin yönlendirdiği bir dünyada, olan budur.

Küresel ekonomide belli bir anda olup bitenlerin büyük çoğunluğu, geçmişte yaşanmış ve o dönemde tahmin edilmesi neredeyse imkânsız olmuş olan, bir avuç olaya bağlanabilir.

Ekonomi tarihinin en yaygın konusu, sürprizlerin rolüdür. Sürprizlerin nedeni, modellerimizin yanlış veya zekâmızın düşük olması değildir. Çünkü, Adolf Hitler'in anne ve babasının, onun doğumundan dokuz ay önceki o akşam tartışmış olma ihtimali, çocuk sahibi olma ihtimaliyle aynıydı. Teknolojiyi tahmin etmek zor, çünkü Jonas Salk huysuzlanıp aşı bulma arayışından vazgeçse, Bill Gates çocuk felcinden ölmüş olabilirdi. Öğrenci kredilerindeki artışı tahmin edemememizin nedeni, 11 Eylül'de havaalanındaki güvenlik görevlilerinden birinin, bir hava korsanının bıçağına el koyamamış olmasıdır. Hepsi bu.

Sorun şu ki, gelecekteki yatırım getirileri bağlamında düşünürken, Büyük Buhran ve İkinci Dünya Savaşı gibi olayları, en kötü durum senaryoları türünden görüşlerimize rehberlik etmesi için sıklıkla kullanıyoruz. Ancak rekor kıran bu hadiseler meydana geldiklerinde, daha önce yaşanmış emsalleri yoktu. Yani geçmişin en kötü (ve en iyi) olaylarının, geleceğin en kötü (ve en iyi) olaylarıyla eşleşeceğini varsayan tahminciler, tarihi takip etmiyor; aslında farkında olmaksızın, tarihte emsali bulunmayan olayların, gelecekte olmayacağını varsayıyorlar.

Nassim Taleb, *Aldatıcı Rastlantısallık* (Fooled By Randomness) adlı kitabında şöyle yazıyor:

> Eski Mısır'da, Firavunlar döneminde... katipler Nil'in sularının yükselmesini izliyor ve bunu, gelecekteki en kötü durum senaryosunu öngörmede kullanıyorlardı. Aynı şey, 2011'de tsunami vurduğunda Fukushima nükleer reaktöründe meydana gelen feci arızada da kendini gösterdi. Tarihte yaşanmış en kötü depreme dayanacak şekilde inşa edilmişti; inşaatçılar daha kötüsünü hayal edememişlerdi ve geçmişteki en kötü olayın bir sürpriz olmuş olabileceğini düşünememişlerdi; çünkü emsali yoktu.

Bu bir analiz hatası değildir. Bu bir hayal gücü başarısızlığıdır. Geleceğin geçmişe hiç benzemeyebileceğinin farkına varmak, finans alanındaki tahminci camiası tarafından genelde pek dikkate alınmayan özel bir beceri türüdür.

2017 yılında New York'ta katıldığım bir akşam yemeğinde Daniel Kahneman'a tahminlerimiz yanlış olduğunda yatırımcıların nasıl tepki vermesi gerektiği soruldu. Kahneman bu soruya şöyle yanıt verdi:

> Sürpriz bir şeyle karşı karşıya kaldığımızda, hata yaptığımızı kabul etsek bile, "Ah, bu hatayı bir daha asla yapmayacağım" deriz. Ama aslında, hata yaptığınızda asıl öğrenmeniz gereken şey, dünyayı öngörmenin zor olduğunu öngörmemiş olduğunuzdur. Sürprizlerden alınacak doğru ders budur: Dünya, sürprizler yapar.

*Sürprizlerden alınacak doğru ders, dünyanın sürprizler yaptığıdır.* Burada öğrenmemiz gereken, geçmişteki sürprizlerden gelecekteki sınırların rehberi olarak faydalanmamız gerektiği değildir; geçmişteki sürprizlerden, bundan sonra ne olabileceğine dair hiçbir şey bilmediğimizin itirafı olarak faydalanmamız gerekir.

Geleceğin en önemli ekonomik olayları -ibreyi en çok hareket ettirecek hadiseler- tarihin bize çok az rehberlik ettiği veya hiç etmediği şeylerdir. Bunlar geçmişte emsali olmayan hadiseler olacaklar. Emsali görülmemiş doğaları, bu hadiselere hazırlıklı olmayacağımız anlamına geliyor ve bu da onları bu kadar etkili kılan şeyin bir parçası. Ayrıca hem ekonomik durgunluklar ve savaşlar gibi korkutucu olaylar, hem de inovasyon gibi olumlu gelişmeler için geçerli.

Bu tahminden eminim; çünkü ibreyi en çok harekete geçirenin sürprizler olduğu öngörüsü, pratik olarak tarihin hemen her noktasında doğru çıkmış olan tek tahmindir.

**2. Günümüz dünyasını ilgilendiren yapısal değişiklikleri hesaba katmadığından tarih, ekonominin ve hisse senedi piyasalarının geleceği için yanıltıcı bir rehber olabilir.**

Birkaç büyük hadiseyi düşünün.

401(k) 42 yaşında. Roth IRA daha genç, 1990'larda hayata geçti. Dolayısıyla da, Amerikalıların bugün emeklilik için nasıl birikim yapması gerektiğine dair kişisel finans tavsiyeleri ve analizler, doğrudan doğruya sadece bir kuşak önce mantıklı olanla kıyaslanamaz. Yeni seçeneklerimiz var.

İşler değişti.

Veya girişim sermayesini örnek alalım. Bundan 25 yıl önce yok gibi bir şeydi. Bugün boyut itibariyle bir kuşak önce sektörün tamamına eşit büyüklükte girişim sermayesi fonları var.[40] Nike'ın kurucusu Phil Knight, anılarında iş hayatındaki ilk günleri hakkında şöyle yazıyor:

> Girişim sermayesi diye bir şey yoktu. Hevesli ve genç bir girişimcinin yönelebileceği çok az alan vardı ve bu alanların hepsi de sıfır hayal gücüne sahip, riskten kaçınan gardiyanların gözetimi altındaydı. Başka bir deyişle, bankacıların.

Bunun anlamı, esasen, start-up girişimlerin nasıl finanse edildiğine dair sadece birkaç on yıl öncesine giden tüm tarihsel verilerin, bugün güncel olmadığıdır. Yatırım döngüleri ve start-up şirketlerin başarısızlık oranları hakkında bildiklerimiz, bir şeyler öğrenebileceğimiz kadar derin bir tarihsel temele sahip değil; çünkü bugün şirketlerin finanse edilme şekli, son derece yeni bir tarihsel paradigmadır.

Veya halka açık piyasaları ele alalım. S&P 500, 1976 yılına kadar finansal hisseleri içermiyordu; bugün, finansallar endeksin yüzde 16'sını oluşturuyor. Bundan 50 yıl önce teknoloji hisseleri pratik olarak yok gibi bir şeydi. Bugün, endeksin beşte birinden fazlasını oluşturuyorlar. Muhasebe kuralları zamanla değişti. Kamuya yapılan açıklamalar, denetimler ve piyasanın likidite miktarı da öyle. İşler değişti.

ABD'de ekonomik durgunluk dönemleri arasında geçen süre, son 150 yılda çarpıcı bir değişim geçirdi:

ABD ekonomisinde durgunluk dönemleri

Durgunluklar arasındaki ortalama süre 1800'lerin sonlarında yaklaşık iki yıl iken, Yirminci Yüzyıl'ın başlarında beş yıla, son 50 yılda ise sekiz yıla çıktı.

Ben bu satırları yazdığım sırada, durgunluğa giriyor gibiyiz; Aralık 2007'de başlayan son durgunluktan bu yana 12 yıl geçmiş. Ve bu, İç Savaş'tan bu yana iki durgunluk arasında geçen en uzun süre.

Durgunlukların görülme sıklığının eskisine göre niçin seyreldiğine dair birçok teori var. Bunlardan birine göre, Fed iş döngüsünü yönetmede veya en azından uzatmada daha iyi. Bir diğer teoriye göre, son 50 yılda egemen olan hizmet sektörlerine kıyasla, bugün ağır sanayi, üretimde patlamalara ve kasılmalara daha yatkın. Kötümser görüş ise "Artık daha az durgunluk yaşıyoruz, ancak durgunluklar eskisinden daha güçlü oluyor" şeklinde. Bizim argümanımız açısından, bu değişime neyin yol açtığının özel bir önemi yok. Önemli olan, işlerin bariz bir şekilde değişmiş olması.

Bu tarihi değişikliklerin yatırım kararlarını nasıl etkilemesi gerektiğini göstermek için, birçok kişinin tüm zamanların en büyük yatırım beyinlerinden biri olarak gördüğü Benjamin Graham'ın çalışmasını ele alalım.

Graham'ın klasik kitabı *Akıllı Yatırımcı* teoriden fazlasını kapsar. Yatırımcıların akıllı yatırım kararları vermek için kullanabilecekleri formüller gibi pratik talimatlar içerir.

Graham'ın kitabını ergenlik dönemimde, yatırım işini öğrenmeye başladığım sıralar okudum. Kitapta sunulan formüller bana çekici geldi; çünkü nasıl zengin olunacağı konusunda, kelimenin gerçek anlamıyla adım adım talimatlar veriyordu. Bu talimatları izleyin, yeter. Çok kolay görünüyordu.

Ancak o formüllerden bazılarını uygulamayı denediğinizde bir şey netleşiyor: Gerçekte, içlerinden birkaçı işe yarıyor.

Graham, net değerinin altında işlem gören hisseleri almayı savunuyordu -esas olarak, bankadaki nakit, eksi tüm borçlar. Bu kulağa harika geliyor; ancak gerçekte -muhasebe sahtekârlığıyla suçlanan kuruşluk hisseler* dışında- sadece birkaç hisse senedi bu kadar ucuza işlem görüyor.

Graham'ın kriterlerinden biri, muhafazakâr yatırımcılara, defter değerinin 1.5 katının üzerinde işlem gören hisse senetlerinden kaçınmalarını söylüyor. Son on yılda bu kuralı izleseydiniz, sigorta ve banka hisseleri dışında neredeyse hiçbir şeye sahip olmayacaktınız. Buna tamam diyebileceğiniz bir dünya yok.

---

* Penny stocks: Kuruşluk hisse senetleri, hisse başına bir doların altında işlem yapan küçük halka açık şirketlerin ortak hisseleridir.

*Akıllı Yatırımcı*, tüm zamanların en iyi yatırım kitaplarından biridir. Ancak Graham'ın yayınlanmış formüllerini başarıyla uygulayan tek bir yatırımcı tanımıyorum. Kitap, belki de bugüne dek yayınlanmış hiçbir yatırım kitabının içermediği kadar bilgelikle dolu. Ancak "nasıl yapılır" rehberi bağlamında, nihayetinde sorgulayabiliriz.

Peki neydi? Graham tavsiyeleri kulağa hoş gelen, ama işe yaramaz bir şovmen miydi? Kesinlikle değil. Müthiş başarılı bir yatırımcıydı.

Fakat pratikte düşünüyordu. Ve gerçek bir karşıttı. Yatırım fikirlerine, çok sayıda başka yatırımcı o teorileri kavrayıp, içerdikleri potansiyeli artık işe yaramaz olana dek popülerleştirdiğinde de sadık kalacak kadar bağlı değildi. Graham'ın kitabının revize edilmiş baskısına açıklayıcı notlar ekleyen Jason Zweig bir yerde şöyle yazmıştı:

> Graham varsayımlarını sürekli deniyor, yeniden test ediyor ve neyin işe yaradığını bulmaya çalışıyordu; dün neyin işe yaradığını değil, bugün neyin işe yaradığını. Graham, *Akıllı Yatırımcı*'nın gözden geçirilmiş her baskısında, önceki baskıda sunduğu formülleri çıkarıp yenilerini koyuyordu; Böyle yaparak da bir anlamda, "Bunlar artık işe yaramıyor veya eskisi kadar iyi sonuç vermiyor; şimdi bu formüller daha iyi görünüyor" diyordu.
>
> Graham'a yapılan yaygın eleştirilerden biri, 1972 baskısındaki tüm formüllerin antika olduğudur. Bu eleştiriye verilecek tek doğru yanıt şudur: Elbette öyleler! O formülleri, 1965 baskısındaki formüllerin yerine koymuştu; 1965 baskısındaki formülleri de 1954 baskısındaki formüllerin yerine koymuştu. 1954

baskısındaki formüller, 1949 baskısındaki formüllerin yerini almıştı; 1949 baskısındaki formülleri de 1934 tarihli *Menkul Kıymet Analizi* (Security Analysis) adlı kitabında sunduğu ilk, yani orijinal formülleri güçlendirmek için kullanmıştı.

Graham 1976 yılında öldü. Savunduğu formüller 1934 ile 1972 yılları arasında beş kez çıkarılıp güncellendiyse, 2020'de ne kadar alâkalı olduklarını düşünüyorsunuz? Ya da 2050'de?

Ölümünden çok kısa bir süre önce Graham'a, tekil hisse senetlerinin ayrıntılı analizinin -kendisinin ünlü olduğu bir taktik- bugün de tercih ettiği bir strateji olarak kalıp kalmadığı sorulmuştu. Verdiği yanıt şuydu:

> Genel olarak, hayır. Artık üstün değer fırsatları bulmak için menkul kıymet analizinde gelişmiş teknikler kullanılmasının savunucusu değilim. Bu, aşağı yukarı 40 yıl önce, kitabımız ilk yayınlandığı zaman, ödüllendirici bir faaliyetti. Ancak o zamandan beri durum çok değişti.[41]

Değişen şuydu: Fırsatlar iyi bilinir oldukça rekabet arttı; teknoloji, bilgiyi daha erişilebilir kıldı; ve ekonomi sanayiden, iş döngüleri ve sermaye kullanımları farklı olan teknoloji endüstrisine geçerken, sektörler değişti.

İşler değişti.

Yatırım tarihinin ilginç yönlerinden biri, ne kadar geriye bakarsanız, bugüne uyarlanamayacak bir dünyayı inceliyor olma ihtimalinizin o kadar yüksek olmasıdır. Pek çok yatırımcı ve ekonomist, tahminlerinin onlarca, hatta yüzlerce yıllık verilerle desteklendiğini bilmenin rahatlığını yaşıyor. Ancak ekonomiler evrildiğinden, gelecek için en iyi rehber, genellikle yakın tarihtir; çünkü gelecekte geçerli olacak önemli koşulları içermesi daha olasıdır.

Yatırım konusunda, genelde de alaycı bir şekilde kullanılan yaygın bir söz var: *"Bu defa farklı."* Geleceği tahmin eden birine, geleceğin geçmişi mükemmel bir şekilde yansıtmayacağını söylemeniz gerekiyorsa "Oh, ne yani... bu sefer farklı mı?" der ve mikrofonu bırakırsınız. Bu söz, yatırımcı John Templeton'ın görüşünü ifade ederken söylemiş olduğu bir cümleden geliyor: "Yatırım işindeki en tehlikeli üç kelime 'bu defa farklı'dır."

Templeton, yine de, zamanın en az yüzde 20'sinde farklı olduğunu kabul etmiş bulunuyor. Dünya değişiyor. Elbette, değişiyor. Ve zaman içinde en çok önem taşıyan şey de bu değişiklikler. Michael Batnick bunu şöyle ifade ediyor: "Yatırım işindeki en tehlikeli dokuz kelime, 'Yatırım işindeki en tehlikeli üç kelime 'bu defa farklı' demektir."

Bu durum, parayla ilgili fikir yürütürken tarihi dikkate almamak gerektiği anlamına gelmez. Ancak önemli bir nüans var: Tarihte ne kadar geriye bakarsanız, çıkarımlarınız o kadar genel olmalıdır. İnsanların açgözlülük ve korkuyla ilişkisi, stres altında nasıl davrandıkları ve nelerden motive oldukları gibi genel şeyler, zaman içinde aynı kalma eğilimindedir. Paranın tarihi, bu tür şeyler için yararlıdır.

Ancak belli trendler, belli alım-satım işlemleri, belli sektörler, piyasalarla ilgili belli neden-sonuç ilişkileri ve insanların paralarıyla ne yapmaları gerektiği konusu daima, ilerleme halindeki evrimin bir örneğidir. Tarihçiler kahin değildir.

O halde, soru şu: Geleceği nasıl düşünmeli ve planlamalıyız? Bir sonraki bölümde bu konuya bir göz atalım.

# 13

# Hataya Yer Bırakma

Her planın en önemli kısmı,
planın plana göre gitmeyeceğini planlamaktır.

AKILLI FİNANSAL DAVRANIŞIN en iyi örneklerinden bazılarını, beklenmedik bir yerde, Las Vegas kumarhanelerinde bulabiliriz.

Tabii ki bu, tüm oyuncular için geçerli bir şey değil. Ancak kart sayma yöntemini uygulayan küçük bir grup blackjack* oyuncusu, olağan insanlara, para yönetimi konusunda olağanüstü önemli bir şey öğretebilir: Hataya yer bırakmanın önemi.

---

Blackjack'te kart saymanın temelleri basittir:

- Krupiyenin hangi kartı çekeceğini kimse kesin olarak bilemez.
- Ancak dağıtılan kartları takip ederek, destede hangi kartların kaldığını hesaplayabilirsiniz.
- Bunu yapmak size, krupiyenin belli bir kartı çekme olasılığını gösterebilir.

Bir oyuncu olarak da, istediğiniz kartın size gelme ihtimali lehinize olduğunda daha fazla, aleyhinize olduğunda ise daha az para koyarsınız.

* Blackjack: Yirmibir olarak da bilinir. (ÇN.)

Bunun nasıl yapıldığının mekaniği önemli değil. Önemli olan, blackjack'te kart sayan birinin, kesinlik değil bir olasılık oyunu oynadığını bilmesidir. Herhangi bir elde haklı olma şansının yüksek olduğunu düşünür, ama yanılma ihtimalinin de yüksek olduğunu bilir. Meslekleri göz önüne alındığında size garip gelebilir, ama stratejileri tamamen alçakgönüllülüğe -sonrasında ne olacağını bilmedikleri ve bilemeyecekleri, bu yüzden de ellerini ona göre oynama tevazusuna- dayanır. Kart sayma sistemi işe yarar, çünkü olasılıkları, son derece hafif bir şekilde kasadan oyuncuya doğru çevirir. Ancak, olasılıklar lehinize görünse bile, bahisi çok yüksek tutuyor ve yanılıyorsanız, o kadar çok kaybedebilirsiniz ki, oynamaya devam edecek paranız kalmaz.

Önünüzdeki bütün fişleri ortaya sürecek kadar haklı olduğunuz bir an, asla yoktur. Dünya kimseye karşı o kadar nazik değil; en azından tutarlı olarak. Kendinize hata payı bırakmalısınız. Planınızın plana göre gitmeyebileceğini planlamalısınız.

Başarılı bir kart takipçisi olan ve *Bringing Down the House* (Kasayı Yere Sermek)* adlı kitapta görüşlerine yer verilen Kevin Lewis, sonradan bu felsefe konusunda bazı şeyler daha yazdı:

> Kart saymanın işe yaradığı istatistiksel olarak kanıtlanmış olsa da, kumarhaneye her gidişiniz şöyle dursun, her eli kazanacağınızı bile garanti etmez. Şansımızın

* MIT'nin Blackjack Takımı olarak bilinen altı MIT öğrencisinin bir Las Vegas kumarhanesinde kart sayarak muazzam paralar kazanmasını anlatan bu kitap büyük ses getirmişti. Gerçek olaylardan esinlendiği belirtilen kitap, daha sonra 21 ve The Last Casino (Son Kumarhene) adlı filmlere uyarlanmıştı. *Bringing Down the House* ifadesi, aynı zamanda sahne performanslarında "salon alkıştan inledi" anlamında kullanılan bir deyim olmasına rağmen, başlığı birebir çevirmeyi uygun gördüm. Ancak yazar bu deyime gönderme yaparak, iki anlamı bir arada vermek istemiş olabilir ya da sadece ikisinden birini kullanmış olabilir. (ÇN.)

kötüye doğru her salınışında, dayanacak kadar paramız olduğundan emin olmalıyız.

Kumarhanede kasaya karşı kabaca yüzde iki avantajınız olduğunu varsayalım. Bu yine de, kumarhanenin zamanın yüzde 49'unda kazanacağı anlamına gelir. Dolayısıyla da, herhangi bir değişkenin aleyhinize dönmesine dayanacak kadar paranız olması gerekir. Genel kurallardan biri, en az yüz temel birime sahip olmanız gerektiğidir. On bin dolarla başladığınızı varsayarsak, yüz dolarlık bir birimi rahatlıkla oynayabilirsiniz.

Tarih çok ileri götürülen ve kötü fikirlerden ayırt edilemeyen iyi fikirlerle dolu. Hataya yer bırakma bilgeliği, belirsizliğin, rastlantısallığın ve şansın, yani "bilinmeyenlerin" her zaman hayatın bir parçası olduğunu kabul etmektir. Bunlarla başa çıkmanın tek yolu, olacağını düşündüğünüz şeyler ile olabilecek olanlar arasına koyduğunuz mesafeyi geniş tutarak, bir başka gün yine savaşabilecek durumda olmanızı sağlamaktır.

---

Benjamin Graham, güvenlik marjı kavramıyla tanınır. Bu konuyu kapsamlı ve matematiksel ayrıntılarıyla yazmıştır. Ancak teorisinin en sevdiğim özeti, kendisiyle yapılan bir söyleşide söylediği şu cümledir: "Güvenlik marjının amacı, tahmini gereksiz kılmaktır."

Bu basit ifadenin içerdiği gücü hafife almak zor.

Güvenlik marjı -hata payı veya zarar/hasar marjı da diyebilirsiniz- kesinliklerle değil olasılıklarla yönetilen bir dünyada güvenle yol almanın tek etkili yoludur. Ve parayla ilgili hemen her şey, bu tür bir dünyada var olur.

Kesin tahminler yapmak zordur. Kart sayan oyuncu için bu bariz bir şeydir; çünkü karıştırılmış bir destede belirli bir kartın nerede olduğunu hiç kimse tam olarak bilemez. "Önümüzdeki 10 yılda borsanın ortalama yıllık getirisi ne olacak?" veya "Hangi tarihte emekli olabileceğim?" diye soran biri içinse, bu o kadar bariz değildir. Oysa, temelde aynılar. Elimizden gelen en iyi şey, olasılıkları düşünmektir.

Graham'ın güvenlik marjı, önümüzde duran dünyayı siyah-beyaz, öngörülebilir ya da saçmalık olarak görmemiz gerekmediğine dair basit bir önermedir. Gri alan -bir dizi potansiyel sonuç kabul edilebilir olduğunda bir şeylerin peşinden gitmek- yola devam etmenin akıllıca yoludur.

Ancak insanlar, paranın dahil olduğu hemen her şeyi yaparken, hataya yer verme gereğini hafife alıyorlar. Hisse senedi analistleri, müşterilerine fiyat aralıkları değil, fiyat hedefleri verirler. Ekonomik tahminciler olayları kesin rakamlarla tahmin ederler; nadiren geniş olasılıklara yer verirler. Sarsılmaz kesinliklerle konuşan bilgin "Emin olamayız" diyen ve olasılıklarla konuşan bir diğerinden fazla takipçi kazanacaktır.[42]

Bunu her türlü finansal girişimimizde, özellikle de kendi kararlarımızla ilgili olanlarda yapıyoruz. Harvard psikoloğu Max Bazerman, insanların evlerini yenilerken bütçeyi nasıl öngördüklerini araştırmış ve şunu kanıtlamıştı: Çoğu insan, başkalarının ev yenileme planlarını analiz ederken, projenin sonuç olarak, öngörülen bütçenin yüzde 25 ila yüzde 50 üzerine çıkacağını tahmin ediyor.[43] Ancak kendi projelerine gelince, tadilatların zamanında ve bütçe dahilinde tamamlanacağını öngörüyorlar. Ah, sonunda da hayal kırıklığına uğruyorlar.

Hata payı bırakmaktan kaçınmamıza iki şey neden olur. Birincisi, geleceğin ne getireceğini birilerinin bilmesi gerektiği fikridir ve bu esasen, aksini kabul etmenin verdiği rahatsız edici duygunun güdümünde gelişen bir şeydir. İkincisi ise, tam da bu nedenle, geleceğin ne getireceğini doğru öngören bir görüşten bütünüyle yararlanacak eylemlerde bulunmamakla kendinize zarar verdiğiniz düşüncesidir.

Ancak hata payı, hafife alınmakta ve yanlış anlaşılmakta. Genellikle, fazla risk almak istemeyen veya görüşlerinden emin olmayanların başvurduğu muhafazakâr bir hedge, yani korunma yöntemi olarak görülüyor. Ama doğru kullanıldığında, bunun oldukça tersi oluyor.

Hata payı, bir dizi olası sonuca dayanmanızı sağlar ve dayanıklılık, düşük ihtimalli bir sonuçtan yararlanma olasılığının lehinize düşmesine izin verecek kadar uzun süre oyunda kalmanıza yardımcı olur. En büyük kazanımlar ya sık sık gerçekleşmediklerinden ya da bileşip bütünleşmeleri zaman aldığı için nadiren meydana gelir. Bu nedenle, stratejisinin bir kısmında (nakit) tutup, diğer kısmında (hisse senetlerinde) karşısına çıkabilecek zorluklara dayanmasını sağlayabilecek kadar hata payı bırakan kişi, yanıldığında sıfırı tüketen, oyun bitti, jeton ekle durumunda kalan kişi karşısında avantajlıdır.

Bill Gates bunu çok iyi anlamıştı. Microsoft genç bir şirketken, "inanılmaz derecede muhafazakâr bir yaklaşımla" hareket ettiğini söylüyor: "Herhangi bir ödeme alamamız durumunda bile çalışanların bir yıllık maaş bordrosunu ödemeye yetecek kadar paranın bankada olmasını istiyordum." Warren Buffett, 2008'de Berkshire Hathaway hissedarlarına hitaben konuşurken benzer bir fikri dile getirdi: Size, derecelendirme kuruluşlarına ve kendime, Berkshire'ın her zaman bol miktarda nakitten daha fazlasına sahip olacağı konusunda söz verdim... Seçmek zorunda kaldığımda, ekstra kâr şansını, tek bir gecelik uykuya bile değişmeyeceğim.[44]

Yatırımcıların hata payını düşündükleri birkaç belli nokta vardır.

Bunlardan biri, volatilite. Varlıklarınız yüzde 30 azaldığında ayakta kalabilir misiniz? Hesap tablosu üzerinde belki evet; yani faturalarınızı ödemek ve nakit akışınızın pozitif kalması açısından. Peki ya zihinsel olarak? Yüzde 30'luk bir düşüşün psişik durumunuzu nasıl etkileyeceğini hafife almak kolaydır. Güveniniz, fırsat olasılığının tam da en yüksek olduğu anda kırılabilir. Siz -veya eşiniz- yeni bir plan yapma veya yeni bir kariyere yönelme zamanının geldiğine karar verebilirsiniz. Zarara uğradıktan sonra tükendikleri için bu işi bırakan yatırımcılar tanıyorum. Fiziksel tükenmeden söz ediyorum. Hesap tabloları size, rakamların ne zaman birbirine eklendiğini veya eklenmediğini söyleme konusunda iyidir. Ne var ki, geceleri çocuklarınızı yatağa yatırırken, almış olduğunuz yatırım kararlarının onların geleceğine zarar verecek bir hata olup olmadığını merak ettiğinizde nasıl hissedeceğinizi modellemede iyi oldukları söylenemez. Teknik olarak dayanabilecekleriniz ile duygusal açıdan mümkün olanlar arasına mesafe koymak, hataya yer vermenin gözden kaçan biçimlerinden biridir.

Bir diğeri ise emeklilik için birikim yapmaktır. Tarihe bakabilir ve örneğin, ABD hisse senedi piyasalarının 1870'lerden bu yana enflasyondan sonra yıllık ortalama yüzde 6.8 getiri sağladığını görebiliriz. Bunu emeklilik için birikim yaparken kendi çeşitlendirilmiş portföyünüzden ne bekleyebileceğinize ilişkin bir tahmin aracı olarak kullanmak, ilk yaklaşım açısından makûldür. Bu getiri varsayımlarını, hedeflediğiniz noktaya ulaşmak için her ay biriktirmeniz gereken para miktarını görmek için kullanabilirsiniz.

Peki ya gelecekteki getiriler düşük olursa? Peki ya uzun vadeli geçmiş, uzun vadeli geleceği tahmin etmede iyi bir veri olur, ancak hedeflediğiniz emeklilik tarihi 2009 gibi acımasız bir ayı piyasasının ortasına düşerse? Peki ya gelecekteki bir ayı piyasası sizi ürkütür de hisse senetlerinden çıkar ve gelecekteki bir boğa piyasasını kaçırırsanız, böylece de fiilen kazanmış olduğunuz getiriler piyasa ortalamasının altında kalırsa? Peki ya tıbbi bir aksilik yaşayıp da emeklilik hesabınızı 30'larınızda nakde çevirmeniz gerekirse?

"Peki ya" diye başlayan bütün bu soruların yanıtı "Bir zamanlar öngördüğünüz gibi emekli olamayacağınızdır" ki, bu da felaket olabilir.

Çözüm basit: Gelecekteki getirilerinizi tahmin ederken hataya yer bırakın. Bu bilimden çok, sanattır. Yirminci Bölüm'de daha fazla anlatacağım gibi, ben kendi yatırımlarımda, hayatım boyunca elde edeceğim gelecekteki getirilerin tarihsel ortalamanın 1/3 altında olacağını varsayıyorum. Bu yüzden de geleceğin geçmişe benzeyeceğini varsaymam durumunda biriktireceğimden daha fazlasını biriktiriyorum. Bu benim güvenlik marjım. Gelecekteki getiriler, geçmişten 1/3 değil, daha da düşük olabilir, ancak hiçbir güvenlik marjı yüzde 100 garanti vermez. Geceleri iyi uyumamı sağlaması için üçte birlik tampon yeterli. Ve eğer gelecek geçmişe benzerse, benim için hoş bir sürpiz olur. Charlie Munger, "Mutluluğa ulaşmanın en iyi yolu, hedefi düşük tutmaktır" der. Harika.

Hata payının önemli bir kuzeni vardır ve o da risk almada iyimserlik önyargısı denen veya benim "Rus ruleti, istatistiksel olarak sonuç vermeli" sendromu dediğim şey, yani olumsuz taraf hiçbir koşulda kabul edilemez olduğunda, olumlu olasılıklara bağlanmadır.

Nassim Taleb, "Riski sevebilir ve buna rağmen yıkımdan tamamen kaçınan biri olabilirsiniz" diyor. Ve gerçekten de, öyle yapmalısınız.

Buradaki fikir, ilerlemek için risk almanız gerektiği; ancak sizi yok edebilecek hiçbir riski almaya değmeyeceğidir. Rus ruleti oynarken olasılıklar sizin lehinizedir. Ancak tersi durumda içerdiği dezavantaj, potansiyel avantajına değmez. Riski telafi edebilecek hiçbir güvenlik marjı yoktur.

Para konusunda da öyle. Diyelim ki, kazanç bağlamında birçok şeyde olasılıklar sizin lehinize. Emlak fiyatları çoğu yıl artıyor ve çoğu yıl boyunca iki haftada bir maaş çeki alıyorsunuz. Ancak bir şeyin doğru olma olasılığı yüzde 95, yanlış olma olasılığı yüzde 5 ise, bunun anlamı, hayatınızın bir noktasında dezavantaj deneyimlemenizin neredeyse kesin olduğudur. Ve eğer dezantajın maliyeti yıkım ise, zamanın geri kalan yüzde 95'lik kısmını riske atmaya muhtemelen değmez, ne kadar çekici görünürse görünsün.

Burada, kaldıraç şeytandır. Kaldıraç -paranızı büyütmek için borç almak- rutin riskleri, yıkıma neden olabilecek bir şeye iter. Buradaki tehlike, rasyonel iyimserliğin, bazı zamanlar yıkımla karşılaşma olasığını çoğu kez maskelemesidir. Sonuç ise, riski sistematik olarak hafife almamızdır. Konut fiyatları son on yılda yüzde 30 geriledi. Birkaç şirket borç ödemelerinde temerrüde düştü. Kapitalizm, bu. Böyle şeyler olur. Ancak yüksek oranda kaldıraçlı olanlar, çifte yıkım yaşadı: Çöküntüye uğramakla sadece parasız kalmadılar, aynı zamanda da fırsat olgunlaştığı anda oyuna geri dönmelerini sağlayacak her türlü şansı da yitirdiler. 2009'daki çöküntüyü yaşayan bir konut sahibinin, 2010'daki ucuz mortgage oranlarından yararlanma şansı yoktu. Lehman Brothers'ın 2009'da ucuz borçlanmayla yatırım yapma şansı yoktu. Onlar için olay bitmişti.

Bundan kaçınmak için, kendi paramı dengeli ağırlıklandırıyorum. Bir kısmında risk alıyorum, diğer kısmında ise korkuyorum. Bu tutarsızlık değil; ancak paranın psikolojisi, insanı bunun tutarsızlık olduğuna inanmaya iter. Ben sadece, risklerimin karşılığını alacak kadar uzun süre ayakta kalabileceğimden emin olmak istiyorum. Başarmak için ayakta kalmalısınız. Bu kitapta birkaç kez değindiğimiz bir noktayı tekrarlamak gerekirse: İstediğinizi, istediğiniz zaman, istediğiniz sürece yapabilme yeteneğinin sonsuz yatırım getirisi vardır.

---

Hataya yer bırakmak, olabileceklere dair hedefinizi genişletmekle kalmaz. Ayrıca, asla hayal edemeyeceğiniz, ama karşı karşıya kaldığınızda son derece sıkıntılı olabilecek hadiselerden korunmanıza da yardımcı olur.

İkinci Dünya Savaşı sırasındaki Stalingrad Çarpışması, tarihin en büyük savaşıydı. İnsanların riskle nasıl başa çıktıkları konusunda bir o kadar şaşırtıcı hikâyeleri de beraberinde getirdi.

Bunlardan biri, 1942 yılı sonlarında, bir Alman tankçı birliği şehrin dışındaki otlaklarda yedekte beklediği sırada yaşananlardı. Ön saflarda tanklara umutsuzca ihtiyaç duyulduğunda, herkesi şaşırtan bir şey oldu: Neredeyse hiçbiri çalışmadı.

Birlikteki 104 tankın 20'sinden azı çalışabilir durumdaydı. Mühendisler sorunu çabucak buldular. Tarihçi William Craig şöyle yazıyor: "Cephe gerisinde hareketsiz geçen haftalar boyunca, tarla fareleri tankların içine yuva yapmış ve elektrik sistemlerini kaplayan yalıtımı yiyip bitirmişti."

Almanlar dünyanın en gelişmiş donanımına sahipti. Gelin görün ki, tarla farelerine yenilmişlerdi.

Düşünsenize, nasıl da gözlerine inanamamışlardır. Böyle bir şeyin akıllarından bile geçmemiş olduğuna kesin gözüyle bakabiliriz. Ne tür bir tank tasarımcısı farelere karşı korumayı düşünür? Makûl düşünen birinin aklına gelmez. Tankların tarihini okumuş birinin de öyle.

Ama bu tür şeyler her zaman olur. Aklınızdan geçemeyecek kadar çılgınca şeyler dışında, her riski planlayabilirsiniz. Ve size en büyük zararı, o çılgınca şeyler verebilir; çünkü düşündüğünüzden daha sık meydana gelirler ve nasıl başa çıkacağınıza dair bir planınız yoktur.

Warren Buffett 2006 yılında yerine geçecek kişi için arayışa geçtiğini duyurdu. "Daha önce hiç karşılaşılmamış olanlar da dahil, ciddi riskleri tanımak ve bunlardan kaçınmak için genetik olarak programlanmış birine" ihtiyacı olduğunu söyledi.[45]

Bu becerinin önemini, şirketim Collaborative Fund'ın yatırım yaptığı start-up girişimlerle çalışırken gördüm. Bir şirketin kurucusundan karşılaştıkları en büyük riskleri sıralamasını istersiniz, size olağan şüphelilerden söz ederler. Ancak yatırım yaptığımız şirketlerde, bir start-up şirketi yönetmenin öngörülebilir zorluklarının ötesinde meselelerle de uğraşmak durumunda kaldık. Bunlardan birkaçı şöyleydi:

- Bir şirkette su boruları kırıldı, su bastı ve şirketin ofisi mahvoldu.
- Bir şirketin ofisine üç kez zorla girildi.
- Bir şirket faaliyetini yürüttüğü üretim tesisinden atıldı.
- Bir mağaza, bir müşteri başka bir müşterinin içeri köpek getirmesini beğenmeyip Sağlık Bakanlığı'na başvurması üzerine kapatıldı.
- Bir CEO'nun aldığı e-posta, tüm dikkatini vermesini gerektiren bir fon toplama operasyonunun ortasında sahte çıktı.
- Bir kurucu, zihinsel çöküntü yaşadı.

Bu olayların çoğu şirket için varoluşsal nitelikteydi. Ancak hiçbiri öngörülebilir değildi; çünkü CEO'ların veya tanıdıkları herhangi birinin başına bu tür sorunlar gelmemişti. Keşfedilmemiş topraklardı.

Bu tür bilinmeyen risklerden kaçınmak, neredeyse tanım gereği imkânsızdır. Hayal edemediğiniz şeye hazırlanamazsınız.

Meydana getirecekleri hasara karşı korunmanın bir yolu varsa, o da çökmesi halinde tüm sistemin işleyişini çökertecek olan "zayıf halkalardan" kaçınmaktır.

Kırılabilecek her şeyin sonunda kırılacağı, hayattaki birçok şey için geçerli bir yordamdır. Yani birçok şey, bir şeyin çalışmasına bağlıysa ve o şey bozulursa, felaket için gün sayıyorsunuz demektir. Bu bir zayıf halkadır.

Bazı insanlar, zayıf halkalardan kaçınmakta fevkalâde iyidir. Uçaklardaki en kritik sistemler yedeklidir ve genelde, yedeklerin de yedekleri vardır. Modern jetlerde dört yedekli elektrik sistemi bulunur. Tek motorla uçabilir ve teknik olarak motorsuz iniş yapabilirsiniz; çünkü her jet, motorlarının ters itişi olmaksızın, yalnızca frenleriyle pistte durabilmelidir.

Asma köprüler de benzer şekilde, bağlantı kablolarının çoğu kopsa da yıkılmadan ayakta durabilir.

Parayla ilgili en büyük zayıf halka, kısa vadeli harcama ihtiyaçlarını finanse etmek için yalnızca maaş bordronuza güvenip, ne kadar harcadığınızı ve gelecekte ne kadar harcayabileceğinizi düşünürken, bu ikisi arasına mesafe koyacak hiçbir birikim yapmamanızdır.

Çoğu zaman -en varlıklıların bile- gözden kaçırdığı püf noktası, Onuncu Bölüm'de gördüğümüz şeydir: Birikim yapmak için belirli bir nedene ihtiyacınız olmadığını anlamak. Bir ev veya araba almak ya da emeklilik için para biriktirmek iyidir. Ancak, muhtemelen tahmin edemeyeceğiniz ve hatta kavrayamayacağınız şeyler için -tarla farelerinin finansal eşdeğeri - tasarruf etmek de aynı derecede önemlidir.

Birikimlerinizi ne için kullanacağınızı öngörmek, gelecekte ne kadar harcama yapacağınızı tam olarak bildiğiniz bir dünyada yaşadığınızı varsayar; ki, bunu hiç kimse bilmez. Ben çok birikim yapıyorum ve bu birikimlerimi gelecekte ne için kullanacağımı bilmiyorum. Sadece bilinen risklere hazırlıklı olan planların pek azı, gerçek dünyada ayakta kalabilmek için yeterli güvenlik marjına sahiptir.

Nitekim, her planın en önemli kısmı, planınızın plana göre gitmemesini planlamaktır.

Şimdi izin verirseniz, bunun sizin durumunuzda nasıl geçerli olduğunu göstereyim.

# 14

# Değişeceksiniz

Uzun vadeli planlama göründüğünden zordur, çünkü insanların amaçları ve arzuları zaman içinde değişir.

KÜÇÜKLÜĞÜMDE BİR ARKADAŞIM vardı. Ne doğuştan zeki biriydi, ne de ayrıcalıklı bir zümreden geliyordu; ama tanıdığım en çalışkan çocuktu. Bu tür insanlardan öğrenecek çok şey vardır; çünkü başarıya giden yolun her santimine dair görüşleri birebir yaşayarak oluşmuştur.

Ergenlik dönemimizde bu arkadaşımın bütün hayali ve hayatının misyonu doktor olmaktı. Şansın ona karşı olduğunu söylemek, merhametli davranmak olur. O sırada makûl düşenen tek bir kişi bile, bunun olası olduğunu düşünmezdi.

Ama o zorladı. Ve sonunda -sınıf arkadaşlarından on yaş daha büyük olsa da- doktor çıktı.

Sıfırdan başlamak, tıp fakültesinin zirvesine giden yolu buldozerle geçmek ve bütün olasılıklara karşın, en asil mesleklerden birine ulaşmak sizce ne kadar tatmin edicidir?

Birkaç yıl önce konuştuk. Aramızdaki konuşma şöyle geçti:

Ben: "Uzun zamandır konuşmuyoruz! Nasılsın... nasıl gidiyor?"

O: "Berbat kariyer."

Ben: "Haha, peki... nasıl yani?...."

O: Berbat bir kariyer, arkadaş..."

On dakika boyunca böyle devam etti. İşin stresi ve uzun mesai saatleri onu bitirmişti. Onbeş yıl önce bugün bulunduğu noktaya ulaşmak için ne kadar istekliyse, bugün aynı oranda hayal kırıklığına uğramış görünüyordu.

Psikolojinin temellerinden biri, insanların gelecekteki benliklerini tahmin etmekte kötü olmalarıdır.

Bir hedef hayal etmek kolay ve eğlencelidir. Fakat bir hedefi, rekabetçi arayışlarla giderek artan gerçekçi yaşam stresleri bağlamında hayal etmek tamamen farklı bir şeydir.

Bunun gelecekteki finansal hedeflerimizi planlama yeteneğimiz üzerinde büyük bir etkisi vardır.

---

Beş yaşındaki her çocuk büyüdüğünde traktör sürmek ister. İyi bir işe dair fikri "Vroom vroom, bip bip, hey koca traktör, işte geliyorum!" ile başlayan ve biten küçük bir çocuğun gözüne, pek az iş bundan daha iyi görünür.

Sonra büyürler ve çoğu traktör kullanmanın en iyi kariyer olmayabileceğini anlar. Belki daha prestijli veya kazançlı bir şey isterler.

Böylece ergenlik çağında hukukçu olmayı hayal ederler. Artık planlarının hazır olduğunu düşünürler, emindirler. Hukuk fakültesi, eğitim masrafları derken o gün gelir ve hukukçu olurlar.

Sonra, hukukçu olarak o kadar uzun çalışma saatleriyle karşılaşırlar ki, ailelerini nadiren görürler.

Böylece, belki de esnek çalışma saatleri olan daha düşük ücretli bir işe girerler. Sonra çocuk bakımının çok pahalı olduğunu ve maaşlarının çoğunu alıp götürdüğünü fark edip, evde oturup çocuklarına bakmayı seçerler. Bunun, nihayet doğru seçim olduğu sonucuna varırlar.

Sonra, 70 yaşında, ömür boyu evde durmanın, emekliliğe hazırlıksız oldukları anlamına geldiğini anlarlar.

Birçoğumuz yaşam boyunca benzer bir yörüngede ilerleriz. Federal Reserve'e göre, üniversite mezunlarının sadece yüzde 27'si ana dallarıyla ilgili bir işte çalışmakta.[46] Ev dışında bir işte çalışmayan ebeveynlerin yüzde 29'u üniversite diplomalı.[47] Tabii ki bunlardan bazıları almış oldukları eğitimden pişmanlık duyuyor olabilir. Ancak, 30'lu yaşlarında, yeni ebeveyn olmuş birinin yaşamdaki hedeflerini, 18 yaşındaki benliğinin asla hayal edemeyeceği şekilde düşünebileceğini kabul etmeliyiz.

Uzun vadeli finansal planlama esastır. Ancak işler değişir; sadece sizi çevreleyen dünya değil, kendi hedefleriniz ve arzularınız de başka yerlere gidebilir. "Geleceğin ne getireceğini bilmiyoruz" demek bir şeydir. Ancak bugün, gelecekte ne isteyeceğinizi kendinizin bile bilmediğini kabul etmek, başka bir şeydir. Ve gerçek şu ki, pek azımız biliriz. Gelecekte ne isteyeceğinize dair görüşünüz muhtemelen değişeceğinden, uzun vadeli kalıcı kararlar vermek zordur.

Psikologların *Geçmişin Sonu Yanılsaması* dediği bir eğilim var: Yani insanların geçmişte ne kadar değiştiklerinin keskin bir şekilde farkında olmaları, ancak kişiliklerinin, arzularının ve hedeflerinin gelecekte ne kadar değişebileceğini hafife almaları. Harvard psikoloğu Daniel Gilbert bir keresinde bunu şöyle anlatmıştı:

> Hayatımızın her aşamasında, olacağımız insanların hayatlarını derinden etkileyecek kararlar alırız ve sonra o insanlar olduğumuzda, verdiğimiz kararlardan her zaman heyecan duymayız. Bu nedenle, ergenler dövme yaptırmak için bayağı iyi para ödüyorlar, gençler

> de onları sildirmek için bayağı iyi para ödüyor. Genç yetişkinler evlenmek için acele ederken, orta yaşlı insanlar boşanmak için acele ediyorlar. Yaşlı yetişkinler, orta yaşlı yetişkinlerin kazanmak için çok çalıştıkları şeyleri, kaybetmek için çok çalışıyorlar. Bu böyle devam edip gidiyor.[48]

"Hepimiz," diyor Gilbert, "Bir yanılsama içinde yol alıyoruz; geçmişin, kendi kişisel geçmişimizin şimdi sona erdiğine, olmamız gereken kişi olduğumuza ve yaşamımızın sonuna kadar da böyle olacağımıza dair bir yanılsama yaşıyoruz." Bu dersi asla öğrenmeme eğilimindeyiz. Gilbert'ın araştırması, 18 ila 68 yaş arasındaki insanların gelecekte ne kadar değişeceklerini hafife aldıklarını gösteriyor.

Bunun uzun vadeli bir finansal planı nasıl etkileyebileceğini görebilirsiniz. Charlie Munger, bileşiklendirmenin ilk kuralının asla gereksiz yere ara vermemek olduğunu söylüyor. Ne var ki, hayattan istedikleriniz değiştiğinde parayla ilgili bir planı -kariyer, yatırım, harcamalar, bütçeleme, her neyse- nasıl kesintiye uğratmazsınız? Zor. Ronald Read -kitabın başında tanıştığımız varlıklı hademe- gibi insanların ve Warren Buffett'ın bu kadar başarılı olmasının bir nedeni, on yıllardır aynı şeyi yapmaya devam etmeleri ve bileşiklendirmenin coşmasını sağlamalarıdır. Ancak çoğumuz ömrümüz boyunca o kadar evriliriz ki, on yıllarca aynı şeyi yapmaya devam etmek istemeyiz. Ya da ona yakın bir şey olur. Yani 80 küsur yıllık bir ömür yerine, paramızı belki de birbirinden ayrı, 20'şer yıllık dört blok halinde düşünmeliyiz.

Az gelirle, isteyerek sade hayatlar yaşayan ve bundan son derece memnun olan insanlar tanıyorum. Lüks bir hayat yaşamak için didinen ve bundan son derece memnun olanlar da var. Her iki seçim de farklı riskler içeriyor: Birinci gruptakilerin riski, aile kurmaya veya emekliliklerini finanse etmeye hazırlıksız olmaları; ikinci gruptakilerin riski ise genç ve sağlıklı yıllarını bir hücrede geçirdirdikleri için pişmanlık duymak.

Bu sorunun kolay bir çözümü yok. Beş yaşındaki bir çocuğa traktör sürücüsü yerine avukat olması gerektiğini söylerseniz, buna bütün gücüyle karşı çıkacaktır.

Ancak, uzun vadeli olduğunu düşündüğünüz kararları verirken aklınızda bulundurmanız gereken iki şey var.

Finansal planlamanın uç noktalarından kaçınmalıyız. Çok düşük bir gelirle mutlu olacağınızı varsaymak veya yüksek bir gelir peşinde, bitmek bilmeyen saatler boyunca çalışmayı seçmek, günün birinde kendinizi pişmanlık noktasında bulma olasılığınızı artırır. Geçmişin Sonu Yanılsaması'nı besleyen şey, insanların çoğu ortama uyum sağlamasıdır; dolayısıyla da uçlardaki bir planın faydaları -neredeyse hiçbir şeye sahip olmamanın basitliği veya neredeyse her şeye sahip olmanın heyecanı- yavaş yavaş azalır veya biter. Ancak bu aşırı uçların dezavantajları -emeklilik dönemini finanse edememe ya da para peşinde koşulmuş bir hayata dönüp bakma- kalıcı pişmanlıklar haline gelebilir. Pişmanlıklar, özellikle de önceki planınızı bir kenara bıraktığınızda ve kaybettiğiniz zamanı telafi etmek için şimdiki hedefinize iki kat daha hızlı koşmanız gerektiğini hissettiğinizde acı verir.

Bileşiklendirme, bir plana büyümesi için yıllar veya on yıllar tanıyabildiğiniz zaman en iyi sonucu verir. Bu sadece tasarruflar değil, kariyerler ve ilişkiler için de geçerlidir. Dayanıklılık, kilit önem taşır. Ve kim olduğumuzu zaman içinde değiştirme eğilimimizi düşünürsek, hayatınızın her noktasında denge, gelecekteki pişmanlıklardan kaçınmaya ve dayanıklılığı teşvik etmeye yönelik bir strateji haline gelir.

Çalışma hayatınızın her noktasında, orta düzeyde yıllık tasarruf, orta düzeyde boş zaman, orta düzeyi aşmayan mesai saatleri ve ailenizle en azından orta düzeyde zaman geçirmeyi hedeflemek, bir plana bağlı kalma ve pişmanlıktan kaçınma olasılığını, sözünü ettiğim bütün bu şeylerden herhangi birinin yelpazenin aşırı uçlarına düşmesi halinde deneyimleyeceğinizden daha çok artırır.

Ayrıca fikrimizi değiştirme gerçeğini de kabul etmeliyiz. Tanıştığım en acınası durumdaki çalışanlardan bazıları, kariyerlerine sırf henüz 18 yaşında, üniversitede ne okuyacaklarına karar verirken o alanı seçmiş oldukları için bağlı kalan ve sürdüren insanlar. Geçmişin Sonu Yanılsaması'nı kabul ettiğinizde, henüz içki içme izninizin bile olmadığı yaşta seçtiğiniz bir işten, Sosyal Güvenlik kapsamında emekliliği hak edecek yaşa geldiğinizde de hâlâ keyif alma ihtimalinin düşük olduğunu fark ediyorsunuz.

İşin püf noktası, değişim gerçeğini kabul etmek ve olabildiğince hızlı bir şekilde yola devam etmektir.

Psikolog Daniel Kahneman *Thinking, Fast and Slow* (Hızlı ve Yavaş Düşünme) adlı kitabını yazarken, *Wall Street Journal*'ın yatırımlarla ilgili bölümünün köşe yazarı Jason Zweig da onunla birlikte çalışmıştı. Zweig bir yazısında, Kahneman'da gördüğü ve kendisine de çok faydalı olduğunu söylediği küçük bir kişilik daprisine değinmişti: "Danny ile ilgili hiçbir şey, beni henüz bitirmiş olduğumuz bir şeyi bir kenara fırlatması kadar şaşırtmadı" diye yazmıştı. Kahneman ile bir bölüm üzerinde sonsuza dek sürecekmiş gibi uzun uzun çalıştıktan sonra olanları, şöyle anlatmıştı:

> Bildiğiniz bir sonraki şey, şu olur: [Kahneman] o kadar farklı, tamamen dönüştürülmüş bir versiyon gönderir ki, yaptığınız şey tanınmaz hale gelir: Farklı başlar, farklı biter, asla aklınıza gelmeyecek anekdotları ve kanıtları dahil etmiştir ve daha önce hiç duymadığınız araştırmalardan yararlanmıştır.

Zweig şöyle devam etmişti:

> Danny'ye, önceki taslağı hiç yazmamışız gibi nasıl yeniden başlayabildiğini sorduğumda hiç unutamadığım bir şey söyledi. "Batık maliyetim yok" dedi.[49]

Batık maliyetler -yani alınan kararları, geçmişte harcanan ve geri alınamayacak çabalara bağlamak- insanların zaman içinde değiştiği bir dünyada şeytandır. Gelecekteki bizi, geçmişteki farklı bizin tutsağı yaparlar. Bu, hayatınızla ilgili büyük kararları sizin adınıza bir yabancının vermesiyle eş anlamlıdır.

Yaşam destek ünitesine bağlı yaşayıp gitmektense, farklı bir insanken benimsenmiş olan finansal amaçları hiç acımadan terk etmek gerektiği fikrini benimsemek, gelecekteki pişmanlığı en aza indirmek için iyi bir strateji olabilir. Ne kadar hızlı yapılırsa, bileşiklendirmeye o kadar çabuk geri dönebilirsiniz.

Şimdi de, bileşiklendirmenin giriş fiyatını konuşalım.

# 15

# Hiçbir Şey Bedava Değildir

---

Her şeyin bir fiyatı vardır,
fakat bütün fiyatlar
etiketlerde yazılı değildir.

---

HER ŞEYİN BİR fiyatı vardır ve parayla ilgili birçok şeyin en önemli unsurlarından biri, sadece bu bedelin ne olduğunu bulmak ve onu ödemeye istekli olmaktır.

Sorun şu ki, birçok şeyin bedeli ilk elden deneyimleyinceye, yani faturanın vadesi geçinceye kadar bariz değildir.

---

General Electric, 2004 yılında dünyanın en büyük şirketiydi ve değeri yaklaşık 330 milyar dolardı. Önceki on yıl boyunca da her yıl birinci ya da ikinci olmuştu; kapitalizmin kurumsal aristokrasinin en parlak yıldızlarından biriydi.

Sonra her şey paramparça oldu.

2008 finans krizi, şirketin kârının yarısından fazlasını sağlayan GE'nin finans bölümünü kaosa sürükledi. Sonunda hurda fiyatına satıldı. Bunun ardından petrol ve enerji sektöründeki girişimler felaket oldu ve milyarlarca dolar zararla sonuçlandı. 2007 yılında 40 dolar olan GE hissesi, 2018'de 7 dolara düştü.

2001 yılından beri şirketin başında bulunan CEO Immelt hemen suçlu ilan edildi ve ağır suçlamaların hedefi oldu. Liderliği ve yaptığı satın almalar, kâr paylarında kesintiye gitmesi, işten çıkarmalar ve tabii ki hisse senedi fiyatının dibi boylaması nedeniyle sert bir şekilde eleştirildi. Haklı olarak, iyi zamanlarda hanedanın servetiyle ödüllendirilenler, dalga çekildiğinde sorumluluğun yükünü taşırlar. Immelt 2017 yılında istifa ederek şirketten ayrıldı.

Fakat giderayak son derece akıllıca bir şey söyledi.

Immelt, halefine -esasen, yanlış işler yaptığını ve yapması gerekenin açık olduğunu söyleyerek eleştirenlere yanıt olarak- şöyle dedi: "Yapan siz olmayınca, her iş kolay görünüyor."

Yapan siz olmadığınızda her iş kolay görünür; çünkü sahadaki birinin karşılaştığı zorluklar, kalabalıktakiler tarafından genelde görülmez.

Dallanıp budaklanarak büyümek, kısa vadeli yatırımcıların, düzenleyicilerin, sendikaların ve yerleşik bürokrasinin çatışan talepleriyle uğraşmak, sadece bütün bunları yapmak anlamında değil, aynı zamanda bizzat kendiniz meşgul olmadıkça sorunların ciddiyetini görmek açısından da zordur. Immelt'in 14 ay iş başında kalan halefi de bunu öğrendi.

Çoğu şey pratikte, teoride olduğundan daha zordur. Bu bazen kendimize fazla güvendiğimiz için olur. Daha sıklıkla da, başarının bedelini belirlemede iyi olmamamızdan ve bunun da o bedeli ödeyebilmemizi engellemesinden kaynaklanır.

---

2018'de biten 50 yılda S&P 500 Endeksi 119 kat yükseldi. Tek yapmanız gereken, arkanıza yaslanıp paranızın bileşerek büyümesine izin vermekti. Ancak elbette ki, başarılı yatırımlar gerçekleştirmek, yapan siz olmadığınızda kolay görünüyor.

"Hisse senedi yatırımlarınızı uzun vadeli tutun" derler. Bu, iyi bir tavsiye.

Fakat hisse senetleri çökerken uzun vadeli bir bakış açısını korumanın ne kadar zor olduğunu biliyor musunuz?

Değen ve değerli olan her şey gibi, başarılı yatırım da bir bedel gerektirir. Ama para birimi dolar ve sent değildir. Oynaklık (volatilite), korku, şüphe, belirsizlik ve pişmanlıktır; ve gerçek zamanlı olarak uğraşıncaya kadar bunların hepsini gözden kaçırmak kolaydır.

Yatırımın bir bedeli olduğunu görememek, aklımızın çelinmesine, böylece de hiçbir karşılık ödemeden bir şeyler elde etmeye kalkışmamıza yol açabilir; ki bu da, dükkân soymak gibi nadiren iyi biter.

Diyelim ki yeni bir araba istiyorsunuz. Arabanın maliyeti 30,000 dolar. Üç seçeneğiniz var: 1) O arabaya 30,000 dolar ödeyeceksiniz, 2) daha ucuza, kullanılmış bir araba bulacaksınız veya 3) çalacaksınız. Bu durumda, insanların yüzde 99'u üçüncü seçenekten kaçınması gerektiğini bilir; çünkü araba çalmanın olumsuz sonuçları, bu eylemin sağlayacağı faydaya ağır basar.

Fakat diyelim ki, huzur içinde emekli olabilmek için önünüzdeki 30 yıl boyunca yıllık yüzde 11 getiri elde etmek istiyorsunuz. Bu ödül bedava mı geliyor? Elbette, değil. Öyle güzel bir dünya yok. Bunun bir fiyat etiketi, ödenmesi gereken bir fatura var. Bu durumda o fatura, piyasanın biteviye sürdürdüğü alaycı tutum; yani büyük getiriler sağlayarak ve onları aynı hızla alıp götürerek oynadığı oyundur. Dow Jones Sanayi Ortalaması, 1950'den 2019'a kadar kâr payları dahil yılda yaklaşık yüzde 11 getiri sağladı, ki bu harika. Ancak bu dönem süresince başarının bedeli korkunç derecede yüksekti. Grafikteki gölgeli çizgiler, piyasanın bir önceki en yüksek seviyesinden en az yüzde 5 düşük olduğu dönemleri gösteriyor.

Bu, piyasa getirilerinin bedelidir. Ücret diyebiliriz. Giriş fiyatı diyebiliriz. Ve acıtır.

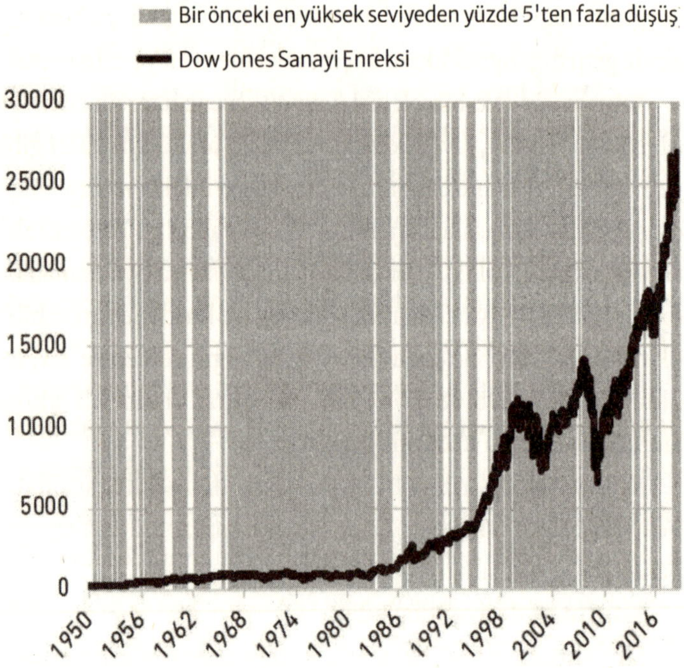


Çoğu ürün gibi, getiri ne kadar büyükse, fiyat da o kadar yüksek olur. Netflix hissesi 2002 yılından 2018'e kadar yüzde 35,000'in üzerinde getiri sağladı; ancak söz konusu dönemdeki işlem günlerinin yüzde 94'ünde tarihsel olarak bir önceki en yüksek seviyesinin altında işlem gördü. Monster Beverage, 1995'ten 2018 yılına kadar yüzdc 319,000 -tarihin en yüksek oranlarından biri- getiri sağladı; ancak bu sürenin yüzde 95'inde bir önceki en yüksek seviyesinin altında işlem gördü.

Şimdi önemli kısıma gelelim. Araba örneğinde olduğu gibi, burada da birkaç seçeneğiniz var: Oynaklığı ve çalkantıları kabullenerek bu fiyatı ödeyebilirsiniz. Veya getirisi daha düşük, ama belirsizliği de daha az olan, yani yukarıdaki ikinci el arabaya eşdeğer bir varlık bulabilirsiniz. Veya otomobil soygunculuğu ile eş anlamlı bir şeye girişir ve getiriyi, beraberinde getirdiği oynaklıktan kaçınarak elde etmeye çalışırsınız.

Yatırım işindeki birçok kişi üçüncü seçeneği tercih eder. İyi niyetli ve yasalara saygılı olsalar da, tıpkı araba hırsızları gibi getiriyi bedel ödemeksizin elde etmek için hileler ve stratejiler oluştururlar. Piyasalarda alım ve satım yaparlar. Bir sonraki ekonomik durgunluktan önce satmaya, bir sonraki patlamadan önce alım yapmaya çalışırlar. Çok küçük bir deneyim sahibi olan yatırımcılar bile çoğunlukla, oynaklığın gerçek ve yaygın olduğunu bilir. Böylece birçoğu, bir sonraki mantıklı adımı atar: Oynaklıktan kaçınmaya çalışır.

Ancak Para Tanrıları, bedelini ödemeden ödül arayanlara pek iyi gözle bakmazlar. Bazı araba hırsızları paçayı sıyırır. Fakat çoğu yakalanıp cezalandırılır.

Yatırım işi de aynı böyledir.

Morningstar bir dönem, taktiksel yatırım fonlarının, yani stratejileri uygun görünen zamanlarda portföy dağılımındaki hisse senetleri ile tahviller arasında geçiş yaparak, piyasa getirilerinde aşağı yönlü riski düşük tutmak olan fonların performansını incelemişti.[50] Bedelini ödemeden getiri istiyorlardı. Bu çalışma, ABD borsalarının yeni bir ekonomik durgunluk korkusuyla çılgına döndüğü ve S&P 500 Endeksi'nin % 20'nin üzerinde düştüğü 2010 yılı ortasından 2011 sonlarına odaklanıyordu. Tam da taktiksel fonların iyi iş çıkarması gereken türden bir ortamdı. Parlamaları gereken andı.

Morningstar'ın hesabına göre, bu dönemde 112 taktiksel yatırım fonu vardı. Bunlardan sadece dokuzunun riske göre düzeltilmiş getirisi, hisse senetleri ile tahviller arasında 60/40 dağılım uygulayan sıradan bir fondan daha iyiydi. Maksimum düşüş açısından ise taktiksel fonların dörtte birinden azı, kendi haline bırakılmış bir endeksten daha iyi sonuç deneyimlemişti. Morningstar şöyle yazıyordu: "Birkaç istisna dışında, [taktik fonlar] daha az kazandı, daha oynaktılar, ve onlar da kendi haline bırakılmış fonlarla aynı oranda aşağı yönlü riske maruz kaldılar."

Bireysel yatırımcılar da kendi yatırımlarında bu hataya düşüyorlar. Morningstar'a göre, hisse senedi fonlarına yatırım yapan ortalama yatırımcı, esasen yatırım yapmış olduğu fonlardan yılda yüzde yarım daha düşük performans gösteriyordu; bu da alıp elde tutmaları gerekirken, aldıktan kısa bir süre sonra satmalarının sonucuydu.[51]

Buradaki ironi, yatırımcıların bedel ödemekten kaçınmaya çalışırken, iki katını ödemeleridir.

GE'ye geri dönelim. Yaptıkları pek çok hatadan biri, eski CEO Jack Welch'in yönetimindeki dönemden kaynaklanıyordu. Welch hisse başına üç aylık kazançların, Wall Street tahminlerinin üstüne çıkmasını sağlamakla ünlenmişti. O büyük ustaydı. Wall Street analistleri hisse başına 0.25 dolar bekliyorsa, şirketin veya ekonominin durumu ne olursa olsun, Jack 0.26 dolar verirdi. Bunu rakamlara masaj yaparak -inanın bu merhametli bir ifade- ve genellikle de itaatkâr rakamların efendilerinin emirlerini yerine getirip selam durması için gelecekteki çeyrek dönemlerin kazançlarını mevcut çeyrek döneme çekerek sağlardı.

> Forbes dergisi, bu tür düzinelerce örnekten birini şöyle haber yapmıştı: [General Electric], riskin iyi yönetildiğini garanti etmede mülkiyet riskini GE'ye yükleyen işlemlerle, iki yıl üst üste, son kullanıcılar yerine isimsiz partnerlere lokomotifler sattı.[52]

Welch bu oyunu hiçbir zaman reddetmedi. *Straight From the Gut* (Doğrudan İçgüdülerimle) adlı kitabında şöyle yazıyordu:

> İş dünyasındaki liderlerimizin krizlere tepkisi GE kültürünün tipik bir örneğiydi. O çeyreğin defterleri kapanmış olsa da, birçoğu, aradaki açığı [kazanç] kapatmak için yardım teklifi alırdı. Kimileri, sürprizleri bertaraf etme işinde 10 milyon dolar, 20 milyon dolar, hatta 30 milyon dolar ekstra çıkarabileceğini söylüyordu.

Sonuç, Welch'in liderliği döneminde hissedarların bunun bedelini ödemek zorunda kalmamış olmasıydı. Onlar için tutarlılık ve öngörülebilirlik vardı: Belirsizliğin sürprizleri olmaksızın her yıl arka arkaya yükselen bir hisse senedi. Sonra, her zaman olduğu gibi faturanın vadesi geldi. GE hissedarları, on yıl boyunca, daha önce muhasebe manevralarının kalkan olduğu devasa kayıplardan zarar gördü. Welch döneminin bir kuruşluk kazancı, 10 kuruşluk zarar haline gelmişti.

Bunun en tuhaf örneği, ipotekli konut kredisi sektörünün iflas etmiş iki devinden, 2000'lerin başında, yatırımcılara "pürüzsüzlük ve öngörülebilirlik" yanılsaması vermek için kazançları gelecek dönemlere yayan, bu amaçla da mevcut kazançlarını milyarlarca dolar eksik beyan eden Freddie Mac ve Fannie Mae'den geliyor.[53] Bedel ödemek zorunda olmama yanılsaması.

---

Soru şu: Arabaların, evlerin, yemeklerin ve tatillerin bedelini ödemeye razı olan bunca insan, iyi yatırım getirilerinin bedelini ödemekten kaçınmak için neden bu kadar uğraş veriyor?

Yanıt basit: Yatırımda başarının bedeli, ilk anda belli değildir. Hemen görebileceğiniz bir fiyat etiketi yoktur; bu nedenle de faturanın vadesi geldiğinde, iyi bir şey almak için ücret ödediğiniz hissini vermez. Yanlış bir şey yapmanın karşılığında kesilen para cezası gibi gelir. Ve insanlar genellikle ücret ödemeyi sorun etmezken, para cezalarından kaçınılması gerektiğini düşünürler. Para cezasını önleyecek ve bundan kaçınmanızı sağlayacak kararlar vermeniz gerekmektedir. Trafik cezaları ve Maliye'nin kestiği cezalar, yanlış bir şey yaptığınız ve cezalandırılmayı hak ettiğiniz anlamına gelir. Servetlerinin gerilediğini deneyimleyen ve bu düşüşü ceza olarak gören herkes için geçerli olan doğal tepki, gelecekteki cezalardan kaçınmaktır.

Kulağa basit veya önemsiz bir şey gibi gelse de, piyasaların oynaklığını ceza yerine ücret olarak düşünmek, yatırım kazançlarının lehinize işlemesini bekleyebilecek kadar uzun süre oyunda kalmanızı sağlayan zihniyeti geliştirmenin önemli bir parçasıdır.

Çok az yatırımcı "Paramın yüzde 20'sini kaybetmeyi sorun etmem" deme eğilimi gösterir. Bu dediğim, yüzde 20'lik bir düşüşü hiç yaşamamış olan yeni yatırımcılar için iki kat daha doğrudur.

Ancak oynaklığa ücret olarak bakarsanız, işler farklı görünür.

Disneyland biletleri 100 dolar. Ama çocuklarınızla asla unutamayacağınız, harika bir gün geçiriyorsunuz. Geçen yıl 18 milyonu aşkın insan, bu ücretin ödemeye değer olduğunu düşündü. Pek az kişi ödediği 100 doları bir tür cezalandırma ya da para cezası olarak gördü. Bir şeyin ödediğiniz ücrete değip değmediği, siz onu ödedikten sonra açıklık kazanır.

Oynaklığın neredeyse her zaman para cezası değil, ücret olduğu yatırım işinde de böyledir.

Piyasa getirileri hiçbir zaman bedava değildir ve hiçbir zaman da olmayacaktır. Diğer bütün ürünler gibi piyasa da sizden bir bedel ödemenizi ister. Kimse sizi Disneyland'e gitmeye zorlamadığı gibi, piyasaya da bu ücreti ödemek zorunda değilsiniz. Biletlerin 10 dolar olabileceği yerel bir fuara gidebilir veya bedavaya evde oturabilirsiniz. Ve her koşulda, hangisini seçerseniz seçin, iyi vakit geçirebilirsiniz. Fakat genellikle, ödediğinizin karşılığını alırsınız. Piyasalar için de aynı şey geçerli. Oynaklığa/belirsizliğe ödenen ücret -getirilerin bedeli- nakit ve tahvil/bono gibi düşük ücretli parklara kıyasla daha çok getiri elde etmenin giriş maliyetidir.

İşin püf noktası, kendinizi piyasanın ödenen ücrete değdiğine ikna etmektir. Oynaklık ve belirsizlikle gerektiği gibi başa çıkmanın tek yolu budur; sadece dayanmak veya katlanmak değil, bunun ödemeye değer bir giriş ücreti olduğunun farkına varmak gerekir.

Elbette bunun her zaman böyle olacağının garantisi yok. Bazen Disneyland'de yağmur yağar.

Ancak giriş ücretini ceza olarak görürseniz, sihirin tadını asla çıkaramazsınız.

Önce fiyatı bulmalı, sonra da ödemelisiniz.

# 16

# Siz ve Ben

Sizden farklı bir oyun oynamakta olan insanlardan finansal ipuçları almaktan sakının.

HANE HALKININ SERVETİ, 2000'lerin başında nokta-com balonunun patlamasıyla, 6.2 trilyon dolar azaldı.

Konut balonunun sonunda, 8 trilyon doların üstünde bir servet eridi.

Finansal balonların toplumsal açıdan ne kadar yıkıcı olabileceğini hafife almak zor. Hayatları mahvediyorlar.

Peki balonlar neden oluyor?

Ve niçin olmaya devam ediyorlar?

Neden ders alıp öğrenemiyoruz?

Bu sorulara verilen yaygın yanıt, insanların açgözlü, açgözlülüğün de insan doğasının ayrılmaz bir özelliği olduğudur.

Bu çoğu için doğru olabilir; ayrıca da yeterince iyi bir cevaptır. Ancak Birinci Bölüm'de ne dediğimizi hatırlayın: Hiç kimse çılgın değildir. İnsanlar pişmanlık duyacakları finansal kararlar verirler ve genellikle de kıt bilgiyle ve mantıksızca böyle yaparlar. Ama o kararlar, verildikleri dönemde onlar için anlamlıdır. Açgözlülüğün suçunu balonlara yüklemek ve orada durmak, insanların sonradan, geriye bakışta açgözlü kararlar olarak görünen şeyleri nasıl ve neden rasyonelleştirdiklerine dair önemli dersleri gözden kaçırmak olur.

Balonlardan ders çıkarmanın zorluğu kısmen, biyopsinin bize net bir uyarı işareti ve teşhis sunduğu kanser gibi bir şey olmamasından kaynaklanır. Balonları, bir siyasi partinin yükselişi ve düşüşüne daha yakın bir şey olarak görebiliriz;

geriye bakıldığında sonucu bilinir, ancak nedeni ve suçlusu konusunda asla görüş birliği olmaz.

Yatırım getirileri bağlamında şiddetli bir rekabet vardır ve zamanın her noktasında, her varlığa birilerinin sahip olması gerekir. Bu esasen balon fikrinin kendisinin, her zaman tartışmalı olacağı anlamına gelir; çünkü hiç kimse değerinin çok üzerinde bir fiyattan işlem gören, aşırı fiyatlanmış bir varlığa sahip olduğunu düşünmek istemez. Sonradan geriye dönüp baktığımızda, ders almaktan çok, suçlama olasılığımız daha yüksektir.

Balonların niçin oluştuğunu hiçbir zaman tam olarak açıklayabileceğimizi sanmıyorum. Bu, savaşların niçin yaşandığını sormak gibi bir şey; hemen her zaman, çoğu birbiriyle çelişen ve tümü tartışmaya açık olan birkaç neden vardır.

Basit yanıtlar için fazlasıyla karmaşık bir konu.

Ancak, her ikisinin de gözden kaçırılan ve kişisel düzeyde sizin için geçerli olan bir sebebini önermeme izin verin: Yatırımcılar sık sık, kendilerinden farklı bir oyun oynamakta olan diğer yatırımcılardan masumca ipuçları alırlar.

---

Finansta masum görünen ama hesaplanamayacak zararlar veren bir fikir vardır.

Bu da, yatırımcıların farklı amaçlara ve farklı zaman ufkuna sahip olduğu bir dünyada, varlıkların tek bir rasyonel fiyatı olduğu nosyonudur.

Kendinize şu soruyu sorun: Bugün Google hissesi için ne kadar ödemelisiniz?

Yanıt "sizin" kim olduğunuza bağlıdır.

Otuz yıllık bir zaman ufkunuz var mı? Eğer öyleyse, ödenecek akıllıca fiyatı belirlemek için önümüzdeki 30 yıl boyunca Google'ın iskontolu nakit akışlarını ciddi bir şekilde analiz etmeniz gerekir.

On yıl içinde nakite geçmek mi istiyorsunuz? O halde, ödeyeceğiniz fiyatı, teknoloji sektörünün önümüzdeki on yıldaki potansiyelini ve Google yönetiminin vizyonunu hayata geçirip geçiremeyeceğini analiz ederek bulabilirsiniz.

Bir yıl içinde satmayı mı düşünüyorsunuz? O halde, Google'ın mevcut ürün satış döngülerine ve bir ayı piyasasının gündeme gelip gelmeyeceğine dikkat etmeniz gerekir.

Günlük işlem yapan bir trader mısınız? O halde, ödenecek akıllı fiyat "kimin umurunda?" olur. Çünkü sadece şu an ile öğle yemeği arasında olacak herhangi bir şeyden birkaç dolar koparmaya çalışıyorsunuzdur ve bu da her fiyata yapılabilecek bir şeydir.

Yatırımcıların amaçları ve zaman ufku farklı olduğunda -ki her varlık sınıfında böyledir- birine saçma görünen fiyatlar, bir başkasına mantıklı gelebilir; çünkü bu yatırımcıların dikkate aldığı faktörler farklıdır.

1990'lardaki nokta-com balonunu örnek alalım.

İnsanlar Yahoo! hissesinin 1999 yılında işlem gördüğü fiyatlara bakıp "Çılgınca bir şeydi! Zilyon katı kazanç! Değerlemenin hiç anlamı yoktu!" diyebilirler.

Ancak 1999 yılında Yahoo! hisseleri alan birçok yatırımcının zaman ufku o kadar kısaydı ki, gülünç bir bedel ödemeleri anlamlıydı. Günlük işlem yapan bir trader, o gün Yahoo! hisse başına 5 dolardan da 500 dolardan da işlem görse, doğru yönde hareket ettiği sürece ihtiyacı olan şeyi elde ederdi. Ve yıllarca böyle oldu.

Finansın bükülmez kurallarından biri, paranın olabildiğince büyük getiri peşinde koşmasıdır. Bir varlığın momentumu varsa -bir süredir tutarlı bir şekilde yükseliyorsa- kısa vadeli işlem yapan bir grup trader'ın yükselmeye devam edeceğini varsaymasının çılgınlık olduğu söylenemez. Sonsuza dek değil; sadece ihtiyaç duydukları o kısa süre için yükselsin yeter. Momentum, kısa vadeli yatırımcıları makûl bir şekilde cezbeder.

Böylece, yarışa start verilir.

Balonlar, kısa vadeli getirilerdeki ivmenin piyasadaki yatırımcı yapısını, çoğunlukla uzun vadeliden, çoğunlukla kısa vadeliye yöneltmeye yetecek kadar parayı çektiğinde oluşur.

Bu süreç kendi kendini besler. Trader'lar kısa vadeli getirileri yukarı ittikçe, daha da fazla trader'ı cezbeder. Bir vakit sonra -genellikle de uzun sürmez- daha kısa zaman ufkuyla işlem yapan fiyat belirleyiciler, daha fazla otorite geliştirerek piyasaya egemen olurlar.

Balonların, değerlemelerin yükselmesiyle pek ilgisi yoktur. Bu sadece başka bir şeyin belirtisidir: Oyun alanına giren kısa vadeli trader'ların sayısı arttıkça, zaman ufku daralır.

Nokta-com balonunun geleceğe dair mantık dışı iyimserlik dönemi olduğu, yaygın bir söylem. Ancak o dönemin en yaygın gazete başlıklarından biri, rekor seviyedeki işlem hacimlerini, yani yatırımcıların bir günde yaptıkları alım ve satımların ulaştığı rekor düzeyi duyurmaktı. Yatırımcılar -özellikle de fiyatları belirleyenler- gelecek 20 yılı düşünmüyorlardı. 1999'da ortalama bir yatırım fonunun yıllık getirisi yüzde 120 idi; yani en fazlası, önlerindeki sekiz ayı düşünüyorlardı. Bu yatırım fonlarını satın alan bireysel yatırımcılar da öyleydi. Maggie Mahar, *The Bull* (Boğa) adlı kitabında şöyle yazıyor:

> Doksanların ortalarında basın, yıllık rakamlar yerine, üç ayda bir çıkan raporları yayınlamaya başlamıştı. Bu değişiklik, yatırımcıları performansın peşinden koşmaya, fonları grafiklerin tepe noktasında, tam da en pahalı oldukları sırada satın almak için koşturmaya itti.

Bu dönem, günlük işlemler ve kısa vadeli opsiyon sözleşmeleriyle şekillenen, piyasaların dakikası dakikasına yorumlandığı zamanlardı. Uzun vadeli görüşlerle ilişkilendireceğiniz türden bir şey değildi.

2000'lerin ortalarındaki konut balonu sırasında da aynı şey oldu.

Önümüzdeki 10 yıl içinde çocuk sahibi olup ailenizi büyütme niyetiyle, Florida'da iki yatak odalı prefabrik bir eve 700,000 dolar ödemeyi haklı çıkarmak zor. Ancak, fiyatların sürekli yükseliş halinde olduğu bir piyasada, o evi birkaç ay içinde elden çıkarıp hızlıca kâr etmeyi planlıyorsanız, tamamen anlamlı. Balon sırasında birçok insanın yaptığı, tam olarak buydu.

Gayrimenkul işlemlerini takip eden bir şirket olan Attom'dan aldığım veriler, Amerika'da 12 ay içinde birden fazla kez el değiştirmiş -fırsatçılar tarafından alınıp satılmış- konutların sayısının balon sırasında beş kat arttığını gösteriyor; bu sayı 2000 yılının ilk çeyreğinde 20,000 iken, 2004'ün ilk çeyreğinde 100,000'in üzerine çıkmış.[54] Konut fırsatçılığı balonun ardından çeyrek dönem başına 40,000'in altına düşmüş ve o zamandan beri kabaca aynı düzeyde kalmış bulunuyor.

Bu fırsatçıların uzun vadeli fiyat-kira oranlarını umursadığını düşünüyor musunuz? Veya ödedikleri fiyatların uzun vadeli gelir artışıyla desteklenip desteklenmediğini? Tabii ki değil. Bu rakamların onların oynadığı oyunla ilgisi yoktu. Fırsatçılar için önemli olan tek şey, evin fiyatının gelecek ay, bu aydan daha fazla olacağıydı. Ve yıllarca, öyle oldu.

Bu yatırımcılar hakkında çok şey söyleyebilirsiniz. Spekülatör diyebilirsiniz. Sorumsuz diyebilirsiniz. Çok büyük riskler almaya istekli olmaları karşısında hayrete düşüp başınızı iki yana sallayabilirsiniz.

Ama hepsine mantık dışı diyebileceğinizi sanmıyorum.

Balonların oluşmasının uzun vadeli yatırımlara irrasyonel bir şekilde katılan insanlarla pek de ilgisi yoktur. Kendi kendini besleyen momentumu yakalamak için öyle ya da böyle rasyonel olarak, kısa vadeli işlemlere yönelen insanlarla ilgilidir.

Momentum kısa vadede büyük bir getiri potansiyeli yarattığında insanların ne yapmasını beklersiniz? Oturup sabırla izlemelerini mi? Asla. Dünyanın işleyişi böyle değil. İnsanlar her zaman kâr peşinde koşacak. Dahası, kısa vadeli trader'lar, uzun vadeli yatırımları yöneten kuralların -özellikle de değerlemeyle ilgili kuralların- göz ardı edildiği bir alanda faaliyet gösterirler; çünkü bunlar oynanmakta olan oyunla alâkasız şeylerdir.

İşlerin ilginçleştiği ve sorunların başladığı yer burasıdır.

Balonlar esasen, bir oyun oynamakta olan uzun vadeli yatırımcılar ipuçlarını, başka bir oyun oynamakta olan kısa vadeli trader'lardan almaya başladığında hasar verir.

Cisco hissesi 1999'da yüzde 300 yükselerek hisse başına 60 dolara çıktı. O fiyattan şirketin değeri 600 milyar dolardı, ki bu delilikti. Aslında pek az kişi şirketin değerinin o kadar ettiğini düşünüyordu; günlük işlem yapan trader'lar eğleniyorlardı, hepsi bu. Ekonomist Burton Malkiel bir keresinde, bu değerlemede ima edilen büyüme oranının, Cisco'nun 20 yıl içinde Amerikan ekonomisinin tamamından daha büyük olacağı anlamına geldiğine dikkat çekmişti.

Ancak 1999 yılında uzun vadeli bir yatırımcıysanız, satın alabileceğiniz tek fiyat 60 dolardı. Ve birçok insan, bu fiyattan alıyordu. Yani etrafınıza bakıp kendinize, "Vay canına, belki bu diğer yatırımcılar benim bilmediğim bir şey biliyorlar" demiş olabilirdiniz. Belki siz de onlar gibi düşünebilirdiniz. Hatta, bu konuda kendinizi akıllı hissetmiş bile olabilirdiniz.

Burada fark edemediğiniz şey, hissenin marjinal fiyatını belirleyen trader'ların sizden farklı bir oyun oynadığıdır. Hisse başına 60 dolar, trader'lar için makûl bir fiyattı; çünkü o hisseyi gün sonunda, kapanıştan biraz önce satmayı planlıyorlardı ve fiyat da muhtemelen daha yüksek bir seviyede olacaktı. Ama 60 dolar sizin için bir felaket demekti; çünkü hisseleri uzun vadede elinizde tutmayı planlıyordunuz.

Bu iki yatırımcı, birbirinin varlığından nadiren haberdar olur. Ne var ki, aynı sahadadırlar ve birbirlerine doğru koşarlar. Yolları körü körüne kesişip de çarpıştıklarında, biri incinir. Birçok finans ve yatırım kararının kökeni, diğer insanların ne yaptığını izlemeye ve onları kopyalamaya veya karşı bahis oynamaya dayanır. Ancak birinin neden böyle davrandığını bilmediğinizde, bunu ne kadar sürdüreceklerini, fikirlerini neyin değiştireceğini veya derslerini alıp almayacaklarını bilemezsiniz.

*CNBC*'de bir yorumcu, "Bu hisseyi almalısınız" dediğinde onun sizi tanımadığını, kim olduğunuzu bilmediğini unutmayın. Henüz yirmilerine gelmemiş, biraz eğlenmek için işlem yapan biri misiniz? Kısıtlı bütçeyle geçinen yaşlı bir dul musunuz? Çeyrek dönem bitmeden defterlerini sağlamlaştırmaya çalışan bir hedge fon yöneticisi misiniz? Bu üç kişinin önceliklerinin aynı olduğunu ve işlem gördüğü seviye ne olursa olsun, belli bir hisse senedinin her üçü için de doğru olduğunu mu düşünmemiz gerekiyor?

Bu çılgınlık.

Diğer yatırımcıların bizden farklı amaçları olduğunu anlamak zor; çünkü psikolojinin temel referans noktalarından biri, rasyonel insanların dünyayı sizinkinden farklı bir mercekten görebildiğini fark etmemektir. Fiyatlardaki yükseliş, bütün yatırımcıları, en iyi pazarlamacıları bile kıskandıracak kadar ikna eder. Bir tür uyuşturucu etkisi geliştirerek, değer bilincine sahip yatırımcıları, farklı bir oyun oynamakta olan başkalarının yaptıkları yüzünden kendi gerçekliklerinden kopan ve kolayca inanan naif iyimserlere dönüştürebilir.

Farklı bir oyun oynayan insanların aklınızı çelmesi, aynı zamanda paranızı nasıl harcamanız gerektiğine dair düşünce yapınızı da değiştirebilir. Tüketici harcamalarının büyük bölümü, özellikle de gelişmiş ülkelerde, toplumsal güdümlüdür: Hayran olduğunuz insanlardan içten içe etkilendiğiniz ve içten içe, insanların size hayran olmasını istediğiniz için öyle yaparsınız.

Ancak diğer insanların arabalara, evlere, giysilere ve tatillere ne kadar para harcadığını görebilsek de, onların amaçlarını, endişelerini ve özlemlerini göremeyiz. Prestijli bir hukuk firmasına ortak olmayı hedefleyen genç bir hukukçunun, eşofmanla çalışabilen bir yazar olarak benim ihtiyaç duymadığım bir dış görünümü koruması gerekebilir. Ancak onun satın aldığı şeyler, benim kendi beklentilerimi belirlediğinde, potansiyel bir hayal kırıklığı yoluna doğru amaçsızca ilerlerim; çünkü ben parayı harcarken, kariyerimde yükselme gibi bir motivasyonum yoktur. Tarzlarımız bile farklı olmayabilir. Fakat farklı bir oyun oynamaktayız, hepsi bu. Bunu anlamam yıllarımı aldı.

Buradan çıkarmamız gereken sonuç şudur: Para konusunda son derece önemli birkaç şeyden biri, kendi zaman ufkunuzu iyi bilmek ve sizden farklı oyunlar oynamakta olan insanların eylem ve davranışlarından etkilenip ikna olmamaktır.

Verebileceğim başlıca tavsiye, hangi oyunu oynadığınızı belirlemek için elinizden gelen her şeyi yapmanızdır.

Ne kadar azımızın bunu yapıyor olması, şaşırtıcı. Sanki aynı oyunu, aynı kurallarla oynayan basketbolcularmış gibi, parasıyla yatırım yapan herkese "yatırımcı" diyoruz. Bu nosyonun ne kadar yanlış olduğunu fark ettiğinizde, hangi oyunu oynadığınızı belirlemenin ne denli hayati önem taşıdığını görürsünüz. Kendi paramla nasıl yatırım yaptığımı Yirminci Bölüm'de ayrıntılı olarak anlatıyorum; ancak yıllar önce şöyle yazmıştım: "Dünyanın gerçek ekonomik büyüme yaratma kabiliyeti konusunda iyimser düşünen, pasif bir yatırımcıyım ve önümüzdeki 30 yıl içinde bu büyümenin yatırımlarıma yansıyacağından eminim."

Tuhaf görünebilir ama, bu misyonu bir kez kağıda döktüğünüzde, onunla alâkasız her şeyin -piyasanın bu yıl ne yaptığının veya gelecek yıl ekonomide bir durgunluk yaşayıp yaşamayacağımızın- oynamadığımız bir oyunun parçası olduğunu anlıyorsunuz. Bu yüzden de, ben bu tür konularla ilgilenmiyorum ve beni ikna edip caydırmaları gibi bir tehlikeyle karşı karşıya değilim.

Şimdi, kötümserlik hakkında konuşalım.

# 17

# Kötümserliğin Baştan Çıkarıcılığı

İyimserlik kulağa satış konuşması gibi gelir.
Kötümserlik ise size uzanmış yardım eli gibidir.

*Asla anlamadığım nedenlerle, insanlar dünyanın cehenneme döneceğini duymayı seviyor.*

– Tarihçi Deirdre McCloskey

İYİMSERLİK ÇOĞU İNSAN için en iyi seçimdir; çünkü dünya çoğu insan için, çoğu zaman daha iyi olma eğilimindedir. Ancak kötümserliğin kalbimizde özel bir yeri vardır. Kötümserlik, iyimserlikten daha yaygındır. Ayrıca kulağa daha akıllıca gelir. Zihinsel çekiciliği vardır ve genellikle de riske karşı kayıtsızlık olarak görülen iyimserlikten daha çok ilgi çeker.

Bu konuya biraz daha eğilmeden önce, iyimserliğin tam olarak ne anlama geldiğini tanımlamamız doğru olur. Gerçek iyimserler, her şeyin harika olacağına inanmazlar. Bu, halinden memnun olma durumudur, gönül rahatlığıdır. İyimserlik, yol boyunca aksilikler çıksa bile, iyi sonuç olasılığının zaman içinde sizin lehinize olacağına inanmaktır. İyimserliğin temeli basit bir fikre, çoğu insanın sabah uyandığında sorun yaratmak yerine, her şeyi biraz daha iyi ve verimli kılmaya çalışmasına dayanır. Karmaşık değildir. Garanti de değildir. Çoğu insan için, çoğu zaman en makûl seçim budur. Merhum istatistikçi Hans Rosling bunu farklı bir şekilde ifade ediyor: "Ben iyimser değilim. Çok ciddi bir olasılıkçıyım."

Şimdi iyimserliğin ondan daha zorlayıcı bir yapısı olan kardeşini, yani kötümserliği tartışabiliriz.

---

Tarih 29 Aralık, 2008.

Modern tarihin ekonomideki en kötü yılı sona ermek üzereydi. Tüm dünyada hisse senedi piyasaları çökmüştü. Küresel finans sistemi her günü yaşam destek ünitesine bağlı geçirmekteydi. İşsizlik yükseliyordu. Bundan daha kötüsü olamazmış gibi görünürken *The Wall Street Journal*, henüz hiçbir şey görmediğimizi savunan bir makale yayınladı. Gazetenin birinci sayfadan verdiği bu makalede, ekonomik görüşleri bilim kurgu yazarlarının yeteneklerine rakip olabilecek Rus profesör Igor Panarin'in bakış açısı aktarılıyordu.

*Journal* şöyle yazıyordu:

> [Panarin], 2010 yılının Haziran ayı sonunda veya Temmuz başlarında ABD'nin altı parçaya bölüneceğini; böylece Alaska'nın Rus kontrolüne geri döneceğini... Kaliforniya'nın ise kendisinin 'Kaliforniya Cumhuriyeti' dediği yapının çekirdeğini oluşturacağını ve Çin'in bir parçası olacağını veya Çin etkisi altına gireceğini söylüyor. Panarin'e göre Teksas, Meksika'ya gidecek ya da Meksika'nın etkisi altına girecek eyaletlerin oluşturacağı "Atlantik Amerikasının" kalbi olacak. Washington, D.C. ve New York, "Teksas Cumhuriyeti'nin" parçası olacaklar ve Avrupa Birliği'ne katılmaları muhtemel. Kanada, Prof. Panarin'in "Orta Kuzey Amerika Cumhuriyeti" adını verdiği bir grup Kuzey eyaletini ele geçirecek. Panarin, Hawaii'nin Japonya

veya Çin'in himayesinde olacağını, Alaska'nın da Rusya'ya tabi olacağını öne sürüyor.[55]

Bunlar isimsiz bir blogda ya da komplo teorileri üreten bir bültende yer alan saçmalıklar değildi. Dünyanın en prestijli finans gazetesinin birinci sayfasındaydı.

Ekonomi konusunda kötümser görüşte olabilirsiniz. Kıyamet tellalığı bile sorun değil. Tarih sadece ekonomik durgunluklarla değil, parçalanmış ülkelerin örnekleriyle dolu.

Panarin türü hikâyelerin ilginç yanı, bunun zıt kutbunda yer alan aşırı iyimser tahminlerin, nadiren kıyamet tellalları kadar ciddiye alınmasıdır.

1940'ların sonlarındaki Japonya'yı örnek alalım. Ülke her yönden -ekonomik, endüstriyel, sosyal, kültürel- İkinci Dünya Savaşı yenilgisinin enkazı altındaydı. 1946 yılındaki acımasız kış, kişi başına gıdayı günde 800 kalorinin altıyla sınırlayan müthiş bir kıtlığa yol açmıştı.[56]

O dönemde bir Japon akademisyenin şöyle bir gazete makalesi yazdığını düşünün:

> Hey millet, doğrulun ve ayağa kalkın. Bizim ömür süremiz içinde ekonomimiz, savaş sonundaki boyutunun neredeyse 15 katı büyüyecek. Yaşam beklentimiz neredeyse iki katına çıkacak. Hisse senedi piyasamız tarihte bir ülkenin nadiren gördüğü getirileri üretecek. Kırk yılı aşkın bir süre işsizliğin yüzde 6'nın üzerine çıkmadığını göreceğiz. Elektronik inovasyonlarda ve kurumsal yönetim sistemlerinde dünya lideri olacağız. Çok geçmeden o kadar zengin olacağız ki Amerika Birleşik Devletleri'ndeki en değerli gayrimenkullerden bazılarını biz alacağız. Bu arada Amerikalılar en

yakın müttefikimiz olacaklar; aynı zamanda da ekonomiye dair görüş ve öngörülerimizi kopyalamaya çalışacaklar.

Özetle, bu akademisyenin söylediklerine kimse itibar etmezdi; dalga geçilir, hatta tıbbi bir değerlendirme için doktora görünmesi istenirdi.

Unutmayalım ki, yukarıda yazılanlar savaş sonrası kuşağın Japonya'da gerçekten yaşadığı şeylerdi. Ancak Panarin'in tam tersi bir aynadan bakıyorsanız, söyledikleriniz bir kıyamet tahmini için hiçbir zaman söz konusu olamayacak kadar saçma görünür.

Kötümserlik, insanlara iyimserlikten daha akıllıca ve daha olası gelir.

Birine her şeyin harika olacağını söyleyin, muhtemelen sizi umursamaz veya şüpheyle bakar. Fakat tehlikede olduğunu söyleyin, bütün dikkatiyle sizi dinleyecektir.

Akıllı biri bana gelip de, gelecek yıl 10 kat değerlenecek bir hisse senedi bildiğini söylese, saçmalık der geçerim.

Saçma sapan biri bana gelip de, benim elimdeki bir hissenin muhasebe hilesi çıktığını ve şirketin batmak üzere olduğunu söylese, bütün randevularımı iptal eder ve ağzından çıkan her sözcüğü can kulağıyla dinlerim.

Diyelim ki, büyük bir durgunluk dönemindeyiz ve gazeteler sizi arayıp görüş istedi. Ortalama bir büyümeye doğru gittiğimizi söylerseniz, kimsenin özellikle umurunda olmaz. Yeni bir Büyük Buhran'a yaklaştığımızı söylerseniz, televizyona çıkarsınız. Buna karşılık iyi zamanların geleceğini veya piyasaların işleyişine devam edecek bir manevra alanı bulunduğunu anlatırsanız ya da bir şirketin büyük bir potansiyeli olduğundan söz ederseniz, yorumcuların ve izleyicilerin ortak tepkisi, sizi ya bir satıcı olarak görmek ya da komik bir şekilde riske karşı kayıtsız biri olarak yorumlamak olur.

Yatırım bültenleri sektörü bunu yıllardır biliyor ve hisse senedi piyasalarının geçtiğimiz yüzyılda (kâr payları dahil) 17,000 kat arttığı bir ortamda faaliyet göstermelerine rağmen, bugün sektör kıyamet tellallığı yapan kahinlerle dolu.

Bu, finansın ötesinde de doğru.

Matt Ridley, *Rational Optimist* (Rasyonel İyimser) adlı kitabında şöyle yazıyor:

> Sürekli çalmakta olan kötümserlik davulu, genellikle bütün zafer şarkılarını bastırır... Dünyanın eskisine göre daha iyiye gittiğini söylüyorsanız, naif ve duyarsız biri olarak tanımlanmakla kurtulabilirsiniz. Dünyanın şimdikinden daha iyiye gideceğini söylüyorsanız, tam bir zırdeli olarak görülürsünüz. Öte yandan, ufukta bir felaket gördüğünüzü söylüyorsanız, bir McArthur dahi ödülü, hatta Nobel Barış Ödülü bekleyebilirsiniz. Benim yetişkinlik yaşamımda... kötümserliğin moda olan nedenleri değişti, ancak kötümserlik hep aynı kaldı.

Hans Rosling, *Factfulness* (Olgusallık) adlı kitabında, "Soru yöneltiğim insan gruplarının her biri, dünyayı olduğundan daha korkutucu buluyor, daha çok şiddet içerdiğini ve daha umutsuz bir yer olduğunu düşünüyor; kısacası dünyayı olduğundan daha dramatik görüyorlar" diye yazıyor.

İnsanların ortalama bir ömür süresi boyunca, ekonomik büyümeden tıptaki atılımlara, hisse senedi piyasalarındaki kazançlardan toplumsal eşitliğe kadar her konuda ne kadar ilerleme kaydedebileceğine bakınca, iyimserliğin kötümserlikten daha çok ilgi göreceğini düşünürsünüz. Ama öyle değil.

Kötümserliğin zihinsel çekiciliği çok uzun zamandır bilinmekte. John Stuart Mill 1840'larda şöyle yazmış: "Başkaları umutsuzluğa düştüğünde umut edenlerin değil, başkaları umut ederken umutsuzluğa kapılan kişilerin, geniş bir insan sınıfı tarafından bilge olarak görüldüğünü, takdir ve hayranlık kazandığını gözlemledim."

Soru şu: Neden? Ve bu, paraya ilişkin düşünce biçimimizi nasıl etkiliyor?

---

Kimsenin çılgın olmadığını bir kez daha tekrarlayalım.

Para konularında kötümserliğin baştan çıkarıcı olmasının bazı geçerli nedenleri vardır. Bunları bilmek, kötümserliğin dozunu kaçırıp fazla ileri götürmememize yardımcı olur.

Kötümserlik kısmen içgüdüseldir ve kaçınılmazdır. Kahneman, kayıptan asimetrik kaçınmanın evrimsel bir kalkan olduğunu söylüyor ve şöyle yazıyor:

> Doğrudan karşılaştırıldığında veya birbiriyle ağırlıklandırıldığında, kayıplar kazançlardan daha büyük görünür. Olumlu ve olumsuz beklentilerin ya da deneyimlerin gücü arasındaki bu asimetrinin evrimsel bir geçmişi vardır. Tehditlere fırsatlardan daha çok önem verip daha hızlı tepki gösteren organizmaların hayatta kalma ve üreme şansı daha yüksektir.

Ancak finansal kötümserliğin iyimserliğe göre daha kolay, daha yaygın ve daha ikna edici olmasının birkaç nedeni daha vardır.

**Birincisi, para her yerdedir; bu nedenle de kötü bir olay genelde herkesi etkiler ve herkesin dikkatini çeker.**

Bu başka bir alan, örneğin hava durumu için geçerli değildir. Florida'yı vuran bir kasırga, Amerikalıların yüzde 92'si için doğrudan risk oluşturmaz. Ancak ekonominin üzerine çökecek bir durgunluk, siz dahil herkesi tek tek etkileyebilir; bu yüzden de *ilgi gösterirsiniz.*

Hisse senedi piyasaları gibi özel bir alan için de tamamen geçerlidir. Amerikan hanelerinin yarısından fazlasının doğrudan hisse senedi yatırımı var.[57] Piyasadaki döngüler ve dalgalanmalar medyada o kadar yoğun bir şekilde yer alıyor ki, Dow Jones Sanayi Ortalaması, borsada yatırımı olmayan hane halkı arasında bile en çok izlenen ekonomik barometre olabilir.

Hisse senetlerinde yüzde 1'lik bir yükselişten akşam haberlerinde kısaca söz edilebilir. Buna karşılık yüzde 1'lik bir düşüş kalın puntolu, genellikle de kan kırmızısı renkte büyük harflerle duyurulur. Asimetriden kaçınmak zordur.

Ayrıca piyasanın neden yükseldiğini pek az kişi sorgularken veya açıklamaya çalışırken, -ki zaten yükselmesi beklenmiyor muydu?- hemen her zaman niçin düştüğünü açıklamaya yönelik hummalı bir girişim vardır.

Yatırımcılar ekonomik büyüme konusunda endişeli mi?

Fed yine işleri batırdı mı?

Politikacılar kötü kararlar mı veriyor?

Yine başımıza kötü bir olay mı gelecek?

Bir düşüşün nedenine ilişkin anlatılar, bunlar üzerinde konuşmayı, endişelenmeyi ve daha sonra olacaklara dair bir hikâye oluşturmayı kolaylaştırır; genellikle de hepsi birbirinin aynıdır.

Hisse senedi yatırımınız olmasa bile, bu tür şeyler dikkatinizi çekecektir. 1929 yılında, Büyük Buhran'ı ateşleyen büyük çöküşün arifesinde Amerikalıların sadece yüzde 2.5'inin hisse senedi yatırımı vardı. Ancak Amerikalıların çoğunluğu, hatta bütün dünya, piyasaların çöküşünü şaşkınlık içinde izledi ve bunun kendi kaderleri açısından neyin işareti olduğunu merak etti. İster avukat, ister çiftçi, ister araba tamircisi olsun, herkes için böyleydi.

Tarihçi Eric Rauchway şöyle yazıyor:

> Borsadaki değer düşüşü ilk anda sadece az sayıda Amerikalıyı etkiledi. Ancak diğerleri piyasayı o kadar yakından izlemişler ve bu çöküşü kaderlerinin bir göstergesi olarak görmüşlerdi ki, ekonomik faaliyetlerinin büyük bölümünü aniden durdurdular. Ekonomist Joseph Schumpeter'in daha sonra yazdığı gibi, "insanlar ayaklarının altındaki zeminin kaymakta olduğunu hissediyorlardı."[58]

Siz ilgilenseniz de ilgilenmeseniz de hayatınızı etkileyecek iki konu vardır: Para ve sağlık. Sağlık konuları bireysel olma eğilimindeyken, para meseleleri daha sistematiktir. Bir kişinin kararlarının diğer herkesi etkileyebildiği bağlantılı bir sistemde, finansal risklere niçin bu kadar çok spot ışığı doğrultulduğu ve bunun niçin böylesine ilgi gösterilen pek az konudan biri olduğu anlaşılabilir.

**İkincisi, kötümserler mevcut trendleri geleceğe yansıtarak tahmin yürütürken, piyasaların nasıl uyum sağladığını çoğu zaman hesaba katmazlar.**

Çevre bilimci Lester Brown 2008'de şöyle yazmıştı: "2030 yılında Çin'in günlük petrol ihtiyacı 98 milyon varil olacak. Dünya şu anda günde 85 milyon varil petrol üretiyor ve bundan fazlasını asla üretemeyebilir. Dünyanın petrol rezervleri o noktaya doğru gidiyor."[59]

Haklı. Bu senaryoya göre dünyanın petrolü biterdi.

Ne var ki, piyasalar böyle işlemiyor.

Ekonomide sarsılmaz bir yasa vardır: Aşırı derecede iyi ve aşırı derecede kötü koşullar nadiren uzun süre aynı kalır; çünkü arz ve talep, öngörülmesi zor bazı şekillerde uyum sağlar.

Brown'ın yaptığı bu tahminden hemen sonra petrolde neler olduğuna bakalım.

Çoğu Çin'den gelen küresel talebin artması ve giderek potansiyel üretim seviyesine ulaşmasıyla birlikte, petrol fiyatları 2008 yılında yükseldi. 2001 yılında 20 dolar olan bir varil petrol, 2008'de 138 dolara satılıyordu.[60]

Bu yeni fiyat seviyesinde petrol çıkarmak, topraktan altın çıkarmak gibi oldu. Petrol üreticilerinin karşısındaki teşvikler muazzam değişti. Varil başına 20 dolar fiyatla onca mücadeleye değmeyen petrol kaynakları -satabilecekleri fiyat, sondaj maliyetini karşılamıyordu- şimdi varili 138 dolarla üreticiler için hayatlarının talih kuşu, tam anlamıyla Bonanza olmuştu.

Bu durum hidrolik kırma ve yatay sondaj teknolojilerinde yükselişi getirdi.

Dünyanın petrol rezervleri, insanlık tarihi boyunca yaklaşık aynı miktarda olmuştur. Ayrıca büyük petrol yataklarının nerelerde olduğunu bir süredir biliyoruz. Değişen şey, petrolü yerin altından ekonomik olarak çıkarmamızı sağlayan teknolojidir. Petrol tarihçisi Daniel Yergin şöyle yazıyor: "Amerika Birleşik Devletleri'ndeki petrol rezervlerinin yüzde 86'sı, keşif sırasında gerçekleştirilen tahminlerin değil, teknolojinin gelişmesiyle ortaya çıkan revizyonların sonucudur."

Hidrolik kırma teknolojisinin 2008 yılında hayata geçmesiyle birlikte, aynen böyle oldu. Yalnızca Amerika Birleşik Devletleri'nin petrol üretimi, 2008'de günde yaklaşık beş milyon varilken, 2019'da 13 milyon varile çıktı.[61] Dünya petrol üretimi şu anda günde 100 milyon varilin üstünde; yani Brown'ın öngördüğü en yüksek seviyeyi yüzde 20 dolayında aşmış bulunuyor.

2008 yılındaki petrol trendlerini geleceğe yansıtarak tahmin yürüten bir kötümser için, elbette ki durum vahim görünüyordu. İhtiyacın tüm icatların anası olduğunu anlayan bir gerçekçi içinse, o kadar korkutucu değildi.

Çirkin bir şeyin çirkin kalacağını varsaymak, kolay bir tahmin yürütmedir. Ayrıca ikna edicidir; çünkü dünyanın değiştiğini hayal etmeyi gerektirmez. Ancak sorunlar düzelir ve insanlar uyum sağlar. Tehditler, eşit büyüklükteki çözümleri teşvik eder. Bu, ekonomi tarihinde, düz çizgilerle tahmin yürüten kötümserlerin kolayca unuttuğu, yaygın bir hikâyedir.

**Üçüncüsü, ilerleme fark edilemeyecek kadar yavaş, aksilikler ise görmezden gelinemeyecek kadar hızlı gerçekleşir.**

Bir sürü gece yarısı trajedisi var. Fakat bir gecede gerçekleşen mucizeler nadiren yaşanır.

*Detroit Free Press* gazetesi 5 Ocak 1889'da yayınladığı bir haberde, insanların günün birinde kuşlar gibi uçabileceğine dair uzun zamandır kurulan düşü çürüttü ve uçağın "imkânsız göründüğünü" yazdı:

> Gerekli yakıt ve mühendisleri de hesaba kattığınızda, uçan bir makinenin asgari ağırlığı 136-182 kilo arasında

> olmalıdır; bunun altında olamaz... Fakat uçma olayında asgari ağırlık sınırı var ve bu da kesinlikle 22.5 kiloyu aşamaz; bu kilonun üzerinde hiçbir hayvan uçamaz. Doğa bu sınıra ulaşmış ve tüm çabalarına rağmen geçememiştir.

Altı ay sonra, Orville Wright, tamircilikle uğraşan ve evlerinin arka bahçesinde bir matbaa makinesi yapmaya çalışan kardeşi Wilbur'a yardım etmek için liseden ayrıldı. Bu makine, Wright kardeşlerin ilk ortak buluşuydu. Fakat sonuncusu olmayacaktı.

Yirminci Yüzyıl'ın en önemli icatlarının listesini yapmanız gerekseydi, uçak birinci sırada olmasa bile, en azından ilk beşte yer alırdı. Uçak her şeyi değiştirdi. Dünya savaşlarını başlattı, dünya savaşlarını bitirdi. Şehirler ve kırsal topluluklar arasında, okyanuslar ve ülkeler arasında köprü işlevi görerek dünyayı birbirine bağladı.

Ancak Wright Kardeşlerin ilk uçağı icat etme arayışının son derece ilginç bir yönü vardı.

Uçmayı başardıkları halde, kimse bunu fark etmemiş gibiydi. Kimse umursamıyordu sanki.

Frederick Lewis Allen Amerikan tarihini konu alan 1952 tarihli kitabında şöyle yazıyor:

> Halkın Wright'ların ne yaptığını anlaması birkaç yıl aldı; insanlar uçmanın imkânsız olduğuna o kadar inanmışlardı ki, Wright kardeşleri 1905 yılında Dayton [Ohio] civarında uçarken görenlerin çoğu, bunun önemsiz bir göz yanılması -bugün çoğu insanın telepatik bir durum, mesela durugörü olarak tanımlayabileceği türden bir şey- olduğu sonucuna vardı. Ta ki

> Mayıs 1908'de, yani Wright'ın ilk uçuşundan yaklaşık dört buçuk yıl sonra, ne yaptıklarını gözlemlemek için deneyimli muhabirler gönderilinceye kadar. Deneyimli editörler, bu muhabirlerin gönderdiği heyecanlı haberlere tamamen güvendiler ve dünya nihayet, insanın uçuşunun başarıyla hayata geçirildiği gerçeğine uyandı.

İnsanlar uçağın mucizesini anladıktan sonra bile, yıllarca hafife aldılar.

Önceleri esas olarak askeri bir silah olarak görüldü. Sonra, zenginlerin oyuncağı olarak bakıldı. Sonra, belki de birkaç kişiyi taşımak için kullanılabileceği düşünüldü.

*Washington Post* gazetesi 1909 yılında şöyle yazıyordu: "Havada ticari kargo taşımacılığı gibi bir şey asla olmayacak. Taşımacılık sektörü yükünü, sabırlı yeryüzünde yavaşça sürüklemeye devam edecek..." Bu haberden beş ay sonra ilk kargo uçağı havalandı.

Şimdi uçak konusunda iyimser düşünme yolunda yıllar süren bu yavaş uyanışı, insanların bir şirketin iflası gibi kötümserlik itkilerine ne kadar çabuk ilgi gösterdikleri gerçeğiyle karşılaştırın.

Ya da büyük bir savaşa.

Ya da bir uçak kazasına. Wright'ın uçağıyla ilgili sözü edilen ilk şeylerden biri, Thomas Selfridge adlı bir teğmenin 1908 yılında, gösteri uçuşu sırasında ölmesi oldu.[62]

Büyümeyi bileşiklenme yönlendirir ve bu da hep zaman alır. Yıkım ise, saniyeler içinde etkisini gösterebilecek tek bir zayıf halka ve bir anda gerçekleşebilecek güven kaybı tarafından yönlendirilir.

Kötümserlik etrafında bir anlatı oluşturmak daha kolaydır; çünkü hikâyeyi oluşturan parçalar genelde taze ve yenidir. İyimser anlatılar, insanların unutmaya meyilli olduğu ve parçaları bir araya getirmek için daha fazla çaba harcadığı uzun bir geçmişe ve geçmişteki gelişmelere bakmayı gerektirir.

Tıp alanındaki ilerlemeleri düşünün. Geçen yıla bakmak size pek az şey verir. Herhangi bir on yıla baktığınızda da ondan daha iyi bir şey çıkmaz. Ancak son 50 yıla bakmak, olağanüstü bir şey gösterecektir. Örneğin, National Institute of Health'e (Ulusal Sağlık Enstitüsü) göre, kalp hastalıklarından yaş itibarıyla kişi başına ölüm oranı 1965 yılından bu yana yüzde 70'in üzerinde gerilemiş durumda.[63] Kalp hastalığına bağlı ölümlerde yüzde 70'lik bir düşüş, her yıl yaklaşık yarım milyon Amerikalının hayatını kurtarmaya yeter. Atlanta nüfusu kadar insanın her yıl ölümden kurtarıldığını düşünsenize. Ne var ki, bu ilerleme çok yavaş gerçekleştiği için terörizm, uçak kazaları veya doğal afetler gibi hızlı ve ani kayıplar kadar dikkat çekmiyor. Her hafta, haftada beş kez bir Katrina Kasırgası olabilir - ne kadar ilgi göreceğini düşünün- ve bu, son 50 yılda kalp hastalıklarındaki düşüş sayesinde her yıl kurtarılmakta olan hayat sayısıyla bir tutulmaz.

Aynı şey, bir ürünün veya bir şirketin ne kadar önemli olduğunu anlamanın yıllar aldığı, buna karşılık iflasların bir gecede gerçekleşebileceği iş dünyası için de geçerlidir.

Ve altı ay içinde meydana gelen yüzde 40'lık bir düşüşün Kongre soruşturmalarını başlatacağı, buna karşılık altı yıl içinde gerçekleşen yüzde 140'lık bir kazancın neredeyse fark edilmeyebileceği hisse senedi piyasaları için de geçerlidir.

Ve itibar oluşturmak bir ömür alırken, tek bir e-posta bütün kariyeri, bir anda yok edebilir.

İyimserliğin güçlü çekimi fark edilmeden geçip giderken, kötümserliğin küçücük dozu ağırlığını hissettirir.

Bu da, kitapta daha önce değindiğimiz önemli bir noktanın altını çiziyor: Yatırım yaparken, başarının bedelini -uzun dönemli büyüme sürecinde oynaklık ve kayıpları- belirlemeli ve bunu ödemeye hazır olmalısınız.

---

*New York Times* 2004 yılında, tedavisi olmayan motor nöron hastalığı nedeniyle felç geçiren ve 21 yaşında konuşamaz hale gelen bilim insanı Stephen Hawking ile bir söyleşi yaptı. Söyleşiyi gerçekleştiren muhabirle bilgisayarı aracılığıyla konuşan Hawking, sıradan insanlara kitap satmaktan ne büyük heyecan duyduğunu söyledi.

*Times* "Hep böyle neşeli misiniz?" diye sordu.

Hawking şu yanıtı verdi: "Beklentilerim 21 yaşımdayken sıfıra indi. O zamandan beri de her şey bonus oldu."

Her şeyin harika olmasını beklemek, insana pek de heyecan vermeyen en iyi senaryo anlamına gelir. Kötümserlik, beklentileri azaltır; olası sonuçlar ile kendinizi harika hissedeceğiniz sonuçlar arasındaki mesafeyi daraltır.

Belki de bu yüzden, bu kadar baştan çıkarıcıdır. Bir şeylerin kötü olmasını beklemek, öyle olmadığında hoş bir sürpriz yaşamanın en iyi yoludur.

Ve bu da, ironik bir şekilde, aslında iyimser olunacak bir şey.

Şimdi, hikâyelere dair kısa bir hikâyeye geçebiliriz.

# 18

# Her Şeye İnandığınızda

Çekici kurgular ve hikâyelerin
neden istatistiklerden
daha güçlü olduğuna dair bir deneme.

DÜNYA'YA BİR UZAYLI gönderildiğini hayal edelim. İşi, ekonomimizi izleyip, gözlemlemek olsun.

Uzaylımız, New York şehrinin üzerinde daireler çizerek ekonomiyi değerlendirmeye ve 2007 ile 2009 arasında nasıl bir değişim olduğunu anlamaya çalışır.

2007'nin Yılbaşı Gecesi, Times Meydanı üzerinde gezinir. Parlak ışıklar, devasa reklam panoları ve TV kameralarıyla çevrili meydanda, on binlerce mutlu insanın havai fişekler altında eğlendiğini görür.

2009'un Yılbaşı Gecesi, yine Times Meydanı'na gelir. Yine parlak ışıklar, devasa reklam panoları ve TV kameralarıyla çevrili meydanda, on binlerce mutlu insanın havai fişekler altında eğlendiğini görür.

Her şey aynı gibidir. Pek fark göremez.

Yaklaşık aynı sayıda New Yorklunun şehirde koşuşturduğunu görmüştür. Bu insanların etrafı aynı sayıda ofis binasıyla çevrilidir; bu ofislerde aynı sayıda masa, aynı sayıda bilgisayar vardır ve aynı sayıda bilgisayar internete bağlıdır.

Şehrin dışına çıktığında, aynı otoyollarla birbirine bağlanmış aynı sayıda fabrika ve depo görmüştür; o otoyolların üzerinde aynı sayıda kamyon gidip gelmektedir.

Yere biraz daha yaklaşır ve aynı üniversitelerin aynı konuları öğrettiğini, aynı sayıda kişiye, aynı diplomaları dağıttığını görür.

Aynı çığır açan fikirleri koruyan aynı sayıda patent vardır.

Teknolojinin daha gelişmiş olduğunu fark eder. 2009'da herkesin elinde 2007'de olmayan akıllı telefonlar vardır. Bilgisayarlar şimdi daha hızlıdır. Tıp daha iyidir. Arabaların kilometre başına benzin tüketimi daha verimlidir. Güneş enerjisi sistemleri ve hidrolik kırma teknolojisi gelişmiştir. Sosyal medya katlanarak büyümüştür.

Ülkeyi baştan sona dolaşır, aynı şeyleri görür. Dünyayı dolaşır, yine aynıdır.

Ekonominin 2009'da da hemen hemen 2007 ile aynı durumda, hatta belki daha da iyi olduğu sonucuna varır.

Sonra rakamlara bakar.

ABD'de hane halkının 2009 yılında 2007'ye göre 16 trilyon dolar yoksullaştığını görünce şok olur. On milyon Amerikalının daha işsiz kalmış olmasına inanamaz. Borsanın değerinin iki yıl öncesinin yarısına inmiş olmasını aklı almaz.

İnsanların ekonomik potansiyellerine ilişkin tahminlerinin bu kadar aşağılara düşmüş olmasına inanamaz.

"Anlayamıyorum" der. "Şehirleri gördüm. Fabrikalara baktım. Aynı bilgiye, aynı araçlara, aynı fikirlere sahipsiniz. Değişen hiçbir şey yok! Neden daha yoksulsunuz? Niçin daha kötümsersiniz?"

2007 ile 2009 yılları arasında Uzaylının göremediği bir değişiklik vardı: Ekonomiye dair kendimize anlattığımız hikâyeler değişmişti.

2007'de konut fiyatlarının istikrarına, bankacıların ihtiyatlılığına ve finansal piyasaların riski doğru fiyatlama kabiliyetine dair bir hikâye anlattık.

2009'da bu hikâyeye inanmaktan vazgeçtik.

Değişen tek şey buydu. Ama dünyadaki bütün farkı da, bu yarattı.

Konut fiyatlarının yükselişini sürdüceğine ilişkin anlatı bozulduğunda; ipotekli konut kredilerinde temerrütler arttı, sonra bankalar para kaybetti, böylece şirketlere verdikleri kredileri azalttılar, bu durum işten çıkarmalara yol açtı, bu da harcamaların azalmasını, sonrasında daha fazla işten çıkarmayı beraberinde getirdi ve böyle devam edip gitti.

Yeni bir anlatıya tutunmanın dışında, aslında 2009'da da 2007'dekiyle aynı -belki de daha büyük- büyüme ve servet kapasitemiz vardı. Buna rağmen, ekonomi 80 yılın en büyük darbesini aldı.

Bu durum, 1945'te üretim tabanı tamamen yok edilen Almanya'dan farklıdır. Ya da 2000'lerde çalışma çağındaki nüfusu küçülen Japonya'dan. Almanya ve Japonya örneklerinde elle tutulur, somut bir ekonomik zarar vardı. 2009'da ise kendimize anlatısal hasar verdik ve çok kötüydü. Bu, ekonominin en güçlü kuvvetlerinden biridir.

Ekonomilerin, şirketlerin ve yatırımların büyümesi veya kariyerlerde ilerleme üzerinde fikir yürütürken "elimizde ne var, ne kadar var ve neler yapabiliriz?" gibi elle tutulur, somut şeyleri düşünme eğilimindeyiz. Ancak hikâyeler, ekonominin açık ara en kuvvetli gücüdür. Hem ekonominin elle tutulur kısımlarının çalışmasını sağlayan yakıt, hem de yeteneklerimizi engelleyen fren olabilirler.

Kendi paramızı yönetirken hikâye güdümlü bir dünya hakkında aklımızda tutmamız gereken iki şey vardır.

**1. Bir şeyin gerçek olmasını ne kadar çok isterseniz, o şeyin gerçek olma olasılığını abartan bir hikâyeye inanma olasılığınız o denli artar.**

Hayatınızın en mutlu günü hangisiydi?

Bu masum soru, *How to Live Forever* (Sonsuza dek nasıl yaşanır?) adlı belgeselde 100 yaşında bir hanıma soruluyor ve karşılığında inanılmaz bir yanıt geliyor.

"Ateşkes Günü" diyor asırlık hanım, 1918 yılında Birinci Dünya Savaşı'nı sona erdiren anlaşmanın imzalandığı günü kastederek.

Yapımcı "Neden?" diye soruyor.

"Çünkü bir daha savaş olmayacağını biliyorduk" diyor asırlık hanım.

İkinci Dünya Savaşı 21 yıl sonra başladı ve 75 milyon insan öldü.

Hayatta gerçek olmasını çok istediğimiz için doğru olduğunu düşündüğümüz birçok şey var.

Ben bunlara "çekici kurgular" diyorum. Bu çekici kurguların paraya, özellikle de yatırımlara ve ekonomiye ilişkin düşünce biçimimiz üzerindeki etkisi çok büyük.

Akıllıysanız, çözümler bulmak istiyorsanız, buna karşılık tehlike büyükse ve sizin kontrolünüz sınırlıysa, bu bileşim çekici kurguların ortaya çıkmasına yol açıyor.

Bunlar son derece güçlü kurgular olabilir. Sizi hemen her şeye inandırabilirler.

Kısa bir örnek verelim.

Ali Hajaji'nin oğlu hastaydı. Yemen'deki köyünün yaşlıları ona halk arasında kullanılan bir çare önermişlerdi: Yanan bir çubuğu oğlunun göğsüne saplarsa, hastalığı bedeninden çıkarıp atardı.

Hajaji bu işlemden sonra *New York Times*'a şöyle söyledi: "Paranız yoksa ve oğlunuz hastaysa, her şeye inanırsınız."[64]

Tıbbın kökeni, faydalı tıptan binlerce yıl öncesine dayanır. Mikropların keşfedilmesinden ve bilimsel yöntemlerin bulunmasından önce, kan akıtma, açlık tedavisi, kötülükleri dışarı atmak için bedeninizde delikler açma gibi ölümünüzü hızlandırmaktan başka hiçbir işe yaramayan diğer tedaviler uygulanıyordu.

Çılgınca görünüyor. Ancak çaresizce bir çözüm arıyorsanız ve iyi bir çözüm bilinmiyorsa veya siz o çözüme erişemiyorsanız, karşınızdaki en kolay, en az direnç gösteren yol, Hajaji'nin muhakemesine giden yoldur: Her şeye inanmayı istemek. Sadece her şeyi denemek değil, aynı zamanda her şeye inanmak.

Daniel Defoe Londra'da yaşanan Büyük Veba'yı 1722 yılında tarihe geçirirken şöyle yazmış:

> İnsanlar kehanetlere ve astrolojik işaretlere, rüyalara ve yaşlı kadın masallarına her zamankinden de çok bağımlı olmuşlardı... Almanaklar onları çok korkutuyordu... Evlerin posta kutuları ve sokak köşeleri doktor faturaları ile insanları çare için onlara gelmeye davet eden cahillerin el ilanlarıyla kaplıydı. Genelde de "Vebaya karşı birebir etkili haplar", "Enfeksiyona karşı yanılmaz koruyucular", "Havadaki kirliliğe karşı muhteşem iksir" gibi şeyler yazan ilanlardı.

Veba, 18 ayda Londra nüfusunun dörtte birini öldürdü. Tehlike bu kadar büyük olduğunda, hemen hemen her şeye inanırsınız.

Şimdi aynı oranda sınırlı bilginin ve yüksek risklerin finansal kararlarımızı nasıl etkilediğini düşünün.

İnsanlar TV'de yayınlanan ve başarı geçmişine dair pek az şey bilinen yatırım yorumlarını niçin dinliyor? Kısmen, yatırımda riskler çok yüksek olduğu için. Birkaç hisse senedinde doğru seçim yaparsınız ve fazla çaba harcamadan zengin olabilirsiniz. Birinin tahmininin gerçekleşme olasılığı yüzde 1 ise ve gerçekleşmesi hayatınızı değiştirecekse, -her ihtimale karşı- ilgi göstermek çılgınlık değildir.

Ayrıca o kadar çok finansal görüş var ki, bir stratejiyi veya tarafı seçtiğinizde, bunlara hem finansal hem de zihinsel olarak yatırım yapmış olursunuz. Belli bir hisse senedinin 10 kat yükselmesini istiyorsanız, artık o takımdansınızdır. Belli bir ekonomi politikasının hiperenflasyonu tetikleyeceğini düşünüyorsanız, artık o taraftasınızdır.

Bunlar düşük olasılıklı bahisler olabilir. Sorun şu ki, izleyiciler yüzde 1'lik şans gibi düşük oranları tartmaz veya tartamaz. Büyük bölümü, doğru olmasını istediği şeyin kesinlikle doğru olduğuna dair sarsılmaz bir inanç geliştirmiştir. Ancak böylesine güçlü bir inanca sahip olmalarının tek nedeni, karşılarında çok büyük bir sonuç olasılığı bulunmasıdır.

Yatırım günlük bazda ekstrem ödül fırsatları sunan nadir alanlardan biridir. İnsanlar finansal şarlatanlığa birçok başka şey, örneğin hava durumu şarlatanlığı için hiçbir zaman söz konusu olmayacak kadar çok inanırlar; çünkü borsanın gelecek hafta ne yapacağını doğru tahmin etmenin getireceği ödüller, gelecek hafta havanın güneşli mi yoksa yağmurlu mu olacağını tahmin etmenin ödüllerinden çok farklı bir evrendedir.

Aktif yatırım fonlarının yüzde 85'inin 2018'de sona eren 10 yılda, kriter alınan eşiğin altında performans göstermesini bu duruma örnek verebiliriz.[65] Bu rakam kuşaklar boyunca oldukça istikrarlı bir şekilde hep düşük oldu. Böylesine düşük performans gösteren bir sektörün niş bir hizmet alanı olacağını ve varlığını sürdürmekte zorlanacağını düşünürsünüz. Ancak bu fonlara neredeyse beş trilyon dolar yatırılmış bulunuyor.[66] Birilerine "yeni Warren Buffett" ile yatırım yapma şansı verin, o kadar büyük inançla sarılırlar ki, milyonlarca insan yaşam boyu birikimlerini oraya yatırır.

Ya da Bernie Madoff'u örnek alalım. Geriye dönüp bakıldığında yaptığı Ponzi planı bariz olmalıydı. Asla değişmeyen getiriler açıklıyordu; bunlar görece bilinmeyen bir muhasebe şirketi tarafından denetleniyordu ve getirilerin nasıl elde edildiği konusunda fazla bilgi vermeyi reddediyordu. Buna rağmen Madoff, dünyanın en sofistike bazı yatırımcılarından milyarlarca dolar topladı. İyi bir hikâye anlattı ve insanlar o hikâyeye inanmak istedi.

Önceki bölümlerde tartıştığımız üç önemli temanın, yani hataya yer bırakma, esneklik ve finansal bağımsızlığın niçin vazgeçilmez olduğunun en büyük nedenlerinden biri budur.

Doğru olmasını istediğiniz şey ile kabul edilebilir bir sonuç elde etmeniz için doğru olması gerekenler arasındaki aralığı ne kadar geniş tutarsanız, kendinizi çekici bir finansal kurgunun kurbanı olmaktan o kadar koruyorsunuz demektir. Bir tahminin içerebileceği hata payını düşünürken, potansiyel sonuçları, yeterince haklı olmanızdan başlayıp çok, çok haklı olmanız durumuna kadar geniş bir aralıkta değerlendirmek caziptir. Ancak en büyük risk şudur: Siz bir şeyin doğru olmasını müthiş istediğinizde, tahminlerinizin aralığı gerçeklikle aynı oyun sahasında bile olmayabilir.

Federal Reserve (Fed) 2007 yılındaki son toplantısında, 2008 ve 2009 yıllarına ilişkin ekonomik büyüme tahminlerini değerlendirdi.[67] Ekonominin zayıflamasından zaten yorulmuş oldukları için iyimser bakmıyorlardı. Büyüme potansiyelini en düşük yüzde 1.6 ile en yüksek yüzde 2.8 aralığında öngördüler. Bu Fed'in güvenlik marjı, bir diğer ifadeyle hata payıydı. Gerçekte ekonomi yüzde 2'nin üzerinde daraldı, yani Fed'in asgari tahmini neredeyse üç kat düştü.

Bir politika yapıcının doğrudan doğruya ekonomik durgunluk öngörmesi zordur; çünkü durgunluk kariyerlerinde güçlüklere neden olur. Bu yüzden de en kötü durum tahminleri bile nadiren "yavaş" büyümeden daha kötü bir şey öngörür. Bu çekici bir kurgudur ve inanması kolaydır; çünkü daha kötü bir şey bekleme düşüncesi fazlasıyla acı verir.

Politika yapıcılar eleştiri okları için kolay hedeflerdir; ne var ki, hepimiz bunu bir ölçüde yapıyoruz. Dahası, her iki yönde de yapıyoruz. Ekonominin durgunluğa girmek üzere olduğunu düşünüyorsanız ve bu beklenti temelinde elinizdeki hisse senetlerini satıp nakde geçerseniz, olmasını istediğiniz şey, ekonomiye bakışınızı bir anda çarpıtır. Ana trendden en küçük bir sapma, her küçük hareket, her anekdot, kıyametin geldiğinin işareti gibi görünür -belki öyle olduğu için değil, siz öyle istediğiniz için.

Teşvikler güçlü bir motivasyon kaynağıdır ve teşvik unsurlarının kendi finansal hedeflerimizi, ayrıca genel finansal durumumuzu nasıl etkilediğini her zaman hatırlamalıyız. Bu hafife alınacak bir şey değildir: Finansta hata payı bırakmaktan daha büyük bir güç yoktur ve riskler ne kadar yüksekse, hata payı o kadar geniş olmalıdır.

**2. Herkesin dünyaya bakışı biraz eksiktir. Fakat o boşlukları doldurmak için eksiksiz bir anlatı oluştururuz.**

Ben bunları yazdığım sırada, kızım yaklaşık bir yaşında. Her şeyi merak ediyor ve çok çabuk öğreniyor.

Ama bazen düşünüyorum da, anlayamadığı ne çok şey var.

Babasının niçin her sabah işe gittiğine dair hiçbir fikri yok.

Fatura, bütçe, kariyer, terfi ve emeklilik için tasarruf kavramlarına tamamen yabancı.

Federal Reserve, kredi türevleri veya NAFTA'yı ona açıklamaya çalıştığınızı hayal edin. İmkânsız.

Ama dünyası karanlıklar içinde değil. Kafa karışıklığı içinde sürüklenip gitmiyor.

Bir yaşında bile, her şeyin nasıl işlediğine dair kendi iç anlatısını yazmış bulunuyor. Battaniyeler sıcak tutar, anne kucağı güven verir ve hurmaların tadı güzeldir.

Karşılaştığı her şey, öğrenmiş olduğu birkaç düzine zihinsel modelden birine uyuyor. Ben işe gittiğimde, gelecek ayın maaşını ve ödenecek faturaları düşünüp kafası karışmıyor. Onun bu durumla ilgili çok net bir açıklaması var: Babam benimle oynamıyor; oysa ben benimle oynamasını istiyordum; bu yüzden de üzgünüm.

Çok az şey bildiği halde, henüz bunun farkında değil; çünkü neler olup bittiği konusunda bildiği birkaç şeyle uyumlu bir hikâye anlatıyor kendine.

Kaç yaşında olursak olalım, hepimiz aynı şeyi yapıyoruz.

Tıpkı kızım gibi, ben de neyi bilmediğimi bilmiyorum. Bu yüzden de dünyayı, elimdeki sınırlı sayıda bir dizi zihinsel model aracılığıyla açıklamaya onun kadar yatkınım.

Ben de aynı onun gibi, karşılaştığım her şeyde en anlaşılır nedenleri arıyorum. Ve yine onun gibi, birçoğu hakkında yanılıyorum; çünkü dünyanın işleyişi konusunda sandığımdan çok daha az şey biliyorum.

Bu durum en gerçek olgulara dayalı konular için de geçerli.

Tarihi örnek alalım. Tarih yaşanmış şeylerin anlatılması, kayda geçirilmesidir. Açık ve objektif olması gerekir. Fakat B.

H. Liddell Hart'ın *Why Don't We Learn From History?* (Tarihten Niçin Öğrenmiyoruz?) adlı kitabında yazdığı gibi:

> [Tarih] hayal gücü ve sezginin yardımı olmaksızın yorumlanamaz. O kadar çok kanıt vardır ki, aralarından seçim yapıp ayıklamak, yani seleksiyon kaçınılmaz olur. Seleksiyonun olduğu yerde sanat vardır. Tarihi okuyanlar, kendilerini haklı çıkaran ve kişisel görüşlerini doğrulayan kanıtları arama eğilimindedir. Sadakati savunurlar. Onaylamak veya saldırmak amacıyla okurlar. Herkes meleklerin tarafında olmak istediğinden, buna uymayan gerçeğe direnirler. Tıpkı savaşları bitirmek için hep yeni savaşlar başlatmamız gibi.

Daniel Kahneman bir keresinde bana insanların geçmişi anlamlandırmak için kendilerine anlattıkları hikâyelerden söz etmiş ve şöyle demişti:

> Geriye bakıp da geçmişi açıklama yeteneği, bize dünyanın anlaşılabilir olduğu yanılsamasını getirir. Mantıklı olmadığı durumlarda bile, dünyanın bir anlam ifade ettiği yanılsamasını verir.

Bu, birçok alanda hata üretmemize yol açan önemli bir sorun. Çoğu insan, anlamadığı bir şeyle karşı karşıya kaldığında anlamadığının farkına varmaz; çünkü sınırlı bile olsa kendi benzersiz dünya deneyimi ve bakış açısı temelinde mantıklı bir açıklama bulabilir. Hepimiz içinde yaşadığımız karmaşık dünyanın bir anlam ifade etmesini isteriz. Bu yüzden de hepimiz, gerçekte kör noktalarımız olan boşlukları doldurmak için kendimize hikâyeler anlatırız.

Bu hikâyeler bize finansal açıdan hem büyüleyici, hem de korkunç şeyler yapabilir.

Dünyanın işleyişiyle ilgili bazı konularda kör olduğumda, hisse senedi piyasalarının niçin böyle davrandığını tamamen, üstelik bir sonraki aşamada neler olacağını bilme yeteneğime aşırı güvenmeme yol açacak şekilde yanlış anlayabilirim. Hisse senedi piyasalarını ve ekonomiyi öngörmenin bu kadar zor olmasının bir nedeni, yeryüzünde, dünyanın sizin düşündüğünüz şekilde işlediğine inanan tek kişi olmanızdır. Benim hiç anlayamadığım nedenlerle kararlar verdiğinizde, sizin için doğru, benim içinse felaket olacak bir karara körü körüne katılabilirim. Onaltıncı Bölüm'de gördüğümüz gibi, balonlar böyle oluşur.

Ne kadarını bilmediğinizi kabul etmek, dünyada olup bitenlerin ne kadarının sizin kontrolünüz dışında olduğunu kabullenmek anlamına gelir. Ve bunu kabul etmek, zor olabilir.

Piyasa tahminlerini düşünün. Bu işte çok, gerçekten çok kötüyüz. Bir keresinde bir hesap yapmıştım ve piyasanın her yıl tarihsel ortalamasına göre yükseldiğini varsaymamız halinde, Wall Street'in büyük bankalarındaki en iyi 20 piyasa stratejistinin ortalama yıllık tahminlerine göre hareket etmekten daha doğru bir sonuca ulaşacağımızı bulmuştum. Ekonomik durgunlukları öngörme yeteneğimiz de bundan çok daha iyi değil. Üstelik çoğu sonucu, öngörülemeyen olayların kontrol ettiği bir dünyada, tahminler öngörülebilirlik yanılsaması verebilir ve büyük olaylar birdenbire ortaya çıktığı için de yarardan çok zarar getirebilir. Carl Richards şöyle yazıyor: "Risk, her şeyi düşündüğünüzü sandığınızda geriye kalanlardır."

İnsanlar bunu biliyor. Piyasa tahminlerinin bütününde doğru veya faydalı olduğunu içtenlikle düşünen bir yatırımcıyla karşılaşmadım. Ancak gerek medyanın, gerekse finansal danışmanların tahminlerine yönelik muazzam bir talep var.

Peki niçin?

Psikolog Philip Tetlock bir keresinde şöyle yazmıştı: "Tutarlı, öngörülebilir ve kontrol edilebilir bir dünyada yaşadığımıza inanma ihtiyacı duyuyoruz; bu yüzden de o ihtiyacı karşılamayı vaat eden ve bize yetkiliymiş gibi görünen insanlara yöneliyoruz."

*O ihtiyacı karşılamak*, mükemmel bir ifade biçimi. Kontrolün bizde olduğuna inanmayı istemek, hesaplanıp çözülmesi gereken analitik bir problemden ziyade, kaşınması gereken duygusal bir kaşıntıdır. Kontrol yanılsaması, belirsizlik gerçeğinden daha ikna edicidir. Böylece de, sonuçların kontrolümüz altında olduğunu anlatan hikâyelere tutunuruz.

Bu kısmen, kesinlik alanlarını belirsizlik alanlarıyla karıştırmakla ilgili bir mesele.

NASA'nın uzay aracı Yeni Ufuklar iki yıl önce Plüton'un yanından geçti. Dokuz buçuk yıl süren, üç milyar millik bir yolculuktu. NASA'nın verdiği bilgiye göre, yolculuk "Ocak 2006'da, araç uzaya fırlatıldığı zaman öngörülenin yaklaşık bir dakika altında bir sürede gerçekleşti."[68]

Bunu bir düşünün. Yaklaşık 10 yıl süren, üstelik daha önce hiç denenmemiş bir yolculukta, NASA'nın tahmini yüzde 99.99998 doğruydu. Bu, New York-Boston arasındaki bir yolculuğu, saniyenin dört milyonda biri kadar yanılma payıyla doğru tahmin etmek gibi bir şey.

Ancak astrofizik bir devinim alanıdır. Finans gibi insan davranışlarının ve duygularının kaprislerinden etkilenmez. İş dünyası, ekonomi ve yatırım, ağırlıklı olarak Plüton'a yapılacak bir yolculuk gibi net formüllerle kolayca açıklanamayan kararların yönlendirdiği belirsizlik alanlarıdır. Ne var ki, bizler umutsuzca, Plüton'a yapılan yolculuk gibi olmasını istiyoruz; çünkü bir NASA mühendisinin bir sonucu yüzde 99,99998 kontrol edebildiğini düşünmek, bize güzel ve rahatlatıcı geliyor. O kadar rahatlatıcı ki, kendimizi kaptırıyor ve para gibi hayatımızın diğer yönlerinin de ne denli kontrolümüz altında olduğuna dair kendimize hikâyeler anlatmaya yöneliyoruz.

Kahneman bir keresinde bu hikâyelerin izlediği yolu şöyle ifade etmişti:

- Planlar geliştirirken, ne yapmak istediğimize ve ne yapabileceğimize odaklanırız; buna karşılık başkalarının planlarını ve becerilerini, onların vermiş oldukları kararların bizim sonuçlarımızı etkileyebileceğini yeterince göz önüne almayız.
- Geçmişi açıklarken de, geleceği öngörürken de, becerinin nedensel rolüne odaklanır ve şansın rolünü ihmal ederiz.
- Bildiklerimize odaklanır, bilmediklerimizi ihmal ederiz ve bu da inançlarımıza aşırı güvenmemize neden olur.

Kahneman bunun şirketler üzerinde etkisini de şöyle anlatmıştı:

> Çeşitli vesilelerle, yenilikçi start-up'ların kurucularına ve katılımcılarına şöyle bir soru sorma fırsatım oldu: Çabalarınızın sonucu ne ölçüde şirketinizde yaptıklarınıza bağlı olacak? Bu açıkçası kolay bir sorudur; yanıt çabuk gelir ve asla yüzde 80'in altında olmamıştır. Bu cesur insanlar, başaracaklarından emin olmasalar bile, kaderlerinin neredeyse tamamen kendi ellerinde

> olduğunu düşünüyorlar. Fakat kesinlikle yanılıyorlar: Bir girişimin alacağı sonuç, kendi çabaları kadar rakiplerinin başarılarına ve piyasadaki değişimlere de bağlıdır. Buna rağmen, girişimciler doğal olarak, en iyi bildikleri şeye, yani kendi planlarına, kendi kararlarına ve eylemlerine, finansmana erişim gibi hemen o anda karşılarında bulunan tehdit ve fırsatlara odaklanıyorlar.

Rakipleriyle ilgili çok şey bilmedikleri için de, rekabetin rolünün düşük olduğu bir gelecek hayal etmeyi doğal buluyorlar.

Bunu, hepimiz bir ölçüde yapıyoruz.

Ve tıpkı kızım gibi, bizi biraz olsun rahatsız etmiyor.

Kör ve şaşkın bir halde dolanmakta değiliz. İçinde yaşadığımız ve faaliyet gösterdiğimiz dünyanın, bizim bildiklerimiz temelinde anlamlı ve mantıklı olduğunu düşünmek durumundayız. Aksini düşünsek, sabahları yataktan kalkmak fazlasıyla zor olurdu.

Peki ya Dünya'nın üzerinde daireler çizen Uzaylı?

Gördüklerine bakıp neler olup bittiğini bildiğinden emin olan, ama başkalarının kafasındaki hikâyeleri bilemediği için sonunda tamamen yanılan biri mi?

O biri, hepimiziz.

# 19

# Şimdi Her Şeyi Toparlayalım

Sizin paranızın psikolojisi hakkında öğrendiklerimiz.

TEBRİKLER, HÂLÂ OKUYORSUNUZ.

Öğrendiğimiz birkaç şeyi birleştirip toparlama zamanı geldi.

Bu bölüm biraz özet niteliğinde; daha iyi finansal kararlar almanıza yardımcı olabilecek kısa ve uygulanabilir birkaç ders de diyebiliriz.

Fakat önce, korkunç bir şekilde ters giden bir dişçi randevusunu anlatmak isterim. Bu hikâye, size paranızla ilgili tavsiye vermenin tehlikeleri konusunda son derece önemli bir şey öğretiyor.

---

Clarence Hughes, 1931 yılında dişçiye gider. Ağzının tamamına yayılan, dayanılmaz bir ağrı içinde kıvranmaktadır. Diş hekimi ağrısını hafifletmek için genel anestezi uygular. Clarence saatler sonra uyandığında 16 dişi eksiktir ve bademcikleri alınmıştır.

Ve sonra her şey ters gider. Clarence bir hafta sonra, ameliyat sonrasında gelişen komplikasyonlar nedeniyle ölür.

Eşi, dişçiyi mahkemeye verir; fakat açtığı davanın konusu, ameliyatın kötü gitmesi değildir. 1931 yılında her ameliyatta ölüm riski vardı.

Eşi mahkemede, her şey bir yana, Clarence'in yapılan işlemlere hiçbir zaman rıza göstermediğini ve kendisine sorulmuş olsa izin vermemiş olacağını söyler.

Dava duruşmadan duruşmaya taşınır, ancak hiçbir yere varamaz. 1931 yılında doktorların hastalarının rızasını alması, siyah ve beyaz gibi net değildi. Bir mahkeme, doktorların en iyi tıbbi kararları verebilme özgürlüğü olması gerektiğine ve "Bu özgürlük olmaksızın, bilimde ilerleme yaşanamayacağına" hükmetmişti.

Tarihin büyük bir bölümünde tıpta etik, doktorun işinin hastayı iyileştirmek olduğu ve uyguladığı tedavi yöntemleri hakkında hastanın ne düşündüğünün konuyla alâkası bulunmadığı yönündeydi. Jay Katz, *The Silent World Between Doctor and Patient* (Doktor ve Hasta Arasındaki Sessiz Dünya) adlı kitabında bu felsefeye değiniyor:

> Doktorlar, hastalarını iyileştirmek olan asli görevlerini yerine getirmek için onların fiziksel ve duygusal ihtiyaçlarıyla ilgilenmek zorunda olduklarını ve bu süreci kendi yetkileri dahilinde yürütmeleri gerektiğini, yani alınacak kararlarda hastalarına danışma gibi bir sorumlulukları bulunmadığını düşünüyorlardı. Hastanın da kararların yükünü doktorlarla paylaşma hakkına sahip olabileceği fikri, asla tıp etiğinin bir parçası olmamıştı.

Bu ego ya da kötülük değildi. İki yönlü bir inançtı:

1. Her hasta tedavi olmak ister.
2. Hastayı iyileştirmenin doğru ve evrensel tek bir yolu vardır.

Bu iki unsura inanıyorsanız, tedavi planlarının hastanın onayını gerektirmemesi mantıklıdır.

Ama tıp böyle işlemiyor.

Son 50 yılda tıp fakültelerinde öğretim yavaş yavaş, hastalıkları tedavi etmekten hastaları tedavi etmeye yöneldi. Bu da, tedavi planlarındaki seçeneklerin belirlenmesi, sonrasında da kendisi için en iyi yönteme hastanın karar vermesi anlamına geliyor.

Bu eğilim kısmen hasta koruma yasalarıyla, kısmen de "hastaların tıpta neyin değerli olduğu ya da denemeye değdiği konusunda son derece farklı görüşler sergilediğini, dolayısıyla da onların fikirlerinin dikkate alınması gerektiğini" savunan Katz'ın etkili kitabıyla yönlendirildi. Katz kitabında şöyle yazıyor:

> Hekimlerin bilimlerini ve sanatlarını icra ederken kendi iyiniyetlerine ve doğru olana karar verme yeteneklerine güvenebileceklerini iddia etmek tehlikeli bir saçmalık... O kadar kolay değil. Tıp karmaşık bir meslektir ve doktorlar ile hastalar arasındaki etkileşimler de karmaşıktır.

Bu son satır önemli. "Tıp karmaşık bir meslektir ve doktorlar ile hastalar arasındaki etkileşimler de karmaşıktır."

Hangi meslek aynen böyle, biliyor musunuz? Finansal danışmanlık.

Ben size paranızla ne yapacağınızı söyleyemem, çünkü sizi tanımıyorum.

Ne istediğinizi bilmiyorum. Ne zaman istediğinizi bilmiyorum. Niçin istediğinizi bilmiyorum.

Bu yüzden de, size paranızla ne yapacağınızı söylemeyeceğim. Ben size, dişçinin Clarence Hughes'e davrandığı gibi davranmak istemiyorum.

Fakat elbette ki, doktorların ve diş hekimlerinin faydasız olduğu söylenemez. Bilgilidirler. Olasılıkları bilirler. Hastalar kendileri için doğru olan tedavi konusunda farklı sonuçlara varsalar bile, hekimler neyin işe yarayacağını bilir.

Finansal danışmanlar da aynı şekilde. Para konusunda evrensel gerçekler vardır; ve insanlar bu gerçekleri kendi finansal durumlarına nasıl uygulamak istediklerine dair farklı sonuçlara varsalar bile, o evrensel gerçekler değişmez.

Bu uyarıyı yaptıktan sonra, paranızla ilgili daha iyi kararlar almanıza yardımcı olabilecek birkaç kısa tavsiyeye göz atalım.

---

**İşler yolunda giderken alçakgönüllü, ters gittiğinde ise merhametli ve affedici olmak için elinizden geleni yapın.** Çünkü hiçbir zaman göründüğü kadar iyi ya da göründüğü kadar kötü değildir. Dünya büyük ve karmaşıktır. Şans ve risk hem gerçektir, hem de ikisini de belirleyip tanımlamak zordur. Gerek kendinizi, gerekse başkalarını yargılarken bunu düşünün ve öyle davranın. Şansın ve riskin gücüne saygı gösterin; o zaman gerçekten kontrol edebileceğiniz şeylere odaklanma olasılığınız daha yüksek olur. Ayrıca doğru rol modellerini bulma şansınız da artar.

**Daha düşük ego, daha çok servet.** Para biriktirmek, egonuz ile geliriniz arasındaki mesafedir ve servet, sizin görmediklerinizdir. Bu nedenle servet, gelecekte daha fazla şeye veya daha fazla seçeneğe sahip olmak için bugün satın alabileceklerinizi baskılamakla yaratılır. Ne kadar kazanırsanız kazanın, bugün paranızla ne kadar eğlenebileceğiniz konusunda kendinize sınır koymadığınız sürece, hiçbir zaman servet oluşturamazsınız.

**Paranızı geceleri iyi uyumanızı sağlayacak şekilde yönetin.** En yüksek getiriyi elde etmeyi veya gelirinizin belirli bir yüzdesini biriktirmeyi hedeflemelisiniz demekten farklı bir şey söylüyorum. Bazı insanlar en yüksek getiriyi elde etmedikçe iyi uyuyamazlar; bazıları ise ancak temkinli ve muhafazakâr yatırım yaptıkları zaman rahat uyuyup dinlenebilirler. Herkesin doğrusu kendinedir ve herkes kendi için doğru gördüğünü yapar. Fakat "Bunu yapmak, geceleri iyi uyumamı sağlar mı?" ilkesi, tüm finansal kararlar için en iyi evrensel rehberdir.

**Yatırımcı olarak daha iyisini başarmak istiyorsanız, yapabileceğiniz en güçlü şey zaman ufkunuzu genişletmektir.** Zaman, yatırım işindeki en kuvvetli güçtür. Küçük şeyleri büyütür ve büyük hataları silikleştirir. Şansı ve riski nötralize edip etkisiz kılamaz; ancak sonuçları, insanların hak ettiği noktaya doğru iter ve yaklaştırır.

**Birçok şeyin yanlış gitmesini sorun etmeyin. Zamanın yarısında yanılabilir, buna rağmen bir servet kazanabilirsiniz;** çünkü, sonuçların büyük çoğunluğunu, küçük bir azınlık oluşturur. Paranızı nasıl değerlendirirseniz değerlendirin, birçok şeyin sonuç vermemesi karşısında rahat olmalısınız. Dünya böyle bir yer. Bu nedenle de, aldığınız sonuçları değerlendirirken her zaman için yatırımlarınıza tek tek odaklanmamalı, portföyünüzün tamamına bakmalısınız. Çok sayıda zayıf yatırımınızın olması, buna karşılık birkaç tanesinin gayet başarılı sonuç vererek öne çıkması iyidir. Genellikle de, en iyi senaryo budur. Aldığınız sonuçları değerlendirirken yatırımlarınıza tek tek odaklanmak, kazananları olduğundan daha parlak gösterir; kaybedenlerin ise olduğundan daha üzücü ve pişmanlık verici görünmesine yol açar.

**Parayı zamanınız üzerinde kontrol geliştirmek için kullanın;** çünkü zamanınızı kontrol edememek, mutluluğu frenleyen son derece güçlü ve evrensel bir faktördür. İstediğiniz şeyi, istediğiniz zaman, istediğiniz kişiyle, istediğiniz sürece yapabilme yeteneği, finans alanındaki mevcut en yüksek kâr payını öder.

**Sempatik olun ve gösterişe rağbet etmeyin.** Hiç kimse, sahip olduklarınızdan sizin kadar etkilenmez. Lüks bir araba ya da güzel bir saat istediğinizi düşünebilirsiniz. Ama muhtemelen, asıl istediğiniz saygı ve hayranlık olabilir. Üstelik bu tür şeyleri beygir gücü ve metalden ziyade, nezaket ve alçakgönüllülük sayesinde kazanmanız çok daha olasıdır.

**Tasarruf edin. Siz sadece tasarruf etmeye bakın.** Birikim yapmak için belli bir nedeninizin olması gerekmez. Araba almak, bir şeyin peşinatını ödemek veya sağlıkla ilgili acil durumlar için tasarruf etmek, harika. Ancak öngörülmesi veya bilinmesi imkânsız olan şeyler için birikim yapmak, tasarruf etmenin en iyi nedenlerinden biridir. Herkesin hayatı birbiri ardına eklenmiş sürprizler zinciridir. Belli bir şeyi hedeflemeyen birikimler, hayatın kaçınılmaz bir kabiliyetine, olabilecek en kötü anda dünyanızı cehenneme çevirme yeteneğine karşı kendinizi korumaya almak, yani finans tabiriyle hedge yapmaktır.

**Başarının maliyetini tanımlayın ve onu ödemeye hazır olun.** Çünkü, değerli hiçbir şey bedava değildir. Ayrıca çoğu finansal bedelin gözle görülür fiyat etiketi taşımadığını unutmayın. Belirsizlik, şüphe ve pişmanlık finans dünyasındaki yaygın maliyetlerdir. Genellikle de o maliyetleri ödemeye değer. Ancak bunları size kesilmiş para cezası (veya kaçınmanız gereken bir ceza) olarak değil, ücret (yani karşılığında güzel bir şey edinmek için ödemeye değer fiyat) olarak görmelisiniz.

**Hata payı ilkesine saygı gösterin.** Size dayanıklılık veren ve sağlam durmanızı sağlayan şey, gelecekte olabilecekler ile sizin iyi bir sonuç elde etmeniz için olması gerekenler arasına mesafe koymaktır; ve dayanıklılık, zaman içinde bileşiklenmeyi sihirli kılar. Hata payı genellikle muhafazakâr bir korunma yöntemi gibi görünür; ancak sizi oyunda tutarsa, defalarca karşılığını verebilir.

**Finans konusunda uç kararlar almaktan kaçının.** Herkesin hedefleri ve arzuları zamanla değişir ve geçmişteki kararlarınız ne denli uçlardaysa, evrildiğiniz süreç içinde o kadar pişman olabilirsiniz.

**Riski sevin, çünkü zamanla karşılığını verir.** Ancak yıkıcı risklere karşı paranoid olmalısınız; çünkü bu, gelecekte risk almanızı engeller ve zaman içinde karşılığını verecek olan risklere girmek istemeyebilirsiniz.

Oynadığınız oyunu tanımlayın ve kararlarınızın/eylemlerinizin farklı bir oyun oynamakta olan insanlardan etkilenmediğinden emin olun.

**Fikir kargaşasına ve farklı görüşlere saygı gösterin.** Akıllı, bilgili ve makûl insanlar finans konusunda fikir ve görüş ayrılığına düşebilir; çünkü insanların amaçları ve arzuları çok farklıdır. Tek bir doğru yanıt yoktur; sizin işinize yarayan, sizin için sonuç veren hangisiyse, doğru yanıt odur.

Şimdi izninizle, benim durumumda neyin işe yaradığını anlatayım.

# 20

# İtiraflar

Benim paramın psikolojisi.

FIRST MANHATTAN DANIŞMANLIK grubunun kurucusu, milyarder yatırımcı Sandy Gottesman'ın yatırım ekibine dahil olacak adaylarla görüşürken şu soruyu sorduğu söylenir: "Sende neler var ve neden?"

"Hangi hisselerin daha ucuz olduğunu düşünüyorsun?" veya "Hangi ekonomi durgunluğun eşiğinde?" değil.

Bana kendi paranla ne yaptığını göster. Hepsi bu.

Bu soruyu seviyorum; çünkü mantıklı olan (insanların yapmanızı önerdiği şey) ile onlara doğru gelen (kendilerinin yaptıkları şey) arasında çoğu kez bir kilometre fark olabileceğinin altını çiziyor.

---

Morningstar'a göre, ABD'deki tüm yatırım fonlarındaki portföy yöneticilerinin yarısı, kendi paralarının bir kuruşunu dahi kendi fonlarına yatırmıyor.[69] Bu iğrenç görünebilir ve söz konusu istatistiğin bu alandaki ikiyüzlülüğü ortaya çıkardığı kesin.

Ancak bu tür şeyler, düşündüğümüzden daha yaygın. Güney California Üniversitesi (University of Southern California, USC) tıp fakülkesi profesörlerinden Ken Murray, 2011 yılında yazdığı *"Doktorlar Nasıl Ölür"* başlıklı tezde, doktorların kendileri için seçtikleri yaşam sonu tedavilerinin, hastalarına tavsiye ettiklerinden ne kadar farklı olduğunu ortaya koyuyor.[70]

Murray tezinde, "[Doktorlar] bizler gibi ölmüyor" diye yazıyor. "Doktorlarla ilgili sıradışı olan şey, Amerikalıların çoğunluğuna kıyasla ne kadar tedavi gördükleri değil, ne kadar az tedavi gördükleridir. Başkalarının ölümlerinin önüne geçmek için onca zaman uğraş verdikten sonra, sıra onlara gelip de kendi ölümleriyle yüz yüze kaldıklarında oldukça sakin karşılama eğilimindeler. Ne olacağını çok iyi biliyorlar, seçenekleri biliyorlar ve genelde istedikleri her türlü tıbbi bakıma erişimleri var. Ancak sakince gidiyorlar." Bir doktor, hastasının kanserini yenmek için her yolu deneyebiliyor, ancak kendisi için palyatif bakımı seçebiliyor.

Birinin size önerdikleri ile kendisi için yaptıklarının farklı olması, her zaman kötü bir şey değildir. Burada altını çizmek istediğim nokta, sizi ve ailenizi etkileyen karmaşık ve duygusal sorunları yönetirken tek bir doğru yanıt olmadığıdır. Bu konuda evrensel bir gerçek yoktur. Sadece siz ve aileniz için işe yarayan şey vardır; bu da işaretlemek istediğiniz kutucukları, sizi rahat hissettirecek ve geceleri iyi uyumanızı sağlayacak şekilde işaretlemekle olur.

Finansta da tıpta da uyulması gereken bazı temel ilkeler olduğu doğrudur; ancak önemli finansal kararlar hesap tablolarına veya ders kitaplarına bakarak alınmaz. Sofrada alınır. Genellikle de amaç, getirileri en üst düzeye çıkarmak değil, bir eşi veya çocuğu hayal kırıklığına uğratma olasılığını en aza indirmektir. Bu tür şeyleri tablolarda, grafiklerde veya formüllerde özetlemek zordur ve kişiden kişiye büyük farklılıklar gösterir. Biri için işe yarayan bir şey, bir başkası için sonuç vermeyebilir.

Sizin için neyin doğru olduğunu ve işe yarayacağını kendinizin bulmanız gerekir. Şimdi benim için neyin doğru olduğuna ve işe yaradığına bakalım.

## Ailemin tasarufa bakışı

Charlie Munger bir keresinde şöyle demişti: "Zengin olmak gibi bir niyetim yoktu. Sadece bağımsız olmak istedim."

Benim açımdan zenginliği bir kenara bırakabiliriz, ancak finansal hedefim daima bağımsızlık olmuştur. En yüksek getirilerin peşinde koşmak veya en lüks hayatı yaşamak için elimdeki varlıkları kullanmak beni pek ilgilendirmiyor. Her ikisi de insanların arkadaşlarını etkilemek için oynadığı bir oyun gibi geliyor ve her ikisinin de gizli riskleri var. Benim en çok istediğim şey, her gün, benim ve ailemin, istediğimiz her şeyi kendi koşullarımızla, bizim arzu ettiğimiz gibi yapabileceğimizi bilerek uyanmak. Verdiğimiz her finansal kararda ana hedefimiz budur.

Benim ebeveynlerim yetişkinlik yıllarını iki evrede geçirdi: İlk evrede yoksul, ikinci evrede ise ortanın biraz üstünde bir yaşam sürdüler. Babam 40 yaşında doktor oldu ve mezun olduğunda üç çocuk babasıydı. Doktor maaşı almak, tıp fakültesine gittiği dönemde evdeki üç aç çocuğa bakma zorunluluğunun dayattığı tutumlu zihniyeti yok etmedi; böylece de ailem iyi yıllarını, imkânlarının çok altında bir hayat sürerek ve yüksek oranda tasarruf ederek geçirdi. Bu onlara bir ölçüde bağımsızlık verdi. Babam Acil Servis doktoruydu; bu benim hayal edebileceğim en stresli mesleklerden biri; ayrıca nöbetlerin, gece ve gündüz vardiyalarında dönüşümlü çalışmanın getirdiği son derece zorlu bir biyolojik ritm düzensizliği söz konusuydu. Yirmi yılın sorunda artık dayanamayacağına karar verdi ve bitirdi. Öylece bıraktı ve çıktı. Hayatının bir sonraki evresine geçti.

Bu durum benim üzerime adeta yapıştı. Bir sabah uyanıp da yaptığınız şeyi, kendi koşullarınıza göre, siz ne zaman hazırsanız değiştirebilme yeteneği, benim gözüme tüm finansal hedeflerin büyükannesi gibi görünüyor. Benim için bağımsızlık, işi bırakıp çalışmamak değil. Sevdiğiniz işi, sevdiğiniz kişilerle, sizin istediğiniz zamanlarda ve siz istediğiniz sürece yapmak.

Ve bir ölçüde bağımsızlık elde etmek, doktor maaşı kazanmayı gerektirmiyor. Bu daha çok, beklentilerinizi kontrol altında tutmak ve imkânlarınızın altında bir yaşam sürebilmekle ilgili bir konu. Gelir düzeyi ne olursa olsun, bağımsızlığı yönlendiren itki tasarruf oranınızdır. Ve belli bir gelir düzeyini geçtikten sonra, tasarruf oranınızı yönlendiren itki, yaşam tarzı beklentilerinizin yüksekten uçmasını önleme yeteneğinizdir.

Eşim ve ben üniversite döneminde tanıştık ve evlenmeden önce yıllarca birbirimizin evlerine taşınıp durduk. Üniversiteden sonra ikimiz de giriş seviyesinde ücretler aldığımız işlerde çalıştık ve orta halli bir yaşam tarzı sürdük. Yaşam tarzı yelpazesi çok geniştir ve birinin normal bulduğu bir tarz, başka birinin gözünde krallar gibi yaşamak olabilir, bir başkasına ise yoksulluk gelebilir. Fakat biz kendi gelirimize göre iyi olduğunu düşündüğümüz bir daire ve bir araba edindik; kendimizce iyi kıyafetler giydik ve gıdamızı iyi aldık. Rahat yaşadık, ama lükse kaçmadık.

On yılı aşkın bir süredir gelirimiz artmış olmasına rağmen -ben finans, eşim sağlık sektöründe çalışmaktayız- yaşam tarzımız aşağı yukarı değişmedi. Bu da, tasarruf oranımızı sürekli olarak yukarı çekti. Neredeyse aldığımız her kuruş zam, tasarruflarımızda, yani bizim "bağımsızlık fonumuzda" birikti. Şimdi, imkânlarımızın oldukça altında bir yaşam sürüyoruz; bu size gelirimizle ilgili pek bir şey söylemese de, 20'li yaşlarımızda oluşturduğumuz yaşam tarzını sürdürme kararımıza dair çok şey anlatabilir.

Bizim hanemizin finansal planının gurur duyduğum bir yönü varsa, o da yaşam tarzıyla ilgili arzularımızın hedefini genç yaşta belirlememiz ve sonrasında da değiştirmememizdir. Tasarruf oranımız oldukça yüksek; ancak daha fazlasını edinmeye yönelik özlemlerimiz pek değişmediği için baskıcı bir şekilde tutumlu olduğumuz duygusunu nadiren yaşıyoruz. Özlemlerimiz olmadığından değil; güzel şeyleri seviyoruz ve rahat yaşıyoruz. Sadece hedeflerimizi yerinden oynatmıyoruz.

Bu herkes için iyi sonucu vermez, ama bizde iyi sonuç veriyor; çünkü ikimiz de bu fikre eşit oranda katılıyoruz, ikimiz de birbirimiz için ödün vermiyoruz. Zevk aldığımız şeylerin (yürüyüş yapmak, okumak, podcast'ler) çoğu düşük maliyetli; bu yüzden de bir şeyleri kaçırıyormuşuz duygusunu nadiren yaşıyoruz. Tasarruf düzeyimizi yüksek bulup sorguladığım ender zamanlarda, yıllar boyunca yüksek oranda birikim yapmanın annemle babama kazandırdığı bağımsızlığı düşünüyorum ve çabucak kendime geliyorum. Bağımsızlık, bizim en büyük hedefimiz. Olanaklarınızın altında bir yaşam tarzı sürdürmenin ikinci bir yararı da "filancalara ayak uydurma" yarışının getirdiği psikolojik iniş-çıkışlardan kaçınmayı sağlaması.

İmkânlarınızın altında, ama daha fazlasını istemeden rahat bir yaşam sürmek, modern birinci dünya ülkelerinde birçok insanın kendini maruz bıraktığı muazzam toplumsal baskıyı ortadan kaldırıyor. Nassim Taleb bunu şöyle açıklıyor: "Gerçek başarı, kişinin iç huzuru için faaliyetlerini düzenleyerek bazı kedi-fare yarışlarından çıkmasıdır." Bu ifadeyi seviyorum.

Biz bağımsızlık kampına o kadar bağlıyız ki, kağıt üzerinde pek de mantıklı olmayan şeyler yaptık. Evimizi peşin aldık, ki bu şimdiye kadar verdiğimiz en kötü finansal karardı; öte yandan paramızla ilgili bugüne dek aldığımız en iyi karar da bu oldu. Biz evimizi aldığımız dönemde ipotekli konut kredilerinde faiz oranları saçma denecek kadar düşüktü. Rasyonel düşünen her danışman, o dönemde ucuz paradan yararlanmamızı ve elimizdeki ekstra birikimi hisse senetleri gibi daha yüksek getirili varlıklara yatırmamızı tavsiye ederdi. Ama bizim amacımız buz gibi bir soğukkanlılıkla rasyonel olmak değil, psikolojik olarak mâkul ve mantıklı olanı yapmak.

Evimizi peşin almanın bana verdiği bağımsızlık duygusu, ucuza alınmış ipotekli konut kredisiyle kaldıraç kullanmanın bilinen finansal kazançlarını çok aşıyor. Aylık ödemeyi ortadan kaldırmak bana, varlıklarımızın uzun vadeli değerini maksimize etmekten daha iyi geliyor. Bağımsız hissettiriyor.

Bu kararı, kusurlarına işaret edenlere ya da asla aynısını yapmayacak olanlara karşı savunmaya çalışmıyorum. Kağıt üzerinde savunulacak bir tarafı yok. Ama bize doğru geliyor ve bizim için iyi sonuç veriyor. Memnunuz. Önemli olan da bu. İyi kararların her zaman rasyonel olması gerekmiyor. Bir noktada mutlu olmak ile "doğru olanı" yapmak arasında bir seçim gerçekleştirmek zorundasınız.

Ayrıca, çoğu finansal danışmanın önerdiğinden daha yüksek bir yüzdeyi - evimizin değeri hariç varlıklarımızın yüzde 20'sini- nakitte tutuyoruz. Bu da yine kağıt üzerinde savunulamaz bir şey ve başkalarına tavsiye etmiyorum. Ama bize böylesi doğru geliyor ve iyi sonuç veriyor.

Biz böyle yapıyoruz, çünkü nakiti bağımsızlığın oksijeni olarak görüyoruz ve -daha da önemlisi- elimizdeki hisse senetlerini hiçbir zaman satmak zorunda kalmak istemiyoruz. Çok büyük bir masrafla karşılaşmamız halinde hisse senetlerimizi satmak zorunda kalma olasılığını olabildiğince sıfıra yakın tutmak istiyoruz. Belki de, risk toleransımız başkalarına göre daha düşük.

Fakat kişisel finans hakkında öğrendiğim her şey bana, istisnasız herkesin, günün birinde beklemediği büyük bir masrafla karşı karşıya kalacağını ve özellikle de hiç beklemediği bir masraf olduğu için buna hazırlıksız yakalanacağını söylüyor. Finansal durumumuzun ayrıntılarını bilen birkaç kişi, "Ne için biriktiriyorsunuz? Ev mi? Tekne mi? Yeni bir araba mı?" diye soruyor. Hayır, bunların hiçbiri için değil. Ben umulmadık yerden gelen eğri topların, beklediğimizden daha yaygın olduğu bir dünya için birikim yapıyorum. Bir masrafı karşılamak için hisse senedi satmak zorunda kalmamak, aynı zamanda elimizdeki hisselerin olabildiğince uzun bir süre boyunca bileşiklenme olasılığını yükseltmek anlamına geliyor. Charlie Munger bunu çok iyi ifade etmiş: "Bileşiklenmenin ilk kuralı, asla gereksiz yere ara verip kesintiye uğratmamaktır."

## Ailemin yatırıma bakışı

Kariyerime hisse senedi seçicisi olarak başladım. O dönemde yalnızca bireysel hisse senetlerimiz vardı; çoğunlukla Berkshire Hathaway ve Procter&Gamble gibi büyük şirketlerin hisseleri ile değer yatırımı olarak gördüğüm bazı küçük şirketlerin hisselerinden oluşan bir karışım yapmıştım. Yirmili yaşlarımdan beri, her zaman aşağı yukarı 25 ayrı hisse senedim oldu.

Hisse seçici olarak nasıl bir iş çıkardığımı bilmiyorum. Piyasayı yendim mi? Emin değilim. Deneyenlerin çoğu gibi ben de iyi bir skor elde edemedim. Sonuçta, bir şekilde fikrimi değiştirdim ve şimdi hisse senetlerimizin hepsi düşük maliyetli bir endeks fonunda.

İnsanların aktif hisse senedi seçicisi olarak kendileri adına yatırım yapmasına veya paralarını aktif bir fon yöneticisine verip seçimi onlara bırakmasına hiçbir şekilde karşı değilim. Bazı insanların piyasa ortalamalarından daha iyi performans gösterebileceğini düşünüyorum; fakat bu zor, hatta çoğu insanın sandığından daha zor.

Yatırım konusundaki görüşlerimi özetlemem gerekirse: Her yatırımcı, hedeflerine başarıyla ulaşma bağlamında en yüksek olasılık içeren strateji hangisiyse, onu seçmelidir. Ve bence çoğu yatırımcı açısından, düşük maliyetli bir endeks fonunun ortalama dolar maliyeti, uzun vadede en yüksek başarı olasılığını sağlayacaktır.

Fakat bu, endeks yatırımının her zaman işe yarayacağı anlamına gelmez. Herkes için doğru olacağı anlamına da gelmez. Ayrıca, aktif hisse senedi seçiciliğinin başarısızlığa mahkûm olduğu da söylenemez. Bu sektör genel olarak, bu iki yönden birinde, daha çok da aktif yatırıma şiddetle karşı çıkanların tarafında fazlasıyla kökleşmiş durumda.

Piyasayı yenmek *zor olmalı*; başarı olasılığı *düşük olmalı*. Öyle olmasa herkes yapardı, herkes yapsa fırsat olmazdı. Dolayısıyla da, piyasayı yenmeye çalışanların büyük çoğunluğunun başarısız olmasına kimse şaşırmamalı. (İstatistikler, büyük sermayeli aktif yöneticilerin yüzde 85'inin, 2019'da sona eren on yılda S&P 500'ün üzerine çıkmadığını gösteriyor.)[71]

Piyasayı yenmeye çalışmanın delilik olduğunu düşünen, buna karşılık çocuklarını yıldızlara ulaşmaya ve profesyonel sporcu olmaya teşvik eden insanlar tanıyorum. Herkesin doğrusu kendine. Hayat olasılıklara oynamakla ilgili bir şey ve hepimiz olasılıklar konusunda biraz farklı düşünüyoruz.

Yıllar geçtikçe, on yıllar boyunca sürekli olarak düşük maliyetli bir endeks fonuna yatırım yaparsak ve o paraya dokunmadan bileşiklenmesini sağlarsak ailemizin tüm finansal hedeflerini gerçekleştirme şansımızın yüksek olacağı görüşüne vardım. Bu vizyonun büyük bölümü, tutumlu harcamaya dayalı yaşam tarzımızdan geliyor. Piyasadan daha iyi performans göstermeye çalışmanın getireceği ek riski almak zorunda kalmadan tüm hedeflerinizi gerçekleştirebiliyorsanız, böyle bir şeyi denemenin ne anlamı var? Dünyanın en büyük yatırımcısı olmayabilirim, ama kötü bir yatırımcı olmama izin veremem. Bu şekilde düşündüğümde, endeksi satın alıp beklemek, bizim için çocuk oyuncağı gibi kolay bir seçim oluyor. Herkesin bu mantığa katılmayacağını biliyorum, özellikle de işi piyasayı yenmek olan arkadaşlarımın. Yaptıklarına saygı duyuyorum. Ama bizim için işe yarayan yöntem bu.

Her ay maaşlarımızın bir bölümünü, Amerikan ve uluslararası hisse senetlerinden oluşan bu endeks fonlarına yatırıyoruz. Belirli bir hedefimiz yok; bütün harcamalarımızı yaptıktan sonra elimizde ne kaldıysa, onu aktarıyoruz. Aynı fondaki emeklilik hesaplarımızı büyütüyoruz ve çocuklarımızın "529 üniversite tasarruf planına"* katkıda bulunuyoruz.

Sonuç olarak, hepsi bu. Esasen tüm net değerimiz bir ev, bir banka hesabı ve Vanguard'daki birkaç endeks fonundan ibaret. Bizim için bundan daha karmaşık bir şey olması gerekmiyor. Basiti seviyorum. Yatırıma gösterilen çaba ile yatırım sonuçları arasında çok az korelasyon olduğuna inanıyorum; bu benim yatırım konusundaki en köklü inançlarımdan biri. Çünkü dünyayı kuyruklar yönlendirir; getirilerin büyük bölümünü, birkaç değişken oluşturur. Ne kadar uğraş verirseniz verin, stratejinizde ibreyi hareket ettiren iki veya üç şeyi

---

* 529 Üniversite Tasarruf Planı: ABD'de anaokulundan yüksek lisanstan mezuniyete kadar eğitim masraflarını karşılamak üzere oluşturulmuş, vergi avantajlı tasarruf planı. (ÇN.)

kaçırırsanız yatırım işinde başarılı olamazsınız. Bunun tersi de doğrudur. Basit yatırım stratejileri, o stratejinin başarısı için önemli olan birkaç şeyi yakaladığı sürece harika sonuçlar verebilir. Benim yatırım stratejim, doğru sektörü seçmeye veya bir sonraki ekonomik durgunluğu zamanlamaya dayanmıyor. Yüksek tasarruf oranına, sabıra ve küresel ekonominin önümüzdeki birkaç on yıl içinde değer yaratacağına dair iyimserliğime dayanıyor. Esasen, yatırım konusundaki bütün çabalarımda bu üç şeyi, özellikle de kontrol edebildiğim ilk ikisini düşünerek hareket ediyorum.

Geçmişte yatırım stratejimi değiştirdim. Yani elbette ki, gelecekte de değiştirme olasılığım var.

Fakat nasıl tasarruf edersek edelim veya yatırımlarımızda nasıl bir strateji uygularsak uygulayalım, bağımsızlık hedefimizden hiç vazgeçmeyeceğimizden ve geceleri en iyi şekilde uyumamızı sağlayacak olan ne ise onu yapacağımızdan eminim.

Biz bunun nihai hedefimiz olduğunu düşünüyoruz ve paranın psikolojisinde ustalaşmak olarak görüyoruz.

Ama herkesin doğrusu kendine. Kimse çılgın değil.

# SONSÖZ

# Amerika'da Mevcut Tüketici Zihniyetinin Kısa Tarihi

Modern tüketicinin psikolojisini ve bundan sonra nereye yönelebileceğini anlamak istiyorsak, bu noktaya nasıl gelindiğini bilmemiz gerekir.

Hepimiz buraya nasıl geldik.

1945 yılında uyuyakalmış ve 2020'de uyanmış olsaydınız, sizi çevreleyen dünyayı tanıyamazdınız.

Bu süreçte yaşanan ekonomik büyüme kelimenin gerçek anlamıyla eşsiz ve benzersizdi. New York ve San Francisco'daki zenginlik seviyesini görseniz, şok olurdunuz. O zenginliği Detroit'in yoksulluğuyla karşılaştırsanız, şok olurdunuz. Konut fiyatlarını, üniversite harçlarına ve sağlık hizmetlerine ödenen fiyatları işitseniz, şok olurdunuz. Ortalama Amerikalının tasarruf ve harcamalar hakında genelde nasıl düşündüğünü duysanız, şok olurdunuz. Ve bütün bunların nasıl olduğuna dair makûl bir anlatı oluşturmaya çalışsanız, tahminimce tamamen yanılırdınız. Çünkü bu sezgisel olarak kavranabilecek bir durum olmadığı gibi, öngörülebilir bir şey değildi.

İkinci Dünya Savaşı sonundan bu yana Amerika'da yaşananlar, Amerikan tüketicisinin hikâyesidir. İnsanların para konusunda neden bugünkü gibi düşündüğünü açıklamaya yardımcı olan uzun bir hikâye.

Hikâyeyi kısaca özetlersek: İşler önce çok belirsizdi, sonra çok iyiydi, sonra oldukça kötü, sonra gerçekten iyi, sonra gerçekten kötü oldu ve bu noktaya geldik. Ben kendimce, tüm bu evreleri ve o dönemlerde yaşanan hadiseleri birbirine bağlayan bir anlatı oluşturdum. Detaylı bir anlatı değil. Ama her şeyin nasıl içiçe geçip birbirine bağlandığını anlatan bir hikâye çıktı ortaya.

Hikâyemiz büyük olayları birbirine bağlamaya yönelik bir girişim olduğu için bu dönemde yaşananlara ilişkin birçok ayrıntıyı dışarıda bırakıyor. Şimdiden söyleyeyim, neleri kaçırdıysam, bana bunları hatırlatacak olan herkese muhtemelen katılıyorumdur. Ancak benim buradaki amacım, tek tek her oyunu anlatmak değil; bir oyunun diğerini nasıl etkilediğine ışık tutmak.

Bakalım modern tüketici bu noktaya nasıl gelmiş.

---

### 1. Ağustos, 1945: İkinci Dünya Savaşı sona eriyor

*New York Times*, Japonya'nın teslim oluşunu "Amerikan Tarihinin En Mutlu Günü" başlığıyla duyurmuştu.

Ancak "Tarih birbiri ardına gelen lanetler silsilesidir" diye bir söz var.

Savaşın sona ermesinin sevinci, çok geçmeden yerini "Şimdi ne olacak?" sorusuna bırakmıştı.

On altı milyon Amerikalı -nüfusun yüzde 11'i- savaşta görev yapmıştı. Sonuçta bunların yaklaşık sekiz milyonu denizaşırı görevlerdeydi. Yaşları ortalama 23'tü. Çok değil, 18 ay içinde 1.5 milyonu hariç hepsi eve dönecek ve üniformasını üzerinden çıkaracaktı.

Peki ya sonra?

Ondan sonra ne yapacaklardı?

Nerede çalışacaklardı?

Nerede yaşayacaklardı?

Bunlar, iki nedenle o günlerin en önemli sorularıydı. Birincisi, yanıtları kimse bilmiyordu. İkincisi, hızlı bir şekilde yanıtlanmadıkları takdirde, birçok ekonomistin gözündeki en olası senaryo, ekonominin Büyük Buhran'ın derinliklerine geri kaymasıydı.

Savaş sırasında üç kuvvet birikmişti:

1. Üretim kapasitesi esas olarak savaş malzemelerinin üretimine kaydırıldığından, konut inşaatı durma noktasına gelmişti. 1943 yılında ayda 12,000'den az ev inşa edilmişti; yani şehir başına bir ev bile düşmüyordu. Savaştan dönen askerler, ciddi bir konut sıkıntısıyla karşı karşıyaydı.
2. Gemi, tank, uçak yapımı gibi savaş sırasında yaratılan belirli işler, savaştan sonra birdenbire gereksiz kalmış ve özel sektörde ender görülen muazzam bir hızla ve muazzam ölçekte durmuştu. Eve dönen askerlerin nerede çalışacağı belli değildi.
3. Evlilik oranı savaş sırasında ve savaştan hemen sonra tırmanışa geçmişti. Askerler annelerinin bodrumuna dönmek istemiyorlardı. Bir an önce aile kurup kendi

evlerine geçmek, bunun için de iyi bir iş bulmak istiyorlardı.

Bu durum, özellikle de üzerinden henüz beş yıl geçmiş olan Büyük Buhran'ın anıları bu kadar tazeyken, politika yapıcıları endişelendiriyordu.

Ekonomi Danışmanları Konseyi, 1946 yılında Başkan Truman'a sunduğu raporda "önümüzdeki bir ila dört yıl içinde tam kapsamlı bir buhran" gelebileceği uyarısında bulunmuştu. Truman ile 1947 yılında yaptığı bir toplantıyı özetleyen ayrı bir bilgilendirme raporunda da şöyle yazmışlardı:

> Ekonomimizin içinden geçtiği durgunluk süreci, durgunluk güçlerinin kontrolden çıkma tehlikesiyle karşı karşıya olup olmadığımız konusunda bulunduğumuz zeminden çok emin olmamızı gerektiriyor... Ekonomide yeni bir gerilemenin buhran koşullarına doğru aşağı yönlü bir sarmal tehlikesini artırabileceğine dair büyük çaplı bir beklenti mevcut.

Bu korku, en büyük ekonomilerden ikisi, Avrupa ve Japonya'nın insani krizlerin enkazı altında ezildiği bir ortamda, büyüme yolunda ilk etapta ihracata güvenilemeyeceği gerçeğiyle daha da şiddetlenmişti. Kaldı ki, Amerika'nın kendisi de tarihinde hiç olmadığı kadar borca gömülmüş ve doğrudan hükümet teşviklerini sınırlamıştı.

Böylece bu konuda bir şeyler yaptık.

### 2. Düşük faiz oranları ve Amerikan tüketicisinin bilinçli bir şekilde hayata getirilişi

Yaptımız ilk şey, savaş sonrasında ekonomi gemisini yüzdürmek için faiz oranlarını düşük tutmak oldu. Bu kolay bir karar değildi; çünkü askerler vatana döndüğünde giysiden otomobile kadar her şeyde kıtlık vardı ve bu da enflasyonu geçici olarak çift haneli rakamlara taşımıştı.

Federal Reserve 1951 yılına kadar siyasi olarak bağımsız değildi.[72] Başkan ve Fed politikayı birlikte yürütüyordu. Fed 1942 yılında, savaşın finansmanına yardımcı olmak için kısa vadeli faiz oranlarını yüzde 0.38'de tutacağını açıklamıştı. İzleyen yedi yıl boyunca da faiz oranları tek bir baz puan bile değişmemişti. Üç aylık Hazine bonolarının getirileri 1950'lerin ortalarına kadar yüzde 2'nin altındaydı.

Faizleri düşük tutmanın bariz nedeni, savaş için harcadığımız 6 trilyon doların finansman maliyetini düşük tutmaktı.

Ne var ki, bu düşük oranlar, evlerine dönen tüm Gaziler için bir şey daha yaptı. Ev, araba, alet-edevat ve oyuncak almak için borçlanmayı gerçek anlamda ucuzlattı.

Paranoid bir politika yapıcının bakış açısından baktığınız zaman, bu harika bir şeydi. Tüketim, İkinci Dünya Savaşı'nı izeyen yıllarda bariz bir ekonomik strateji haline geldi.

Savaşı finanse etmek için tutumluluğu ve tasarrufu teşvik eden bir dönem hızla, harcamaları canla başla teşvik eden bir döneme dönüştü.

Princeton tarihçisi Sheldon Garon şöyle yazıyor:

> Amerika 1945 yılından sonra, Avrupa ve Doğu Asya'daki tasurrufu teşvik modellerinden bir kez daha uzaklaştı... Politikacılar, işadamları ve işçi sendikalarının liderleri, ekonomik büyümeyi teşvik etmek için Amerikalıları harcama yapmaya cesaretlendirdi.[73]

Bu baskıyı, iki şey besledi.

Bunlardan birincisi, ipotekli konut kredisinde eşi görülmemiş fırsatlar sunan Gazi Yasası idi. Bu yasayla birlikte, 16 milyon gazi, genellikle hiç peşinat vermeden, ilk yıl faiz ödemeden ve aylık ödemeleri kiradan bile düşük olabilecek sabit oranlarla konut alabilme olanağına kavuştu.

İkinci faktör, Buhran dönemi düzenlemelerinin gevşetilmesiyle birlikte tüketici kredilerinde yaşanan patlama oldu. İlk kredi kartı 1950 yılında hayata geçti. Mağaza kredisi, taksitli alışveriş kredisi, bireysel krediler, nakit avans kredileri derken, her şey bir anda uçuşa geçti. O dönemde, kredi kartları dahil olmak üzere bütün borçların faizi vergiden düşülebiliyordu.

Tadından geçilmiyordu. Böylece hepimiz bol bol yedik. Aşağıdaki basit tablo bu basit hikâyeyi gayet net ortaya koyuyor.

| Yıl | ABD'de hane halkının toplam borcu |
|---|---|
| 1945 | 29,4 milyar $ |
| 1955 | 125,7 milyar $ |
| 1965 | 331,2 milyar $ |

1950'lerde hane halkı borcu, 2000'lerin borç savurganlığı döneminden bile 1.5 kat hızlı büyüdü.

**3. Kredilerdeki patlama ve 1930'lardaki gizli üretkenlik patlamasının beslediği tüketime yönelik bastırılmış talep, ekonomide patlamayı getirdi.**

1930'lar Amerikan tarihinin ekonomideki en zor on yılıydı. Fakat olumlu bir yönü de vardı; fark edilmesi yirmi yıl süren bir gümüş kaplamayla sıvanmıştı: Büyük Buhran, tamamen ihtiyaçtan dolayı, girişimciliği, üretkenliği ve inovasyonları çok büyük ölçüde beslemişti.

1930'lardaki verimlilik patlamasına o kadar dikkat etmedik, çünkü herkes ekonominin ne kadar kötü olduğuna odaklanmıştı. 1940'larda da dikkat etmedik, çünkü herkes savaşa odaklanmıştı.

Sonra 1950'ler geldi ve aniden gözümüz açıldı. "Vay canına, harika yeni icatlarımız var. Ve biz onları üretmekte gerçekten iyiyiz!" dedik.

Cihazlar, çeşitli aletler, arabalar, telefonlar, klima, elektrik, vesaire vesaire.

Savaş sırasında evlerde kullanılan birçok ürünü satın almak imkânsıza yakındı; çünkü fabrikalar silah ve gemi üretmek üzere dönüştürülmüştü. Bu durum, savaşın sona ermesiyle birlikte Gazilerden gelen bastırılmış bir talep yarattı.

Evli, hayata devam etmeye hevesli ve ucuz tüketici kredileriyle cesaret bulmuş olan Gaziler, ülkenin o güne dek görmediği bir satın alma çılgınlığına yöneldi.

Frederick Lewis Allen *The Big Change* (Büyük Değişim) adlı kitabında şöyle yazıyor:

> Savaş sonrasındaki o yıllarda çiftçiler yeni traktörler, mısır toplama aletleri, elektrikli süt sağma makineleri aldılar; esasen her çiftçi ve komşuları, ortak kullanımları için muazzam bir tarım makineleri donanımı oluşturdu. Çiftçinin eşi, her zaman özlemini duyduğu ve Büyük Buhran sırasında hiçbir zaman güçlerinin yetmediği bembeyaz elektrikli buzdolabına, modern çamaşır makinesine ve derin dondurucuya kavuştu. Banliyöde yaşayan aile, mutfağına bulaşık makinesi aldı, bahçesi için elektrikli çim biçme makinesi edindi. Kentli aile, çamaşırhanelerin müşterisi oldu ve evinin oturma odasına televizyon koydu. Kocaların ofisi klimalıydı.
>
> Ve biteviye böyle devam edip gitti.

Bunun ne denli büyük bir yükseliş olduğunu hafife almak zor.

Ticari otomobil ve kamyon üretimi 1942 yılından 1945'e kadar gerçek anlamda durmuştu. Sonra 1945 yılından 1949'a kadar 21 milyon otomobil satıldı. Ardından 1955 yılına dek 37 milyon otomobil daha satıldı.

İnşa edilen konut sayısı 1940 yılından 1945'e kadar iki milyonun altında kalmıştı. Sonra 1945 yılından 1950'ye kadar yedi milyon konut inşa edildi. Ardından 1955 yılına dek sekiz milyon konut daha inşa edildi.

Eşyaya yönelik bastırılmış talep ve henüz keşfetmiş olduğumuz eşya yapma yeteneğimiz, savaştan dönen Gazilerin tekrar çalışmaya başlamasını sağlayan işleri yarattı. Üstelik, iyi işlerdi. Bu iyi işlerin tüketici kredileriyle birleşmesiyle de, Amerika'nın harcama kapasitesi patladı.

Federal Reserve 1951 yılında Başkan Truman'a şöyle yazmıştı: "1950 yılı itibarıyla, konut inşaatları dahil olmak üzere toplam tüketici harcamaları yaklaşık 203 milyar dolar oldu; bir diğer ifadeyle, 1944'teki seviyesinin yaklaşık yüzde 40 üzerine çıktı."[74]

"Bütün bu Gaziler savaştan sonra ne yapacak?" sorusunun yanıtı, artık belliydi. Yeni şeyler yaparak işlerinden kazandıkları parayla ve ucuza borçlandıkları paranın da yardımıyla, yeni şeyler alacaklardı.

### 4. Kazançlar hiç olmadığı kadar eşit paylaşılıyor.

1950'lerin ekonomisinin belirleyici özelliği, yoksulların eskiye göre iyileştirilmesi yoluyla ülkenin zenginleşmesiydi.

Ortalama ücretler, 1940'tan 1948 yılına kadar iki katına çıktı, sonra 1963'te tekrar ikiye katlandı.

Ve bu kazançlar, onlarca yıl önce geride bırakılmış olanlara odaklandı. Zengin ile yoksul arasındaki uçurum olağanüstü daraldı.

Lewis Allen 1955 yılında şöyle yazıyordu:

> Hali vakti yerinde olanların ekonomik yarıştaki muazzam liderliği önemli ölçüde azaldı.
>
> Bu gelişmede en iyisini başaran grup sanayi işçileri oldu; yani eskiden 2500 dolarla geçinen, şimdi ise 4500 dolar kazanan bir çelik işçisinin ailesi veya eskiden yılda 3000 dolar harcayabiliyorken, şimdi yılda 5500 dolar veya üzerinde harcama yapabilecek durumda olan vasıflı makine işçilerinin aileleri.
>
> En üstteki yüzde 1'lik dilimin, yani 16,000 doların üzerinde kazanan ve gerçekten de hali vakti yerinde ve zengin olarak sınıflandırabileceğimiz grubun toplam milli gelir içindeki vergi sonrası payı önceden yüzde 13 iken, 1945'te yüzde 7'ye düşmüştü.
>
> Bu kısa vadeli bir trend değildi. 1950 yılından 1980'e kadar ücretlilerin en alttaki yüzde 20'lik kesiminin reel geliri, en tepedeki yüzde 5 ile yaklaşık aynı miktarda arttı.

Eşitlik, ücretlerin ötesine uzandı.

Rekor sayıda kadın ev dışında iş edindi. Kadınların iş gücüne katılım oranı, savaştan sonra yüzde 31 iken, 1955 yılında yüzde 37'ye, 1965 yılında ise yüzde 40'a yükseldi.

Azınlıklar da kazandı. Eleanor Roosevelt, Afrika kökenli bir Amerikalı muhabirin 1945 yılındaki yemin töreni resepsiyonu sırasında kendisine söylediklerini aktarırken şöyle yazmıştı:

> On iki yılda neler olduğunun farkında mısınız? 1933 yılı resepsiyonunda, bir grup renkli insan bugün olduğu gibi çizgiyi aşmış ve diğerlerinin arasına karışmış olsaydı, ülkedeki her gazete bunu haber yapardı.

> Bugün haber değeri olduğu aklımızdan bile geçmiyor ve hiçbirimiz bundan söz etmeyeceğiz.

Kadın ve azınlık hakları bugünkü düzeyine göre diplerdeydi. Ancak 1940'ların sonlarında ve 50'lerde eşitlik yolunda kaydedilen ilerleme olağanüstüydü.

Sınıfların eşitlenmesi, yaşam tarzlarının da eşitlenmesi anlamına geliyordu. Normal insanların altında Chevy'ler vardı. Zenginler Cadillac kullanıyordu. Televizyon ve radyo, insanların zevk aldığı eğlence ve kültürü, sınıf farkı olmaksızın eşitledi. Postayla sipariş olanağı sağlayan kataloglar, her nerede yaşarlarsa yaşasınlar, insanların giydiği giysileri ve satın aldığı ürünleri eşitledi. *Harper's Magazine* 1957'de şöyle yazıyordu:

> Zengin adam, yoksul adamla aynı sigarayı içiyor, aynı jiletle tıraş oluyor, aynı tür telefonu, elektrikli süpürgeyi, radyoyu ve televizyonu kullanıyor; evlerindeki aydınlatma ve ısınma donanımları aynı ve bu böyle sürüp gidiyor. Zenginin otomobili ile yoksulun otomobili arasındaki farklar gayet önemsiz. Esasen üzerlerindeki motor ve teknik donanım aynı. Oysa yüzyılın başlarında otomobilde hiyerarşi vardı.

Paul Graham, 2016 yılında, yalnızca üç TV kanalı olması kadar basit bir şeyin kültürü nasıl eşitlediğini dile getirirken şöyle demişti:

> Şimdi bunu hayal etmek zor, ama o dönemde on milyonlarca aile, her gece televizyonun karşısında oturarak yan komşularıyla aynı anda, aynı programı izliyordu. Şimdi Süper Bowl Kupası'nda olan şey, eskiden her gece

yaşanıyordu. Kelimenin gerçek anlamıyla senkronize olmuştuk.[75]

Bu önemliydi. İnsanlar refah düzeylerini emsalleriyle kıyaslayarak ölçerler. Ve 1945-1980 döneminin büyük bölümünde, insanların kendilerini kıyasladıkları emsalleriyle pek çok ortak noktası vardı. Birçok insan -çoğu insan- çevresindekilerle ya eşit ya da en azından makûl bir yaşam sürüyordu. İnsanların gelirleri kadar hayatlarının da eşitlendiği fikri, hikâyemizin önemli bir noktasını oluşturuyor ve bu konuya tekrar döneceğiz.

**5. Borç muazzam yükseldi. Ama gelirler de aynı şekilde yükseldiği için borcun etkisi pek önemli olmadı.**

Yeni tüketim kültürünün, yeni borç ürünlerinin ve Federal Reserve'in düşük tuttuğu, hükümet programlarıyla sübvanse edilen faiz oranlarının bir araya gelmesiyle, hane halkının borcu 1947'den 1957'ye kadar beş kat arttı.

Ancak bu dönemde gelir artışı o kadar güçlüydü ki, borçlardaki yükselişin haneler üzerinde sert bir etkisi olmadı. Ayrıca savaş sonrasındaki başlangıç noktasında, hane halkının borç seviyesi çok düşüktü. Büyük Buhran'ın birçok haneyi meteliksiz bırakması ve savaş sırasında hane halkı harcamalarının son derece kısılmış olması nedeniyle, borç birikimi sınırlı kalmıştı. Dolayısıyla da 1947-1957 yılları arasındaki 10 yıllık dönemde, hane halkı borcunun gelire oranla artışı yönetilebilir düzeydeydi.

Bugün hane halkı borcunun gelire oranı yüzde 100'ün biraz üzerinde. Oysa 1950'lerde, 1960'larda ve 1970'lerdeki yükselişlerden sonra bile yüzde 60'ın altında kalmıştı.

Bu borç patlamasına yol açan ana itki, konut sahibi olma oranındaki artıştı.

1900 yılında konut sahibi olma oranı yüzde 47 idi. İzleyen 40 yıl boyunca da o düzeyde kaldı. Sonra 1945'te yüzde 53'e, 1970'te ise yüzde 62'ye ulaştı. Artık nüfusun önemli bir kısmı, önceki kuşakların erişimi olmayan -olamayan- miktarlarda borç kullanmaktaydı. Ve çoğunlukla da bunu sorun etmiyorlardı.

David Halberstam, *Fifties* (Elliler) adlı kitabında şöyle yazıyor:

> Kendilerine ve geleceklerine, daha zor zamanlarda büyüyenleri şaşırtacak kadar çok güveniyorlardı. Onlar ebeveynleri gibi borçtan korkmuyorlardı... Sadece kazandıkları para ve sahip oldukları şeyler anlamında değil, geleceğin çoktan geldiğine duydukları inançla da ebeveynlerinden farklıydılar. Ailelerinde ev sahibi olan ilk birey onlardı ve mobilya veya beyaz eşya almak için girdikleri mağazalara yeni bir heyecanı ve gururu da beraberlerinde getiriyorlardı; eskiden olsa, bu tür duyguları, belki ilk bebeklerine kıyafet seçen genç çiftler sergileyebilirdi. Bir eve sahip olma başarısı o kadar büyük bir atılımı yansıtıyordu ki, o eve ne alınsa azdı.

Giderek daha da önem kazanacağından, birkaç şeyi birbirine bağlamak için iyi bir noktada olduğumuzu düşünüyorum:

- Amerika patlıyor.
- Hep birlikte, daha önce hiç olmadığı kadar topyekûn patlıyor.
- Borçla birlikte patlasa da o dönemde bu sorun olmuyor; çünkü borç seviyesi gelire göre hâlâ düşük ve

borcun korkulacak bir şey olmadığı kültürel olarak genel kabul görüyor.

### 6. Bazı şeyler çatırdamaya başlıyor

1973, ekonominin artık yeni bir yolda yürüdüğünün netleştiği yıl oldu.

O yıl başlayan ekonomik durgunluk, işsizliği 1930'lardan beri en yüksek seviyesine çıkardı.

Enflasyon fırladı. Ancak savaş sonrasındaki ani yükselişlerin aksine, bu defa yüksek kaldı.

On yıl önce yüzde 2.5 olan kısa vadeli faiz oranları, 1973'te yüzde 8'i gördü.

Ve bütün bunları Vietnam savaşı, büyük çaplı protesto gösterileri, Martin Luther King, John ve Bobby Kennedy suikastleri ışığında düşünürsek, toplumdaki korku düzeyinin ne denli yüksek olduğunu anlayabiliriz.

Böylece karanlık çöktü.

Amerika, savaştan sonraki yirmi yılda dünya ekonomisine egemen oldu. Birçok büyük ülkenin üretim kapasiteleri bombardımanlarla enkaz haline getirilmişti. Ancak 1970'lerle birlikte bu durum değişti. Japonya patlıyordu. Çin ekonomisi dışa açılıyordu. Ortadoğu, petrol kaslarını esnetiyordu.

Büyük Buhran'ın zorluklarıyla sertleşip güçlenen ve savaşla birlikte sistemli iş birliği ve yardımlaşma ruhuna sıkı sıkıya tutunan Muhteşem Kuşağın* kültürü ile şanslı ekonomik avantajların bileşiminden oluşan yapı, Baby Boomer** kuşağının

---

* Muhteşem Kuşak (Greatest Generation): Büyük Buhran döneminde büyüyen, dolayısıyla da dönemin zorlu ekonomik koşullarında biçimlenen, ardından İkinci Dünya Savaşı'nda verdiği mücadele ile büyük takdir toplayan kuşak. (ÇN.)

** Baby Boomer: İkinci Dünya Savaşı sonrasındaki nüfus patlaması döneminde, ge-

yetişkinliğe adım attığı dönemde değişti. Normale dair farklı bir vizyonu olan bu yeni kuşak, aynı zamanda önceki yirmi yılda ekonomide esen olumlu rüzgârların artık büyük ölçüde esmez olduğu bir zamana denk geldi.

Finansta her şey, *beklentilerle şekillenir*. Önceki yüzyılın en büyük yön değişimlerinden biri, ekonomi rüzgârlarının farklı yönden ve eşitlik anlamında düzensiz esmeye başladığı, buna karşılık insanların beklentilerinin hâlâ savaş sonrası dönemin eşitlik kültüründe kökleşmiş olduğu dönemde gerçekleşti. O da vardı tabii, ama tamamen gelir eşitliği meselesi değildi. Asıl önemlisi, yaşam tarzı ve tüketim beklentilerinde eşitlik fikrinin yerleşip kökleşmiş olmasıydı: Yani gelir dağılımında 50'inci yüzdelik dilimde olan birinin, 80'inci veya 90'ıncı yüzdelik dilimdeki birinden önemli ölçüde farklı bir hayat yaşamaması gerektiği ve 99'uncu yüzdelik dilimdeki birinin belki daha iyi bir yaşam sürebileceği, ancak bunun da yine 50'inci yüzdelik dilimdeki birinin anlayabileceği türden, makûl bir hayat olacağı kavramı toplumun içine içlemişti. Amerika, 1945-1980 yılları arasındaki dönemin büyük bölümünü böyle bir düzen içinde yaşadı. Bunun ahlâki olarak doğru veya yanlış olduğunu düşünmeniz, konumuz açısından önemli değil. Önemli olan, olmuş olması.

Beklentiler her zaman gerçeklerden daha yavaş hareket eder. 1970'lerin başından 2000'li yılların başlarına kadar olan dönemin ekonomik olguları, büyümenin sürdüğünü, ancak eşitlik anlamında daha dengesiz hale geldiğini; buna karşılık insanların yaşam tarzlarının emsallerinden pek farklı olmaması yönündeki beklentilerinin değişmediğini ortaya koyuyordu.

---

nel olarak 1946-1964 yılları arasında doğmuş olan kuşak. (ÇN.)

## 7. Canlanma yeniden başlıyor, fakat bu defa öncekinden farklı.

Ronald Reagan 1984 yılında yayınlattığı "Amerika'da Sabah" başlıklı ilan metninde şöyle diyordu:

> Amerika'da yine sabah oldu. Bugün ülkemiz tarihinde hiç görmediğimiz kadar çok sayıda kadın ve erkek işe gidecek. 1980'deki rekor seviyelerin yaklaşık yarısına inmiş olan faiz oranlarıyla, son dört yılda hiç görmediğimiz kadar çok sayıda, yaklaşık 2000 aile yeni ev alacak. Bugün öğleden sonra 6500 genç erkek ve kadın evlenecek ve dört yıl öncesine göre yarıdan fazla düşmüş olan enflasyonla geleceğe güvenle bakabilecekler.

Bu ilanda yazılanlar abartı değildi. Gayri safi yurtiçi hasıladaki (GSYH) artış, 1950'lerden bu yana en yüksek seviyesindeydi. 1989 yılında Amerika'da işsiz sayısı, yedi yıl öncesine göre altı milyon kişi azalmıştı. S&P 500, 1982 ile 1990 yılları arasında neredeyse dört kat artmıştı. 1990'larda GSYH'daki toplam reel artış, yüzde 40'a karşı yüzde 42 ile, kabaca 1950'lerdekine eşitti.

Başkan Clinton 2000 yılının ilk günü ulusa hitaben yaptığı Yeni Yıl konuşmasında şöyle diyordu:

> Yeni yüzyıla, 20 milyondan fazla yeni istihdam pozisyonuyla; 30 yılı aşkın süredir gördüğümüz en hızlı ekonomik büyümeyle; son 30 yılın en düşük işsizlik oranlarıyla; son 20 yılın en düşük yoksulluk oranlarıyla; Afrikalı kökenli Amerikalılar ve İspanyol kökenliler arasındaki en düşük kayıtlı işsizlik oranlarıyla; 42 yıl aradan sonra ilk defa arka arkaya gelen ticaret fazlalarıyla başlıyoruz ve Amerika gelecek ay, tarihimizdeki

> en uzun ekonomik büyüme dönemine ulaşacak. Yeni bir ekonomi kurduk.

Son cümlesi önemliydi. Yeni bir ekonomiydi. 1945-1973 dönemi ekonomisi ile 1982-2000 dönemi ekonomisi arasındaki en büyük fark, aynı miktarda büyümenin tamamen farklı ceplere girmesiydi. Şimdi aktaracağım rakamları muhtemelen duymuşsunuzdur, ancak burada tekrar ele almaya değeceğini düşünüyorum. *Atlantic* dergisine göre:

> 1993-2012 yılları arasında, en tepedeki yüzde 1'lik kesimin geliri yüzde 86.1 yükselirken, en alttaki yüzde 99'luk kesimde sadece yüzde 6.6 gelir artışı oldu.

Joseph Stiglitz 2011 yılında şöyle yazıyordu:

> En tepedeki yüzde 1, son on yılda gelirinin yüzde 18 oranında arttığını görürken, ortadaki kesimin gelirleri fiilen düştü. Elinde sadece lise diploması olan erkeklerde gelir düşüşü daha hızlı oldu; bu kesimin geliri, yalnızca son 25 yılda yüzde 12 geriledi.

Savaştan sonra meydana gelen eşitlenmenin neredeyse tam tersiydi.

Bunun niçin böyle olduğu ekonomideki en sevimsiz tartışmalardan biridir; ayrıca sadece bu konuda neler yapmamız gerektiğine odaklanır. Neyse ki, bizim buradaki tartışmamız açısından her ikisi de önemli değil.

Önemli olan tek şey, keskin eşitsizliğin son 35 yılda bir güç haline gelmesi ve bunun da Amerikalıların İkinci Dünya Savaşı sonrası ekonomisinde kültürel olarak kökleşip yerleşen iki fikre tutunmuş olduğu bir dönemde gerçekleşmesiydi: Amerikalıların çoğunluğuyla aynı yaşam tarzını sürmelisin ve o yaşam tarzını finanse etmek için borçlanmak kabul edilebilir bir şeydir.

### 8. Büyük esneyiş

Küçük bir grup Amerikalının gelir düzeyindeki artış, bu grubun yaşam tarzı bağlamında çoğunluktan kopmasına neden oldu.

Daha büyük evler, daha güzel arabalar alıyorlar, pahalı okullara gidiyorlar ve lüks tatiller yapıyorlardı.

Ve herkes onları izliyordu; 1980'ler ve 90'larda Madison Avenue, sonrasında da internet bunu besledi.

Meşru anlamda zengin Amerikalıların küçük bir bölümünün sürdüğü yaşam tarzı, gelirleri artmayan çoğunluğun özlemlerini şişirdi.

1950'lerden 1970'lere kadar uzanan eşitlik ve birlik-beraberlik kültürü, masum bir şekilde "Filancalara ayak uydurma" etkisine dönüştü.

Artık sorunu görebiliriz.

Yılda 900,000 dolar kazanan yatırım bankacısı Joe, yaklaşık 370 metrekarelik bir ev ve iki Mercedes satın alır; üç çocuğunu Pepperdine'e gönderir. Maddi gücü bütün bunları karşılayabilecek durumdadır.

Bir banka şubesinde müdürlük yapan ve yılda 80,000 dolar kazanan Peter, Joe'yu görür ve bilinçaltında, benzer bir hayat yaşamanın onun da hakkı olduğunu düşünür; çünkü Peter'ın anne-babası, farklı işlerde çalışsalar bile Amerikalıların yaşam tarzının çok da farklı olmayacağına inanmışlar ve bunu ona da aşılamışlardır. Peter'ın anne-babası kendi dönemlerinde haklıydı, çünkü gelir dağılımı dengeliydi. Ama bu, o zamanlardı. Peter şimdi farklı bir dünyada yaşıyor. Gelin görün ki, gerçekler değişmiş olsa da beklentileri anne-babasınınkilerden pek farklı değil.

Peki Peter ne yapar?

Çok büyük miktarda ipotekli konut kredisi alır. Kredi kartı borcu 45 bin dolardır. Leasing yöntemiyle iki araba kiralar. Çocukları yüklü miktarda öğrenci kredisi borcuyla mezun olacaktır. Joe'nun yaptıklarına ve edindiklerine gücü yetmediği halde, aynı yaşam tarzını sürebilmek için sınırlarını zorlamış ve sürekli esnetmiştir. Bu, büyük bir esneyiştir.

1930'larda olsa, insanlar bu duruma akıl sır erdiremeyebilirdi. Ama savaştan bu yana 75 yılımızı hane halkı borcunun kültürel olarak kabul görmesini teşvik etmekle geçirdik.

Ortalama ücretlerin aynı kaldığı bir dönemde, ortalama düzeydeki yeni Amerikan evi yüzde 50 büyüdü.

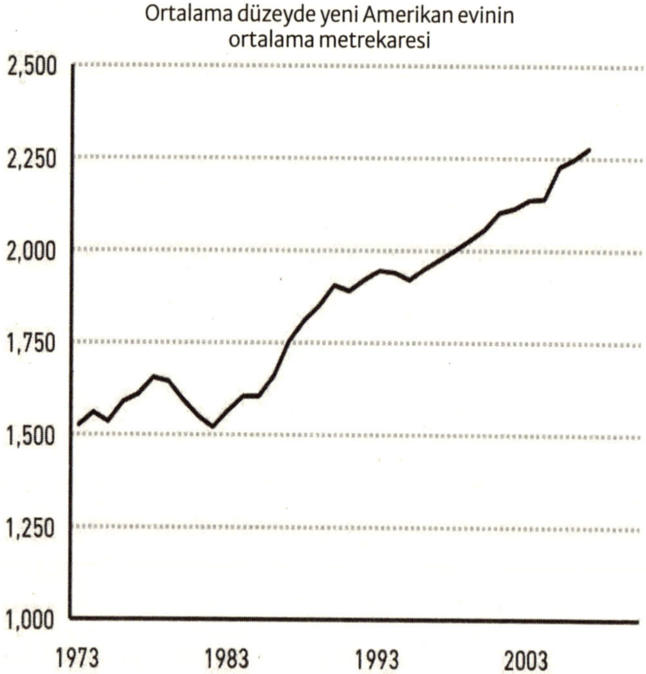

Ortalama bir Amerikan evinin artık sakinlerinden çok banyosu var. Bu evlerin neredeyse yarısı dört veya daha fazla yatak odalı; bu oran 1983 yılında yüzde 18 idi.

Enflasyona uyarlı ortalama otomobil kredisi, 1975-2003 yılları arasında iki katından fazla artarak, 12,300 dolardan 27,900 dolara çıktı.

Bu arada üniversite ücretlerinde ve öğrenci kredilerinde neler olduğunu biliyorsunuz.

Hane halkı borcunun gelire oranı 1963 yılından 1973'e kadar sabit kaldı. Sonra tırmandı, tırmandı ve 1973'te yaklaşık yüzde 60 düzeyindeyken, 2007'de yüzde 130'un üzerine çıktı.

Faiz oranları 1980'lerin başından 2020'ye kadar düşerken bile, gelirin borçların geri ödemesine giden yüzdesi yükseldi. Üstelik bu yükseliş, alt gelir gruplarına yöneldi. Gelirlerin borç ve kiralama (leasing) ödemelerine giden payı, en yüksek gelir gruplarında yüzde 8'in biraz üzerindeyken, 50'inci yüzdelik dilimin altındakilerde yüzde 21'in üstünde bulunuyor.

Borçlardaki bu artış ile 1950'ler ve 60'larda meydana gelen borç artışı arasındaki fark, son sıçramanın yüksek bir tabandan başlamış olmasıdır.

Ekonomist Hyman Minsky, borç krizlerinin başlangıcını şöyle anlatıyor: İnsanların geri ödeyebileceklerinden daha fazla borçlandıkları an. Çok kötü ve acı verici bir durum. Wile E. Coyote'un aşağı bakması ve işinin bittiğini anlayıp hızla düşmesi gibi bir şey.*

Elbette ki, 2008'de yaşanan buydu.

---

* Wile E. Coyote: Animasyon yönetmeni Chuck Jones ile yazar Michael Maltese'nin 1948 yılında yarattığı Çakal (Coyote) karakteri. Çakal ve Roadrunner (Çölkuşu) ikilisi arasındaki kovalamaca etrafında dönen hikâye çok sevilmiş ve bugüne dek 49 çizgi film çekilmiştir. Filmlerde Çakal sürekli olarak avının peşine düşmek için ayrıntılı planlar yapar, olmadık yöntemler dener ve senaryo genellikle Çakal'ın bir uçurumdan aşağı yuvarlanma sahnesini içerir. (ÇN.)

**9. Paradigma bir kez yerleştiğinde, tersine çevirmek çok zordur.**

2008'den sonra çok sayıda kredi dağıtıldı. Sonra faizler düştü. Hane halkının borç ödemelerinin gelire yüzdesi, şimdi 35 yılın en düşük seviyelerinde.

Ancak 2008'e verilen tepki, her ne kadar gerekli olsa da, bizi bu noktaya getiren bazı trendleri devam ettirdi.

Parasal genişleme (kantitatif genişleme) bir yandan ekonomik çöküşü önlerken, bir yandan da varlık fiyatlarını artırdı; bu, o varlıkların sahipleri -çoğunlukla zengin insanlar- için bir nimet.

Fed, 2008 yılında kurumsal borçlara arka çıkarak destek verdi. Bu, o borçların yükümlülerine -çoğunlukla zengin insanlara- yardımcı oldu.

Son 20 yılda vergi indirimleri ağırlıklı olarak daha yüksek gelirlilere gitti. Yüksek gelirli insanlar çocuklarını en iyi üniversitelere gönderiyor. Bu çocuklar ileride daha yüksek gelirler elde edebilirler ve Fed'in arka çıkacağı kurumsal borçlara, çeşitli hükümet politikalarıyla desteklenecek hisse senetlerine yatırım yapmaya devam edebilirler, vesaire, vesaire.

Bunların hiçbiri kendi başına sorun değildir; zaten bu yüzden değişmeyip olduğu yerde kalıyorlar.

Fakat bunlar, 1980'lerin başından beri yaşanmakta olan daha büyük bir şeyin belirtileridir: Ekonomi, bazı insanlar için diğerlerine göre daha iyi sonuç veriyor. Başarı eskisi kadar liyakata dayalı olmadığı gibi, önceki dönemlerden daha yüksek kazanımlarla ödüllendiriliyor.

Bunun ahlâki olarak doğru veya yanlış olduğunu düşünmek zorunda değilsiniz.

Ve yine belirteyim, bunun niçin olduğu da hikâyemiz açısından önemli değil.

Önemli olan, *yaşanmış olması* ve ekonominin, insanların savaş sonrası dönemde belirlenen beklentilerinden uzaklaşmasına yol açması: Sistematik eşitsizliğin olmadığı, komşularınızın ve yolun birkaç kilometre aşağısında yaşayanların sizinkine çok benzer yaşamlar sürdüğü büyük bir orta sınıf var.

Bu beklentilerin, gerçeklikten uzaklaştıktan sonra 35 yıl boyunca öylece takılıp kalmasının bir nedeni, geçerli olduğu durumlarda pek çok insana kendini iyi hissettirmesidir. O kadar iyi bir şeyi -ya da en azından o kadar iyi olduğu izlenimi veren bir şeyi- bırakmak kolay değil.

Bu yüzden de insanlar peşini bırakmadı. Geri istiyorlar.

**10. Çay Partisi*, Wall Street'i İşgal**, Brexit ve Donald Trump olaylarının her biri, "Durdurun dünyayı, inecek var" diye haykıran bir grubu temsil ediyor.**

Haykırışlarının detayları farklı da olsa, bütün bu gruplar -en azından kısmen- savaş sonrası beklentiler bağlamında, yani sistemin kabaca herkes için kabaca aynı şekilde işlemesi açısından, bu düzenin onlara yarar sağlamadığını haykırıyor.

Trump'ın yükselişini yalnızca gelir eşitsizliğine bağlayıp burun kıvırabilirsiniz. Kıvırmalısınız da. Bu tür şeyler her

---

* Çay Partisi (Tea Party): 2009 yılında ABD'nin birçok bölgesinde gerçekleşen kitlesel protesto eylemleriyle gündeme gelen ultra liberal, milliyetçi ve aşırı sağcı siyasi hareket. Adını 1773 yılında Boston'da gerçekleşen ve sömürgecilerin limana çay dökmesi nedeniyle "Çay Partisi" olarak bilinen ayaklanmadan aldı. (ÇN)

** Wall Street'i İşgal: Kanadalı aktivist grup Adbusters'ın 17 Eylül 2011'de, ABD'de finansın kalbinin attığı yer olarak bilinen Wall Street'te başlattığı ve "Wall Street'i İşgal" sloganıyla öne çıkan toplumsal hareket. Bu eylemler barışçıldı ve eylemcilerin çoğunluğunu eğitimli gençler oluşturmuştu. (ÇN)

zaman derinlerdeki karmaşıklığın katmanlarıdır. Ancak insanları "Beklediğim gibi bir dünyada yaşamıyorum" diye düşünmeye iten şeyin de önemli bir parçasıdır: "Bu düzen beni kızdırıyor. Lanet olsun! Kahrolsun! Ben tamamen farklı bir düzen için savaşacağım, çünkü bu -her ne ise- işe yaramıyor."

Bu zihniyeti alın ve insanların başkalarının nasıl yaşadığını her zamankinden de çok gördüğü Facebook, Instagram ve kablolu yayın ağlarının içerdiği gücün seviyesine taşıyın. Yangına körükle gitmek, ateşe benzin atmak gibi bir şey. Benedict Evans şöyle diyor: "İnternet insanların karşısına yeni bakış açıları çıkardıkça, insanlar o bakış açılarının var olmasına giderek daha çok öfkeleniyor." Bu durum, gerek sonuçların gerçek aralığının daha düşük olması, gerekse diğer insanların ne düşündüğünü ve nasıl yaşadığını görüp öğrenmenin bugünkü kadar kolay olmaması nedeniyle, ekonomik görüş yelpazesinin de daha dar kaldığı savaş sonrası ekonomiden büyük çaplı bir yön değişikliği anlamına geliyor.

Ben kötümser değilim. Ekonomi dalgaların ve döngülerin hikâyesidir. Bir şeyler gelir ve gider.

İşsizlik oranı şu anda onyıllardan bu yana en düşük seviyesinde. Şimdi düşük gelirli çalışanların ücretleri zenginlere göre daha hızlı artıyor.[76] Bursları da hesaba katarsak, üniversite masraflarındaki artış büyük ölçüde durdu.[77] Muhteşem 1950'lerden bu yana sağlıkta, iletişimde, ulaşımda ve sivil haklar alanında gerçekleşen ilerlemeleri inceleyenlerin çoğu, tahminimce geçmişe geri dönmek istemez.

Ancak bu hikâyenin ana temalarından biri, beklentilerin sahadaki gerçeklikten daha yavaş hareket etmesine odaklanıyor. İzleyen 35 yılda ekonomi değişirken insanların 1950'lerin beklentilerine tutunup kalmasında bunu görüyoruz. Dahası, bugün bir orta sınıf patlaması başlamış olsa bile, olasılıkların en tepedekiler hariç herkesin aleyhine olacağına yönelik beklentiler değişmeyebilir.

Dolayısıyla da "Bu düzen işlemiyor" dönemi devam edebilir.

"Her ne olursa olsun tamamen yeni bir şeye ihtiyacımız var; hemen şimdi!" dönemi de aynı şekilde devam edebilir.

Bu da bizi bir bakıma, İkinci Dünya Savaşı gibi olayların yolunu açan hadiselerin başladığı yere, yani hikâyemizin en başına götürüyor.

Tarih, birbiri ardına gelen lanetler silsilesidir.

# Dipnotlar

1. J. Pressler, "Former Merrill Lynch Executive Forced to Declare Bankruptcy Just to Keep a $14 Million Roof Over His Head," *New York* dergisi (9 Nisan, 2010).
2. Aynı yerde.
3. L. Thomas Jr., "The Tale of the $8 Million 'Bargain' House in Greenwich," *New York Times* (25 Ocak, 2014).
4. U. Malmendier, S. Nagel, "Depression Babies: Do Macroeconomic Experiences Affect Risk-Taking?" (Ağustos 2007).
5. "How large are 401(k)s?" *Investment Company Institute* (Aralık 2019).
6. R. Butler, "Retirement Pay Often Is Scanty," *New York Times* (14 Ağustos, 1955).
7. "Higher education in the United States," *Wikipedia.*
8. K. Bancalari, "Private college tuition is rising faster than inflation .... again," *USA Today* (June 9, 2017).
9. "How Many People Die Rock Climbing?" *Rockulus.*
10. A. T. Vanderbilt II, Fortune's Children: The Fall of the House of Vanderbilt (William Morrow Paperbacks, 2012).
11. D. McDonald, "Rajat Gupta: Touched by scandal," *Fortune* (1 Ekim, 2010).
12. "Did millionaire Rajat Gupta suffer from billionaire envy?" *Economic Times* (27 Mart, 2011).
13. J. Nicas, "Facebook Connected Her to a Tattooed Soldier in Iraq. Or So She Thought," *New York Times* (28 Temmuz, 2019).
14. T. Maloney, "The Best-Paid Hedge Fund Managers Made $7.7 Billion in 2018," *Bloomberg* (15 Şubat, 2019).
15. S. Weart, "The Discovery of Global Warming," history.aip.org/climate/cycles.htm (Ocak 2020).

16 S. Langlois, "From $6,000 to $73 billion: Warren Buffett's wealth through the ages," *MarketWatch* (6 Ocak, 2017).

17. D. Boudreaux, "Turnover in the Forbes 400, 2008–2013," Cafe Hayek (16 Mayıs, 2014).

18. M. Pabrai, www.youtube.com/watch? time_continue=200&v=Ym-mIbrKDYbw.

19. "Art Dealers: The Other Vincent van Gogh," *Horizon Research Group* (Haziran 2010).

20. https://www.collaborativefund.com/uploads/venture-returns.png

21. "The Agony and the Ecstasy: The Risks and Rewards of a Concentrated Stock Position," *Eye on the Market, J.P. Morgan* (2014).

22. L. Eadicicco, "Here's Why You Probably Won't Get Hired At Google," *Business Insider* (23 Ekim, 2014).

23. "What is the offer acceptance rate for Facebook software engineering positions?" *Quora.com.*

24. 24 W. Fulton, "If You Want to Build a Great Team, Hire Apple Employees," *Forbes* (22 Haziran, 2012).

25. J. Berger, "How to Change Anyone's Mind," *Wall Street Journal* (21 Şubat, 2020).

26. D. Sivers, "How I got rich on the other hand," sivers.org (30 Ekim, 2019).

27. N. Chokshi, "Americans Are Among the Most Stressed People in the World, Poll Finds," *New York Times* (25 Nisan, 2019).

28. Russell Sage Foundation-Chartbook of Social Inequality.

29. D. Thompson, "Why White-Collar Workers Spend All Day at the Office," *Atlantic* dergisi (4 Aralık, 2019).

30. "Rihanna's ex-accountant fires back," News24 (24 Mart, 2014).

31. B. Mann, "Want to Get Rich and Stay Rich?" *Motley Fool* (7 Mart, 2017).

32. "U.S. energy intensity projected to continue its steady decline through 2040," U.S. Energy Information Administration (1 Mart, 2013).

33. Julius Wagner-Jauregg/Biographical, nobelprize.org.. 34 J. M. Cavaillon, "Good and bad fever," *Critical Care* 16

34. J. M. Cavaillon, "Good and bad fever," *Critical Care* 16:2 (2012).

35. "Fever—Myths Versus Facts," Seattle Children's.

36. J. J. Ray, and C. I. Schulman, "Fever: suppress or let it ride?" Journal of Thoracic Disease 7:12 (2015).

37. A. LaFrance, "A Cultural History of the Fever," *Atlantic* dergisi (16 Eylül, 2015).

38. J. Zweig, "What Harry Markowitz Meant," jasonzweig.com (2 Ekim, 2017).

39. L. Pleven, "In Bogle Family, It's Either Passive or Aggressive," *Wall Street Journal* (28 Kasım, 2013).

40. C. Shapiro and M. Housel, "Disrupting Investors' Own Game," Collaborative Fund.

41. https://www.bylo.org/

42. Washington State University, "For pundits, it's better to be confident than correct," *ScienceDaily* (28 Mayıs, 2013).

43. "Daniel Kahneman's Favorite Approach For Making Better Decisions," Farnham Street (Ocak 2014).

44. W. Buffett, Letter to the Shareholders of Berkshire Hathaway Inc. (2008).

45. W. Buffett, Letter to the Shareholders of Berkshire Hathaway Inc. (2006).

46. B. Plumer, "Only 27 percent of college grads have a job related to their major," *Washington Post* (20 Mayıs, 2013).

47. G. Livingston, "Stay-at-home moms and dads account for about one-in-five U.S. parents," *Pew Research Center* (24 Eylül, 2018).

48. D. Gilbert, "The psychology of your future self," TED 2014.

49. J. Zweig, "What I Learned From Daniel Kahneman," jasonzweig.com (30 Mart, 2014).

50. J. Ptak "Tactical Funds Miss Their Chance," *Morningstar* (2 Şubat, 2012).

51. R. Kinnel, "Mind the Gap 2019," Morningstar (15 Ağustos, 2019).

52. M. Desmond. "Accounting Tricks Catch Up With GE," *Forbes* (4 Ağustos, 2009).

53. A. Berenson, "Freddie Mac Says It Understated Profits by Up to $6.9 Billion," *New York Times* (25 Haziran, 2003).

54. "U.S. Home Flipping Rate Reaches a Nine-Year High in Q1 2019," *Attom Data Solutions* (4 Haziran, 2019).

55. A. Osborn, "As if Things Weren't Bad Enough, Russian Professor Predicts End of U.S.," *Wall Street Journal* (29 Aralık, 2008).

56. "Food in the Occupation of Japan," *Wikipedia.*

57. J. M. Jones, "U.S. Stock Ownership Down Among All but Older, Higher-Income," *Gallup* (27 Mayıs, 2017).

58. E. Rauchway, The Great Depression and the New Deal: A Very Short Introduction (Oxford University Press, 2008).

59. L. R. Brown, Plan B 3.0: Mobilizing to Save Civilization (W. W. Norton & Company, 2008).

60. FRED, Federal Reserve Bank of St. Louis.

61. "U.S. Crude Oil Production—Historical Chart," Macro Trends.

62. "Thomas Selfridge," *Wikipedia*.

63. https://www.nhlbi.nih.gov/

64. D. Walsh, "The Tragedy of Saudi Arabia's War," *New York Times* (26 Ekim, 2018).

65. B. Pisani, "Active fund managers trail the S&P 500 for the ninth year in a row in triumph for indexing," *CNBC* (15 Mart, 2019).

66. 2019 Investment Company Factbook, Investment Company Institute.

67. "Minutes of the Federal Open Market Committee," *Federal Reserve* (30–31 Ekim, 2007).

68. https://www.nasa.gov/

69. A. Ram, "Portfolio managers shun investing in own funds," *Financial Times* (18 Eylül, 2016).

70. K. Murray "How Doctors Die," Zócalo Public Square (30 Kasım, 2011).

71. B. Pisani, "Active fund managers trail the S&P 500 for the ninth year in a row in triumph for indexing," *CNBC* (15 Mart, 2019).

72. "Treasury-Fed Accord," federalreservehistory.org..

73. S. Garon, "Beyond Our Means: Why America Spends While the World Saves," St. Louis Federal Reserve Bankası (1 Temmuz, 2012).

74. "Economic Report of the President," FRASER, St. Louis Federal Reserve (1951).

75. P. Graham, "The Refragmentation," paulgraham.com (2016).

76. P. Davidson, "Jobs in high-wage industries are growing fastest," *USA Today* (14 Aralık, 2019).

77. R. Channick, "Average college costs flat nationwide, at just under $15K, as universities increase grants," *Chicago Tribune* (16 Ekim, 2018).

# TEŞEKKÜR

Tüm kitaplar gibi *Paranın Psikolojisi* de bana bu yolda destek veren sayısız insanın yardımları olmaksızın gerçekleşemezdi. O kadar çok insanın desteğini gördüm ki, burada hepsini sıralamam imkânsız olacak. Ancak özellikle destekleyici olan birkaç kişiyi saymam gerek:

Bana herkesten önce inanan Brian Richards.

Mecbur olmadığı halde bana inanan Craig Shapiro.

Desteği hiçbir zaman sarsılmayan Gretchen Housel.

Hiçbir karşılık beklemeden yardımlarını esirgemeyen Jenna Abdou.

Beni cesaretlendiren, yol gösteren ve bir temel oluşturmamı sağlayan Craig Pearce.

Geri bildirimleri çok değerli olan Jamie Catherwood, Josh Brown, Brent Beshore, Barry Ritholtz, Ben Carlson, Chris Hill, Michael Batnick, James Osorne.

Teşekkürler.

YORUMLARINIZI BEKLIYORUZ

https://www.scalakitapci.com/paranın-psikolojisi

SCALA Kitapçı
"Dünyanıza değer katar"
30 yıl
her kitap başka
bir yolculuk...
yeni yollara
yeni yolculuklara
hoşgeldiniz...
www.
scalakitapci.
com
ScalaKitapci
Scala_Kitapci
scalakitapci